THE

APOSTOLICAL FATHERS:

A CRITICAL ACCOUNT OF THEIR

GENUINE WRITINGS AND OF THEIR DOCTRINES.

THE

APOSTOLICAL FATHERS:

A CRITICAL ACCOUNT OF THEIR

GENUINE WRITINGS AND OF THEIR DOCTRINES.

BY

JAMES DONALDSON, LL.D.

WIPF & STOCK · Eugene, Oregon

Wipf and Stock Publishers
199 W 8th Ave, Suite 3
Eugene, OR 97401

The Apostolical Fathers
A Critical Account of Their Genuine Writings and of Their Doctrines
By Donaldson, James
Softcover ISBN-13: 978-1-6667-6468-0
Hardcover ISBN-13: 978-1-6667-6469-7
eBook ISBN-13: 978-1-6667-6470-3
Publication date 11/10/2022
Previously published by Macmillan and Co., 1874

This edition is a scanned facsimile of the original edition
published in 1874.

TO

JOHN STUART BLACKIE,

PROFESSOR OF GREEK IN THE UNIVERSITY OF EDINBURGH,

THIS BOOK

Is Dedicated,

FROM FEELINGS OF AFFECTION, GRATITUDE,

AND ADMIRATION,

BY HIS OLD PUPIL,

THE AUTHOR.

NOTE.

This book was published in 1864 as the first volume of a 'Critical History of Christian Literature and Doctrine from the death of the Apostles to the Nicene Council.' The intention was to carry down the history continuously to the time of Eusebius, and this intention has not been abandoned. But as the writers can be sometimes grouped more easily according to subject or locality than according to time, it is deemed advisable to publish the history of each group separately. The Introduction in the present volume serves as an Introduction to the whole period.

CONTENTS.

INTRODUCTION.

CHAPTER I. *Advantages of the Study of Early Christian Literature.* Object of the work.—Importance of the subject.—Nature of the work.—Criticism of literature.—Criticism of opinions.—Dogma.—Use for present age.—Early writers as witnesses.—As interpreters of the New Testament. —As philosophers.—Of great use to the classical scholar.—A part of classical scholarship, page 3.

CHAPTER II. *External Testimony.* The only proper evidence contemporary.—The character of the witnesses.—The critical powers of the ancients.—Their treatment of external testimony.—External witnesses. —Eusebius.—Jerome.—Historians of the Church.—Historians of Heresies. —Chroniclers.—Photius, p. 12.

CHAPTER III. *Internal Evidence.* Nature of internal evidence.— Number of dubious and anonymous works in first three centuries.— Forgeries.—Interpolations.—Main principle of internal evidence.—Effects of lapse of time.—Every age produces changes.—Illustrated in the case of Eusebius, p. 26.

CHAPTER IV. *Literature of the Subject.* Roman Catholic books.— Greek Church.—Tone of Roman Catholic writers.—Protestant writers.— Collections of the Fathers.—Translations.—Lexicons, p. 34.

CHAPTER V. *The Tübingen School.* Baur.—Hegel.—Disregard of historical evidence.—Schwegler's Nachapostolisches Zeitalter.—Criticism of the School, p. 45.

CHAPTER VI. *Early Christian Theology. Mode of Treatment.* Mode of presentation.—Temptations in the treatment of doctrines.—The starting-point.—Oral Christianity.—Its main truths.—No system.—Its unspeculative character acknowledged by various writers.—Greater precision as history advances.—The lesson which the history of dogma teaches, p. 57.

CHAPTER VII. *Historical Survey of the Mode of Treatment.* Roman Catholic writers.—Some refuse to discuss the subject,—The rest anxious to find the doctrines of the Fathers in entire agreement with their own,— Petavius,—Newman,—Döllinger.—Protestant writers took their stand on the Scriptures,—Daillé,—Milton.—Burton.—Defenders of the Faith,— Horsley,—Jamieson,—Lord Hailes,—Barbeyrac,—Whiston,—Lardner.— Evangelical School,—Goode,—Isaac Taylor,—Dr. W. L. Alexander.—The theology of the Fathers an obstacle.— Dr. Bennet,—Vaughan,—Stoughton.—Anti-Romanists,—Scultetus,— Forbes of Corse.—English Church,—Closely allied in doctrine to the early writers,—Waterland,—Blunt,—Bull,—Burton.—Defenders of the Faith,— Progress of the study.—Mosheim,—Semler,—Schleiermacher,—Neander,— Bunsen,—Miss Cornwallis,—Maurice,—Milman,—Davidson,—Westcott.— The Tübingen School, p. 67.

CONTENTS

BOOK I. THE APOSTOLICAL FATHERS.

CHAPTER I. *Introduction.* The name Apostolical.—The works.—Their character.—Deal with the inner workings of the Church.—Show little or nothing of the contact with heathenism, philosophy, and heresy.—Are pervaded by deep piety.—The doctrines are stated in a broad, general manner.—Opinions in regard to their theology.—Literature, 101.

CHAPTER II. *Clemens Romanus: Life.* Bishop in the Church in Rome.—The date.—His place in the line of bishops.—Is he the person mentioned in the Epistle to the Philippians?—Death of Clemens.—His nationality, p. 113.

The Writings of Clemens. The Epistle to the Corinthians.—Its authorship.—Its genuineness.—Its incompleteness.—Interpolations.—Date of the letter.—Circumstances in which the letter was written.—Character of the letter.—Abstract of the letter.—Opinions on its theology.—Abstract of the letter.—Other writings ascribed to Clemens.—Epistle to the Hebrews.—Literature.—Theology.—God.—Christ.—The Holy Spirit.—The Trinity.—Angels.—Man.—His original state.—Salvation.—The Church.—Its office bearers and rites.—Future state.—The Scriptures.—Morality, p. 124.

CHAPTER III. *Polycarp: Life.* The authorities.—Irenaeus.—Eusebius.—Jerome.—Polycarp's visit to Rome.—Paschal controversy.—The Martyrium.—Its genuineness to be determined by internal testimony.—The question at issue.—Claims to be written by eye-witnesses.—The claim discussed.—The date of the Martyrium.—Interpolations.—The narrative given in it.—Date of Polycarp, p. 191.

The Writings of Polycarp. The letter.—Its genuineness.—Interpolations.—His other letters.—The object of the letter.—Its character.—Abstract.—The Doctrines of the letter.—God.—Christ.—Holy Spirit.—Angels.—Sin.—Salvation.—The Church.—Future State.—Scriptures.—Morality.—Literature, p. 224.

CHAPTER IV. *The Epistle of Barnabas.* Its authorship.—External testimony in favour of Barnabas the Apostle.—The internal evidence strongly against the authorship of Barnabas.—Its conception of Judaism.—Mistakes in regard to Judaism.—Other arguments.—To whom was the letter addressed?—Locality of the writer.—The date of the letter.—Object of the letter.—Its integrity.—Opinions on its theology.—Abstract.—Doctrines.—God.—Christ.—The Holy Spirit.—Angels.—Man.—The Church.—Future State.—The Scriptures.—Morality.—Literature, p. 248.

CHAPTER V. *The Pastor of Hermas.* Its authorship.—External testimony.—Regarded as inspired. Hermas the brother of Pius.—Internal evidence.—Account of Hermas in the book.—His position in the Church.—Date of the work.—Place of composition.—Theology of the work.—Its character and object.—Abstract.—Doctrines.—God.—Christ.—Holy Spirit.—Angels.—Man.—Conduct of Christians.—The Church.—Future State.—Scriptures.—Literature.—The Sinaitic Codex, p. 318.

CHAPTER VI. *Papias: Life.* Writings.—Doctrines.—Editions, p. 393.

INDEX, p. 403.

INTRODUCTION.

CHAPTER I.

ADVANTAGES OF THE STUDY OF EARLY CHRISTIAN LITERATURE.

THIS work professes to be a Critical History of Christian Literature and Theology from the death of the Apostles till the period of the Nicene Council. It is an attempt to investigate the authorship of the various works which have come down to us from that era, and to ascertain the influences which led to their production and determined their character. It also makes an effort to state exactly what were the theological opinions of each writer. The work is therefore an introduction to the study of the Christian writers, and prepares the way for a full consideration of the mode in which Christian theology was developed.

Such studies as these ought not to require any defence in the present day. Men have generally come to recognise the fact that every period of history contains a message from God to man, and that it is of vast importance to find out what that message is. Moreover it is ever a valuable exercise of the mind, to throw oneself into modes of thought and feeling widely different from our own. If we conduct our study in an honest spirit, we come forth from it more conscious of our own ignorance and weakness, and consequently much more charitable towards the failings of others. At the same time our whole range of thought is widened.

These advantages flow in an especial manner from the unprejudiced study of early Christian literature. The point from which we start is the most momentous in the world's history. The fact which we have to consider is the greatest. Even to the most callous mind Christianity must appear a movement of gigantic importance. The student of early Christian literature traces this great moral movement in the words of those who were influenced by it. He as it were speaks with those who felt the first waves of Christ's influence; and he examines their modes of thought that he may see how Christ's Gospel changed their whole being, and how in consequence they worked in and on the world. At the same time he has to rid himself of most of his modern associations. He has to transport himself into a time when the very modes of conception and expression were widely different from those of this age, and he has to realize a thousand influences which acted most powerfully on them, but which have now vanished for ever. If he really feels that he is of one spirit with those old workers for Christ, if he is ready to stretch forth the right hand of fellowship to them, his sympathies will flow largely with most divisions of the present Christian Church, however diverse on some points their beliefs.

A work like the present, as however being merely an

introduction to this profitable study, is necessarily defective in several aspects.

It is defective in that it has to deal with the lives of those earnest men in a purely critical manner. It has to examine carefully every statement made in regard to them—it has to weigh the credibility of it; and thus it sifts the true from the false. It cannot therefore in many instances attempt a portraiture of the men as they lived and moved.

Besides this, the actual life of those men cannot be properly realized unless we realize the heathenism in the midst of which they lived and worked. A man's history is not merely an account of his religious life, but must embrace the whole of his relations, his political and intellectual aims and struggles. Still more so is this the case with the history of an age. And so in truth the history of the Church fails to be a true history, if we cannot bring up before our minds the physical, intellectual, and political features of the ages in which the Church is depicted as living and acting[a].

Yet no satisfactory History of the Church, either by itself or as working amidst heathenism, is possible without such preliminary works as the present. Literary criticism is the foundation on which ecclesiastical histories must rest. In a work like this we deal with the sources from which these histories derive their materials. We try to ascertain how far they are trustworthy. Unless this introductory work is carefully done, the history will rest on an insecure foundation. In no department of study has the character of the authorities been less sifted, and most histories of the Church abound

[a] See Dean Stanley's Introductory Lectures, first published separately, and now prefixed to his History of the Eastern Church.

in baseless statements and serious misrepresentations. Even those writers who have made careful investigations, as Mosheim and Neander, have often omitted to state the reasons of their conclusions, and the reader is left at the mercy of the historian.

Still more necessary is it that we should have exact information as to the opinions of the early Christian writers. Here nothing but the utmost care and impartiality will enable us to reach the truth. And here the misconceptions and mistakes that prevail are innumerable, and act on the present Christian life with injurious effect. My main effort has been simply to record the theological doctrines of the early Christian writers with an anxious desire to state accurately, without exaggeration or distortion, what they thought. I have occasionally attempted to throw light on the mode in which doctrines were developed. Let not the reader however be misled by this word " developed." A statement of the New Testament is often said to be the germ of a doctrine. The image used here is misleading. A doctrine is not a living thing, like a germ. And moreover, even if it were, it has to be remembered that even a germ is developed by attracting and assimilating to itself many foreign elements which are around it. It is by additions from without, and different from itself, that it grows. So in the case of a doctrine. The first statement of it is usually general, just as the first perception of an object by the eye is general[b]. Thus we see and know a face before we have made any definite observation of the colour of the eyes, or the form of the nose and chin. We know that the face is beautiful before we have examined it in detail. This

[b] See Sir W. Hamilton's Lectures on Metaphysics, vol. ii. p. 149.

is the first stage of the doctrine, if I may so call it. But we develope it by ascertaining exactly what is the character of each feature. It is to be noticed that our developments may be all wrong, while our general statement is correct. I may assert in an indefinite way that Ben Ledi is high. If pressed for the exact height in feet, I may be unable to give it, or if I do give it I may be wrong, and yet my first statement is quite correct. So in the case of doctrines. They generally present themselves first in history as broad indefinite truths. Subsequent generations try as it were to fill up these truths by endless particulars, explanations, and additions. And in our efforts to ascertain the particular opinions of a writer, we have to take the greatest care not to give greater precision and definiteness to his thoughts than he himself gave to them. We are to be on our guard against supposing that he was aware of difficulties which only the long course of time discovered, or of shades of difference which only the most searching thought was after long endeavour able to distinguish. Especially in starting we must take care not to identify broad general statements with those minute theories which are called their developments. We shall thus be fitted in some measure for one of the great tasks of the age, namely, to distinguish between what is essential and what is non-essential in Christianity.

There is one advantage which some will expect from a study of early Christian theology in regard to which they will be disappointed. Many theological questions agitate men's minds in these days; and some will turn to investigations like ours, in hopes that new light may be thrown upon them. This is a mistake. The questions which agitate one age are never precisely the same as those which agitate another[c]. They may be fundamentally the same; but the circumstances in which they are taken up are so widely different, that they require different solutions. Thus the question of inspiration as it presents itself to us, never so presented itself to any previous generation. In former times there was not the same strictness in regard to historical criticism; there was a vast amount of carelessness in regard to textual criticism; there was not the same desire for uniformity in history as in nature; there was not the same chronological accuracy; and many other such circumstances, the results of the civilization and thought of this and past centuries, unite to present this question of Inspiration in a light different from that in which it appeared to the early Christian writers. Therefore their decisions are nothing to us, because they did not feel our difficulties, nor had they our desire for precision.

The case is completely altered when these writers are adduced as witnesses to facts. Here we have to deal with them as vouchers for the statements they make. And hence the vast importance of a critical study of early Christian writings in relation to a knowledge of the authorship of the New Testament. It is from them alone that we get any information we have in regard to some of the writers of the New Testament books; and in them alone can we trace the history of these books, and find external testimony to their genuineness. Before this work can be done satisfactorily, we must

---

[c] Hegel has put this well in his Philosophy of History: "Jede Zeit hat so eigenthümliche Umstände, ist ein so individueller Zustand, dass in ihm aus ihm selbst entschieden werden muss, und allein entschieden werden kann." (p. 9.)

know the early Christian writers well, and we must ascertain their characters.

We may also expect some light from them in the interpretation of the New Testament. Too much stress is not to be laid on this point. The Christian writers were not generally men of profound thought, nor were even men of profound thought in those days capable of exact interpretation. It is absurd therefore to speak of the *authority* of the early Christian writers in the interpretation of the New Testament. Yet still as these men lived near the New Testament times, and as the thoughts of one generation propagate themselves through the next, we prepare ourselves for an accurate interpretation of the New Testament by careful interpretation of the writers that followed those of the New Testament, and by a thorough knowledge of their modes of thought.

Besides the interest which the writings of the early Christians possess for the student of history and for the Christian, they have also strong claims to the study of the philosopher and the scholar.

The early Christian writers frequently discuss the philosophical opinions of previous heathen thinkers. Their works are therefore necessary to the historian of Greek philosophy. Thus Eusebius has preserved many fragments of the Stoics not to be found elsewhere. Besides, several of them were philosophers themselves. When they were such, I give an exposition of their peculiar ideas in the sections which treat of their character and merits. Philosophy occupies ever a more and more prominent place in Christian writings and thought, as we advance from the Apostolic days; and the intermixture of philosophy with religion in those times has received and is receiving a good deal of attention from modern philosophers[d].

A knowledge of the early Christian writers is also of great importance to the scholar. The works of Clemens Alexandrinus are a storehouse of fragments of the Greek comic writers. They also contain curious information with regard to the mysteries, as do those of some others. And indeed both in regard to the Greek and Roman religions the writings of the early Christians are invaluable. They were enabled from their position to see many things which heathens never thought of observing.

We also derive from them, and especially from Tertullian and Clemens Alexandrinus, much information in regard to heathen manners and customs. We have sometimes important literary notices in them; and in one of them, Tatian, considerable light is thrown on the history of ancient art.

But a farther claim on the scholar's attention may be made for these Christian writings. Scholarship aims at entering into the thoughts and realizing the lives of the men of antiquity, and from this point of view the distinction between pagan and Christian vanishes. The Christian writings of the second and third centuries are as much in the province of the scholar as Plutarch and Lucian, Athenæus and Dion Cassius, Tacitus and

---

[d] There are three works especially devoted to the philosophy of the Fathers: volume fifth of Ritter's Geschichte der Philosophie; A. Stöckl's Geschichte der Philosophie der patristischen Zeit, Würzburg, a Roman Catholic work; and Die Philosophie der Kirchenväter, von Dr. Johannes Huber, München 1859. A good account is also given in Ueberweg: Grundriss der Geschichte der Philosophie, Berlin 1864, and Erdmann: Grundriss der Geschichte der Philosophie, Berlin 1866.

Juvenal. Christianity grew up from the midst of heathenism, the interaction between the two was strong and powerful, and no continuous or accurate explanation of the one can be given without a close study of the other. The Christian writings therefore form an essential portion of the scholar's work, and accordingly the best histories of Latin and Greek literature, Bähr, Teuffel, Bernhardy, Müller and Donaldson, take the Christian writers within the scope of their criticism.

CHAPTER II.

PRINCIPLES OF CRITICISM—EXTERNAL TESTIMONY.

In this and the following chapters we state the main principles of our criticism. We ascertain the genuineness of a work, either by historical testimony or by internal evidence, or by both.

In regard to testimony, we set out with the principle, that the only proper historical evidence is contemporary testimony. Even the assertions of contemporaries are not always to be trusted. How few, for instance, of those alive at the present day could be called competent witnesses in regard to the birthday of the Duke of Wellington or of the Ettrick Shepherd. And if we examine the facts of our own consciousness and the reports of daily life, we shall see that even individuals themselves are not always to be relied on for the facts of their own history. The uncertainty which thus attaches to even proper historical statements, must not drive us into complete unbelief. We receive the statements of contemporaries as true, unless there is some reason to look upon them as false. We do not hold these statements as absolutely certain, but we take them for the most likely we can get, and we rely on them just as we rely every day on assertions that are not based on incontestable evidence. As we move away from the particular period into testimony of a later period, we are not warranted in rejecting it entirely, for the testimony of a later period may be, and generally is, the testimony of contemporaries handed down from one generation to another. But we must be more cautious. We have now to take into account the exaggerations and distortions which result from the passage of a thought or statement through various minds. We must remember the marvellous proneness of human beings to mistake one thing for another, especially when they are under any influence which may blind them to the naked truth. These and many such considerations must be ever present to the mind in the estimate of evidence. A previous examination of all these considerations [a] would be useless. The discussion of particular cases brings them out into clearer light than any formal investigation. Only this important principle is to be continually kept in mind—that all past evidence is to be measured and estimated by our experience of evidence in the present time. "Historical evidence," says Sir George Cornewall Lewis, " like judicial evidence, is founded on the testimony of credible witnesses. Unless these witnesses had personal and immediate perception of the facts which they report, unless they saw and heard what they undertake to relate as having happened, their evidence is not entitled to credit. As all original witnesses must be contemporary with the events which they attest, it is a necessary condition for the credibility of a witness that he be a contemporary; though a con-

[a] Various writers have devised and arranged canons, in order to determine the genuineness or spuriousness of books. For a list, see Walchii Bibliotheca Patristica, p. 258.

temporary is not necessarily a credible witness. Unless therefore an historical account can be traced by probable proof to the testimony of contemporaries, the first condition of historical credibility fails[b]." The forgetfulness of this principle has retarded the ascertainment of the exact truth, in regard to many points of early Christian literature, to a degree that is scarcely conceivable. A factitious reverence for some of the Christian writers has brought along with it a too great facility of belief. And there is added to this the circumstance that our information is often so scanty that there is a strong temptation to supply what is defective by the help of statements that have not the shadow of historical evidence in their favour. The various attempts at a history of early Christian literature, which we shall notice subsequently, all signally fail in carrying out this first and essential principle of historical evidence.

Before we can deal satisfactorily with evidence in a particular case, we must know the character of the witnesses. I deem it therefore appropriate to take a short survey of the authorities on whom we have to rely in the history of Christian literature, and my method of treating them.

At the outset it may be remarked of all our witnesses, that it is utterly absurd to expect from men of the first five centuries of the Christian era anything like an adherence to the principles of modern historical criticism. In individual cases, where controversy and its frequent concomitant persecution raged keenly and men's minds were sharpened, we may sometimes meet with an ap-

[b] Inquiry into the Credibility of the Early Roman History, vol. i. p. 16. See the whole section, and the notes to it.

proach to it: but where there is nothing to rouse the critical faculty, we may generally expect an amount of credulity and arbitrariness which surpasses the capacities of most moderns. This statement applies not only to Christian writers, but to the very best thinkers of ancient times[c], to the very best critics of Alexandria, and, not least, to the great Aristarchus in his own department[d]. It applies with especial force however to the era in which Christian literature arose, and we meet with the same easiness of belief and arbitrariness of procedure in Plutarch, Diogenes Laertius, and Lucian, as in Hegesippus and Eusebius.

The want of a critical faculty exhibits itself in not clearly estimating the value of external testimony. There is a certain contentedness in all ancient writers which allows them to put faith in the most improbable assertions; and sometimes their power of belief is coextensive with their power of fancy, so that a guess with them easily crystallises into a fact. This state of mind, where facts and fancies meet with the same ready welcome, occurs most frequently in the case of those men who were much conversant with speculation. Thus we find in Clemens Alexandrinus, and in Origen, an exceeding readiness to identify with the persons mentioned in the New Testament any Christian individuals of the same name who had existed before their own time.

[c] See Zeller's estimate of Aristotle in his Platonische Studien, p. 131, quoted by Schwegler in the introductory chapter of his Nachapostolisches Zeitalter, vol. i. p. 45, where he exhibits fully the uncritical character of all the ancients. For the Latin historians, see Merivale's History of the Romans under the Empire, vol. vii. p. 307.

[d] See Wolf's Prolegomena ad Homerum, c. xlvi. 'Is critico judicio maxime pollere putabatur qui optimum poëtam proprio ingenio emendare poterat.'

The examination of the genuineness of early Christian literature is a matter of great difficulty, because there is little of contemporary testimony. No one set about composing a history of the Church and its affairs until Eusebius. We have accordingly only scattered notices which have to be pieced together. The great danger in such a case is, that the modern critic give reins to his imagination, and out of the few scattered facts or likelihoods patch together, by the help of fancy, a complete whole. Hence the history of Christian literature has been overloaded with innumerable conjectures. It has been my object to avoid as much as possible conjecture itself, and the record of conjectures. The statements of contemporaries and those later writers who may be supposed to have had access to good sources, are set down and examined. And no attempt is made beyond this to settle points that it is utterly impossible to settle without evidence. This remark applies especially to dates, few of which can be fixed with anything like certainty in the first or second centuries.

I have proceeded in a peculiar way with the writers subsequent to the first three centuries. My first, my best, and almost my only authority is Eusebius. Eusebius wrote his history just at the point of time when there was still some sympathy for the true spirit of the early writers, but when that sympathy was soon to be utterly absorbed in sympathies for thoughts of a very different kind. He was devotedly attached to the study of the early writers; he had ample opportunities; and he was capable of using them well. The immense value of his book arises from the circumstance that he was careful in recording his proofs and in quoting from the writers of whom he was giving an account. Like all the rest of his own age, he was utterly uncritical in his estimate of evidence, and where he as it were translates the language of others into his own, not giving their words, but his own idea of their meaning, he is almost invariably wrong. Every statement therefore which he makes himself, is to be received with caution. But there can be no question about the trustworthiness of his quotations. Some indeed have accused him of a wish to conceal the truth; but it seems to me that the charge is utterly unfounded, and is based on a total misconception of the meaning of one or two passages in his writings. It need scarcely be observed that, like all of his own age, he does not realize the various stages of thought and practice through which the Church passed. He generally gives the old thoughts and the old practices the clothing and names which they had in his own day.

Eusebius did his work well; and his history became henceforth the standard book on the subject. All subsequent writers have simply repeated his statements, sometimes indeed misrepresenting them. Eusebius therefore stands as my first and almost only authority. When statements additional to those of Eusebius are found in subsequent writers, I have looked on them with suspicion. No doubt many things did escape the notice of Eusebius. We have one remarkable instance in his omission of all mention of Athenagoras. We know also that he was very imperfectly acquainted with the Latin Christian writers. But we have no reason to suppose that his omissions in regard to the early Greek Christian writers can be made up for by the unattested statements of subsequent historians. The assertion of Maximus in his Preface to the works of Dionysius the

Areopagite[f], that he had seen many books not known to Eusebius, is worthless in itself. For the works he was recommending were forgeries, and all the books which he had in view may have been spurious. We know that to have been the case in at least one instance, for he finds fault with Eusebius because he omits mention of all the works of Clemens Romanus, except his two letters. I agree entirely with the principle laid down by Evans[g] in speaking of Eusebius: "Later authors supply useful subsidiary information, but no fact should be insisted upon, nor any weighty inference drawn, where they are the sole authority."

The only work that was professedly composed on the same subject as the history of Eusebius was Jerome's book "De Illustribus Viris." As far as he has Eusebius for his guide, Jerome simply translates him, now and then misconstruing his sentences[h], occasionally contracting, and sometimes adding a few sentences of fresh matter.

Any additions he makes are invariably to be looked on with suspicion, as we shall see. Jerome has often been called the greatest critic of the Fathers, but certainly his critical powers never come out in his historical treatises. He intended at one time to write a history of the Church; and one should have inferred from this that he had examined the subject; but there is nowhere in his writings proof of his being acquainted with writers unknown to Eusebius, or of his having made more minute investigations. And in the few historical

[f] Tom. i. p. xxxvi. ed. Corderii.

[g] Biography of the Early Church, series i. p. 11.

[h] See instances of Jerome's mistakes in Greek in Pearson, Vind. Ign. part ii. c. x.

treatises which he has left, especially in his Life of Hilarion, we have convincing proof that he could be deluded by the most absurd stories, that in fact he had no idea of examining critically circumstances which took place even in his own time and his own neighbourhood. Besides all this, we know from his violent harangues against Helvidius, Jovinian, and Vigilantius, that, if his anger were roused, truth and decency were cast to the winds. We have also to take into account the rapidity of his production. He wrote at an inordinate rate, not having time to consider his thoughts or statements, and not caring to marshal his authorities[i]. To such inconvenience did his rashness sometimes put him, that he had to retract statements which he made in regard to incidents in his own life[k].

Several after Jerome took up the subject of the illustrious writers of the Church, but their productions do not deserve attention. Most of them indeed do not discuss the writers of the first three centuries, and the few that do are hasty uncritical short sketches based on Jerome[1].

---

[i] See Daillé, De Vero Usu Patrum, p. 236.

[k] For some of Jerome's wilful mistakes and exaggerations, see Maitland's Church in the Catacombs, p. 229, note; Isaac Taylor's Ancient Christianity, vol. i. p. 343 ; Daillé, De Vero Usu Patrum, p. 153 ; and especially Dr. Gilly's Vigilantius and his Times, p. 93 ; and Zöckler's Hieronymus, p. 383. Notwithstanding the plainest proofs of Jerome's want of critical power, Roman Catholic writers have placed him even above Eusebius as an authority. See Möhler's Patrologie, p. 21.

[1] The works of these writers are collected by Fabricius in his Bibliotheca Ecclesiastica, in qua continentur De Scriptoribus Ecclesiasticis S. Hieronymus, Gennadius Massiliensis, Isidorus Hispalensis, Ildefonsus Toletanus, Honorius Augustodunensis, Sigebertus Gemblacensis, Henricus Gandavensis, Anonymus Mellicensis, Petrus Casinensis, Jo. Trithemii Abbatis Spanhemensis Liber de S. E. Aub. Miraei Auc-

The writers that refer incidentally to the history of the Church are comparatively few. The men of the fourth and later centuries did not busy themselves much with the thoughts of the earliest among their predecessors. The most noteworthy are the ecclesiastical historians and the historians of heresies.

The historians that relate the history of the Church in the first three centuries—Rufinus, Cassiodorus, and Nicephorus—simply translate or compile from Eusebius, often, like Jerome, misunderstanding, and as often wilfully changing. The only historian that can be said to seem to occupy an independent position is Sulpicius Severus, and his work is altogether the merest abstract. The praises and credit which have been yielded to this writer are for the most part undeserved. There is not the slightest proof that he gave a moderate degree of attention to the ante-Nicene writers; and there is the most convincing proof in his Life of St. Martin that he was totally unfit to investigate evidence [m].

The historians of the Heresies are equally uncritical. Epiphanius seems to have been a man whose ideas of geography, history, and chronology were confused to an extraordinary degree. The one quotation which Daillé has made in proof of his ignorance of geography is

tarium de S. E. curante Jo. Alberto Fabricio S. S. Theolog. D. Hamburgi 1718, fol. Fabricius occasionally adds copious notes, especially to the work of Jerome.

[m] Neither Sulpicius Severus nor Cassiodorus deserves the name of historian. Bernays in his monograph Ueber die Chronik des Sulpicius Severus (Berlin 1861), shows that the Historia Sacra of Severus was regarded as a Chronicle by writers who lived not long after his time. Cassiodorus calls his book a Chronicon, and he is more entitled to be noticed in a history of early Christian Literature for two or three chapters in his De Institutione Divinarum Scripturarum than for the few allusions to Christian authors in his Chronicon.

sufficient to show how much we may rely on his statements. We extract it here. "The Pheison," he says, "is called Ganges among the Indians and Ethiopians. The Greeks call it Indus. For it encircles the whole of Evilat, both little and great, even the parts of the Elymeans, and passes through Great Ethiopia, turns to the south, and within Gades flows into the Great Ocean[n]." Of his historical confusions we shall have many instances; and nothing more need be said here, than simply that the preference which some critics have shown for Epiphanius[o], Theodoret, and the later writers, is totally unwarranted. Most of these writers were monks who lived away from the world of realities, who could scarcely distinguish between facts and their own fancies, and who were probably very indifferent whether Hadrian lived ten or a hundred years before Marcus Antoninus. The causes why their statements have been preferred are mainly two. They have sometimes made assertions in harmony with the conjectures of the critics, and they have been looked on as sainted men whose every opinion and affirmation must have been true, or, at the very least, close to the truth.

All that has been said of the uncritical character of such eminent writers as Epiphanius and Theodoret applies with equal force to the accounts of heresies given by such men as Philastrius or in the anonymous or pseudepigraphous libelli collected by Oehler[p].

As we advance in time, our authorities become fewer.

[n] Anchor. p. 60, D, c. 58, Dindorf.

[o] Dodwell, for instance, has fallen into a series of wild conjectures from trusting to Epiphanius. See Dissertat. in Irenæum, iii. 19.

[p] Corporis Hæreseologici Tomus Primus continens Scriptores Hæreseologicos Minores Latinos. Edidit Franciscus Oehler. Berolini 1856-61. The second portion contains the Panarion of Epiphanius.

They consist of the chroniclers, and of several writers who mention the books that come in their way. The chroniclers form a numerous class. They are all more or less dependent on Eusebius. Eusebius published a work called Παντοδαπὴ ἱστορία, consisting of a chronographia and a κανὼν χρονικός. His researches were based on the labours of Julius Africanus. The second part, or Canon Chronicus, was translated into Latin by Jerome; but Jerome took great liberties with his author's text, as he himself informs us in the preface, suppressing some parts and filling out others. In Jerome's translation alone the work came down to us; and it is only within recent times that an Armenian translation has been discovered [q]. Eusebius wrote this work before he wrote his ecclesiastical history. His Ecclesiastical History necessarily treated the matters with which we are concerned more fully than his Canon Chronicus. So that we should have derived little assistance from the work if it had come down to us complete and in Greek. If the Armenian version contains the whole, Eusebius must have treated ecclesiastical matters very concisely indeed, and certainly not with the same care which he afterwards bestowed on that

[q] Eusebii Pamphili Cæsariensis Episcopi Chronicon Bipartitum: nunc primum ex Armeniaco textu in Latinum conversum annotationibus auctum, Græcis fragmentis exornatum. Opera P. Jo. Baptistæ Aucher Ancyrani, Monachi Armeni et Doctoris Mechitaristæ. Venetiis 1818, 4to. It was published also by Mai and Zohrab the same year at Milan. Mai has published an abstract of the Greek which he had discovered, in his Scriptorum Veterum Nova Collectio (Romæ 1825), vol. viii. pars. i. More recently has appeared Eusebi Chronicorum Canonum quæ supersunt edidit Alfred Schoene. Berlin 1866. This contains Jerome's translation, with a Latin translation of the Armenian and of a Syriac epitome, and a collection of the Greek fragments.

part of his subject. In Jerome's translation many additional dates are inserted, and the subject is treated more amply; but the same faults that are evident in his work De Illustribus Viris are manifest here also. From some cause or other there is considerable discrepancy between the numbers as given in the Armenian version and in the translation of Jerome. This circumstance is probably owing to the ease with which one number is mistaken for another, especially by careless transcribers. The principal chronicles which treated of the same periods as that of Eusebius, were the Chronicon Paschale, and the Chronicles of Georgius Syncellus, Georgius Cedrenus, and Joannes Malalas. So convinced was Scaliger that these writers had recourse to Eusebius, that in his restoration of the Eusebian text he thought he was justified in extracting indiscriminately from these writers and setting the extracts down to the account of Eusebius[r]. It is generally allowed now that Scaliger went too far; and that at least some of these writers frequently consulted the sources[s]. Yet they will be found, when we come to examine the information they give additional to that of Eusebius, to have been led astray or to have been

[r] Thesaurus Temporum Eusebii Pamphili: Chronicorum Canonum omnimodæ historiæ libri duo, interprete Hieronymo: item autores omnes derelicta ab Eusebio et Hieronymo continuantes, ejusdem Eusebii utriusque partis Chronicorum Canonum reliquiæ Græcæ, quæ colligi potuerunt. Opera ac studio Josephi Justi Scaligeri, editio altera. Amstelodami 1658, fol.

[s] See for instance in defence of Georgius Syncellus the Præfatio of Goarus in p. 61, vol. ii. of the edition of Syncellus and Nicephorus by Wilhelm Dindorf: Bonn 1829. These volumes form part of the Corpus Scriptorum Historiæ Byzantinæ, got up by Niebuhr. The Chronicon Paschale appeared in the series Bonn 1832, and the Chronicle of Malalas, Bonn 1831; both edited by Louis Dindorf. Cedrenus appeared in 1838-39, edited by Bekker.

rash in their interpretation, rather than to have rested their statements on new authorities. In fact they were a careless set of writers, content with making books of considerable size, without the slightest thought as to what the quality of the books might be. Some of them, like Malalas, committed the most ridiculous blunders, such as calling Sallust and Cicero the wisest poets of the Romans, and making Claudius Cæsar the founder of the city of Britain, not far from the Ocean[t]. Besides, these chroniclers deal very superficially with the history of our period, passing over it in a cursory manner, and often giving us merely untrustworthy lists of bishops. They are most valuable when they supply us with extracts from the early Christian writers; but even then we have to take care that the chronicler has not been betrayed into accepting as genuine what a little critical power would have clearly shown him to be spurious.

Of the other works which throw some light on early Christian literature, the most valuable is the Library of Photius[u]. The notices it contains of books which he read may be relied on. Not so much can be said of the opinions he may express in the course of his narrative. But still, in regard to the doctrines contained in the early writers, he was in a position to speak more fairly than the writers of the fourth and fifth centuries. They wrote at a time when many of the most important doctrines were being discussed. They were not without a wish that the early writers should be on their side,

[t] See Hodius, Prolegomena, sect. xxxvi. p. lxv. in Dindorf's edition. And on the name and character of Malalas, see De Quincey's article on Bentley, in his Works, vol. vi. "Studies on Secret Records."

[u] Photii Bibliotheca: ex recensione Immanuelis Bekkeri. Berolini 1824, 4to.

though sometimes they cared little about them. Photius was entirely free from this desire. His dogmas were to his own mind infallibly certain ; and by them he judged other writings without respect of persons.

A few scattered allusions to early Christian writers, and quotations from their books, occur in other less known works, such as the Ὁδηγός of Anastasius Sinaita, in the Parallels of John of Damascus, and in the works of Anastasius Bibliothecarius. Many of the Martyria have been preserved by Simeon Metaphrastes. All these are credulous and careless.

CHAPTER III.

INTERNAL EVIDENCE.

It will be seen from the short notice of the authorities given in the last chapter, that the external testimony may sometimes fail us entirely, and sometimes be next to worthless. Our only resource then is in the internal evidence. Sometimes internal evidence may be of the most satisfactory nature, but generally it gives us very little. It is often valuable in establishing a negative conclusion. It seldom helps us to definitively positive knowledge. Its negative conclusions are often however of the most important nature; and as this is especially the case with our subject, we must say a few words on the circumstances which compel us to have such frequent recourse to internal evidence.

The productions claiming to belong to the first three centuries, for which there is no satisfactory external testimony, are very numerous. They may be divided into two large classes. The one class includes those works which were undoubtedly written within the first three centuries or shortly after. The origin of these books is a matter for investigation in each particular case. But in general it may be remarked that many productions appeared anonymously, and often in fictitious form, and that later writers attributed them to men who had been eminent in the Church. A large number of these works owe their present state to circumstances of a different nature. The process of their formation seems to have been the following. There was at first some small writing which became the nucleus of interpolations, additions, and emendations. Each transcriber, as he copied, inserted the notes of previous readers into the text, and often from his heated imagination added something himself. This is acknowledged on all hands to be the case in many of the Martyria, in the Apostolical Constitutions, and in the Liturgies. This circumstance makes it a duty to proceed with the utmost caution and circumspection in the treatment of the early writers. We may possibly have before us works of the early writers, but works which at the same time have received additions from later hands.

The second class of writings consists of those which themselves claim to be the productions of men of the first three centuries, but which there is strong reason to suspect were deliberate forgeries. The writers of the first three centuries while they lived gained for their opinions no more authority than the soundness of the truth, the clearness of the style, and their personal character naturally commanded. But at a subsequent period an eager desire was felt to obtain for some practices and dogmas the stamp of a long antiquity. And hence arose a considerable number of forgeries which pretended to be the works of the early writers. Many of these forgeries are so gross that almost all parties have now agreed to treat them as spurious. Such, for instance, are the letters of the so-called early Popes. In some cases, however, considerable difficulty is experienced, and the difficulty is increased by the circumstance that we know for certain that even in the second and third centuries the letters of bishops and others were excised and interpolated in their lifetime. Dionysius mentions that his epistles were mutilated[a], and Cyprian tells how he sent back a letter to the presbyters and deacons in Rome, to see if it were genuine and had not been tampered with[b].

Some are of opinion that many early Christian writers forged writings in the name of the great men of former days with no bad intention. Men in those days, they say, thought more of the reasonableness of the subject-matter than of the authority of the writer, and hence they did not hesitate to issue works in the name of another man, simply because they were in the style or mode of thought peculiar to that man[c]. This liberal theory, however, has not the slightest historical foundation on which to rest. None of the ancient writers seem to have been aware of this peculiar method of expressing tendencies. And perhaps it would not have been so readily proposed in modern times, had not the number of writings which the school who hold the theory suppose to be forged been enormous. If almost all the writings of the New Testament are forgeries, and if nearly all the productions of the second century are also of doubtful character, some mode of palliating at least, if not entirely defending, the procedure of the authors of these works is absolutely necessary.

In addition to all this, an opinion is prevalent that

---

[a] Eus. Hist. Eccl. iv. 23. See Heinichen's First Excursus, vol. iii. p. 354.

[b] Cypriani Opera, Goldhorn, Epist. IX. c. ii.

[c] See Schwegler, Nachapostolisches Zeitalter, p. 80.

the writings of the early Christians were peculiarly open to interpolations and corruptions from transcribers, translators, and editors.

This opinion is not without reason. When we come to treat of Origen, we shall see on what arbitrary principles Rufinus and even Jerome translated from Greek into Latin, correcting the doctrine as well as omitting when it was deemed inexpedient to insert the sentence. Perhaps, however, the corruptions of the early writings have been unduly magnified, and the Roman Catholic editors especially have often been blamed for interfering with the text, where little or no blame was deserved [d]. The early editors unquestionably introduced several expressions of a papistic nature into Cyprian's works. But many of the so-called interpolations were made only in the indexes. And the omissions of which they were guilty were dictated by that hierarchical principle which forbids a full exhibition of everything to popular gaze—a principle which may have been adopted and carried out with the strictest regard to truth and honesty. The fact that the Roman Catholics have not tampered with the early writers is best proved by the circumstance that these writers often bear testimony against the practices of the Roman

[d] There is a work on the subject in English: "A Treatise of the Corruptions of Scripture, Councils, and Fathers, by the Prelates, Pastors, and Pillars of the Church of Rome, for the maintenance of Popery. By Thomas James, Chief Keeper of the Public Library in the University of Oxford. Revised and corrected from the editions of 1612 and 1688 by the Rev. Edmund Cox, M.A., London 1843." James was evidently crazy on the subject of the "foul corruptions;" so much so, that he would at last trust manuscripts only. He did good service, however; and his book is a curiosity worth looking into. For other works of a similar nature, see Walchii Bibliotheca Patristica, p. 307.

Catholic Church, and that the theory of development has been devised to account for the silence of early Christian authors in regard to many dogmas afterwards deemed important[e].

On the whole, then, the approach to the criticism of early Christian literature must be made with suspicion and caution. But we are not to be driven by such considerations into absolute despair. On the contrary, we shall find that most cases admit at least of some kind of solution. The mode of dealing with the internal evidence will of course vary in each particular case.

But the main principle of all such investigations deserves deliberate enunciation here—that a book to which external testimony bears no satisfactory evidence cannot be regarded as genuine if its doctrines or its statements differ materially from the doctrines or statements of the period. It is acknowledged that such a standard is fallible. But the mode of procedure is the only right one. The book is set aside for the time as of uncertain date. All the works which are known to belong to the period to which this one claims or is said to belong are examined carefully, and if modes of expression, evolutions of opinion, indications of controversies, and such like occur in it which do not occur in them, we may set down the book as being of a later date.

In the application of this test we deem it of essential importance ever to keep before our minds the effect of time in modifying opinion and testimony. This has generally been overlooked. The Fathers have been massed together as a whole, and the opinion of one

[e] See Daillé, De Usu Patrum; and especially Blunt, On the Use of the Fathers.

has been appealed to as if that were sufficient to prove that such must have been the opinion of another, if he be but a Father. Now it is to be remembered that the writings of the so-called Fathers extend over a period of four or five hundred years at least; that this period was a period of much excitement, of rapid movement, of great and most momentous change. Christianity at its commencement is working invisibly, hardly noticed by the most keen observer outside. Before its close, it has become the acknowledged religion of the government, and it finally supplants heathenism. It is not possible that such changes should take place in the outward circumstances of Christians without many inward changes, many transformations and mutations in the modes of thought and feeling, among those who called themselves by the name of Christ.

We go farther than this, and maintain that not only every century but every age brought its changes. We perceive this in our own age, and we cannot doubt that it was so in past ages. The remark applies peculiarly to periods which form the commencement of eras. The new idea which is launched is confined at first to a small circle, gradually widens and widens its sphere, comes into contact with more obstacles and subjects of influence, until it penetrates the whole mass, and at the same time has itself been greatly modified. Now this I take to be the case with Christian thought; and I think that every new phase of it produced great changes in each age. The fundamental faith in Christ remains the same in all ages; but the ideas which make up the total of Christian thought are continually altering. The proof of this will be presented throughout the whole of this work. All I wish to maintain at present is, that such a course of matters is the only course agreeable to what we see now.

The errors that result from the forgetfulness of this principle affect the character of testimony and the history of opinion, and accordingly in the application of opinion as a test we must guard against confounding the opinions of one age with those of another. We shall take as an instance the works of Ignatius. If the letters of Ignatius contain doctrines different or additional to those contained in the letters of Clemens and other nearly contemporary writers, we have just reason to doubt their genuineness. Nor is it enough to prove that these doctrines are contained in writings twenty or thirty or forty, much less two or three hundred years after the supposed time of Ignatius. For the very point we maintain is, that the lapse of time brought about changes, that these later writings contain evidence of the changes, and the letters of Ignatius must go into the same age with the writings with which they agree.

A forgetfulness of the effects produced by the lapse of time has also led to a misapprehension of the statements of later writers in regard to earlier. An instance will best explain what is meant.

We take the case of Eusebius. We wish to inquire into the history of a particular writer. Now we may rest assured that whatever Eusebius will say, he will speak in the language of his own time and circle. As Shakspere attributes to Julius Cæsar a belief in the devil, Eusebius will not fail to identify the opinions of his predecessors with his own. If a man is called a bishop, he will understand the term to mean just such a bishop as he saw and was. But it would be a matter of great blame to us if we were to commit the same mistake. We must examine documents contemporaneous with the writer, ascertain from them the state of the Church and the meaning of the word 'bishop' then, and understand Eusebius according to the light which we thus gain.

CHAPTER IV.

THE LITERATURE OF THE SUBJECT.

It is not necessary to devote much space to a consideration of modern works on Patristic literature. There are several works not very inaccessible which are specially designed to convey all requisite information to the student.

The most useful of these is the Bibliotheca Patristica of John George Walch (editio nova ab Jo. Traug. Lebr. Danzio adornata: Jenæ 1834, 8vo; with a supplement by Danz: Jenæ 1839). His criticisms as well as his learning are considerably superior to those of a Roman Catholic writer who has lately gone over the same path: —Dr. Michaelis Permanederi Bibliotheca Patristica: Tomus Primus: Patrologia Generalis (Landishuti 1841). Tomus Secundus: Patrologia Specialis (vol. i. 1842). These works will supply more particular information with regard to the authors now to be mentioned.

The works relating expressly to the history of Christian literature may be divided into two great classes— works of real research and value; and mere sketchy productions or summaries, intended either for prelections or for the masses. Each of these classes may again be divided into Roman Catholic and Protestant.

The first considerable work by a Roman Catholic on the Fathers, is that of Antonius Possevinus, " Apparatus ad Scriptores V. et N. T., eorum Interpretes, Synodos et Patres Latinos ac Græcos, horum Versiones, Theologos Scholasticos quique contra Hæreticos egerunt." (Venet. 1603; Col. Agripp. 1708, ii. fol.) It was followed by a work of Cardinal Bellarmine's, Liber de Scriptoribus Eccl. (Romæ 1613, 4to), which belongs more properly to the sketchy class, and is not much more than a catalogue of the writers and their works. It was however so highly esteemed by the Roman Catholic Church, that several of its able sons—Labbe, Andr. du Saussay, and Casimir Oudin—re-edited the work, and added laborious appendices. Labbe's Dissertations were published in two vols. 8vo, Paris 1660. Casimir Oudin, besides publishing a supplement to Bellarmine (Paris 1682, 8vo), wrote a separate commentary on ecclesiastical writers : " Casimiri Oudini, Commentarius de Scriptoribus Ecclesiæ antiquis illorumque Scriptis tam impressis quam manuscriptis adhuc extantibus in celebrioribus Europæ bibliothecis a Bellarmino, Possevino, Philippo Labbeo, Guilielmo Caveo, Ludovico Ellia du Pin, et aliis omissis ad annum MCCCCLX, vel ad artem typographicam inventam : cum multis dissertationibus, in quibus insigniorum Ecclesiæ autorum opuscula atque alia argumenta notabiliora accurate et prolixe examinantur." (Tom. iii. Lips. 1722, fol.) Before the appearance of Oudin's work, several valuable contributions to Christian literature had been made. Foremost among these is Tillemont's Mémoires pour servir à l'Histoire Ecclésiastique des six premiers siècles (Paris 1693, xvi. 4to), which treat in the fullest manner of the lives of the Christian writers. This was succeeded by a work which has been praised by Protestants for its liberal spirit : Louis Ellies du Pin, Nouvelle Bibliothèque des Auteurs Ecclésiastiques, contenant l'histoire de leur vie, le catalogue, la critique, et la chronologie de leurs ouvrages; le sommaire de ce qu'ils contiennent; un jugement sur leur style et sur leur doctrine; et le dénombrement des différentes éditions de leurs œuvres. (Paris 1686-1714, xlvii. 8vo.)

Du Pin afterwards published the history of the writers of the first four centuries in Latin : "Nova Bibliotheca Auctorum Ecclesiasticorum." (Tom. ii. Paris 1703-15, fol.)

His works were translated into English. (Third ed. Dublin 1722, 3 vols. fol.)

Shortly after this appeared a work of vast research and learning by Nicolas Nourry, which extended however only to the first four centuries. It was called " Apparatus ad Bibliothecam maximam veterum patrum et antiquorum scriptorum ecclesiasticorum Lugduni editam." Paris (1703-15 ; 2 tom. fol.) Many of his dissertations have found their way into the various editions of the Christian writers.

The work of Du Pin, though much praised at its appearance, was felt by the Roman Catholic clergy to be unsatisfactory in its judgments on the Fathers, and it was affirmed that it was also very defective. To remedy these defects, the Benedictine Remy Ceillier undertook a history of the sacred and ecclesiastical writers; but Protestant readers will not regard his production as so fair as that of Du Pin's. Its title is " Histoire Générale des Auteurs Sacrés et Ecclésiastiques, qui contient leur vie, le catalogue, la critique, le jugement, la chronologie, &c. Par le R. P. Dom

Remy Ceillier." (Paris 1729-63, xxiii. 4to.) He gives an account not merely of the lives but of the theology of the writers, always keeping the Roman Catholic dogmas in view. It has found great favour with the French clergy, and is now republishing with additions, principally from Roman Catholic writers. The first volume appeared in 1858, at Paris.

In more modern times there are two works of considerable importance by Roman Catholic writers. They both treat more or less fully of the doctrines as well as of the literature of the Christians. The first of them is voluminous. It is styled " P. Gottfridi Lumper Monachi Benedictini, &c. Historia Theologico-critica de vita, scriptis atque doctrina sanctorum patrum aliorumque scriptorum ecclesiasticorum trium primorum sæculorum ex virorum doctissimorum literariis monumentis collecta.'' (Augustæ Vindelicorum 1783-99, xiii. 8vo.) It is a remarkably learned work. The industry displayed in it is enormous, and the writer has considerable critical powers. But he is fettered by Roman Catholic traditions and sympathies. He devotes considerable space to the detail of the legends which found their way into the unauthenticated narratives of the lives of the early Christians.

The other work is by a man of great religious fervour and high-toned feeling, who laboured diligently and successfully in the field of patristic study, I. A. Moehler. His work is named " Patrologie oder Christliche Literärgeschichte, aus dessen hinterlassenen Handschriften mit Ergänzungen, herausgegeben von Dr. F. X. Reithmayr." (Regensburg 1840.) It was published, as the title implies, after his death. Reithmayr has made considerable additions to the work, and he seems to have taken liberties with the manuscript entrusted to him. It is a decidedly able and interesting work, and pervaded by that spirit of liberality which distinguished Moehler and his school. It is however distinctly Roman Catholic throughout. It extends only to the first three centuries, and is in many respects defective, notwithstanding the additions of Reithmayr. It has the merit, moreover, of being very readable. Remarks are made on the prominent points of the theology of the writers as well as on their lives, and a list of the principal editions is added. The work is not now to be procured in German, but there is a French translation[a] of it, which may be had.

Of the more compendious works by Roman Catholic writers, merely the names of the writers may be given. First on the list, and of some importance because he lived at a time when more MSS. were extant than are now, is John of Trittenheim, whose work, with the additions of Aubertus Miræus relating to the sixteenth and seventeenth centuries, is given in Fabricius. After Miræus were Sixtus Senensis (1575), Stephanus Lusignanus (1580), Simon de Voyon (1607), Suffridis Petri (1630), Sardagna (1772), Wilhelmus (1775), Schleichert (1777), Tobenz (1779), Macarius a S. Elia (1781), Stephanus Wiest (1785), Lang (1809), Winter (1814), Rueff (1828), Busse (1828), Goldwitzer (1829), Kaufmann (1832), Locherer (1836), Annegarn (1839), Fessler (1850–51), Deutinger (1850–51), Charpentier (1853), Magon (1864), and Alzog (1866).

Here should be mentioned also a work, the tone of which is very much in harmony with that of Roman Catholic writers. It is by Constantinus R. Contogones,

[a] Par Jean Cohen, Louvain 1844, 8vo.

Professor of Theology in the university of Athens, and an ardent adherent of the Greek Church. As yet only two volumes have been published of this work. It is able and learned. It gives an account of the theology of the writers as well as of their lives and writings, and it contains short notices of the editions. The title of the work is as follows: Φιλολογικὴ καὶ κριτικὴ ἱστορία τῶν ἀπὸ τῆς α' μέχρι τῆς η' ἑκατονταετηρίδος ἀκμασάντων ἁγίων τῆς ἐκκλησίας πατέρων καὶ τῶν συγγραμμάτων αὐτῶν. ὑπὸ Κωνσταντίνου Κοντογόνου, καθηγητοῦ τῆς θεολογίας ἔν τε τῷ πανεπιστημίῳ ’Οθῶνος καὶ τῇ ἐκκλησιαστικῇ ‘Ριζαρείῳ σχολῇ. τόμος πρῶτος, περιέχων τὰς τρεῖς πρώτας ἑκατονταετηρίδας. (’Εν ’Αθήναις 1851· τόμος δεύτερος, περιέχων τὴν δ' ἑκατονταετηρίδα, 1853.)

The tone of Roman Catholic writers is generally that of profound submission to ecclesiastical tradition. A strong defence is often made for worthless treatises which exalt the Church and praise virginity. Many men however arose among them of a liberal and truthful spirit, though these generally had to suffer for their fairness. Ellies du Pin had to submit to a recantation, and his work was condemned at Rome. Oudin tells us that to avoid like censure he did not discuss opinions, but confined himself to the examination of the genuineness or spuriousness of works. He went farther however than Ellies du Pin, and withdrew entirely from the Roman Church. Those Roman Catholics who have come under the influence of the Tübingen school are also remarkable for the freedom and fairness with which they discuss Patristic subjects. This liberality is very prominent in the work of Moehler, and yet the Roman Catholic respect for tradition and the Fathers of the Church is likewise very strong. Indeed he says in his work that he hopes it will have the effect of arousing a more earnest and deeper attachment to the principles of his Church. We have seen him praise the critical powers of Jerome, and he extols those even of Isidor of Sevilla and Photius[b]. He therefore readily accepts statements from later writers which viewed as historical evidence are utterly worthless.

The only systematic work of importance which Protestants have produced on early Christian literature is the history of Cave. It is styled " Scriptorum Ecclesiasticorum Historia Literaria a Christo nato usque ad sæculum XIV." (First part, Lond. 1688, with an appendix by Wharton, 1689. Second part, with an appendix by Robertus Gerius, Lond. 1698[c].) The whole work was republished after the death of Cave, with additions from his manuscript notes, at Oxford, 1740–43, in two volumes folio. It was reprinted at Basle in 1741–45. Cave wrote a variety of other works on the history of Christian writers in English; but most of the sketches, while characterised by the marked individuality of the writer, by an earnest desire for the truth, and by extraordinary erudition, contain such a curious jumble of stories, credible and incredible, that no reliance can be placed on them. In fact this blemish attaches to his great work. He evidently formed no distinct notion of the nature of testimony, he does not go critically into an examination of the witnesses, and accordingly his work cannot be relied on, nor does it enable the reader to form an opinion for himself.

Among the Protestant writers who have given a more or less sketchy account of the history of Christian

[b] Page 22.

[c] This is the edition quoted in this work for want of the better.

literature, are Melancthon, Joannes Schopf, Joannes Gerhard, Joannes Bottsacus, Joannes Hülsemannus, Joannes Chph. Meelführer, Joannes Gottfr. Olearius, Abraham Scultetus, Varenius, Chph. Sandius, Casp. Heuniseh, G. Stolle, Pestalozzi, Engelhardt, Boehringer. There are several works which treat simply of the lives of the early writers and martyrs, and several which relate only to a particular class of writers. Among these are the works of Tentzel, Ittig, Clericus, and Loescher.

In England, the works expressly on the Fathers, besides those of Cave, are very few.

1. Biographia Ecclesiastica ; or, the Lives of the most Eminent Fathers of the Christian Church who flourish'd in the first four centuries. Adorned with all their effigies, curiously ingraven. London : 1704, 2 vols. 8vo. The writer quotes no authorities. The book is worthless, except for its curiously engraven effigies.

2. Evans: Biography of the Early Church; by the Rev. Robert Wilson Evans, M.A. London 1837. Second series : 1839. This work contains the lives only of some of the most distinguished men who flourished before the Arian controversy. It attempts to realize the circumstances of each. It is well written, conceived in a devout spirit, and does not obtrude High Church views very strongly. There is no attempt to sift evidence, but an exceeding willingness to believe anything said to the credit of the early writers by Eusebius, or writers anterior to him.

3. Narratives of the Lives of the more eminent Fathers of the first three centuries, interspersed with copious quotations from their writings, &c. By the Rev. Robert Cox, A.M. London 1817, 8vo. This work

also is not critical. It is conceived in a devout spirit, and is one of the best of its kind.

4. The Book of the Fathers of the Christian Church, and the Spirit of their Writings. London 1837, 8vo. The writer of this work does not meddle with more than one or two of the Fathers who lived before the Nicene Council. This is the case with another popular but well written and accurate book of the same nature, "The Popular Preachers of the Ancient Church: their Lives, their Manner, and their Work." By the Rev. W. Wilson, M.A.

There are several other works which profess to give accounts of the lives and works of the Fathers of the first three centuries; such as a very small book, called Barecroft's Ars Concionandi (1715, 8vo); Dr. Adam Clarke's Concise View of the Succession of Sacred Literature (London 1830, 8vo), which is very concise indeed; and book first of Riddle's Christian Antiquities (London 1839, 8vo); but they do not require special notice.

All the works which treat directly of the Fathers in English, except Cave's, are professedly popular. They do not discuss the authorities which they cite, and they often dispense with authorities altogether.

Those in England who have busied themselves with the study of the early Christian literature, have almost invariably given the results of their investigations in works devoted to doctrines, or to the history and antiquities of the Church.

Besides the works now mentioned, there are several which treat exclusively of Latin Christian writers. These will be mentioned in their place. There are also several collections of dissertations on the Fathers, the best known of which is Sprenger's Thesaurus Rei Patristicæ, &c. Wirceb. 1784-92, iii. 4to.

I conclude with a notice of the collections of the Fathers. Of course it is generally sufficient to have one of these. If any one has Gallandi, or Migne, he is well furnished; but they do not supersede the use of separate editions. They are generally called Great Libraries.

The first great collection of importance was that of Margarinus de la Bigne (8 vols. fol. Paris 1575), frequently reprinted. The next important work is Henr. Canisii Antiquæ Lectiones (Ingolst. 1601-8, vi. 4to), and afterwards reprinted under the care of Basnage. The library of De la Bigne was published at Cologne, with a supplement, edited principally by Andreas Schottus, 1622; and at Paris 1639, with a supplement by Morellius. Another edition, with additions, was published at Paris in 1654; with still more additions at Lyons 1677. The library of De la Bigne was completely surpassed by the Bibliotheca Veterum Patrum Antiquorumque Scriptorum Ecclesiasticorum, postrema Lugdunensi longe locupletior atque accuratior. Opera et Studio Andr. Gallandii, Presb. Congreg. Oratorii Venet. (Venet. 1765-88, xiv. fol.) A library of the Fathers is publishing in Paris by J. P. Migne, "Patrologiæ Cursus Completus," with notes and many very important dissertations; and in Latin by Caillau and Guillon.

There are also several important translations of the works of the Fathers. They generally discuss the lives of the writers. The two best known of these are Rössler: Bibliothek der Kirchenväter in Uebersetzungen und Auszügen (Leipz. 1776-86, x. 8vo), and Genoude:

Les Pères de l'Eglise, traduits en Français (viii. 8vo); a strongly Roman Catholic work.

In English there is a complete translation of all the ante-Nicene writings with the exception of some of Origen in Clark's ante-Nicene Christian Library, edited by the Rev. Alex. Roberts, D.D., and James Donaldson, LL.D. (in twenty-four volumes, 8vo. 1867-72).

There are also two other works in English, somewhat limited in their aim:—

The Christian Fathers of the First and Second Centuries: their principal remains at large, with selections from their other writings, &c. By the Rev. E. Bickersteth (London 1838.) And—

The Writings of the Early Christians of the Second Century, &c. Collected together and first translated complete by the Rev. Dr. Giles. (London 1857.)

There is no satisfactory lexicon of Patristic Greek. Two efforts have been made to supply the want. The first is the well known work of Suicer, "Thesaurus Ecclesiasticus, e Patribus Græcis, ordine alphabetico, exhibens quæcunque Phrases, Ritus, Dogmata, Hæreses et hujusmodi alia spectant, &c." (Amstel. 1682, fol. editio sec. 1728.) Suicer's work is as much a dictionary of facts as of words. The other attempt is the Greek Lexicon of the Roman and Byzantine Periods, by E. A. Sophocles, Boston 1870, which is substantially the same work as A Glossary of Later and Byzantine Greek, by E. A. Sophocles, forming Vol. VII. New Series, of the Memoirs of the American Academy. (Cambridge and Boston 1860, 4to.) The author deserves the greatest credit for his diligence and learning; and, though necessarily imperfect, his book supplies a very great want.

CHAPTER V.

THE TÜBINGEN SCHOOL.

OUR account of the writers who have dealt critically with early Christian literature would be defective without a special discussion of the Tübingen School. The members of this school are, properly speaking, theologians, and the appropriate place for a review of their works would seem to be in our notice of the treatment of early Christian theology. The school however is remarkable for its want of any Christian theology of its own; and it has in consequence occupied itself with criticising the theology of others, and the documents in which that theology is contained, from an historical point of view.

The Tübingen school is composed of a considerable number of eminent theological scholars, who differ very widely from each other in many opinions, but agree in what they call their critical method. The head and patriarch of the school was the late Dr. Baur, Professor of Evangelical Theology in Tübingen.

Drawing their philosophy from Hegel, they look upon Christianity as an ordinary phenomenon, to be explained as any evolution in history ought to be explained. History, they maintain, has always to exhibit the idea pervading and energising the circumstances. It must ever distinguish between mere appearances and what really and eternally is. These ideas show themselves as tendencies of the human mind running through an age: and a development takes place when contrary tendencies struggle against each other, and a unity arises out of the struggle. Christianity was such a struggle of tendencies: Jewish Christianity on the one hand, and heathen Christianity on the other, being the two great tendencies. Jewish Christianity sought to confine Christianity within the rites of Judaism: it was therefore national, particular, and aristocratic. Heathen Christianity, on the other hand, proclaimed all men alike in God's sight. Paul was the preacher of this universalism. "The Pauline universalism indeed contains nothing that could not be regarded originally as an essential momentum of the self-consciousness of Jesus[a]." Yet Jesus did not give expression to this universalism. Such a course would have repelled those whom he wished to conciliate. Even many of the elder apostles did not attain to the universalism of Paul; and after the apostles died, Jewish Christianity gained the upper hand in wide regions of the world. A new element however made its appearance, seen in the fourth Gospel, which succeeded in reconciling the particularism of Jewish Christianity with the universalism of Paul, and hence arose the Catholic Church. The mission of Gnosis was to give adequate expression to Christianity as the absolute religion. It was thus a definite form of a philosophy of religion. These are the main features of the Baurian explanation of Christianity.

[a] Die Tübinger Schule und ihre Stellung zur Gegenwart, von Dr. F. Ch. Baur, p. 35: Tübingen 1859.

This is not the place to discuss Hegelianism—to show that the philosophy of history is not history, and to exhibit the fatal mistake of Baur in taking the philosophy of Christianity for Christianity itself. I have to do with Baur's theory only as it affects the treatment of early Christian literature by him and the rest of the Tübingen school. Now the great and primary fault of this school in this aspect is their disregard of historical evidence. Their philosophy does not permit them to believe in a miracle. They must therefore dishonour the documents in which miracles are related. But if they can reject the evidence of books so well attested as some at least of our Gospels, what will they not do with other and later documents for which there is only the same kind of testimony but of less amount? The Tübingen school thus have felt themselves forced to throw almost the whole of the documents of the first and second centuries of the Christian era into one general unauthenticated mass. Some have spared a few[b]; some have cast all into uncertainty. To have thus by negative criticism brought these books into the class of the spurious, they reckon no great accomplishment. Previous Rationalism had done as much as this. The task of the school is, by means of ideas, to sift these writings, to determine their origin, to find out their authorship, and to discover their date. Criticsm of this nature they believe is the only sure kind, being based on that which is; on the Idea, not on mere individual appearances[c].

[b] Baur himself regards the letters of Paul to the Galatians, Corinthians, and Romans, as in the main genuine. His scholar Bruno Bauer has rejected all. The only other book in the New Testament which may possibly be genuine, according to Baur, is John's Apocalypse.

[c] See Schwegler's Nachapostolisches Zeitalter, vol. i. p. 10.

Now, however satisfactory the pursuit of dates and authors by means of ideas or tendencies may be to a Hegelian, to a common mortal the work seems utterly useless, and more like an effort of arbitrary fancy and caprice than of sound reason. Let us take an instance. If none of the so-called letters of Paul are well authenticated, if the Acts of the Apostles is not an historical book, how is it possible for Baur to determine what was Paul's character, and from that character to infer that the letters to the Galatians and Romans and Corinthians are in harmony with it, and the letters to the Philippians and the Colossians are not? On the contrary, we should be inclined to suspect that though Baur fancies he is led in his selection of these epistles by his idea, he is misled by a pet theory, and sets them down as genuine because he can find some show of reason in them for the notion that Paul and Peter differed from each other, and that that difference was a serious one, and that therefore, as he infers, it must have continued for a long period. And one is the more confirmed in this idea of the arbitrariness of procedure by the circumstance that the various members of the school differ very widely from each other; that no sooner does one member construct, by means of his conception of the idea, than his neighbour destroys and builds anew in another way. Thus Schwegler's work of construction is most effectively pulled to pieces by Ritschl, who in the first edition of his book proceeded according to the same mode of criticism.

As it is impossible in the body of my work to enter into the reasonings of the Tübingen school, it may be as well here, once for all, to record the main results of this transcendental criticism as given in Schwegler's Nachapostolisches Zeitalter. The very exhibition of these results will show to how great an extent the school is influenced by merely subjective considerations.

Schwegler supposes a remarkable contrariety to exist between the original Christianity and the Pauline doctrines; and that only towards the end of the second or beginning of the third century were these elements reconciled. The reconciliation of these elements was the moving force in the Church. The first form of Christianity was Ebionitism, seen in the apostles Peter, James, and John, and represented by the gospel of the Hebrews, which was the only gospel in use up to the middle of the second century (vol. i. p. 215). The Gospel of Matthew is a form of this gospel (p. 241), marking the Catholic conclusion of the Ebionitic gospel literature. The Church was Ebionitic up to the middle of the second century. Paul's letter to the Roman Church proves that it was in his time Ebionitic; and the first literary document of the Roman Church, the Pastor of Hermas, is Judaic (p. 328). It must have been written before the middle of the second century. In about twenty years after the composition of Hermas, *i.e.* between 150 and 160 A.D., appeared Hegesippus, the earliest historian of the Church, and thoroughly Ebionitic (p. 342 ff), a pet writer with Schwegler. The writings of Justin Martyr exhibit a peculiar phenomenon—a mixture of Ebionitism with Platonism, the Logos-doctrine being Platonic. Schwegler thus speaks of the Ebionitic elements: " Ebionitic is Justin's whole view of the original connection and object of the incarnation of Christ; Ebionitic his complete silence in regard to the Apostle Paul, whose letters he never quotes, into whose peculiar doctrines (*Lehrbegriff*) he nowhere enters, and whose apostolic authority he consequently seems to have rejected; Ebionitic his rough form of Chiliasmus, his Demonology, and the horror at the eating of sacrificial flesh connected therewith; his view of the Holy Ghost, whom he seems to have reckoned among the angels; his angel-worship; his valuing the Old Testament so much above the New." (p. 360.)

The second stage of the Church's progress finds the Church Ebionitic, but arguing with a peaceful tendency. This is seen in the Clementine Homilies, in which the foundation is thoroughly Ebionitic; but they " form an intermediate step in the process of the development of Ebionitism into Catholicism." (p. 378.) He takes the Clementines as " really representing the consciousness of their time. As their writer thought and wrote, so thought the Church (*so dachte man*) in Rome towards the middle of the second century." (p. 405.) The original Apostolic Constitutions are of the same character, and exhibit the same stage of development, as also do the Letter of James and the second Letter of Clemens.

The third stage brings us to Catholicism—a state of neutrality and a peace-conclusion, as he calls it. This stage is represented by the gospel of Mark (p. 455), written towards the end of the second century; in the Clementine Recognitions, written between 212 and 230, which are a Catholic form of the Homilies; and in the Second Epistle of Peter, which he looks on as the "last stone of the Ebionitic development-series." (*Schlussstein der Ebionitischen Entwicklungsreihe*, p. 490.)

Parallel with this Ebionitic development-series runs the Pauline. Also in it there can be distinguished three periods or stages analogous to the Ebionitic: a decidedly

Pauline; an intermediate, conciliatory; and lastly, a catholicizing. (vol. ii. p. 1.)

The type of the first stage is found in the First Letter of Peter. It was written by one of the Pauline party in the time of the Trajan persecution. Along with it goes the Κήρυγμα Πέτρου.

The principal writings of the second stage are the Gospel of Luke, the Acts of the Apostles, and the First Letter of Clemens. In the Gospel of Luke the Pauline element appears as the groundwork of the Gospel, the Judaistic as interpolations and additions. The Gospel must have been written after the Trajan persecution. The Acts of the Apostles is also a work of the same character,—a tendency-writing to conciliate the Petrine to the Pauline party. It is freer in its handling of historical matters. It was written some time between the Trajan persecution and the blossoming of Gnosis. (p. 118.) The First Letter of Clemens is also an intermediate work. Its standpoint is that of a fair middle, of an honourable capitulation. (p. 128.) It cannot have been written by Clemens, nor by a contemporary of the apostles. The Epistle to the Philippians also belongs to this stage.

The types of the third stage are the Pastoral Letters and the Letters of Ignatius. The Pastoral Letters were written some time about 169. They express a desire for unity—the main idea by which the Pauline and Ebionitic elements were reconciled. The Letter of Polycarp is a mere shadow of the Pastoral Letters, written about the same time and in the same circles.

The Ignatian Letters he calls the Programme of Catholicity in the process of growth (*Programm der werdenden Katholicität*). They contain the Pauline idea of universality and the Petrine idea of unity or uniformity worked out in a logical and all-sided manner. The combination of these two ideas resulted in the Catholic Church. (p. 161.)

Schwegler then discusses the moment of Catholicity, and among these Gnosis especially. We pass over this part of his book as having little to do with the present purpose, only remarking that he here finds a place for the Epistle of Barnabas, which he says was written in the first half of the second century. (p. 241.)

Then in the fourth Book he proceeds to show how Ebionitism and Paulinism developed into Catholicism in the churches of Asia Minor. The principle of development is different from what it was in Rome. In Rome it was politico-ecclesiastical; in Asia Minor speculativo-theological. (p. 246.) The Roman Church produced the unity of the episcopal system; the Asiatic Church the Logos-idea and the doctrine of the Trinity. The Letter of Paul to the Galatians gives the first clue to the state of the churches in Asia Minor. They were Ebionitic. (p. 247.) The earliest and most important document of this Ebionitic Church is the Apocalypse of John, written by that apostle before the destruction of Jerusalem. (pp. 249–50.) The age of John continued for a considerable time, and found its most complete expression in Montanism, the successor of the Apocalyptic age.

At the same time the Logos-doctrine sprang up in opposition to the Jewish or Ebionitic notion of Christ. The first representative of this Pauline phase is the Epistle to the Hebrews, and later the so-called Epistles of Paul to the Colossians and Ephesians. In the meantime Montanism added to the elements of thought by the first presentation of the Holy Spirit as divine; and Montanism was thus the first that brought to light the doctrine of the Trinity. (pp. 339-40.) Last and latest of all comes the Gospel of John, entirely Catholic in its spirit, and yet not without traces of a Jewish element, which however is glorified. (p. 346.)

Such is the reconstruction of the early Church history and literature according to the doctrine of tendencies. One is utterly amazed how a man could deliberately sit down, and day after day, casting to the winds every fragment of historical evidence, build, and build after his own fashion, as Schwegler has done. He seldom troubles himself about giving reasons for his opinions. He merely brings out his perceptions or illustrations of the tendencies. Of course he does occasionally appeal to historical testimony—human nature must come out sometimes; but his appeals are generally very perverted and unsatisfactory; and the most signal proof of this is, that almost the whole scheme rests on the statements and thoughts of a work which is purely fictitious, the Clementine Homilies. The tremendous importance of this work to the Baurian school is a damaging sign of its inherent weakness.

I need not say that I regard the whole of the Baurian scheme to be a pure fiction, as Bunsen has justly named it. The difference between Peter and Paul, on which it is based, I believe vanished very soon; and, as I have said, I do not think there is the slightest proof that two gospels were preached by the apostles: the Pauline by Paul, and the Petrine by the rest of the apostles [d].

[d] Baur himself calls it a "doppeltes Evangelium:" Das Christenthum und die Christliche Kirche der drei ersten Jahrhunderte, p. 51. (Second edition, Tübingen, 1860.)

They all preached one and the same Saviour, and therefore one and the same gospel. The only circumstance that gives a colour to Baur's theory is this:—The apostles continued in the practice of their Jewish rites, as far as we know, up to the last. The point is by no means a settled one; but the most likely opinion is, that they did observe the Jewish Law in at least many of its institutions. But this circumstance gives simply an appearance of feasibility to the Baurian theory. When we look at the real state of affairs, every appearance vanishes. The essential belief of Christianity was a belief in Christ—a confidence in Him that He would save from sin. Whoever in early times had this belief was reckoned and treated as a Christian. He might continue his Jewish practices, or he might not. That was a matter of indifference. Faith in Christ alone was absolutely necessary. There is not the slightest shadow of a proof that any of the apostles, or, subsequent to the Jerusalem conference, that any of the members of the Church within the first two centuries, insisted on the observance of Jewish rites as essential to salvation. On the contrary, we have the best of proof that those who did insist on the essential nature of the Judaistic rites felt the Church too liberal for them, and left it. The proof of these statements will appear in the course of this work. And the fact is that both Baur and Schwegler might have seen this if they had defined their Jewish Christianity and their Pauline Christianity. If Jewish Christianity did not insist on the practice of Jewish rites as essential, then it was not opposed to Pauline Christianity. Only on the supposition that it did will the Baurian theory be of any use. But the Tübingen school have entirely failed to prove this point; indeed have intentionally or unintentionally not attempted the proof. In fact in none of the writings which will come under our notice shall we find the least indication that any of the writers were so Jewish-Christian as to condemn the Pauline party for not observing the Jewish rites. And all that Baur and Schwegler have done is simply to point out the traces of certain beliefs which to their minds indicate a Jewish origin. But these very beliefs were perfectly consonant with Paulinism; nay, many of them were the very beliefs of the Apostle Paul[e].

In addition to all this, we have to take into account that beyond the early documents of the New Testament, that is, the Epistle to the Galatians, the First Epistle to the Corinthians, and the Acts of the Apostles, we shall not find in any well authenticated work any statement of any kind to the effect that there existed a Pauline and a Petrine party. Both parties, as far as they belong to the end of the first century and to the second century, are indebted to the tendency-criticism for their origination.

While thus speaking of the Tübingen school, I wish at the same time to state my belief that they are thoroughly honest men, earnest in their search after truth, and that they deserve much praise for their fearlessness and industry. If they were not honest men they would have agreed far more frequently than they have done. And their differences will necessarily increase as they go on in their researches, because the fundamental idea is a wrong one, and their philosophy

[e] Ritschl's work on the Altkatholische Kirche shows this in a very satisfactory manner. See, for instance, his criticism of Schwegler's reasons for regarding Justin Martyr as Ebionitic.

is not well adapted at least for historical purposes. And this too I take to be a reason why, when I glance over their performances and sum up the fruits of their own investigations, I find no tangible progress. There has been a vast deal of industry, of hard study, of honest investigation; but, as far as substantial fruit is concerned, there is not much: rather there is wider and wider confusion, greater and greater perplexity. The only fact which seems to come out plainer and plainer is, that no good can be reached by this new mode of criticism. And this is all the more remarkable that most members of the school are men of considerable powers. Baur himself, when he is not misled by his ideas and tendencies, is clear and forcible; as in his Letter to Bunsen on the Ignatian Epistles, and in part of his work on the Origin of Episcopacy. The same remark might be made of Hilgenfeld and of others. And they all deserve the greatest credit for the fresh life which they have given to the thorough study of the early Christian writers.

CHAPTER VI.

EARLY CHRISTIAN THEOLOGY.—MODE OF TREATMENT.

THE second part of our subject is the exhibition of doctrines. This exhibition differs from what is given in books on the history of dogmas, in that the whole of a man's doctrines are presented at once, and the connection of the opinions of one with those of another is left to the reader's own investigation. An objection also may be taken to the mode of presenting these doctrines, in that it does not bring before the mind the consecution of ideas in the writer's conception of the doctrines. Especially the leading idea of the particular writer is not brought so prominently forward as perhaps some would like[a]. This however is not an objection of any moment. What I wish to present is an accurate statement of what these men did believe; and I venture on an explanation of the central points of these beliefs only when I think that there really were central points, and that these central points are plainly to be seen. It is to be remembered that most of them did not think systematically, and that though it may be of advantage for us to arrange their opinions systematically, yet we do

[a] Hilgenfeld, for instance, has urged this objection against Schliemann's presentation of the Clementine doctrines.

them considerable injustice thereby. For we present as hard intellectual propositions what in them were living and energising truths.

I have made a distinction in my treatment of the opinions of the early and later writers. In the case of the former, up till the time of Irenæus, I have adduced every passage which seemed to me to bear on theological questions. The reason for so doing is, that I wish as far as possible to enable my readers to determine for themselves what doctrines are not mentioned. For the omissions are by far the most significant feature of these writers to our time. Besides this, the language of these writers is more indefinite, and can therefore be more easily distorted, than that of later writers. When we approach the time of Irenæus, doctrines come out more in the shape of direct propositions, and the writers become more conscious not merely of what they believe but of what they do not believe. It is sufficient to adduce these precise statements of theirs, which when once made settle the question of their beliefs.

The one great requisite in the treatment of doctrines is fairness. The temptations to be partial and one-sided are exceedingly strong. One must therefore approach these writers with a single desire for historical truth, with a willingness to enter into the thoughts of the writers, and with a resolution as far as possible to relate the truths held by them without any colouring from his own mind.

The two great temptations in the treatment of doctrines are, to forget the effects of the lapse of time, and to seek merely one's own opinions in the statements of the early writers.

In the first case we are apt to forget how totally

different the age of the early Christians was from ours, how different the modes of thinking that prevailed among them, and how various were the agencies around them that were influencing their modes of thought and expression.

In the second case we go to the Christian writers with the hope of finding confirmation of our own opinions. We look upon these opinions as the only true ones. We trust that the early Christians also held them, and wherever we see the slightest resemblance to them we pronounce an identity of beliefs. We shall have more to say of these causes of error when we survey the history of the treatment of doctrines.

As the same time, however, it must be confessed that it is scarcely possible, perhaps I should say it is impossible, for a man of a sound mind to present an objective view of these doctrines without being somewhat influenced by his opinion of the connection and development of the various beliefs. Gradually as he proceeds in his work, a desire for order arises in his mind, and out of the perception of this order arises a certain directive power to him in estimating beliefs.

Now it seems to me that all sects of Christians can get a fair starting-point for viewing the development of doctrine in what we may suppose to have been the great beliefs which were preached to the early Christians. We at the present day have a complete New Testament before us—we have the light of many ages reflected on it, the most powerful minds have helped to an understanding of its contents, the most powerful philosophical intellects have endeavoured to develope and systematise its principles. We ought therefore to be in a much better position in the present day for interpreting, systematising, and developing the New Testament doctrines than the early Christians were. Many of them could not read, most of them had no philosophic powers, most of them heard the gospel only through the voice of apostles—to the poor the gospel was preached. Many of the books of the New Testament must have been unknown even to those who could read. In fact "there was a spoken Christianity as well as a written Christianity. The former existed before the latter. It was independent, and for the most important ends complete and sufficient[b]." This spoken Christianity, this oral gospel, must have been of such a nature that it could be easily understood by the masses—could have been conveyed from one man to another. This oral gospel is our starting-point. What was it? what were its great truths? They all centred round Christ. The main one was that Christ was the source of a new spiritual life. He was the son of God, the fulness of God in human form. He showed God to men. His will was one with the Divine will: God's power was his power. He came to the world to save men from sin, to lead men to God. He taught in his lifetime the way of life—to love God and keep his commandments. He died for men that He might bring them to God, and He rose again from the dead, sat down at the right hand of God, received all power in heaven and on earth, and from that time was with all those who trusted Him, sustaining them, guiding them, and preparing them for complete holiness. Those who thus trusted Christ would at death go to be with their Lord, would afterwards have their bodies raised up, and would reign with Him in complete sinlessness. Those who rejected Him, on the other hand, could

[b] Professor Godwin: p. 73 of the Essay mentioned afterwards.

expect nothing but God's wrath. Such would be the main truths proclaimed[c].

The existence of a preached Christianity must be ever kept in mind while we treat of the progress of theology. And at the same time we have to remember that the early Christians preferred what they received from living witnesses to what was contained in books. A statement to this effect is made by Papias, and reasons are given for it in Clemens Alexandrinus. What this preached Christianity was, however, we should be utterly unable to realise, had we not had written documents of the age. And accordingly it is in the apostolic writings in which we are to seek for the complete exhibition of the earliest form of Christianity. These writings, as it appears to me, present us with the most astonishing moral phenomenon that human history exhibits. The intensity of the moral heat, if I may so speak, of these writings is something scarcely comprehensible to us. All the philosophers before them sought for some highest good. Even when they allowed that the highest good was to be found in morality, they, by expressing a

---

[c] I refer my readers once for all to Professor Godwin's admirable Essay on the Earliest Form of Christianity, in the Introductory Lectures delivered at the opening of the New College, London, October 1851 (London 1851). Professor Godwin developes at greater length than I have room for, the main topics of this preached Christianity. He sums up thus: "His humble state, his Divine mission, the nature of his miracles, the perfection of his character, the spirituality of his kingdom, his salvation from sin, his sacrificial death, his exaltation to supreme dignity and universal dominion, his constant presence by his Spirit with his Church, his coming again as the Judge of all men—these were subjects on which oral communications could be made, with all the correctness and completeness needful for an intelligent and cordial acknowledgment of Jesus as the Son of God and the Saviour of men."
—P. 94.

possible difference, showed that the idea of happiness was present to their minds. In the case of the apostles, the idea of happiness and every other such notion pass entirely out of sight in their anxious longing for complete holiness, for living, as they called it, for Him who was the Life. There cannot be a doubt that in Christ's salvation freedom from a fearful punishment is implied; yet the apostles never once mention this freedom from punishment. The only possible mode in which they can conceive calamity coming upon them is in the anger of their heavenly Father. To be alienated from Him, to incur his displeasure,—all evils were included within that. In fact that was the one evil. And so when they looked forward to a future life, there is not a single expression of anticipation of mere earthly joy, not the slightest hint of mere pleasure. Their whole longing is to be with that Lord who had died to wipe away their sins. This is the main feature of these writings.

In respect to theology there is not the slightest attempt to systematise. There is the most absolute belief of certain great truths. There is a determined, unwavering confidence in Christ as the author and finisher of their faith. But there is not the remotest desire to unravel the puzzles which afterwards beset the theological world. There is in their childlike faith an utter unconsciousness of them. Thus they speak of Christ invariably as one individual being. They knew He was the Son of God. They knew He was real man. But it was the Son of God that became man, just as the child and the grown up man are the same being. How this took place, whether He had two natures or wills, in what metaphysical relation He stood to the God and Father of all—these and many such questions never occupied their minds. So again in regard to Christ's death. They knew that Christ did die to take away their sins and to bring them to God. They knew that He in his death did conquer death. They knew that He had stripped the principalities and powers of the air of their dominion; but how his death could effect such a grand revolution in the souls of men and in the relations of the universe to man, this was a question which did not occupy their minds. And indeed it might be easy to show that they had a strong disinclination to any such speculations.

This unspeculative character of the apostolic teaching the modern Church has to a considerable extent lost sight of, simply because dogmatic theology has now taken the place of practical in many respects. Still those who have deeply considered the subject have been all but unanimous. And the acknowledgment has been made by all parties; by the thoroughly evangelical Count de Gasparin[d], by the liberal Neander, and by the Roman Catholic Moehler. "The apostles," says the last mentioned, "related the history of the Lord, and with that alone the whole contents of Christianity were given[e]." The fact also was in some measure appreciated by the first man who formed a theological system. "Now we ought to know," says Origen, "that the holy apostles, preaching the faith of Christ, stated in the clearest language certain things which they believed to be necessary, to all, even to those who seemed rather backward in the search after divine knowledge, evidently leaving the reason of the assertion of those things to be

[d] Christianity in the Three First Centuries, p. 82.
[e] Literärgeschichte, p. 49. See also p. 50.

inquired into by those who should deserve the excellent gifts of the Spirit [f]," &c.

With regard to outward forms the apostles verged towards indifference. They did not look on baptism as of great consequence: they came to view the observance of Judaistic rites as a matter of convenience and taste, and they regarded the observance of the eucharist as binding on them, because it was a memorial instituted by Him who was their life, and the object of intensest love. In the administration of their communities it seems to me that there ruled one great principle, viz. that each Christian man was a king and a priest—that by the indwelling of Christ's Spirit within him he had become a free man in the highest sense of the word. The organisation of churches under various office-bearers might proceed in different ways, provided this principle were untouched—and in fact the offices in the Church, if they might be called offices, were not fixed established modes of government, but wise methods of bringing every gift of the Church into active employment.

Such is a general view of the faith and practice of the early Christians. This mode of belief was childlike, and full of trust in God.

But gradually, as we advance in the history of the Church, we find greater precision. This precision is almost invariably the result of opposition to false notions. The fact is, as it appears to me, that the writers of the first three centuries strove unconsciously for the simple practical view of the great truths, but equally unconsciously they gave way to the same speculative tendency

[f] De Princip. lib. i. Præfat. c. iii. See Redepenning, Origenes, part i. p. 393.

to which the heretical opinions of their antagonists owed their origin. As we deal with the individual writers, we shall have more ample opportunity to show this. Here let it be remarked, that the opinion that there was originally only a broad basis of great truths, not too closely defined, and conceived in a purely practical shape, can alone harmonise with many of the circumstances which will present themselves to us, such as the coexistence of a true Christianity with materialism, the frequent discussions of the nature of Christ, and the rejection by some of the doctrine of the divinity of the Spirit. And this broad basis is also the explanation of the extraordinary liberality of the early Church. For I think it will appear that the Church received all who expressed their confidence in Christ and their willingness to obey Him. They might speculate as they liked. They might even believe Christ their great Leader to be of merely human origin. But so long as they were willing to follow Him, and keep in the goodly fellowship of Christians, the Church welcomed them [g]. And I think it will also appear that the early heretics were not expelled from the Church, but that they (the Gnostics among them) first set up certain dogmas, and would fain have confined Christianity to those only who believed these. They went out from the Church because the Church was too liberal for them. The Church however gradually came to adopt the same course; and we then find an agreement, not in faith in Christ, but in belief in certain dogmas insisted on as the essential characteristic of a Christian. More and more were the

[g] A very remarkable instance of this is the way in which Paul dealt with those in the Corinthian Church who denied the Resurrection. He does not once threaten expulsion.

simple views of the early Christians expanded into logical precise propositions by means of a philosophy. These propositions have had the result of showing what human reason can accomplish in the explanation of divine mysteries. They have served the same purpose as the various schemes of metaphysics in regard to knowledge. We have become, or ought to become, conscious of our ignorance, and therefore we ought to be at once more humble and more charitable.

CHAPTER VII.

HISTORICAL SURVEY OF THE MODE OF TREATMENT.

THE literature which in some way or other bears on the doctrines of the early Christians is of enormous extent. In every controversy an appeal has been made to the works of the primitive Christians, and there is not a dogma in the whole of our theological creeds for the defence or destruction of which the Fathers have not been ransacked. We can therefore take only a rapid glance at the prominent features in the treatment of early Christian doctrine.

We begin with Roman Catholic writers. At the time of the Reformation the Romanists appealed to the Fathers as authorities, they paid respect to most of them as saints, and they were inclined to place them in positions of the highest honour. Such a feeling led them to bestow the utmost pains on the proper editing and explanation of their writings; and, as we have seen, they have been by far the most diligent cultivators of patristic literature. The false honour however which they paid to the early Christian writers proved a mighty obstacle to the exact appreciation of their sentiments and character. The Romanists wished to see in the Fathers the doctrines of their Church, and they did see them. Not only so, but the great majority of the Church deem it impossible that there can be any real disagreement in doctrine between the members of the Church, to whatever age they may belong. Consequently development is out of the question, and the history of dogmas is looked on as a questionable attempt [a].

Those who have ventured on the attempt have been strongly biassed by their antipathy to Protestantism. They were far more eager to obtain confirmation of the pope's authority, of the priesthood, of the sacramental efficacy, and other external points which were called in question, than of the Trinity, or the Atonement. And accordingly several Romanist writers are remarkable for the candour with which they state the defects of the early writers. Foremost among these is the Jesuit Petavius, whose work De Theologicis Dogmatibus (Paris 1644–50) [b] was one of the very first attempts at a history of dogmas as a whole [c]. He candidly confesses that a great number of the early writers, especially Athenagoras, Tatian, Theophilus, Tertullian, and Lactantius, believed "the Son to have been brought forth (produc-

[a] Neander states of Professor Hermes of Bonn, that "he scrupled to give lectures upon it." (Lectures on the History of Christian Dogmas, by Dr. Augustus Neander. Edited by Dr. J. L. Jacobi. Translated from the German by J. E. Ryland, M.A. Two vols. London, Bohn, 1858, vol. i. p. 28.) See also Baur, Lehrbuch der Christlichen Dogmengeschichte: zweite Ausgabe, pp. 35 and 57. (Tübingen 1858.) Both these works give an historical account of the treatment of the history of dogma.

[b] This learned work has been lately republished: Dionysii Petavii Aurelianensis e societate Jesu, opus de Theologicis Dogmatibus expolitum et auctum, collatis studiis Car. Passaglia et Clem. Schrader, ex eadem societate. Romæ 1857. Dedicated to the Pope.

[c] See Baur: Lehrbuch der Christlichen Dogmengeschichte, p. 32.

tum) by the Supreme God the Father, when he wished to make the universe, that he might employ him as a helper." He adds, that "some others, like Origen, thought the Father superior to the Word in age, dignity, and power;" and that "they thought he had a beginning not less than creatures, that is, that his personality (ὑπόστασιν) had not been distinct from eternity [d]." The fact is that Roman Catholic writers are not without a motive for exhibiting the defects of the early writers. Maintaining, as Petavius[e] did, that councils alone settled doctrines, they regard these aberrations of individuals as proofs of the uncertainty of individual opinion. Many of them moreover have held to the notion that the Fathers did not state their opinions fully; that they often concealed their true sentiments from the public eye, and occasionally argued to suit circumstances. The great truths which they believed, they handed down by tradition; and only in the Church, the living possessor of these traditions, can we have a complete exposition and authoritative explanation of the sentiments of the great teachers of Christendom. In Newman's Essay on Development, the very defects of the early writers are dwelt on at length, and made the basis of an argument[f]. He sets it down as an unquestionable fact, that it was only by degrees that both the theology and the practice of the Church attained their maturity. And he propounds as his theory that God intended this development to take place, and that He provided for it by arranging that it should take place under the eye of Infallibility. And he maintains that this theory is more feasible than any that has been proposed. His words

[d] De Trin. i. v. 7.   [e] See Prolegomena, c. ii.
[f] See especially pp. 12-15.

are: "Some hypothesis all parties, all controversialists, all historians, must adopt, if they would treat of Christianity at all. Gieseler's text-book bears the profession of being a dry analysis of Christian history; yet on inspection it will be found to be written on a positive and definite theory, and to bend facts to meet it. An unbeliever, as Gibbon, assumes one hypothesis; and an ultramontane, as Baronius, adopts another. The school of Hurd and Newton considers that Christianity slept for centuries upon centuries, except among those whom historians call heretics. Others speak as if the oath of supremacy, as the *congé d'élire*, could be made the measure of St. Ambrose, and they fit the Thirty-nine Articles on the fervid Tertullian. The question is, which of all these theories is the simplest, the most natural, most persuasive. Certainly the notion of development under infallible authority is not a less grave, a less winning hypothesis than the chance and coincidence of events, or the oriental philosophy, or the working of Antichrist, to account for the rise of Christianity and the formation of its theology." (p. 129.)

Döllinger, in his Christenthum und Kirche in der Zeit der Grundlegung (Regensburg 1860), has given expression to much the same train of thought. "The first deposit of teaching," he says, "was a living deposit which was to grow organically, to unfold itself out of its root according to an inner necessity, and at the same time in a manner corresponding to the spiritual wants of believers in different times, and to create for itself the most suitable expression. It consisted more of facts, principles, dogmatic germs and hints, which bore within themselves a constitution adapted to, and a capability of, successive development and instructive cultivation, in which potentially lay shut up a fulness of dogmatic material." (p. 162.) And so he remarks, in regard to the doctrine of the Trinity : " The chief and fundamental doctrine, the doctrine of the Trinity, which was so strange and objectionable to the Jews of that time, and unheard of by the heathen, the dogma whose confirmation and development was to occupy the Church for many centuries, is never fully discussed, continually only presupposed, and scarcely alluded to in passing[g]." (p. 145.)

Protestantism took its stand on the Scriptures. The Roman Catholic Church maintained that the Scriptures were not enough—that, complete as they might be in themselves, the meaning of them was a matter of doubt, and some external authority was required to determine it with certainty. This authority they said lay in the Fathers and the Church. It was natural that Protestants in resisting this claim should examine the writers to whose opinion they were thus to bow—not in order to know what they really thought, but to show how fallible and mistaken many of them had been. The most important work on this subject that appeared was that of Daillé, De Vero Usu Patrum[h].

Daillé had studied the Christian writers most profoundly ; he knew well their merits and their demerits ; and with skilful knife he laid open the putrefactions which the Roman Catholics worshipped, and at the same time exhibited the beauties which Protestants might admire. The exhibition of these errors of the Fathers

[g] See the whole of his Second Book, section 1, Schrift und Tradition.

[h] This treatise was published in French in 1631, translated into Latin by Mattaire, and revised and improved by the author, Geneva 1655. It was translated into English by the Rev. T. Smith, whose translation was re-edited and amended by the Rev. G. Jekyll, LL.B., London 1841. I have made my references to the Latin version.

however was the main work of Daillé which the world cared for. The Protestant world was struggling for emancipation, or was afraid of a return to slavery; and thus the eyes of the most enlightened Protestants dwelt more willingly on the flaws in the characters of the men who had been set up as idols, than on the nobleness and earnestness which they would willingly have seen in them as brethren. We sympathise with them in their feelings. The protest of Milton is a noble protest: "Whatsoever time or the heedless hand of blind chance hath drawn down from of old to this present, in her huge Drag-net, whether Fish or Sea-weed, Shells or Shrubs, unpickt, unchosen, those are the Fathers. Seeing therefore some men, deeply conversant in Books, have had so little care of late to give the World a better account of their reading than by divulging needless Tractates, stufft with the specious names of Ignatius and Polycarpus; with fragments of old Martyrologies and Legends to distract and stagger the multitude of credulous Readers, and mislead them from their strong guards and places of safety under the tuition of Holy Writ, it came into my thoughts to persuade myself, setting all distances and nice respects aside, that I could do Religion and my Country no better Service for the time than doing my utmost endeavour to recall the People of God from this vain foraging after Straw, and to reduce them to their firm Stations under the Standard of the Gospel; by making appear to them first the insufficiency, next the inconveniency, and lastly the impiety, of these gay Testimonies that their great Doctors would bring them to dote on[1]."

[1] Of Prelatical Episcopacy. (Milton's Works, Amsterdam 1698, vol. i. p. 239.) And read at the same time the noble passage beginning "And here withal I invoke the Immortal Deity." (p. 252.)

There cannot be a doubt that the learning of Daillé and the protest of Milton were absolutely required, and the objections which have been taken to the one or the other are made in forgetfulness of the circumstances of the case. It is a disagreeable thing, as Daillé himself remarks, to drag before the light the failings and errors of holy men; but when fallible men like ourselves are exalted as gods over us, and especially when their failings have been praised as virtues, and mistake is exhibited as infallible dogma, the truth must then be set forth. At the time too of Daillé and Milton it must be remembered that the letters of the Popes, all the epistles of Ignatius, and that too in the longer form, and many other such documents, were paraded as genuine. Daillé's critical power in his De Usu Patrum, and in his other works, especially that on Ignatius and Dionysius the Areopagite, were the principal means of ridding the study of early Christianity of many a wearisome discussion. In fact Daillé's merits cannot be easily over-estimated [k]. Those who took up his work cannot be praised so highly: they have scarcely advanced a step. The chapter in which Daillé recorded his opinion of the merits of the Fathers was unheeded, and a prejudice was handed down from one generation to another against all Christian writers of antiquity, and especially the earlier. So powerful has this prejudice been, that, as far as I know, the Evangelical school in this country has not produced one first-rate work on early Christian literature. Their ablest works have been directed against Romanism and Tractarianism, and therefore have been exceedingly one-sided. This fault attaches to two of the

[k] See Bunsen's high opinion of Daillé's work on Ignatius : Ignatius und seine Zeit, p. 239.

most remarkable books which made their appearance in the course of the late Tractarian controversy: the Divine Rule of Faith and Practice, by William Goode, M.A., F.S.A., of Trinity College, Cambridge (second edition, London 1853), and the Ancient Christianity of Isaac Taylor. Goode devotes a large portion of his first volume to show that many of the early Christian writers were heterodox. For instance, he labours to show that Tatian, Athenagoras, Theophilus of Antioch, Hippolytus, and even Justin Martyr, must be heterodox on the generation of the Word, whatever interpretation of their words be adopted. (Vol. i. p. 238.) He does this with the laudable object of proving how absurd it is for a man to hand over his reason to their keeping. But at the same time the book betrays carelessness in the study of these early writers, and unintentionally does them injustice, by assuming a certain standard of orthodoxy. The same fault attaches also to Isaac Taylor's contribution to the controversy, Ancient Christianity. (Third edition, London 1841.) There is little notice taken of the early Christian writings. The writer draws his main arguments from the works of those who flourished in the fourth and fifth centuries, and the impression left on the mind as to the state of their opinions and feelings is one-sided in the extreme. Both Goode and Taylor however caution their readers against the incorrect estimate which might be formed from the facts which they are compelled to adduce to undermine the extravagant authority claimed for the Fathers; and, in what seems to me the best reasoned of the productions that appeared in the Tractarian controversy—Anglo-Catholicism not Apostolical (Edinburgh 1843, 8vo)—Dr. W. L. Alexander treats the whole subject with admirable fairness. He utters the following sound protest against undervaluing the early Christian writers: "It must be admitted, further, that to the writings of the Christian Fathers we stand indebted for much that we venerate as useful, and indeed indispensable, in Christianity. There has been amongst Protestants a great deal of foolish talking, and much jesting that is anything but convenient upon this subject. Men who have never read a page of the Fathers, and could not read one were they to try, have deemed themselves at liberty to speak in terms of scoffing and supercilious contempt of these venerable luminaries of the early Church. Because Clement of Rome believed in the existence of the phœnix, and because Justin Martyr thought the sons of God who are said in Genesis to have intermarried with the daughters of men were angels, who for the loves of earth were willing to forego the joys of heaven; and because legends and old wives' fables enow are found in almost all the Fathers, it has been deemed wise to reject, despise, and ridicule the whole body of their writings. The least reflection will suffice to show the unsoundness of such an inference. What should we say of one who, because Lord Bacon held many opinions which modern science has proved to be false, should treat the Novum Organum with contempt? or of one who should deem himself entitled to scoff at Richard Baxter, because in his Saint's Rest that able and excellent man tries to prove the existence of Satan by quoting instances of his apparitions, and of his power over witches? There is no man, however good or great, that can get quite beyond the errors and credulities of his age. It becomes us therefore, in dealing with the writings of a former generation, to take care that in rejecting the bad we do not also despise the good; and especially that we be not found availing ourselves of advantages which have reached us through the medium of these writings, whilst we ignorantly and ungratefully dishonour the memories of those by whom these writings were penned." (pp. 70, 71.)

There is however another motive, besides antipathy to Romanism, which has powerfully influenced the Evangelical school in their dislike of the early Christian writers. The Evangelical theology is widely different from that of the early Christian writers. Luther's theology was based on the study of the works of Jerome and Augustine[1]. "Among the Fathers of the Christian Church," says M'Crie of Knox, "Jerome and Augustine attracted his particular attention. By the writings of the former he was led to the Scriptures as the only pure fountain of divine truth, and instructed in the utility of studying them in the original languages. In the works of the latter he found religious sentiments very opposite to those taught in the Romish Church, who, while she retained his name as a saint in her calendar, had banished his doctrine as heretical from her pulpits[m]." Even up to this day, of all the Fathers Augustine is the favoured writer with the Evangelical school. But Augustine is widely different from the early writers. His theology is based on a studious, though often inaccurate and uncritical, interpretation of the New Testament and a comparison of its various statements. Some of the early writers knew little of the New Testament, and those who had it in their hands used it rather to build themselves up in holiness than to satisfy the cravings of the intellect for definition and system. Moreover Augustine

---

[1] Leaders of the Reformation, by Principal Tulloch, pp. 8, 10.
[m] Life of John Knox, p. 9.

laboured hard to bring the doctrines which he found in the New Testament, or inferred from it, into logical consistency and mutual support. It is this rationalising element in his writings which has attracted the Evangelical school to him. But this element is totally wanting in the earliest Christian writers, and appears in a comparatively mild form even in those of the third century. Thus a distaste arose and still exists for these early writers. This distaste has been fostered by two circumstances. The first is that the early Christian writers have been judged according to the systematic theology of the Evangelical school. Their test of orthodoxy has been applied to them, and the test being reckoned as infallible or nearly so, they have been found wanting. The distaste however might have been overcome by a more intimate acquaintance with the writings of the early Christians; but unfortunately no attempt has been made to make this acquaintance, no effort to enter into their circumstances, to feel their difficulties, to realise their mode of thought, and to measure the grandeur of their morality by placing it alongside that of the pagan writers of the same age. As a proof of these assertions, I shall take as a specimen of the treatment of the early writers by the Evangelical school, a work called "The Theology of the Early Christian Church," exhibited in quotations from the writers of the first three centuries, with Reflections, by James Bennet, D.D. (London 1841.) This volume formed the Congregational Lecture for that year, and may therefore be taken to represent in some measure the feeling of the past generation of Congregationalists in regard to the Fathers. Dr. Bennet often blames the whole of them for vagueness and what we now call negative theology. Thus he says, "The incarnation, atonement, and intercession of the Redeemer are not taught by the Fathers in the formal systematic manner which professed theologians afterwards adopted; but the elements of a system are scattered with rude simplicity and perplexing vagueness over their works." (p. 152.) In opposition to the reverence paid to the Fathers and the authority ascribed to their opinions, he remarks, "Their theology is often so heterodox, their expositions of Scripture so absurd and contradictory, and their chastity so obscene, that he who would dethrone them has but to bring a blazing torch into their shrines, and show to the crouching multitude what it is they have adored." (p. 397.) And in the same spirit he contrasts the New Testament writings with those of the Fathers, and remarks, "All others, consulted as authorities, would taint a reader not in his dotage with infidelity: such is their ignorance, their imbecility, their conceit, their false philosophy, their demonology, their Buddhist asceticism, their indecency, their prelatical pride, their contests for superiority, their self-righteousness, their contradictions of each other and of the Scriptures on which they profess to build their faith[n]." (p. 427.) There is not a single writer who has left works of any extent who is not accused of some great heterodoxy. Thus of Justin he candidly remarks: "He labours to show that Christ was the God who appeared to the patriarchs, but is so defective in his statement of the Trinity, that after the Council of Nice he would have been deemed an Arian." (p. 24.) Of Irenæus he remarks: "Irenæus himself has not escaped the charge of heresy; for he has said many strange things, and, in a work so large, few good ones."

[n] See the whole context.

(p. 31.) Again he observes: "The charge of Arianism and of teaching the mortality of souls is not proved against Irenæus, though he often talks like a Pelagian." (p. 31.) "Clemens Alexandrinus," he says, "scarcely mentions the atonement, and supposes the design of Christ's becoming man was to teach men to become gods." (p. 34.) Of his morality he remarks, that it "is, like that of Socinian writers, a substitute for the merits of Christ, who is introduced so rarely that he appears as a stranger, and so erroneously that we are as much surprised as delighted when we find him invested with the honours which are his due." (p. 35.)

The same sentiments and animus are evident in Killen's Ancient Church, and in Cunningham's Historical Theology, though the latter work contains many traces of wider sympathy, and the influence of Bull is everywhere visible. A much nobler appreciation of the character of the early writers is to be found in Vaughan's Causes of the Corruption of Christianity (p. 322), and in the sympathetic volume of Stoughton On the Ages of Christendom, both Congregational lectures. In both however the defective theology of the writers of the first three centuries is made a matter of lamentation. Yet surely this subject ought to engross the attention of Evangelical Christians. If it be true, as they say, that the early writers were heterodox on the Trinity; if they knew nothing of a satisfaction of Divine justice, but spoke only in a vague way of this matter; if they wavered in regard to original sin, some denying it entirely and others expressing themselves with great uncertainty; if their testimony to the inspiration of the New Testament is unsatisfactory and inconclusive — where was Christianity in those days? Did it really sleep for three long centuries? Are we to suppose that there were Christians in those days, but that they never wrote books? Or how is the chasm to be bridged? Or may not members of the Evangelical school like Dr. Bennet be wrong in asserting that it is necessary for a man to believe in original sin, the Trinity, the atonement, and similar dogmas before he can be a Christian?

Besides this, are not those very men who are thus accused the evidence which we have for the power and truth of Christianity? Was not Christ's power marvellously shown forth in them? And does not he who attempts to expel them from the Christian Church aim a deadly blow at the brotherhood of Christ's Church?

There is another consideration which the Evangelical community should solemnly ponder. Those men who were so defective in their theology, were strong in faith. They loved Christ with an intense love. As this real faith grows colder, as men begin to trust in outward forms, as they get involved in worldly governments, they also begin to systematise more and more, and to lay stress on belief in their systems; and the theologians who please such men as Dr. Bennet lived in an age of innumerable forms and practices totally foreign to the spiritual Christianity of a Justin, a Clemens, and an Origen. This is a serious consideration. The advance of speculation and system takes place alongside of trust in other things than Christ. Systems have their use; but the Christian Church has paid dearly for them. And an earnest study of the writings of the devoted martyrs and champions of Christianity would be of immense importance to the Evangelical school, as true brotherly sympathy with them would not only increase that fervent zeal in which they abound, but would lead them to extend the hand of fellowship to many an earnest brother for whom Christ died, to whom they now are but too apt to refuse the cup of water.

The appeal made by the Roman Catholics to the Fathers had however a different effect on many Protestants. They examined the writings for which authority was claimed, and, believing that the early Christian sentiments were those of Protestantism, they endeavoured to show that the testimony of the Fathers told against the Roman Catholic Church. Such is, in many parts, the strain of Scultetus's Medulla Theologiæ Patrum. His great object, as he states in the title, is to vindicate the writings of the Fathers from the corruptions of Bellarmine. He is animated by the keenest bitterness against the Jesuits, and in treating of the Eucharist tries every device to make the Christian writers speak against Bellarmine and the Universalists (Ubiquitarii)°. The same opposition to Romanism was the inducement to a very remarkable work by John Forbes of Corse, Professor of Theology in King's College and in the University of Aberdeen, and one of the famous Aberdeen doctors. Baur has placed Forbes's work alongside that of Petavius, as the two great attempts of the seventeenth century to give a history of dogmas. His book was called "Instructiones Historico-Theologicæ de Doctrina Christiana inde a tempore Apostolorum ad sec. 17." (Amsterdam 1645.) It is also contained in the second volume of his collected works. (Amsterdam 1673, fol.) He tells us, in the address to the reader, that the Synod of Aberdeen requested him to deliver lectures to his

---

° See especially his remarks on Justin, p. 46.

students on the history of doctrines, because Romanists were at that time imposing on people, and making them believe that antiquity was entirely on the side of the Roman Catholic Church. The polemical nature of the work however is seen only in certain portions of it. He treats the history of doctrine, like Petavius, not according to ages, but according to subjects. His references to the early writers are exceedingly few, principally in lib. i. cap. iii.; and he regards them as entirely orthodox.

The English Church especially claimed the Fathers as being on its side. It had done so from the earliest times [p]. There were many reasons for this. It had not made such a complete rebound from Romanism as the others. Its prominent doctrine of episcopacy could not be established from the New Testament alone. It had on the whole little sympathy with Calvinism; and its conservative feeling was very strong. While therefore it resisted the pretensions of the Pope, it did not wish entirely to snap asunder the links of history. It claimed the writers of the first three centuries as agreeing with it in all essentials; and again and again in the early apologies for the English Church the early Christian writers were praised and appealed to. In the progress of time the Church of England saw itself divided into various parties. The Evangelical section sympathised in feeling with the sentiments already attributed to them. They were what Newman calls the School of Newton and Hurd. But by far the largest and most distinguished portion of the Church were great in their reverence for the early Fathers, and spoke much

[p] See Blunt on the use of the Fathers.

of the value of tradition. Many of these laboured hard in the study of the early Christian literature; and in truth the English Church furnishes a magnificent list of patristic scholars second only to those of the Roman Catholic Church. Their names will frequently occur throughout these volumes[q]. In opposition alike to other Protestants and to Roman Catholics, they especially took upon themselves to define the exact use of the Fathers. They believed Scripture to contain all that was needful for salvation; but they believed also that the writers of the first three centuries were the safest guides in the interpretation of the Scriptures. "We allow," says Waterland, "no doctrine as *necessary* which stands only on *Fathers*, or on *tradition* oral or written: we admit none for such but what is *contained* in Scripture and *proved* by Scripture *rightly* interpreted. And we know of no way more safe in *necessaries* to preserve the *right* interpretation than to take the *ancients* along with us[r]." They attempted to show that the accusations brought against the Fathers did not apply to the early writers, and how likely it was that the friends, companions, and successors of the Apostles would more fully comprehend the meaning of their words than men

[q] Professor Forbes, mentioned above, should perhaps properly be reckoned along with the English Churchmen. He refused to sign the Covenant, and was in consequence deprived of his professorship. Afterwards he thought it advisable to leave Scotland. His Instructiones was printed at Amsterdam, while he was living in exile. He dedicated the work to Charles the First. In the dedicatory letter he points out on the one hand the error which Roman Catholics committed in paying too great deference to the Fathers, and on the other he rebukes those who contemn them as useless, calling them "inepti Scripturæ laudatores."

[r] On the Use and Value of Ecclesiastical Antiquity: Waterland's Works, vol. v. p. 316. Oxford 1823.

speaking a different language, breathing a totally different atmosphere, and accustomed to very different ideas. These considerations are well set forth in the Essay by Waterland, quoted above, on the Use and Value of Ecclesiastical Antiquity. The whole subject has also been ably discussed by a writer of our own time, Professor Blunt. In the first part of the work called "The Right Use of the Early Fathers: two series of Lectures delivered in the University of Cambridge by the Rev. J. J. Blunt, B.D., late Margaret Professor of Divinity" (London 1857), Blunt tries to do away with what he regards as the misrepresentations of Daillé. He defines the position of the English Church in regard to the Fathers, and he shows with great success how satisfactory the proofs are that they do not sanction the errors of the Roman Catholic Church.

The ideas of the English Churchmen in regard to the use of the early Fathers were unfavourable to a fair study of patristic theology. They set out from a belief in the certainty of the doctrines of their own Church. They wished to have tradition on their side; and they were compelled therefore on all occasions to show that tradition was on their side. They could not have recourse, like Roman Catholics, to any theory of secresy or development. They did not venture, like Evangelical Protestants, to pronounce them heterodox. The only third course remaining for them was to explain away what seemed inconsistent with the Articles of the Church of England. And from the earliest times to this day their efforts have been mainly directed to reconcile inconsistencies and explain away some of their plainest and most positive statements. This is seen in the great controversy which raged within the English

Church itself, and among Arians and Socinians, with regard to the Trinity. The most learned work on the subject, that of Bull, undertakes to show that the writers of the first three centuries held the doctrines set forth in the Nicene Creed. Bull starts with the idea that the Nicene Creed is the truth, and he evidently was of opinion that whatever the early Fathers might have said, they must have believed the doctrines set forth in it. So he goes to work, explaining away multitudes of passages which tell strongly against his preconceived idea, and setting down as the opinions of authors mere inferences of his own from their opinions. So much so is this the case, that, as Newman has remarked, out of thirty authors that he has appealed to, he has, for one cause or another, to explain nearly twenty[s].

At the same time Bull had not so much to twist as might at first sight be imagined. The three points which he undertakes to prove are the pre-existence of Christ, the sameness of his substance with that of the Father, and the co-eternity of the Son. Of the first no one can doubt that the Fathers speak positively enough. In regard to the second and third, they did not so much differ from the Nicene Creed as simply neglect, or fail to see, the points which afterwards came into dispute, and therefore their statements are not so precise as Bull would fain make them. On another point, the subordination of the Son to the Father, in which the Fathers are, according to some Evangelical divines, utterly heterodox, Bull agreed with them. For he maintained that

---

[s] See Newman's criticism of Bull's work, in his Essay on Development, pp. 158–59.

Christ, even in respect to his divinity, was inferior to the Father—that the Father was the fountain and source of the Son's divinity [t]. And in treating of this subject he does not adduce passages from the early writers to show that this was their belief; but regarding this as a settled point, he attempts to show that the most distinguished Fathers of the Nicene period agreed with the early writers.

It is a remarkable circumstance that Bull's work was directed against Petavius, a Jesuit, on the one hand, and Sandius, an Arian, on the other. The honesty of Petavius was especially perplexing to him and other members of the Church of England. Indeed to some it seemed like insulting the Fathers to deny their orthodoxy. This feeling is curiously brought out in a letter which Waterland has quoted in reference to Petavius. "The very pious Mr. Nelson," he says, "in a letter to a popish priest, has some reflections worth the inserting in this place. 'I am not ignorant that two of your great champions, Cardinal Perron and Petavius, to raise the authority of *general councils* and to make the rule of their faith appear more plausible, have *aspersed* not only the holy *Scriptures,* as uncapable, by reason of their *obscurity*, to prove the *great* and *necessary* point of our Saviour's *divinity*, but have impeached also

[t] "Proinde [ut] Pater divinitatis, quæ in Filio est, fons, origo ac principium sit," iv. 1. 1. p. 251. "Catholici doctores, tum qui Synodo Nicæna anteriores fuere, tum qui postmodum vixerunt, unanimi consensu Deum Patrem etiam secundum divinitatem Filio majorem esse statuerunt." (iv. 2. 1.) Petavius the Jesuit denounces the Calvinists as heretical on this point. "Ex iis," he says, "corollarii id loco conficitur inanem, immo vero impiam esse Calvini et Autothcanorum argutiam qui Filium qua Deus est a Patre originem accepisse negant, fatentur autem qua est Filius, sive ratione habita personæ." De Dog. lib. ii. c. iii. 6. De Deo Deique proprietatibus.

the Fathers in the first three centuries as tardy in the same point. Blessed God, that men should be so fond of *human* inventions as to sacrifice to them those *pillars* of our faith which are alone proper and able to support it! I mean *Scripture* and primitive *antiquity*'[u]." The writer adds that he had heard Petavius had retracted his opinion.

The same spirit which pervades Bull's works is seen in Waterland's various writings. The early Fathers must at all hazards be made to agree with the Church of England. It is seen also in Burton's two treatises: "The Testimonies of the Ante-Nicene Fathers to the Divinity of Christ;" "To the Trinity." And even in Blunt's work there is an evident determination to overlook every expression that seems a disagreement. There is not the slightest attempt to enter into the spirit of the Fathers and their modes of thinking. The results of modern criticism compel him to notice the discrepancies; but he makes no attempt to reconcile them. He never dreams that what appears to him inconsistent and even contradictory, might be seen from another point of view to be harmonious. He thus sums up their opinions on the Trinity: " Now, in spite of many unguarded phrases which from time to time fall from the Fathers—unguarded, I say, because entirely at variance with their ordinary teaching—it is not to be denied that the faith of the sub-apostolic Church was Trinitarian." (p. 486.) Besides, all the writers of the first three centuries are appealed to as if they all agreed. The testimony for instance of Tertullian is adduced as evidence in regard to the practice of the Church in the time of Polycarp.

[u] Waterland's Works, vol. v. p. 257 *note.*

Most of the works on the doctrines of the Fathers produced by English Churchmen were controversial. They were directed principally against Arians, Socinians, and disbelievers. The Arian doctrines were often upheld within the Church itself; and three of the greatest Englishmen—Milton, Locke, and Newton [x] expressed opinions on the subject of Christ's divinity different from the common notions. Within the Church, Dr. Clarke especially was accused of anti-Trinitarianism in his work on the Trinity. He appealed to the earliest Fathers; and throughout the controversies which then raged [y] the character of the early Christian writers and their authority were much canvassed. The anti-Trinitarian writers were generally inclined to rate the writers of the second century and onwards very low: they pointed out their numerous mistakes, and they tried to show that they corrupted rather than interpreted Scripture doctrine. This opinion was paraded especially by the Unitarians. Seeing in Christ nothing but a mere man, they could not but feel that the Church at a very early stage made a great departure from the truth. They therefore turned from the Church altogether, and imagined that the sect of the Ebionites ought to have been *the* Church; but, unfortunately, triumphant error had driven them into a corner. The true Church had been suppressed; the great mass of early Christians were not real Christians. Such sentiments prevented the holders of them from

[x] Newton occupied some of his leisure hours in examining the real opinions of Athanasius. See Brewster's Life of Sir Isaac Newton.

[y] For an account of these controversies and the various writings then produced, see the Life of Bishop Bull by Nelson, and that of Waterland by Van Mildert, in their collected works.

taking a living interest in the development of the Church; and accordingly most of the Unitarian works in this country were deficient in scholarship. Priestley, in his History of the Corruptions of Christianity, modestly acknowledged that he took "a good deal of pains to read, or at least to look carefully through, many of the most capital works of the ancient Christian writers [z]." Horsley laid hold of these words, and endeavoured to show how ignorant Priestley was of his subject. Horsley's Charge was a complete and satisfactory refutation of Priestley, though it did not do much more than use Bull's work well. Several other able replies to Priestley were written, one of which deserves especial note here as being among the very few learned works written by Scotsmen on the early Christian writers. Its title is "A Vindication of the Doctrine of Scripture, and of the Primitive Faith concerning the Deity of Christ, in reply to Dr. Priestley's History of Early Opinions; by John Jamieson, D.D., Minister of the Gospel, Forfar." (Edinburgh 1794. 2 vols. 8vo.)

The controversy with the infidelity to which such men as Voltaire and Gibbon had given expression, also evoked from English Churchmen the results of their patristic studies. Most of the works that attack the deistical writers of this country deal in some measure with the writings of the early Christians. In Scotland also we have to note Lord Hailes's Reply to the famous Fifteenth and Sixteenth Chapters of Gibbon's History. Lord Hailes devoted his attention to several portions of patristic study, editing and translating various books of Lactantius, and publishing three volumes of Remains

[z] Preface, p. xxii.

of Christian Antiquity, with explanatory notes. (Edinb. 1776–80.)

The work of Barbeyrac on the Morality of the Fathers (Traité de la Morale des Pères de l'Eglise: Amsterdam 1728, 4to), was thought by many English Churchmen to be directed against the characters of the Fathers. And accordingly Waterland and Blunt have both expended much energy in repelling his attacks on some of their moral doctrines. But Barbeyrac himself states that his object was to raise up a new line of argument against the infallibility of the Fathers. He does not wish to depreciate their real merits, but he labours to show that they erred on various important points of morality, and that consequently they are not entitled to that slavish reverence which Remi Ceillier in particular, and the Roman Catholic party in general, claimed for them. He has often made objections which further investigation has proved to be baseless; but there are several points in which he has shown that they were wrong, and in which most unbiassed people will allow that they were wrong. It is no wonder that they should err; but it is wonderful that men gifted with rational natures should maintain that they could not and never did err.

This is the proper place to notice two works which fostered the study of patristic literature in no ordinary degree. The one was " Primitive Christianity Revived: in four volumes. By William Whiston, M.A." (London 1711.) A fifth volume was published in 1712, containing a translation of the Recognitions. Whiston was a man of great simplicity of mind, and had a most earnest desire for the truth. Unfortunately, however, his scholarship was not great; and his mind, probably through his mathematical training, had become exceedingly crotchety. Accordingly the two great discoveries of his work are mere outrageous fancies. He believed the Apostolical Constitutions to be inspired, and he regarded the longer Greek form of the Epistles of Ignatius as genuine.

The other work was Lardner's Credibility of the Gospel History, the first part of which made its appearance in 1727. Lardner was a man of extraordinary diligence, great candour, and true Christian liberality. His work, though he got little reward for it, has been of incalculable use to the defenders of Christianity, and its contents have been ransacked again and again by men who should have gone to the Fathers themselves. Lardner prefixes discussions on the date and authorship of the writings which he uses; and he then quotes and explains all the passages which bear any resemblance to passages in the New Testament. He has done the work once for all; and I have therefore, in my account of the theology of each writer, given only those passages which are undoubtedly taken from the New Testament, the author being named, or the words being identical.

The revival of literature in Germany opened up a new era in the study of early Christian literature. Mosheim's works on Ecclesiastical history contributed very materially to its formation. For the age in which it appeared, his history was remarkable for its fairness and the power of combining scattered notices into a whole. Walch also treated the heretics with characteristic German honesty. But in many respects the movement was due to those who examined early Christian literature simply to know what it was. These inquirers, who were pervaded with the spirit of indifference then widely prevalent, were in a position to state fairly many points that in the keenness of polemics had been entirely overlooked. Foremost among these was Semler, who recognised the great fact that each age has its own ideas and atmosphere of thought, and that doctrines can be ascertained correctly only when examined in the light of these [a]. Many of his criticisms were necessarily rash, and seldom deserve notice now; but his critical treatment of the subject aroused thought and inquiry. Many followed in his footsteps; and gradually, as a healthier and holier spirit came over German theologians, through the influence of Schleiermacher and men of the same stamp, the German mind was more prepared to understand the history of the early Christians. For, as Neander remarks, only a Christian mind can properly understand the progress of Christianity. Neander himself is the best type of the living Christianity which applied itself to the comprehension of its earliest forms. He set out from the principle that Christianity was a life, and he saw that at the first it had revealed itself only as a life. He looked therefore upon dogma as a growth—a natural growth indeed, but still a growth. Both Roman Catholics and Protestants had for the most part regarded the creed of the Christian as fixed, and any aberration from it had been set down as heterodox. Now dogma was looked upon as a development, and possibly a healthy development, of Christian life.

[a] D. Baumgarten's Untersuchung theologischer Streitigkeiten; erster Band, mit einigen Anmerkungen, Vorrede und fortgesetzten Geschichte der Christlichen Glaubenslehre herausgegeben von D. Johann Salomo Semler. Halle 1762. p. 16. The whole of the introduction of Semler's to his History of Doctrines is replete with modern thought, and well repays perusal.

Neander could thus exhibit the real history of these times with perfect truthfulness, and the results, as seen in his history, are great. He had many fellow workers. Their labours will help us frequently in the shape of monographs. In more recent times, a spirit of the most thorough Christianity, and consequently of great liberality, pervaded all the writings of Baron Bunsen, one of the most profound investigators of Christian literature. There was in him a remarkable union of the purely scientific spirit with the deepest love to Christ; and consequently his Christianity and Mankind is characterised at once by fearlessness of research, a large sympathy with Christians, and hearty earnest piety.

From Neander and Bunsen we may often differ; but the principles that lie at the basis of their investigations seem to me the only sure ones; and when the foundations are secure, the discussion of differences tends towards a well-assured unity. Of the former it may be remarked that his investigations were to some extent influenced by the circumstance that he adopted the developed theology of the Church as in the main his own, and consequently he was inclined to find traces of a certain class of speculations earlier than he would otherwise have done. Besides this, the form of his work often prevented him from going into the reasons of his opinions; and he also felt himself compelled to pass over many matters which are of the deepest interest in the history of Christian literature.

Bunsen occupies in some respects a more independent position. Possessing a liberal Christian heart, he sympathised with all phases of the Church's history. But he threw himself with especial sympathy into the thoughts and feelings of the early ages of Christendom. In almost all the doctrinal results of his investigations I think he is correct; but he has mingled along with these results a peculiar philosophy of them which is, to say the least, difficult of comprehension. His point of view seems to me, if I understand him aright, very nearly that of the Alexandrian Clemens and Origen. Besides this, in his great work, Christianity and Mankind, he has chosen to build up the history and features of the early ages rather than give a critical exposition of the process by which he obtains his results. It seems to me questionable whether our position in the criticism of the early writings is so far advanced as to permit a completely satisfactory reconstruction of the materials.

The same liberal Christian spirit is evident in all the best books that treat of early Christianity. But three writers, all of them now gone from amongst us, deserve special mention. The first is Miss Cornwallis, who gave her opinions anonymously in Nos. XIX. and XX. of Small Books on Great Subjects: "On the State of Man subsequent to the Promulgation of Christianity." (London 1851–52.) These two small volumes are healthy in tone, full of the most valuable material, and the result of vast reading and investigation. The second is Maurice in his Lectures on the Ecclesiastical History of the First and Second Centuries. (1854.) Maurice does not attempt to examine the writers critically, but entering into full sympathy with them, he exhibits their modes of thought and feeling in a masterly manner. Like Bunsen, he prefers to construct rather than to analyse; and we think that in this way both have several times allowed their imagination to carry them farther than a just criticism can approve. A remarkable instance in both is the method in which each builds up the personality of Ignatius out of the different set of letters which each supposes to be genuine. Maurice's position is moreover, like Bunsen's, more that of the Alexandrian Clemens than of the Roman Clemens. It is essentially that of a philosophical Christianity. The third is Milman, who, in his "History of Christianity" and his "History of Latin Christianity," combines the most varied culture with singular fairness and philosophic breadth.

There are two writers of the present day who also claim notice from us, as dealing in an independent and masterly manner with early Christian literature. The one is Dr. Davidson in his "Introduction to the Study of the New Testament" (1868), who, animated by a strong and ardent love of truth, carries his researches fearlessly wherever his evidence leads him. His work is characterized by great independence and by a thorough knowledge of all that has been written on the subjects he discusses. The other work is that of Canon Westcott on the "History of the Canon of the New Testament." (Second ed. 1866.) It is more conservative than that of Dr. Davidson, but it is not the less honest and conscientious. All the materials of the history of the Canon are arranged with great accuracy, the evidence is adduced impartially, and the judgments given are carefully weighed.

Of the Tübingen school not much need be said here. Their expositions of the early Christian theology are often exceedingly fair. In dealing with the Apostles, however, they are anxious to carry out their notion of a difference even to doctrine. But the only great doctrinal difference which they supposed to have existed between the Apostles disappears before a fair interpretation of the passages alleged. The doctrine is that of Justification by Faith. Paul is supposed to have preached a peculiar doctrine on this point. On all hands this peculiar doctrine is allowed to appear in a very modified manner in the subsequent ages; and in the Epistle of James some have supposed that Paul's doctrine is flatly contradicted. The supposition of a difference arises mainly from two circumstances: a false meaning attached to δικαιῶ; and a forgetfulness that Paul speaks principally of trust in God, not in Christ. The word δικαιῶ is not used in the New Testament in its classical sense. We have to fall back on its *etymological* meaning. This meaning is either, to make a person who is sinful righteous, or to declare a person righteous who is righteous. The meaning attributed to it is, to treat a person who is guilty as if he really were not guilty. Only the most concurring evidence of unquestionable examples of such a use of the word would justify a man in giving it this meaning. And no such examples can be found within the first three centuries at least. Now Paul's doctrine was this. He is arguing against Judaism. He maintains that if a man's righteousness is to depend on the performance of the Law, then righteousness is an impossibility. No man can do, or ever has done, all that he ought to do. Can man then be righteous at all? Unquestionably, says Paul. There is a righteousness which consists in trusting God. The person may have sinned, but his hope is in God; and whatever he has to do, the motive is his confidence in God. The case of Abraham was a most pertinent example of this righteousness. How could a man obtain this righteousness—this trust in God? Unquestionably by faith in Christ. Christ was the way to God; and he who trusts Christ will certainly learn to trust God, and attain the righteousness, which is not according to man, but according to God.

Now James's doctrine, instead of being opposed to this, is a representation of the same essential truth, in opposition to a different error. Paul struggled against dead works; James against dead belief. The word πιστεύω has a double construction and a double meaning: πιστεύω Θεῷ (or εἰς Θεόν), "I trust God." Such trust is ever practical, is ever living; and such trust, and such alone, does Paul speak of. Πιστεύω τὸν Θεὸν εἶναι, "I believe that God is." Here we have mere belief, simply the language of a creed. And James refers exclusively to this meaning of the word: "Dost thou believe that there is one God? Thou doest well. Even the demons believe and tremble." A mere consent to creeds is nothing apart from deeds. What is the use of believing that God is, if you do not trust that God, if your belief does not go forth into a practical confidence in God? The basis of true religion is by both apostles recognised to be a living active faith in God. Baur has indeed acknowledged nearly as much as this; but, notwithstanding, he continually speaks of Paul's doctrine of Justification and Propitiation as greatly modified in the next age. But such statement is false, and would not have been made at all, had not a totally erroneous opinion of Paul's doctrine been in his mind.

BOOK I.

THE APOSTOLICAL FATHERS.

THE APOSTOLICAL FATHERS.

CHAPTER I.

INTRODUCTION.

THE name given to the writers who lived in the age succeeding that of the Apostles is objectionable. Westcott calls them Sub-Apostolic—a word which Blunt uses in a wider sense. De Quincey calls the age subsequent to Christ the Epi-Christian; and perhaps here we should not do wrong in calling the Apostolical Fathers the Ep-Apostolic writers. Tertullian calls the followers of the Apostles, Apostolici;[a] hence the name Apostolical Fathers.

Of these writers, investigation assures us only of the names of three, Clemens, Polycarp, and Papias. The works which are ranked beside the writings of these have been supposed by some to belong to apostolic individuals—Barnabas, Hermas, and Ignatius. But a rigid examination of evidence shows that there is no satisfactory ground for attributing the Epistle of Barnabas to Barnabas the friend of Paul, nor the Pastor of Hermas to the Hermas mentioned in the Epistle to the Romans. These two writings however may reasonably be placed in company with the other Ep-Apostolic

[a] De Carne, c. ii. De Præscript. Hær. 32.

writings, as they unquestionably belong to the earliest Christian literature subsequent to the apostolic. The case is different with the letters attributed to Ignatius. There can be no doubt that there was a man belonging to the earliest period of the Christian Church called Ignatius, and that he wrote letters: but the writings now ascribed to him present a problem which has not yet been solved. The letters bearing his name appear in at least three forms: a Syriac, in which there are only three epistles, a shorter Greek, and a longer Greek. Besides these there are Latin translations of the shorter Greek and of the longer Greek: and these contain very remarkable deflections from the Greek. So that we have in reality five forms. And we have to ascertain whether any of these five forms is genuine, and which; and supposing we were to find one form genuine, we should have to prove that the text had not been tampered with in any respect. It seems to me that we have no means of determining these questions, but that it can be proved that in whatever form they be examined, they will be found to contain opinions and exhibit modes of thought entirely unknown to any of the Ep-Apostolic writings. The examination of these letters must therefore be deferred until we meet with similar opinions and thoughts in well authenticated writings.

The character of all the Ep-Apostolic writings is marked. They are simple informal utterances of pious faith. They exhibit no signs of the application of the intellect to the distinction of doctrines. They present the great truths of Christianity in a living, active form. They give us the internal workings of the Christian spirit.

As yet Christianity is seen dealing simply with itself.

There is one slight and perhaps only an apparent exception to this. In the Epistle of Barnabas there are evident signs of a controversy with Judaism. Yet the Judaism brought before us is more that which would suggest difficulties to a Christian reader of the Bible than an actual outward living Judaism which the writer wishes to bring over to Christianity. The subject discussed is not, in fact, the relation of Christianity to the Jews as non-believers in Christ, but the relation of Christianity to the divine revelations given to the Jews in the Old Testament.

These writings reveal nothing of the results of the contact of Christianity with heathenism. We have in Clemens indeed occasional glimpses of a mind that had been trained under heathen influences, and we see already how he naturally sought for confirmation of his Christian opinions and practices in what he regarded as the noble men of heathenism.

These writings also show nothing of direct personal contact with philosophy, or with the philosophy of Philo in particular. In Clemens, and still more in Barnabas, we have allegorical interpretation; but this allegorical interpretation they may have received in the Christian Church. There are unquestionable instances of it in the writings of Paul [b]. Moreover, this allegorical interpretation had been prevalent from a very early date among the philosophers of Greece. Anaxagoras and his friend Metrodorus of Lampsacus systematically applied allegory to the interpretation of the Homeric poems.

---

[b] Stoughton (Ages of Christendom, p. 111) remarks of allegorical interpretation: "It was the injudicious and indiscriminate application of a method which, within limits, is sanctioned by an inspired commentator." See also the Roman Catholic Freppel, Pères Apostoliques, p. 101.

Plato condemns the explanation of mythology by ὑπόνοιαι or hidden meanings[c] (Rep. ii. p. 378), a proof that in his time this mode of explaining away had already been in vogue. The Stoics systematically applied it to the explanation of the prevalent gods. And the same mode of interpretation had long before the Christian era been applied to the Old Testament by Aristobulus[d]. So that before the time of Philo a barely literal interpretation was probably unknown, and Clemens and Barnabas did but join in a mode of thought that was universal.

Very little is said with regard to heretics. Polycarp alludes pointedly to one class, the Docetes. These men, growing up apparently within the Church, were not content with the simple faith of common Christians in Christ. They must find a place for Christianity within their philosophy. Their philosophy, of course, is not to bend. Christianity must bend to it. Matter, they say to themselves, is an evil. The good God could not have made it. The good Christ could not have come in contact with it. And so Christ was not born, and Christ had not a real body, nor did He really die, nor did He really rise again. In one word, the fundamental facts of Christianity are a lie, and faith in Christ a deception. Speculation is to be superior to faith, and we are to trust to our speculative powers, and seek the key of the universe, rather than submit like little children, and attain to holiness through Him who is the way, the truth, and the life. No wonder that Polycarp

---

[c] See Diog. Laërt. ii. 11; Tatian, Orat. ad Græc. c. 21, p. 37; and, for other references, Wolf's Prolegomena to Homer, p. 162, p. 97 of the second edition.

[d] See for a full discussion of this point Gfrörer's Philo und die Jüdisch-Alexandrinische Theosophie, Abtheilung ii. cap. xv. p. 71.

spoke strongly against such men, for they laid the axe to the root of all morality; they withered up the love of God in man's heart. Yet Polycarp does not seem to have uttered his words of denunciation until every means had been used. Cerdo, who is said to be the originator of Docetism, began his speculations within the Church: he taught his views secretly for some time. He was warned, confessed his sin, and was oftener than once received back into the full affection of his Christian brothers. In vain: he could not bear their love. And Irenæus expressly tells us that he withdrew from the assembly of Christians. How Marcion was treated, it is difficult to say; for we have no satisfactory accounts of him. The probability is that he also was brought up within the Church; that he also confessed his sin, and was received back into the brotherhood; but that at last he determined to set up a new Christianity and a new Church for himself. We shall have to examine some of these points afterwards.

The most striking feature of these writings is the deep living piety which pervades them. This piety is not of a morbid character. It consists in the warmest love to God, the deepest interest in man, and it exhibits itself in a healthy vigorous manly morality. This morality cannot in any way be resolved into selfishness. It is an end to itself. These writings speak of no glorious heaven of delights—they know of no joy but the joy of holiness. They do not speak at all of heaven, but of a "place due to man." They do not urge to morality by rewards, but they appeal straight to the heart of man for confirmation of the truths spoken, and they direct to God and Christ as the furnishers of strength against the temptations of life. This intense moral heat and fervour is all the more striking, that in contemporary writings and writings shortly antecedent the mind is sickened with the details of sin and vice which were universally prevalent. The pages of Tacitus, Juvenal, Persius, and Martial are full of the most fearful representations of universal licentiousness and loss of all faith in God and man[e]. And perhaps a student could not receive a more satisfactory impression of the truth that God was working among the Christians in a most remarkable manner, than by turning from the fetid pages of stern Juvenal or licentious Martial to the pure unselfish loving words of Clemens Romanus, Polycarp, or Hermas. The simple reading of these writings by themselves does not strike us so much now, because what was living new earnest morality to them is now familiar to us, and often the very words used by them are now used by men to cloak their deceit and worldliness. But let us not on this account hide from ourselves the marvellous phenomenon here presented—of a morality that has nothing to do with selfish or worldly aims—that seeks its source in God, that fills the whole being, that goes out to all men in love, and that is to itself a boundless good. There is apparently one exception to this total forgetfulness of mere happiness. Papias speaks of the worldly blessings of the millennium. But it is to be remembered that the Christians knew of no heaven as a place set apart for them. In the apostolic

[e] Perhaps the condition of women at this time may be taken as the best index of the general state of morals. This is fully described in Schmidt's Geschichte der Denk- und Glaubensfreiheit im ersten Jahrhundert der Kaiserherrschaft und des Christenthums, p. 266 ff; and in Friedländer's Darstellungen aus der Sittengeschichte Roms in der Zeit von August bis zum Ausgang der Antonine, erster Theil, p. 263 ff.

writings heaven means either the sky or the peculiar dwelling-place of God. And when the Apostles speak of a future state, they speak of it simply as "being with the Lord." Of course the inference might be drawn, that as the Lord was in heaven, Christians would be there. But then there is no indication that the inference was drawn. And, in fact, we shall see that afterwards various opinions arose on the point, and that most probably the phrase "going to heaven" passed from the Stoic philosophy into Christian phraseology. Whenever then Christians would attempt to assign a place to the blessed, that place would most likely be the earth beautified, renewed, and made glorious—and if the words of Papias be carefully examined, they cannot mean more than this. He does not express one word of pleasure at the thought of a sensuous enjoyment, and after all he simply records the words of Christ, without giving us the interpretation which he put upon them. And in these words it deserves notice that the idea of holiness is so permeating, that the trees are said to desire the blessing of the Lord.

In examining the Ep-Apostolic writings for the sake of their doctrines we have to bring them out of a living practical form into an intellectual lifeless shape. The doctrines thus brought out are found to be the same in the main as those of the New Testament. Nowhere is Christ directly called God in them. Nowhere is a relief from punishment spoken of as the result of his life or death. His work from beginning to end is a purely moral work. There is no curious prying into the peculiar nature of Christ's death. The Spirit is mentioned without precision. The great facts relating to man's sin and salvation are introduced in a broad indefinite real manner. No curious questions are discussed. And the final state of man is set forth in plain undefined easily understood language. The Scriptures of the Old Testament are often referred to. The books of the New are never spoken of as inspired, and never mentioned as authorities in matters of belief.

Some indeed have tried to show that there exist great differences between the beliefs of the Apostles and those of the Apostolical Fathers. They suppose that a degeneracy is clearly traceable in the latter, and that dogmatic theology made an " immense retrograde movement in their hands [f]." The forms of the beliefs are often the same, but they " reproduce them without entering into their inner sense [g]." How false these opinions are, we leave the reader to judge from the accounts of their theology which we present.

Literature.

The writings of the Apostolical Fathers have been frequently collected. The first separate collection of them is that of Cotelerius (Paris 1672. II. fol.), which was reprinted and edited with additions by Joannes Clericus, Antwerp 1698. The second edition of Clericus's edition of Cotelerius is the most valuable. It was published at Amsterdam in 1724. It contains the works of Barnabas, Clemens, Hermas, Ignatius, and Polycarp, real and spurious, with many prefaces, notes, and dissertations, some of great length, such as Pearson's Defence of the Ignatian Epistles.

[f] Reuss on Clemens: Theolog. Chret. vol. ii. p. 327.
[g] Pressensé, Histoire des Trois Premiers Siècles de l'Eglise Chrétienne, vol. ii. p. 371.

INTRODUCTION.

The next collection of the Apostolical Fathers was by L. Thomas Ittigius, who prefixed a dissertation on the writers who flourished immediately after the Apostles (Lips. 1699, 8vo). Collections were also edited by Rich. Russel (Lond. 1746, II. 8vo), Frey (Basil 1742, 8vo), Hornemann (Havniæ 1828, II. 8vo), Reithmayr (Munich 1844, 12mo), Grenfell (Rugby 1844), and Muralto (Turici 1847), none of which are of great value. The modern collections which the student will find of great importance are,—

1. S. Clementis Romani, S. Ignatii, S. Polycarpi Patrum Apostolicorum quæ supersunt. Accedunt S. Ignatii et S. Polycarpi Martyria ad fidem codicum recensuit, adnotationibus variorum et suis illustravit, indicibus instruxit Guilielmus Jacobson, A.M., editio tertia denuo recognita. (Oxon. 1847). This work is based upon a careful collation of MSS. It contains a most valuable selection of notes, and has short prolegomena, consisting of annotations on Jerome's biographies of the writers. It also gives a very full list of the editions and translations. It does not give the Pastor of Hermas, and only the shorter Greek form of the Epistles of Ignatius.

2. Patrum Apostolicorum Opera, textum ex editionibus præstantissimis repetitum recognovit, annotationibus illustravit, versionem Latinam emendatiorem, prolegomena et indices addidit Carolus Josephus Hefele, SS. Theolog. Doct. ejusdemque in Acad. Tubing. Prof. P.O. (Tubingæ: editio tertia 1847 [h]; editio quarta 1855). Hefele's notes are judicious and valuable. His prolegomena are clear, and contain an admirable summary

---

[h] I have used the third edition of this work.

of the main points discussed by previous writers. He occasionally trusts too much to the learning of others.

3. Patrum Apostolicorum Opera. Textum ad fidem Codicum et Græcorum et Latinorum, ineditorum copia insignium, adhibitis præstantissimis editionibus, recensuit atque emendavit notis illustravit, versione Latina passim correcta, prolegomenis, indicibus instruxit Albertus Rud. Max. Dressel. Accedit Hermæ Pastor ex fragmentis Græcis Lipsiensibus, instituta quæstione de vero ejus textus fonte, auctore Constantino Tischendorf. (Lipsiæ 1857; editio altera 1863). Dressel does not stand high as contributing to the illustration of his writers, nor are his prolegomena so clear and well reasoned as they might be. Scholars are immensely indebted to him however for the unedited manuscripts which he has brought to light, and many uncollated ones which he has examined. His work is the most complete collection of the genuine Ep-Apostolic works.

4. Novum Testamentum extra Canonem receptum, edidit Adolphus Hilgenfeld (Lipsiæ 1866). This work contains the two Epistles of Clemens, the Epistle of Barnabas and the Pastor of Hermas, with the fragments of the Gospel according to the Hebrews, Egyptians, &c. It is characterized by a thorough knowledge of the subject, a complete acquaintance with all the German literature on it, and by considerable independence and originality of thought.

Besides these editions which throw light on the Apostolical Fathers, mention is to be made here of several important works which have appeared lately in Germany on the state of the Church and of doctrine as exhibited in these writings. The most important are,—

1. Rothe: Die Anfänge der Christlichen Kirche und

ihrer Verfassung. Ein geschichtlicher Versuch von Richard Rothe. (Wittenb. 1837). Baur's work on the Ursprung des Episcopats is a reply to Rothe.

2. Schwegler: Das Nachapostolische Zeitalter in den Hauptmomenten seiner Entwicklung, von Dr. Albert Schwegler. (Tübingen 1846. 2 vols.)

3. Ritschl: Die Entstehung der altkatholischen Kirche; eine kirchen- und dogmengeschichtliche Monographie. (Bonn 1850. Zweite Auflage 1857.)

4. Thiersch: Die Kirche im Apostolischen Zeitalter. (Frankfurt und Erlangen 1850. Zweite Auflage 1858.)

5. Lechler: Das Apostolische und das Nachapostolische Zeitalter dargestellt von Gotthard Victor Lechler. Zweite Auflage: Stuttgart 1857. (The first edition appeared at Haarlem 1851.)

6. Reuss: Histoire de la Théologie Chrétienne au Siècle Apostolique. (Strasbourg, 2nd éd. 2 vols. 1860).

7. Hilgenfeld: Apostolische Väter. 1853.

8. Lange: Das Apostolische Zeitalter dargestellt von Dr. J. P. Lange. (Braunschweig 1854.)

9. A popular description of the Apostolical Fathers, their writings, and the circumstances in the midst of which they lived and wrote, is given in " Les Pères Apostoliques et leur Epoque. Par M. l'Abbé Freppel, Professeur à la Faculté de Théologie de Paris. Cours d'éloquence sacrée fait à la Sorbonne pendant l'année 1857–8. (2nd éd. 8vo. Paris 1859.) It is strongly Roman Catholic.

There are also three important works on the moral teaching of the Apostolical Fathers.

1. Francisci Jani Jacobi Alberti Junius, Lugduno-Batavi Commentatio de Patrum Apostolicorum Doctrina Morali. (Lugduni Batavorum 1833.)

2. Jani van Gilse Zaandamo-Hollandi Commentatio de Patrum Apostolicorum Doctrina Morali. (Lugduni Batavorum 1833.)

3. Stephani Petri Heyns, ex Promontorio Bonæ Spei, Commentatio de Patrum Apostolicorum Doctrina Morali. (Lugduni Batavorum 1833.) These three works were prize essays. Besides these there are various separate writings of Bunsen, Baur, and others, which will be mentioned at the proper time.

There is one work in English which treats of the Apostolical Fathers, but by no means in a satisfactory manner. It is, "A History of the Rise and Early Progress of Christianity, by Samuel Hinds, D.D." (Third edition 1854.) This work has no claims to be regarded as an original production, at least as far as the Apostolical Fathers are concerned. The author is indebted principally to Cave and Bingham, and many of his statements are erroneous and inaccurate.

CHAPTER II.

CLEMENS ROMANUS.

THE first document which comes under our notice is a letter addressed by the Roman Church to the Corinthian. The name of the composer of the letter is not attached to it; but we know what it is most important to know, when we are assured that the sentiments expressed in it are the sentiments of the Roman Church. The composition of the letter was unanimously attributed by the ancients to Clemens Romanus.

Life.

Clemens, called Romanus to distinguish him from Clemens of Alexandria, was an overseer in the Church in Rome. At what period he occupied this position is matter of dispute. The earliest witness on this point is Hegesippus. His testimony admits of a double interpretation. Eusebius[a] remarks: "And that the divisions among the Corinthians took place in the time of the person mentioned (κατὰ τὸν δηλούμενον), Hegesippus is

---

[a] Hist. Eccl. iii. 16.

a trustworthy witness." If we supply to δηλούμενον, τὸν Κλήμεντα, as Lardner[b], Lipsius[c], Dressel[d], and others have done, we get the statement that Clemens was contemporary with the Corinthian disputes. If we supply χρόνον, as Möhler[e] and Contogones[f] have done, and as the usage of Eusebius[g] seems to me to require, then the testimony of Hegesippus is to the effect that the divisions of the Corinthian Church took place in the reign of Domitian. The latter interpretation makes Hegesippus say nothing with regard to Clemens. Nor have we any express testimony that Hegesippus mentioned Clemens. Hegesippus remained for some time at Corinth, and seems to have instituted particular inquiries into the divisions that had taken place there. We know also that in his work he mentioned the letter sent by the Roman Church to the Corinthian[h]; and the words in which Eusebius announces this, "after some things said by him with regard to the letter of Clemens," would incline us to believe that he did mention Clemens; but the description of the letter may possibly have been Eusebius's own. We therefore get from Hegesippus no statement with regard to Clemens: but we learn from him that the circumstances which called forth the Roman letter took place in the reign of Domitian. On

---

[b] Credibility, part ii. ch. ii.

[c] De Clementis Romani Epistola ad Corinthios priore Disquisitio, p. 156.

[d] Patres Apostolici, Prolegg. p. xv.

[e] Patrologie, p. 58.   [f] Vol. i. p. 19.

[g] In Hist. Eccl. ii. 11, iii. 28 and iii. 29, the χρόνος is expressed; in ii. 6, iii. 18, and iii. 32, either χρόνος or the name of the reigning emperor is to be supplied. The passages might be indefinitely increased.

[h] Euseb. Hist. Eccl. iv. 22.

this information we shall be warranted in believing that Clemens flourished at that time, if we get satisfactory testimony to his authorship of the epistle. The first witness to this is Dionysius, an overseer of the Corinthian Church, whose words will be adduced hereafter. We notice here simply that the testimonies of Hegesippus and Dionysius conjoined give Clemens as living in the time of Domitian.

Most of the other writers who mention Clemens supply us with information only in regard to the place he held in the line of the overseers of the Roman Church. The most important is Irenæus. His words are: "The blessed Apostles Peter and Paul, having founded and built up the Church, gave the office of oversight to Linus. This Linus Paul has mentioned in his letters to Timothy. He is succeeded by Anencletus. After him, in the third place from the Apostles, Clemens obtains the oversight, who also saw the Apostles themselves and conversed with them, and who still had the preaching of the Apostles ringing in his ears, and their doctrine before his eyes[i]." The minute accuracy of these statements is open to question. Everything must depend on the critical faculty of Irenæus, which unfortunately was not great. The assertion that Paul and Peter founded the Roman Church and built it up is exceedingly questionable. For that Paul did not found it, we know from his Epistle to the Romans; and that Peter had very little connection with it, is also matter of certainty; and indeed it is not improbable that he had no connection with it at all. Besides this, there is extreme unlikelihood that there was only one overseer in the Roman Church at a time, as the state-

[i] Irenæus, Hæres. iii. c. 3; also in Euseb. Hist. Eccl. v. 6.

ment of Irenæus seems to imply. The Corinthian Church had more than one; most of the churches of which we know anything had more than one; and we may therefore rest assured that the Roman Church had also more than one. In addition to this, we see a perverting influence at work in the minds of Irenæus and his contemporaries, in their strong wish to be able to trace up their doctrines to the days of the Apostles. How powerfully this motive acted, alongside of the inactivity of true historical criticism, on the minds of Clemens Alexandrinus and Origen, will become evident in various parts of this work. In this case Clemens Alexandrinus[k] speaks of Clemens as an Apostle; and Origen calls him a disciple of the Apostles[l], and identifies him with the person mentioned in Philippians iv. 3[m].

The most precise information which we have is in Eusebius. He quotes Irenæus, and elsewhere gives the same succession as he gave, stating that Clemens succeeded Anencletus in the twelfth year of the reign of Domitian, 93 A.D.[n], and died in the third year of the reign of Trajan, 101 A.D.[o] On what authority Eusebius assigned these dates we do not know, but we can have little doubt that he was tolerably careful; and, on the whole, this is the most satisfactory information we can now obtain on the subject[p].

---

[k] Clemens Alexandr. Strom. iv. c. 17. [l] De Princip. lib. ii. c. 3.
[m] Origen in Joann. tom. vi. c. 36.   [n] Euseb. Hist. Eccl. iii. 15.
[o] Euseb. Hist. Eccl. iii. 34. In the Armenian version of the Chronicon the date of his oversight is given as the seventh year of Domitian's reign. Jerome's version agrees with the Ecclesiastical History.

[p] The conjectures of Pearson and Dodwell on this and other chronological points are discussed in Tillemont and Lardner. They do not deserve record here.

The tradition with regard to the position of Clemens in the line of succession from the Apostles was by no means uniform. Eusebius had access only to the Greek form of it given in Irenæus. Tertullian seems to have regarded Clemens as the immediate successor of Peter. In attacking the churches of the heretics, he challenges them to exhibit "the order of their overseers so running down by succession from the beginning, that the first overseer had some one as his ordainer and predecessor who was either an Apostle or an apostolic man that had lived with the Apostles. For this is the way in which the Apostolic Churches hand down their rolls, as the Church of the Smyrneans relates that Polycarp was placed by John, and the Church of the Romans that Clemens was ordained by Peter[q]." The inference from these words, that Tertullian regarded Clemens as the first overseer of the Roman Church, is not absolutely certain. For his argument would be sound, and perhaps stronger, if Clemens were only the third from the Apostles; for then the Roman Church could exhibit, not merely one, but several apostolic men in its roll. But still it has been universally taken to indicate that Tertullian believed Clemens to be the first, and at least the immense probability is that such was his belief. And Jerome expressly states that most of the Latins represented Clemens as the successor of Peter. Schliemann supposes that this belief owed its origin to the Clementines, which introduce Clemens as the disciple of Peter[r]. And he thinks he finds a passage in Origen confirmatory of this idea. For Origen, in quoting from the

[q] Tertull. De Præscriptione Hæret. c. xxxii.
[r] Die Clementinen von Adolph Schliemann, p. 120.

Recognitions, describes the writer as "Clemens the Roman, a disciple of the Apostle Peter[s]." But the testimony of Origen does not help us much here. For Origen merely asserts that Clemens was a disciple, which he might have been even had he been third in the succession. And it is to me extremely doubtful whether we can with security assign the description of Clemens in the Philocalia to Origen. For nothing is more common than for an ancient editor to interpolate explanatory remarks—an instance of which occurs in chapter xxii. of this same Philocalia in relation to the same Clemens. He is there called "a bishop of Rome;" a mode of expression entirely unknown to the time of Origen[t]. There is not however the slightest doubt that the Clementine stories were adopted by later writers as historical[u], and from the preface of Rufinus to the Recognitions[x] we gather that many based the belief in Clemens's immediate succession of Peter on the letter of Clemens to the Apostle James. Tillemont has observed this[y].

The fact probably was, that none of them knew anything about the matter. Writers subsequent to the time of Eusebius indulged in endless conjectures and opinions, some placing him first, some second, some fourth, and some trying to reconcile these various opinions. Of the attempts at reconciliation two may be noticed, more as characteristic of the mode in which these later writers dealt with such matters, than as

[s] Philocal. Spencer, p. 81. c. xxiii. Lommatzsch, p. 226.
[t] Philocal. p. 202. Lommatzsch.
[u] See Schliemann, pp. 118-124.
[x] Recognitiones, ed. Gersdorf, p. 2.
[y] Tome i. part i. p. 484.

likely to throw light on our investigation. Rufinus, in his preface to the Clementine Recognitions, tries to solve the difficulty by supposing that Linus and Anencletus were overseers of the Roman Church while Peter was alive, and after Peter's death it fell to the lot of Clemens to become overseer. This supposition has no testimony to support it, and probably Rufinus did not feel the need of its being thus supported. In one respect it seems to us to hit the truth. It frees Peter entirely from the oversight. It is not likely that either Peter or Paul was an overseer in any church. The other explanation is that of Epiphanius. It is only one of his conjectures on the subject. He supposes that Clemens received the appointment of overseer from St. Peter, but that he did not fill his office as long as Linus and Cletus were alive. This conjecture is based solely on the words of Clemens in the Epistle to the Corinthians. These words are an exhortation to a person filled with love to say, "If on account of me there are division, strife, and schisms, I go out of the way, I retire[z]."

There is one point in the statement with regard to Clemens which has attracted considerable attention. Is he the person mentioned in the Epistle to the Philippians? Now, as far as historical evidence goes, we must without hesitation affirm that it is not sufficient to prove his identity. The first mention of it occurs in Origen[a], whose authority in such a matter is null. The identity of name would be enough for him to warrant him in pronouncing an identity of persons. After his

[z] Hæres. xxvii. §. 6. Pan. lib. i. Tillemont gives a full account of the various attempts at solution, including even that of the Protestant Hammond: tome second, prem. part. p. 484.

[a] Comment. in Joann. tom. vi. c. 36. Lommatzsch.

time writers are unanimous in representing him as the person, and Eusebius oftener than once thus speaks of him[b]. At the same time the objections which have been urged against the supposition (for it cannot be called a tradition,) are utterly weak. That the Clemens mentioned was a Philippian is probable enough, but there is no reason why a Philippian should not find his way to Rome and hold a high position in the Roman Church. Nor is there anything in the letter of the Roman Church inconsistent with the writer of it being a disciple of Paul. In fact the letter informs us thus much, that the writer knew at least some of the writings of Paul. So far as this point then is concerned, the want of positive historical evidence on the one side, and the perfect congruity of the supposition on the other, leave the matter undecided. This determination of the question does not prevent us from giving full credence to the statement of Irenæus, that he had heard the Apostles—a statement most likely in itself, in harmony with the most probable dates, and connected with the whole character of the letter. But there is no real evidence for believing him to be in any especial way a scholar of Peter. The statements of the Clementines are unworthy of credit.

Of the death of Clemens nothing is known. Later writers represented him as a martyr, and there exists a worthless document[c] describing his martyrdom. But from the statement of Eusebius[d] ($\dot{a}\nu a\lambda \acute{v}\epsilon\iota\ \tau\grave{o}\nu\ \beta\acute{\iota}o\nu$), we learn that that historian had heard nothing of it, and

[b] Hist. Eccl. iii. 15.
[c] In Cotelerius, tom. i. pp. 804-811.
[d] Hist. Eccl. iii. 34.

indeed the time at which he died would render any such statement questionable in the extreme.

Some have attempted to gather information with regard to Clemens from the Letter; as it appears to us, unsuccessfully. Tillemont and a host after him have inferred, from such statements as "our father Abraham," and the writer's acquaintance with and admiration of Jewish men and manners, that he was a Jew. But whatever the writer may have been, such words as "our fathers" are applicable not to him, but to the Roman Church, and would in fact prove that the Roman Church was Jewish. And again, a writer's acquaintance with Jewish customs and admiration of the patriarch Jacob may proceed from other causes than the habits of thought peculiar to a born Jew.

More recent writers have inclined to the opinion that he was a Roman[e]. The supposed indications of this are of a more interesting nature, and at first sight seem to have some weight. It is attempted to prove that the writer was well acquainted with Greek and Latin literature, and that in his reception of Christianity he sought to bring some of the beliefs which he had imbibed in the course of his education into harmony with it. Thus he is represented as looking on the Danaids and Dirce, not as mere fictions, or appendages of false divinities, but as martyrs[f], and as placing the writings of the Sibyl alongside of the writings of the Apostles. His acquaintance with Greek and Latin literature is supposed to be shown in the use he makes of the fable of the phœnix[g], in the opinion stated, that there existed worlds beyond the ocean[h], and

[e] Lips. Disq. p. 155.
[f] Hilgenfeld: Apostolische Väter, p. 36. Lips. Disq. p. 151.
[g] c. 25.   [h] c. 20.

in some rather indefinite historical allusions to the history of the Romans, or more correctly, of the nations[i].

If he really did the first two things here noticed, we certainly should be inclined to look on them as strong proofs of his heathen origin. But we do not think there is good reason for believing that he did so. The words " Danaids and Dirce " have up to recent times been universally discarded as either interpolations or corruptions, and the arguments are so strong for this view that it is wonderful any one could for a moment resist them. After mentioning the afflictions to which holy men were exposed on account of jealousy, the letter adds: " On account of envy, women, the Danaids and Dircae, being persecuted, having suffered terrible and unholy torments, reached the sure course of faith, and the weak in body received a noble reward." Is it possible that a Christian writer who must have personally known many noble women who fell victims to the fury of the heathen, would omit all notice of them, and mention specifically only two names, and those two names he could have heard only amid the ribald tales of licentious gods? Nay more, if we take the words in the most inoffensive way in which they can be taken, namely, as a comparison; so far are they from proving the writer to have been acquainted with Greek literature, that they must be regarded as signs of utter ignorance; for it would require more than ingenuity to elevate women that had killed their husbands, and a woman that had tormented another, into heroic martyrs[k].

[i] c. 55.

[k] An admirable emendation of the passage has been proposed by Wordsworth and approved by Bunsen. He would read νεανίδες, παιδίσκαι. See Jacobson's note on the passage.

The statement with regard to the Sibyl is more feasible, but the passage on which it is based is not found in the manuscript. It occurs in a writing falsely attributed to Justin Martyr[1]; and as in later times many letters and writings were attributed to Clemens, we have no means of ascertaining whether it is taken from the genuine or some of the spurious letters. The opinion that the Sibyl was inspired was not uncommon at a very early age; but we must have more proof before we can allow that the Roman Church held it.

The three other passages do not deserve much notice, as they prove nothing at all with regard to the origin of Clemens, and are, as it appears to us, rather unfavourable than otherwise to the notion that the writer was well educated. That he could read and write we can have no doubt, as he would not have been chosen to compose the letter if he could not; and that he had some sense of beauty of style, we think evident from the letter itself. But the opinion with regard to the phœnix seems to us unquestionably indicative of a rather credulous and uncultivated mind. Commentators have generally appealed to Herodotus, and more especially to Tacitus and Pliny, as acquiescing in the common belief; but on a closer examination of what these writers say, a great difference will be seen to exist between them and Clemens. Herodotus[m] relates simply the reports of others, and does not intimate that he believed any part of them, but positively declares that some of the statements were not credible. Pliny states expressly that he does not know whether the accounts of the bird are fabulous or not[n]. And

---

[1] Quæstt. et Respp. ad Orthodoxos, Respons. 74.
[m] Herod. ii. 73.   [n] Pliny, Nat. Hist. x. 2.

Tacitus[o], without denying the existence of the bird, equally plainly declares that the statements with regard to it are uncertain (hæc incerta et fabulosis aucta). Now on the other hand Clemens accepts the whole story as true in its most ridiculous minutiæ.

What indications the letter gives of the time at which the writer lived, will be more appropriately discussed when we inquire into its date.

There are several sources of information in regard to Clemens of which we have taken almost no notice. These are the Clementine Recognitions, the Homilies, and the Constitutions. The reason is, that we believe them to be purely fictitious as far as Clemens is concerned—a proposition which we shall attempt to prove when we come to treat of them.

WRITINGS OF CLEMENS.

I. THE EPISTLE TO THE CORINTHIANS.

This Epistle has come down to us only in one manuscript. It was discovered in 1628 appended to the famous Alexandrian codex of the Old and New Testament. Along with it was another writing with no inscription, but named in the catalogue prefixed to the codex, ... εντος ε ..... λη B, which it is easy to interpret "The Second Epistle of Clemens."

We have now to inquire into the authorship of the first epistle. We have seen already that we have no authority for ranking Hegesippus among the witnesses

[o] Tacitus, Ann. vi. 28.

in this matter. Even if we take the words of Eusebius as Lipsius has done, the amount of information we receive is, that the disturbances among the Corinthians took place in the time of Clemens[p]. To the same effect is the testimony of Irenæus, who says that "in the time of this Clemens (ἐπὶ τούτου τοῦ Κλήμεντος) no small dissension arising among the brethren at Corinth, the Church in Rome sent a most satisfactory letter to the Corinthians[q]." The first ascription of the epistle to Clemens is in a letter of Dionysius, overseer of the Corinthian Church, addressed to the Roman Church and Soter its overseer: "We passed this Lord's holy day," he says, "in which we read your letter," (i. e. the letter of the Roman Church recently sent to the Corinthian Church,) "from the constant reading of which we shall be able to draw admonition even as from the reading of the former one you sent us written through Clemens[r]." This statement of Dionysius carries great weight; for it must be regarded as the opinion of the two principal parties whose ancestors were concerned in the matter. Yet the distance of Dionysius from Clemens prevents us from being certain; and it is not impossible that the ascription of the letter to Clemens arose simply from the circumstance that he was at the time the most prominent overseer of the Roman Church. We need not quote further testimony with regard to the authorship of the Epistle, as subsequent writers are unanimous in

[p] Pearson, in his Vindiciæ Ign. pars. i. c. iii. quotes a passage from Anastasius Bibliothecarius, in which that writer affirms that Hegesippus asserted that the whole Church received the Letter of Clemens as genuine. Pearson clearly shows that Anastasius had no authority for his statement, and it arose entirely from a misinterpretation of Georgius Syncellus.

[q] Adv. Hær. lib. iii. c. 3, n. 3.   [r] Euseb. Hist. Eccl. iv. 23.

ascribing it to Clemens: Clemens Alexandrinus [s], Origen, and Eusebius all speak of Clemens as the unquestionable author. We have not adduced a passage in the Pastor of Hermas which mentions Clemens, because it really gives us no information with regard to him or the letter, and we shall have to discuss it hereafter in another connection.

The next question that has to be considered is, Is the letter which we now have, the letter spoken of by Irenæus and others? A few have attempted to deny its genuineness, especially in early times; but their objections were utterly frivolous, the allusion to the phœnix being especially repugnant to their idea of Clemens. One writer, Bernardus (Anonymus in Cotelerius), maintained that the letter which has come down to us was a forgery, and a mere expansion of a few chapters of Clemens Alexandrinus. This theory was based on the circumstance that Clemens Alexandrinus has summarised many of the chapters of the Roman Clemens, omitting allusions to some chapters altogether, and condensing others within small compass. The notion of Bernardus however is so outrageous, while the summarising of Clemens Alexandrinus is so in harmony with his usual practice, that this theory has been universally rejected in the present day.

Some of the Tübingen school, especially Schwegler, have attempted to throw discredit on the authorship of Clemens, and to remove the date of its composition to a later period. The data on which the attempt is based are so arbitrary, and so intimately connected with the whole Baurian scheme, that they do not require refuta-

[s] Clem. Alex. Strom. i. c. 7, p. 339; iv. c. 17, p. 609, 610; v. c. 12, p. 693; vi. c. 8, p. 773. Origen and Eusebius have been already quoted.

tion here. Baur himself allowed that there was nothing in the letter to warrant our refusing to look on Clemens as its author; but he adds this singular reason for being uncertain: "The point cannot be regarded as absolutely settled, since so many other writings were ascribed to the same Clemens with the greatest injustice, and his name especially became the bearer of so many old traditions and writings relating to the constitution of the Church[t]." Because many writings which were not genuine were ascribed to Clemens, or rather bore his name, this one also is likely not to be genuine, though antiquity was unanimous in regarding the one epistle as genuine, and in early times equally unanimous in rejecting the other as forged. Baur has since expressed his general agreement with Schwegler[u].

Have we the whole of the letter? To this second question we can give a positive reply. We have not the whole of the letter. Towards the conclusion of the manuscript there is a break, and Junius thought that a whole leaf was wanting. We have no means of supplying this defect. Various passages quoted as from Clemens by ancient writers have been assigned a place here; but we have no means of ascertaining whether these passages were taken from this letter or from the spurious writings of Clemens.

[t] Ursprung des Episcopats, p. 69.

[u] The notions of Schwegler are refuted in a very sensible and satisfactory, though not exhaustive, work: Disquisitio Critica et Historica de Clementis Romani Priore ad Corinthios Epistola, by Ecco Ekker Trajecti ad Rhenum, 1854); also by Ritschl, p. 274 ff; and Lechler, p. 476, n. 2. The evidence for the genuineness of the letter is exhibited in a clear and conclusive manner by Conrad Thönnissen: Zwei historisch-theologische Abhandlungen. I. Ueber die Authentizität und Integrität des ersten Briefes des Clemens von Rom an die Corinther. (Trier 1841.)

Is the letter in any way corrupted by changes or interpolations? This question is open to greater doubt. At the first glance the letter seems longer than one would expect in such circumstances, and there is more of full delineation and less of practical home-speaking than the circumstances might be supposed to require. Such objections however are of no weight. They may leave a general hesitancy about the question, but as yet no attempt to impugn any one passage has been successful.

Of these attempts a few deserve notice. Immediately on the publication of the letter, Hieronymus Bignonius (in supremo Senatu Parisiensi Advocatus Regius) wrote to Hugo Grotius to ask his opinion with regard to its genuineness. He himself found difficulties in the writer's use of epithets and his tendency to amplification, in the argument for the resurrection drawn from the phœnix, in the mention of offerings and the use of the word λαϊκός in ch. xl., and in the epithet ἀρχαίαν applied to the Corinthian Church. He supposed moreover that some clauses had been added by transcribers. Hugo Grotius replied to these objections and satisfied Bignonius entirely, except with regard to the phœnix[x]. This can scarcely be called an attack on the integrity of the text.

The ecclesiastical historian Mosheim[y] attacked it mainly on the ground that the chapters did not cohere well. Following what he regarded as the design of the writer, he retained some chapters and excluded others. The best answer to such a mode of treatment is, that letters are not often very systematic, and that no one

[x] Coteler. Patres Apost. vol. i. p. 133.
[y] Instit. Hist. Chr. Majores, p. 214.

can judge beforehand what a writer may introduce into his letters. There is another answer to part of his division, that some of the excluded portions are quoted by Clemens Alexandrinus.

In more recent times Neander has expressed his doubts with regard to the integrity of the letter. He takes particular exception to the fortieth and forty-first chapters, because, as he says, "we find the whole system of the Jewish priesthood transferred to the Christian Church[x]." This objection falls entirely to the ground when the true nature of the passage is ascertained. For then it will appear that Clemens did not transfer the system of the Jewish priesthood to the Christian Church. He merely refers to it as an instance of God's orderly arrangements in his dealings with his people, and he leaves the application of the particulars of the Jewish system entirely to the γνῶσις of each individual. The chapter commences: "Since these things then are manifest to us, even examining into the depths of the divine knowledge, we ought to do all things in order, which the Lord has commanded us," &c. How Clemens himself explained the meaning of the Jewish worship and the Jewish priesthood for Christians he does not say, and though, as we shall notice hereafter, explanations have been hazarded with regard to some parts of his statements, yet there are others that have not been grappled with, and, as far as I can see, do not admit of a satisfactory solution. Thus he affirms that sacrifices are not offered everywhere, but only in Jerusalem; and not in every part of Jerusalem, but only at the altar in

---

[x] Neander's Church History (Bohn's Translation), vol. ii. p. 408. Mosheim had rested his doubts with regard to this passage on the same grounds. (Instit. Major. sæc. I. p. 214.)

front of the shrine (ναοῦ); a statement which he leaves entirely unexplained in its reference to the Corinthians. There can be no doubt then that we have here an instance of the application of Christian γνῶσις to the interpretation of the Old Testament; for the writer expressly says so in introducing and in finishing the subject; and this is now the opinion of the more recent commentators as it was of some ancient [y].

As a set-off to these speculations with regard to the integrity of the epistle, we must take into account that the letter was well known in early times. We have express testimony that it was read in various churches, and was reckoned by some as inspired. We have already seen that it was read in the Corinthian Church on the Sunday towards the end of the second century. Eusebius asserts that it was read publicly in his day [z], and Jerome says the same of his time, "quæ et in nonnullis locis publice legitur [a]." The position, at the end of the Alexandrian codex, in which the only manuscript of it now remaining has been found, is proof that the transcribers of it regarded it at least as not unworthy to be placed as an addition to the Old and New Testament. These circumstances are considerable security for the fidelity of transcribers; but our trust in them would be much greater had we more manuscripts. In addition to this evidence we must take into account the circumstance that the epistle has been largely quoted by Clemens Alexandrinus.

The date of the letter has yet to be settled. It has been variously fixed at 67 or 68, and 96 or 97. Some in more recent times have assigned it to the second

[y] Junius, Lipsius, Bunsen, Hilgenfeld.   [z] Hist. Eccl. iii. 16.
[a] De Viris Illustribus, c. 15.

century[b]; but as this opinion is based almost, if not entirely, on conjecture with regard to the process of development of the Pauline and Petrine controversy, we must dismiss such a subjective test, and consider only the other two opinions.

With this question is mixed up that of the date of Clemens's oversight of the Roman Church, but they are not indissolubly connected. It is easy to conceive that Clemens may have been selected by the Roman Church to be the composer of their letter, even though he were not overseer. It was the most eloquent and persuasive writer that was required, and unquestionably they found in Clemens a suitable man, whatever may be the period at which he wrote. If we accept as the right translation of the passage in Eusebius that which I have given, we have then the authority of Hegesippus for saying that the letter was written in the reign of Domitian. As however a great deal of internal evidence has been brought to bear on this point, we shall examine it in detail. We shall follow Hefele[c], who has well arranged the arguments for the year 68, and replied to the objections taken against it.

1. The writer thus refers to Paul, and probably also to Peter. "But to stop referring to ancient examples, let us come to the athletes who were nearest us. Let us take the noble examples of our own generation. On account of jealousy and envy the greatest and most righteous pillars were persecuted, and even went to death. Let us place before our eyes the good Apostles[d]." Then the writer refers to two Apostles, one of whose

[b] Schwegler: Nachapostolisches Zeitalter, ii. 125 ff. Baur: Streitschrift gegen Bunsen, p. 127 ff.

[c] Prolegomena, p. xix.   [d] c. 5.

names is imperfect in the manuscript, but is probably Peter; the other is Paul. Here it is argued that the word 'nearest' ἔγγιστα, is applicable only if the epistle were written immediately after the deaths of Peter and Paul. But this depends entirely on the objects compared. Now the examples he had just quoted were Aaron and Miriam, Dathan and Abiram, and David. Coming down to what he would call modern times, he might easily apply the term ἔγγιστα to any within a century or two of his own period, when he was dealing with such ancient times as those of David. No argument therefore can be drawn from this expression for fixing the date to A.D. 68.

2. A persecution is mentioned in chapter i. and then there is supposed to be a description of a persecution in chapter vi. which Hefele identifies with that of chapter i. The description in chapter vi. he says, suits only the persecution of Nero, which was unusually severe, and is inappropriate to that of Domitian which was not so terrible. The passage is a continuation of the preceding: "Along with these men (the Apostles) who lived holy lives, were associated a large multitude of the elect, who, having suffered through envy many indignities and tortures, became most beautiful examples in the midst of us." Now it seems to me that we have here no description of a persecution at all. Along with Paul and Peter there was a great number of men who were also Christian athletes. This is all Clemens says; and such a description would be quite appropriate to times when there was no general persecution, but merely much private persecution, such as always existed against the Christians in early times. It seems to me that there is therefore no express reference to any particular period,

but to the annoyances that all the Christian athletes endured. And I am confirmed in this by the turn which Clemens's thoughts take immediately after mentioning this great multitude. He first describes women who endured extreme indignities and gained heavenly reward. Then he adds: "Jealousy has alienated the hearts of wives from their husbands, and altered that which was said by our father Adam, 'This is now bone of my bone and flesh of my flesh.' Jealousy and strife have overturned great cities and rooted out great nations." And so here he ends with his instances of the effects of jealousy and strife.

3. Hefele grounds his third argument on the same passages. If Clemens had written after the persecution of Domitian, would he not have mentioned some of those illustrious men who suffered in it; such as Flavius Clemens, Ancilius Glabrio, Flavia Domitilla, John the Evangelist? The answer to this is, that Clemens would mention only those who were well known to the Corinthians, and that in fact he mentions only two, though many had suffered in the persecution of Nero and before that time; that the three whom Hefele speaks of were not more deserving of notice than hundreds of others of that generation who had been equally persecuted; and that as for John it would be premature speaking of him before he was dead. Besides, Peter and Paul were quite sufficient particular illustrations of what he wished to show, without introducing any more.

4. The fourth argument is derived from chapters xl. and xli. in which Clemens is supposed to speak of the temple as yet standing, and consequently it is inferred that the letter must have been written before the destruction of Jerusalem.

The interpretation of these chapters however ought, as we have seen, to be allegorical. And Clemens speaks of these things as existing, not because they existed in his time, but because they existed in the Old Testament, signs and symbols of everliving truths.

Most of the arguments which have been adduced on the other side are equally unsatisfactory. Clemens, in referring to Paul's First Epistle to the Corinthians, asks the question, "What did he write first to you in the beginning of the Gospel[e]?" From this some have inferred that a long time must have elapsed between Paul's first letter and that of Clemens. The inference is unwarranted. Then in the same chapter Clemens calls the Corinthian Church an "ancient" (ἀρχαίαν) Church, and from this it is inferred that Clemens's time must have been considerably removed from that of the founding of the Church of Corinth. But here everything depends upon the objects compared, and no one can doubt that in comparison with other Churches the Church of Corinth could appropriately be called "ancient," even in the lifetime of the Apostles. Besides, as Dodwell remarks, a Church could well be called ἀρχαία which was founded ἐν ἀρχῇ τοῦ εὐαγγελίου[f]. Some have found an argument for the date of the letter in the passages which correspond to those in the Epistle to the Hebrews. The Epistle to the Hebrews they say must have been written between A.D. 70 and 80. This letter of Clemens quotes from this epistle, and must therefore have been written after it[g]. The argument however is a very

[e] c. xlvii.

[f] Addit. ad Pearsonii Dissert. ii. de Successione Pontif. Rom. cap. vi. § 25. See also Grabe Spicil. vol. i. p. 256.

[g] See Ekker, p. 101.

unsatisfactory one. The writer of the Epistle to the Hebrews may have quoted from Clemens, and not Clemens from him. The Epistle to the Hebrews may have been written by Clemens. And the date of the Epistle to the Hebrews is by no means an easily settled question.

Hilgenfeld has also appealed to the word γενεά, which he considers as meaning only a space of thirty years. The letter therefore could not have been written more than thirty years after the death of the Apostles Peter and Paul. But this limitation of the meaning of γενεά is unwarranted[h].

Volkmar thinks, that the book of Judith, referred to in chap. 55, was not written till after the Jewish war of Trajan; and that consequently the letter of Clemens was not written till then. But we have much more authority and evidence for the date of the authorship of the Epistle of Clemens than for that of the book of Judith; and accordingly the date of the Epistle of Clemens is not determined by it, but is testimony to the date of the book of Judith[i]. Perhaps the only real indication of the date of the letter is contained in some passages that refer to the appointment of overseers. Clemens makes mention of elders "appointed by the apostles or afterwards by other illustrious men," and speaks of them "as borne witness to for a long period." (μεμαρτυρημένους πολλοῖς χρόνοις.) We have here the age of the Apostles, then we have illustrious men after their day, and we have elders living for a long time after these illustrious men had succeeded to the function of the Apostles alluded to. Thirty or forty years after the

[h] Ekker, p. 96.
[i] See Lightfoot, S. Clement of Rome, p. 160.

death of Peter and Paul would not be too much to account for such a statement [j].

There has been much useless discussion as to the circumstances of the Corinthian Church which called forth this letter. The only source of information which we have as to particulars is the letter itself, and ingenious trifling has drawn out of the most innocent assertions the most extraordinary theories [k]. Some have attributed the dissensions to the party of Christ mentioned in Paul's First Epistle to the Corinthians, as if they knew what that was [l]. Gundert assigns them to the Pauline party [m]; and Uhlhorn, in addition to the Christ party, introduces false teachers, especially Docetes [n]. Even Lipsius presses the matter too far when he supposes that the character of the disturbers of the Corinthian Church is to be inferred from every admonition given in the letter. The extreme probability is, that the quarrels were entirely personal and not doctrinal. The letter expressly accuses a few headlong and self-willed individuals as the cause [o]. They were anxious to expel some of the presbyters from their oversight. We are not acquainted with their reasons; but from the tenor of the letter we may infer that they were largely actuated by jealousy and a high

---

[j] See Ekker, p. 99. Ekker refutes both Hefele and Schwegler as to the date in a very honest and satisfactory manner.

[k] Ekker refutes the purely gratuitous suppositions of Rothe, and submits the ideas of Schenkel and Hilgenfeld to a thorough examination, and shows their incorrectness. His conclusions are nearly the same as those given in the text, ch. ii.

[l] Schenkel, Studien und Kritiken (1841), p. 61.

[m] Gundert, Zeitschrift für die gesammte Lutherische Theologie und Kirche, 1854, p. 45.

[n] See, for an exposition of these, Lipsius, p. 119. [o] c. i.

opinion of themselves. We do not think that there is any good reason for supposing that they prided themselves, in contrast with the elders, on their wisdom, strength, riches, chastity, or power of gnostic interpretation. On the contrary, if they had done so, the letter would directly have combated such pretensions, while the allusion to these qualities is merely incidental. Indeed, if there were any doctrine at all on which we could suppose that there was a dispute, it would be that of the resurrection, for the writer is eager to establish it. But as no allusion is made to the dissentients in connection with this doctrine, we must regard the introduction of the subject as intended either to benefit the Church generally, or some portion of it which may or may not have been composed of dissentients, or may have been composed of both parties.

It is important to notice, too, that though the letter lays the blame on a few individuals, it does not hesitate to rebuke the whole Church. It describes in glowing language its extraordinary prosperity and goodness, and then goes on to state that it grew proud of itself, and from this sprung jealousy, strife, and disorder, the dishonoured rising up against the honoured, the foolish against the thoughtful, and the young against the elders[p].

We may now sum up in a few words the results of our investigations, both as to Clemens and the letter. We have most distinct evidence with regard to these two facts, that disputes among the Corinthians arose in the time of Domitian, that the Roman Church then sent a letter to the Corinthians, and that at that time Clemens held office in the Roman Church. Later but

[p] c. 3.

apparently not untrustworthy evidence leads us to believe that Clemens was the writer of the letter, though it is not impossible that because he was known to be connected with the Roman Church at that period, the letter without further investigation was believed to be his. We also have good testimony for believing that Clemens had heard some of the Apostles preach. This is all we know.

We may remark here that Clemens has been the hero of modern historical fancies, as well as of ancient. Especially Kestner, in his Agape (Jena 1819), a work which at the time of its appearance powerfully stirred the German mind, supposed that Christianity was spread by means of a secret society of which our Clemens was the founder. He devised this plan of revolutionizing the world through Christianity [q].

We now proceed to examine the letter itself.

The letter bears a striking resemblance in turn of thought and even in style to the writings of the New Testament. It is, as it has often been called, a truly apostolical writing. The writer never speculates. He forms to himself no complete system of theology. He believes in the truths as facts, and they come out as they have relation to the practice of daily life. And then throughout the whole there runs a continual reference of all matters to God. The writer continually has before him the idea of an ever-present, loving, and providing Father, in whose hands he and all his brethren are. His references to Christ are of the same nature. He always thinks of Him as his Lord. He does not indulge in dry

---

[q] See Baur, Ursprung des Episcopats, p. 98. De Quincey has proposed something of the same nature in connection with Essenism. He does not however meddle with Clemens.

theories regarding Him. He gives no explanation of
any puzzles. He feels Him to be a power working
within him for holiness. Then his phraseology is
strikingly similar to that of the New Testament. He
speaks of the 'elect,' of the 'called,' of 'justification,' of
those 'who fall asleep,' exactly as in the writings of
Paul. There are two points, however, in which there
are striking differences. The first is, that Clemens far
more frequently quotes long passages of the Old Testament. And the second is a more enlarged reference to
the operations of God in nature. It is a curious circumstance that the writers of the New Testament never
indulge in any lengthened descriptions of the beauties
of the world around them, or of the sun, moon, and
stars. Paul mentions the argument for God derived
from his works, and he has one grand burst where he
summons before him the whole creation travailing and
groaning since the introduction of sin. But still he
does not linger on this theme. . Clemens, on the other
hand, has a whole chapter devoted to the order and
harmony of the world; and as it is really a beautiful
piece of writing, and throws light on that tendency
towards expansion of style which gradually makes the
works of Christian writers more voluminous as we travel
from the Apostles, we transcribe it: "The heavens, moved
by his management, are obedient to Him in peace. Day
and night run the course appointed by Him, nowise
hindering each other. Sun and moon and the choruses of
the stars roll on in harmony according to his command,
within their prescribed limits without any deviation.
The pregnant earth, according to his will, sends up at
the proper seasons nourishment abundant for men and
beasts, and all the living things that are on it, neither

hesitating, nor altering any of the decrees issued by Him. The inexplorable parts of abysses, and the inexplicable arrangements of the lower world are bound together by the same ordinances. The vast immeasurable sea, gathered together into various basins according to his fashioning, never go beyond the barriers placed round it, but does as He has commanded. For He said: 'Thus far shalt thou come, and thy waves shall be broken within thee.' The ocean, impassable to men, and the worlds beyond it are directed by the same commands of the Lord. The seasons of spring and summer and autumn and winter give place to each other in peace. The stations of the winds at the proper season perform their service without hindrance. The overflowing fountains, fashioned for enjoyment and health, never fail to afford their breasts to nourish the life of men. And the smallest living things meet together in peace and concord. All these the great Fashioner and Lord of all has appointed to be in peace and concord; doing good to the whole, but exceedingly abundantly to us who have fled for refuge to his mercies through our Lord Jesus Christ, to whom be glory and majesty for ever and ever. Amen."

The theology of Clemens has been a matter of considerable discussion among those who can trace a difference between the thought of Paul and Peter; and there has been keen contention as to how far Clemens followed or abandoned the ideas of Paul. As I do not believe in this difference between Peter and Paul, I leave my readers to judge the matter for themselves in the abstract which I give of Clemens's theology. Meantime I place before them the opinions of some of the best critics of Clemens. Reuss, while contrasting the letter of Clemens with that to the Hebrews, says: "The letter of Clemens is still farther removed from Paul; the evangelic thought grows less and becomes paler; the mysticism has disappeared; there is no longer any question about imputation in respect of regenerating faith; salvation is produced by the action of external causes operating on the will of man; works re-assume an important place, if not the first; God Himself and the angels give an example of this; the fear of judgment is anew the motive of human virtue, as under the ancient law [r]." "Behold then," he says, a few pages farther on, "faith and hope have become synonymous, as we have seen already elsewhere; then faith is attached to God and not to Christ; there is no idea of a direct and intimate relation between Him and the believer; in fine, redemption is a fact accomplished without man who is to profit by it; and it arrives at this last stage in consequence of another act which remains absolutely foreign to the first. This fundamental point of the gospel has become then, at the end of some dozens of years, a vulgar formula, an article of the catechism, which people learn by heart, without at all comprehending it, and above all without having felt in themselves its great importance [s]."

Lipsius traces the agreement and disagreement of Clemens with Paul in the various points of his doctrine. He supposes Clemens to differ from Paul in making faith not so much the source of a new life as a firm conviction of the mind concerning the Divine will; in

[r] Histoire de la Théologie Chrétienne, vol. ii. p. 321. To the same effect Kayser, in the Revue de Théologie, publiée sous la direction de T. Colani. Strasbourg 1851, p. 95.

[s] Histoire de la Théologie Chrétienne, vol. ii. p. 323.

speaking of justification by works, and thus approaching to the opinion of James; in making faith and virtue have the same effect; and, in fact, in making justification not merely the result of faith, but of good works. He maintains that "Clemens did not dare to deny the vicarious death of Christ, for he was unwilling to contradict Paul, but he did not know how it was to be understood[t]." He finds also a difference between Paul and Clemens, in that the latter regarded "the resurrection of Christ not as the cause (principium), but simply as the beginning of the resurrection of the dead[u]." Hilgenfeld finds in Clemens modified Paulinism. The modifications he discovers especially in the stress laid on works, in a more thorough identification of the revelation before Christ with the Christian, and in a reference of the constitution of the Church to the Levitical priesthood; though he agrees with the opinion that the Levitical priesthood was only a typical model[x]. Schwegler[y] thinks that Clemens attempted to reconcile the opinions of Paul and James, Paulinism and Ebionitism; and Köstlin[z] maintains that the letter could not have been written under a Pauline direction, and he infers consequently that a Petrine Jewish-Christianity must have had the preponderance in the Roman Church.

---

[t] Lipsius, p. 82.   [u] Ibid. p. 85.

[x] Hilgenfeld, Apost. Väter, p. 88. For the opinions of others, see Hilgenfeld, p. 86, Lipsius, and Uhlhorn in Herzog's Encyclopædia. Ekker refutes Schwegler, Ritschl, and Hilgenfeld. His opinions are in the main the same as those stated in the text.

[y] Nachapost. Zeitalter, vol. ii. p. 128.

[z] Theolog. Jahrb. Tübingen 1850, p. 247 ff.

II. ABSTRACT OF THE LETTER.

The letter opens thus: "The Church of God that sojourns at Rome to the Church of God that sojourns at Corinth, called, made holy in the will of God, through our Lord Jesus Christ; grace and peace be multiplied to you from Almighty God through Jesus Christ." The church in Rome assures the church in Corinth that they have been prevented by their own troubles from addressing them in regard to the sedition that had arisen among them, and which had caused their good name to be evil spoken of. The church in Corinth was formerly distinguished for every Christian grace, hospitality, humility, prayerfulness and peacefulness. But a change had come over them. They were too prosperous, and began to quarrel, and to be jealous of each other, and full of party spirit. It was this jealousy that brought death first into the world, Cain envying Abel; and the dire effects of it are illustrated in the histories of Jacob and Esau, Joseph and his brethren, Moses, Aaron, Miriam, Dathan, Abiram, David, and in the persecutions of many men of their own generation, Peter and Paul being most striking examples. The church rehearses these for their own sakes as well as for the Corinthians. They have both the same struggle, and ought therefore to be serious and earnest, and then the Corinthians would see that God, in all generations, gave men opportunities to return from their sins to a better state of mind. This they prove from the Old Testament: and therefore both of them ought to lay aside all party spirit and selfishness, looking to the noble examples of faith and obedience which the Old Testament furnishes. Among these examples they instance Enoch and Noah and Abraham; and they show what advantage came to Lot and Rahab on account of faith and hospitality. They therefore exhort themselves and the Corinthians to be humble minded, to obey God, and to side with those who wish for peace and concord. And they enforce their exhortation by quoting from Isaiah liii. the description of the humility and meekness of Christ, and by exhibiting the humility of the most devout men of the Jewish economy—Elijah, Elisha, Ezekiel, Abraham, Job, and Moses. They also quote, as a fine instance of deep contrition of heart and humility, David's Psalm li. If they were to take these men as examples, they would seek peace and concord; but they go to a still higher example. Look how long-suffering God is to men, how noiselessly and yet harmoniously He conducts all the affairs of this world—one thing never opposing another. If they were to act worthily of such a God, all things would have to be done in order and peace. And here they give general directions as to the respect due to the guides of the church and the elders, and the duties to be inculcated on the young men and women and children. These duties and exhortations also are confirmed by faith in Christ, for they ought not to waver in their belief of the coming of the Lord. Indeed, a resurrection is plainly exhibited to us in the resurrection of Christ, in the changes of day and night, in the transformation of the seed into a plant, and in the renewal of the phœnix. A belief in this fact furnishes strong reasons for obedience to God, from whom nothing is hid, and therefore they ought not to delay in giving up sinful desires, appealing to God's mercy, and doing what is pleasing to God. For the indulgence of sin leads to

God's curse, while righteousness has his blessing. They should therefore earnestly inquire after the ways of God's blessing, and they would find it in being made righteous through faith. Not that they were to give up the doing of good works; for, as God delights in his own works, and especially in man his noblest work, so righteous men were always adorned with good works. Besides, God rewards his servants. They should therefore obey God's will, and, contemplating the angels, who cry out "Holy, holy, holy is the Lord of Sabaoth!" they should with one accord entreat Him continually that He would make them partakers of his glorious promises. How glorious are the gifts which God bestows, and how wonderful must those things be which God has prepared for those who wait for Him! Therefore they should wait for Him, and follow that course of conduct which is pleasing to Him, and which will bring them to salvation. But Jesus Christ is their salvation. Through Him they have had their eyes opened, and through Him the Lord has wished them to taste of immortal knowledge. They ought therefore to be earnest in their Christian warfare, noticing how regularly each part of the Roman army works into another; how each part of the body is necessary to the rest. So they ought to let each one have his proper place in the Christian work, and all should be humble. For what is, after all, the power of any earthborn creature? Looking therefore into the depths of divine knowledge, they should do all things in order. Look at the order in the Jewish economy, with special work for the high priest, for the priests, and for the Levites, and special seasons for everything. So in the Church: Christ was sent from God, and the apostles from Christ; and then these apostles appointed their first converts as overseers and deacons of those who were to believe. What can they find astonishing in this, when they look at the mode in which Moses appointed the priesthood? And as the apostles knew there would be a strife about the oversight, they appointed other persons to succeed the persons first appointed should they die. Those presbyters are happy who have died, as they were unmolested in their office, for they (the Roman church) see that some of the Corinthians have been removing holy men from a service which they performed with credit. Such conduct proves them to be fond of strife and party spirit. The Scriptures always represent those men as bad who inflict injury on the good. They should therefore adhere to the good, giving up all dissension, and recognising the unity of the saints in having one God, one Christ, and one Spirit of grace. They (the Corinthians) should look at Paul's letter to them. There they were accused of party spirit. But their conduct now was much worse. Then they had adhered to apostolic men; but now, what were the persons that caused the outbreak against the elders? Only one or two persons of no consequence. And the rumour had reached the ears not of them (the Romans) only, but of those inclined to different courses altogether ($\dot{\epsilon}\tau\epsilon\rho\omicron\kappa\lambda\iota\nu\epsilon\hat{\iota}s$, the heathen according to Hilgenfeld, p. 55, note), so that the Lord's name was evil spoken of. This must not be. They must pray God to be reconciled to them, and they must enter anew the gate of righteousness which is in Christ. And the fact is, the greater a man seems to be, the more humble ought he to be, and the more ought he to seek the common good. For he who has love in Christ keeps Christ's commandments. And the effects of love no one can adequately describe. Those who do God's commandments in the concord of love have their sins forgiven. Therefore those who are the leaders of this sedition should confess their sins, taking warning from what happened to those who hardened their hearts rebelling against Moses, and to Pharoah with his Egyptians. God requires simply confession. If they were to look into the sacred writings, they would find a beautiful instance of self-renunciation in the case of Moses. And the man now who has real love would retire to whatever place the Church might wish him, rather than cause or keep up strife. They (the Romans) would adduce instances of such self-renunciation even from heathens—the kings and leaders who sacrificed themselves for the good of their people. And even women had strength given them, Judith and Esther for instance. Both Romans and Corinthians should pray for those in sin, that they might yield to God's will. Mutual admonition is good for both, for God chastises whom He loves. They therefore advise the Corinthians to be subject to their presbyters, and submit to being found unimportant but of good character among the flock of Christ, rather than, seeming to be above all, to be cast off from the hope of Christ. For in Prov. i. 23–31, Wisdom denounces fearful calamities on those who reject her counsel. They conclude with the wish that God might grant them faith, peace, long-suffering, and other blessings, through their high priest Jesus Christ. And then they mention that they hope the Corinthians will soon send back the three persons, Claudius Ephebus, Valerius Biton, and Fortunatus, whom the Roman Church had commissioned to visit them, with the good news of the restoration of perfect peace and harmony. The last words are: "The grace of our Lord Jesus Christ be with you and with all everywhere who have been called by God and through Him, through whom to Him be glory, honour, power, and greatness, an eternal throne, from the ages to the ages of ages. Amen."

III. WRITINGS ASCRIBED TO CLEMENS.

Eusebius informs us that there were other writings ascribed by some to Clemens, but that no mention was made of these in ancient writers. He gives us the names of two of these productions—a second letter to the Corinthians, and the dialogues of Peter and Apion. Other spurious works, which he does not name, but to which he probably alludes, are still extant. These are, the Recognitions, the Homilies, the Apostolical Constitutions, and two Letters on Virginity preserved in Syriac. We shall discuss all these in the chapter devoted to the dubious literature of the first three centuries.

In the meantime we have one work to notice, as having had Clemens's name connected with it. This is the Epistle to the Hebrews. Some of the early Christian writers attributed this production to Clemens. A full discussion of this subject belongs to a consideration of the Epistle to the Hebrews. We lay before the reader only the statements that refer to Clemens. These occur in two passages in Eusebius, in one of which he speaks in his own person, in the other he quotes Origen. In speaking of the Epistle to the Corinthians, Eusebius remarks that Clemens introduces into it many thoughts similar to those in the Epistle to the Hebrews, and also borrows several expressions from it word for word.

Then he informs us that some in his day said that Paul addressed the Hebrews in his own language, and that Luke translated his writing into Greek; while others said that Clemens was the interpreter. This he thinks would account for the similar style and turn of thought in both epistles[c]. In the passage quoted from Origen it is remarked that the style of the Epistle to the Hebrews is more classical than Paul's, while the thoughts are not inferior to those of his acknowledged Epistles. And then Origen adds: "If I were to express my opinion, I should say that the thoughts are the apostle's, but that the phraseology and composition are those of some one who has recorded the apostle's instructions, and who has as it were written down notes of what had been said by the teacher. If any church then regards this letter as Paul's, let it be commended for this. For not rashly did the ancient men hand it down as being Paul's. But who it was that really wrote the letter God only knows; but the accounts which have come down to us are two: one party saying that Clemens, who was overseer of the Romans, wrote the letter; the other saying that it was written by Luke, who wrote the Gospel and the Acts[d]." The authorship of the Epistle to the Hebrews seems thus even in ancient times to have been traced to Clemens, mainly in consequence of its similarity to the Epistle to the Corinthians in style and thought. Grabe[e] has drawn up a list of the passages that are similar, which we now present as part of the evidence such as it is:—

[c] Euseb. Hist. Eccl. iii. 38.   [d] Ibid. vi. 25.
[e] Quoted in Wotton, pp. 103, 104, of Additional Notes; and in Jacobson, tom. i. p. xiv.

Hebrews.	Clemens.
i. 3, 4. Who being the brightness of his glory . . . . having become so much better than the angels, as he has inherited a more excellent name than they.	xxxvi. Who being the brightness of his greatness, is so much greater than angels, as He has inherited a more excellent name. For it is written thus: "Who maketh his angels spirits (winds), and his ministers a flame of fire." And in the case of his Son thus spoke the Lord: "Thou art my Son, this day have I begotten thee:" . . . . And again He says to him, "Sit on my right hand, until I make thine enemies thy footstool."
i. 7. And of the angels he saith: Who maketh his angels spirits, and his ministers a flame of fire.	
i. 5. For unto which of the angels said He at any time, Thou art my Son, this day have I begotten thee?	
i. 13. But to which of the angels said He at any time, Sit on my right hand, until I make thine enemies thy footstool?	
iii. 2. As also Moses was faithful in all his house. (See also iii. 5.)	xliii. Moses a faithful servant in all his house.
iv. 14. Seeing then that we have a great high priest.	lviii. Through our high priest Jesus Christ.

There is a general resemblance between Heb. xi. 5–20, 31, and Clem. Cor. ix. x. xii., in both of which Enoch, Noah, Abraham, and Rahab, are spoken of as illustrations of faith and obedience.

Hebrews.	Clemens.
xi. 37. They wandered about in sheepskins and goatskins.	xvii. Who walked about in goatskins and in sheepskins.
xiii. 17. Obey them that have the rule over you.	i. Being submissive to them that have the rule over you.

How far also the thoughts agree, the reader may judge for himself by comparing the present exposition of Clemens's doctrine with the Epistle to the Hebrews.

IV. LITERATURE.

The single manuscript of the Epistle of Clemens Romanus has been mentioned already.

The first edition was prepared by Patricius Junius (Patrick Young), and published at Oxford in 1633, quarto. He filled the blank spaces with conjectures, which he printed in red characters; he placed a Latin translation alongside of the Greek; he added admirable notes, largely interspersed with beautiful quotations from the Fathers; and he prefixed a list of testimonies of the ancients to Clemens. He appended the fragment of the so-called second epistle without note or translation. The text of Junius was re-edited by Mader (Helmestadii 1654, 4to), by Bishop Fell (Oxford 1669, 12mo[f]), by Labbé and Cossartius (Paris 1671, fol.), Colomesius (Lond. 1687, 8vo), and in the collections of Cotelerius, Clericus, and Ittigius, already mentioned. Most of these added dissertations of more or less value. Henry Wotton collated the manuscript again (plusquam semel), and gave the results of his recension in an edition published at Cambridge in 1718, 8vo. He was enabled to correct several oversights of Junius. He supplied valuable notes, and added those of Junius, Boisius, and Cotelerius. He prefixed a long preface, exhibiting the authority of the Apostolical Fathers from the English church point of view, and discussing the genuineness of the Apostolic Constitutions and the Ignatian letters. He added dissertations on the clergy

---

[f] Fell remarks in the preface to the edition which he issued in 1677, that a very learned man had collated the text (qui collationem diligentissime instituit), but had been able to detect Junius only in a very few trifling slips.

and the unity of the church. In 1721 (Paris, fol.), Coustantius took his text from Cotelerius; but after that the text of Wotton was followed in the subsequent collections of the Apostolical Fathers. Jacobson collated the manuscript again for his edition of the Apostolical Fathers, and his recension was followed by subsequent editors (Hefele and Dressel and Hilgenfeld).

In 1867 Tischendorf gave a new recension in his "Appendix Codicum Celeberrimorum Sinaitici Vaticani Alexandrini," 4to, Lipsiæ, since published separately. J. C. M. Laurent published an edition based on that of Tischendorf's, containing some conjectures of his own as well as of Tischendorf's, Lipsiæ 1870. The most thorough edition is that of J. B. Lightfoot, D.D., "St. Clement of Rome. The Two Epistles to the Corinthians. A revised text, with introduction and notes," London and Cambridge 1869. For this edition the manuscript has been again carefully collated; and doubtful passages have been examined with great diligence. The introduction and notes are very learned and good.

The second letter is almost always given with the first, and some fragments which are supposed to belong to Clemens Romanus are appended.

"Photographic Facsimiles of the Remains of the Epistles of Clement of Rome, made from the unique copy preserved in the Codex Alexandrinus," have been "published by order of the Trustees of the British Museum," London 1856, 4to.

Several translations of this Epistle have appeared. The best known is that by Archbishop Wake, which has been republished frequently, most recently in an improved form edited by Temple Chevallier. Translations are given in the Ante-Nicene Library and in Hoole's Apostolic Fathers (1872).

V. THEOLOGY.

God.—The doctrines of Clemens, as we have said already, are all found in conjunction with practical thought. Accordingly nothing speculative or merely theoretical is stated with regard to God, nothing of his character or purposes in themselves. But still, as much is said of God's deeds relating to Christ, to man, and more especially to Christians, we can form a tolerably accurate notion of Clemens's idea of God. He speaks of Him as "the great Framer and Lord of all [g]," "the Father and Creator of the whole world [h]," "the all-holy Framer and Father of the ages [i]," "the Almighty [k]," "the All-seeing [l]," "the true and only God [m]," "Lord of spirits and of all flesh [n]." "He comprehends all things [o]," and "his energy [p] pervades all the operations of nature." "He made man in the impress or stamp of his own image [q]." Almost all these statements are made in connection with the effect they are calculated to produce on man. Thus the fact that all things come from God is brought forward as an inducement to doing good; and his hearing and seeing all things, even the thoughts of men, and his possessing all power, are oftener than once adduced for the same purpose [r]. In like manner God's kindness is mentioned as a reason why we should be kind to each

[g] c. 20. [h] c. 19.
[i] c. 35, and c. 55. αἰώνων, 'ages,' should most probably be translated 'worlds.' See commentators on Heb. i. 2.
[k] c. 2; cf. c. 27. [l] cc. 55, 58; cf. c. 28. [m] c. 43.
[n] c. 58. The words in Greek here are, Δεσπότης τῶν πνευμάτων καὶ Κύριος πάσης σαρκός.
[o] c. 28. [p] c. 24. [q] c. 33. [r] cc. 21, 27, 28.

others[s]; his forbearance and freedom from all anger in
his actions towards the whole creation are insisted on
as a cogent argument for cultivating a spirit of forbearance[t], and we are urged to act worthily of God[u].
Clemens always contemplates God from the Christian
point of view. He is absolute and supreme Ruler[v], and
can do what He wishes; but at the same time He is
bound by the laws of morality. "Nothing is impossible with God but to lie[x]." In harmony with this
moral nature His whole providential arrangements are
made out of love to men. He is our kind and merciful
Father[y], who took us to Himself in love[z]. He is
faithful in his promises, and just in his judgments[a].
He loves those who fear Him, and kindly grants his
graces to those who come to Him with simple mind[b].
He needs nothing from those coming to Him except
confession of sin[c]; and in his kindness He urges men
to return to his tender mercies[d]. He is Himself the
source of all moral excellence. He makes men righteous
through faith[e], and He gives room for change of mind
to those who wish to return to Him[f]. He chose Jesus
Christ, and us through Him as an especial people[g].
He is the defender of those who with pure conscience
serve his all-virtuous name[h]. Nevertheless He chastises his own children[i], but this chastisement is for
their good[j]. While such as obey his precepts are
blessed, the wicked are hateful to Him and cursed[k].
He hates those who praise themselves[l]; and He made
it manifest in the case of Lot and his wife that He does

[s] c. 14. [t] c. 19. [u] c. 21. [v] c. 27. [x] Ibid.
[y] c. 29. [z] c. 49. [a] c. 27. [b] c. 23. [c] c. 52.
[d] c. 9.   [e] c. 32. [f] c. 7.   [g] c. 58. [h] c. 45.
[i] c. 56. [j] Ibid.   [k] cc. 30, 35. [l] c. 30.

not abandon those who place their hope in Him, while He punishes and tortures those who turn their minds from Him [m]. In one passage God is said to have been propitiated. "The Ninevites, changing their minds in reference to their sins propitiated (ἐξιλάσαντο) God by their prayers, and received salvation [n]." Frequent mention is made of God's elect.

Christ.—Photius [o] remarked of this letter of Clemens, "that, while naming Jesus Christ our Lord high priest and defender, he did not utter God-becoming and loftier words with regard to Him" (οὐδὲ τὰς θεοπρεπεῖς καὶ ὑψηλοτέρας ἄφηκε περὶ αὐτοῦ φωνάς). This statement is true, though many modern commentators have attempted to force more God-becoming expressions out of it. Indeed the way in which Christ is spoken of is one of the most striking peculiarities of the letter. But we shall let the facts speak for themselves. In only one passage is He called God's Son, and that when the writer adduces the words, "Thou art my Son, this day have I begotten thee [p]." That Clemens regarded Christ as more than human there is most certain evidence, for he describes Him as the reflection or radiance of God's greatness, and as being so much greater than the angels as He has inherited a more excellent name than they [q]. In another place He is spoken of as the Sceptre of God's greatness [r], an expression which seems to mean that Christ is the peculiar manifestation of the regal character, the power, the love of God. By far the most common designation is that of Lord.

He is Lord of the Church, and accordingly the fact

[m] c. 11.   [n] c. 7.   [o] Biblioth. 126, p. 95: Bekker.
[p] c. 36.   [q] Ibid.   [r] c. 16.

answers to our expectation when we see one Church writing to another speaking continually of Christ in that aspect of his work and character which their relation to each other brings out most prominently. They say to each other, "Let us reverence the Lord Jesus Christ[s]." Several doxologies occur in the course of the letter. These some have believed to be ascriptions to Christ, and we therefore lay them before the reader that he may judge. The first is found at the conclusion of chapter xx. which we have already translated (p. 140), and to which we now refer the reader. The second, in c. 50, runs thus: "This blessedness fell to the lot of those who were selected by God through Jesus Christ our Lord, to whom be glory for the ages of the ages. Amen." Wotton and others have asserted that these ascriptions of honour are made to Jesus Christ, and they have tried by means of them to show the untruth of the remark of Photius. We cannot think the passages justify Wotton. If there is clear evidence in the letter that such epithets were applied to Jesus Christ, then we might apply these. But if there is not (and in the other doxologies there is a marked difference), then the relative must be taken to refer to God and not to Christ. Grammatically it may apply to either. Generally it applies to the nearest; but if the sense require it, there is no reason for hesitating to apply it to the more distant of the nouns. The other two doxologies are as follows: "The all-seeing God * * * grant faith, fear, * * * through Jesus Christ; through whom to Him be glory and greatness, strength and honour, now and for ever. Amen[t]." "The grace of our Lord Jesus Christ be with you

[s] c. 21.   [t] c. 58.

and with all everywhere who are called by God and through Him, through whom to Him be glory, honour, power, strength, greatness, an eternal throne, for ever and ever. Amen[u]." In both these instances the ascription of praise is unquestionably to God through Christ. The analogy would lead us to infer that in the other two doxologies the words "through Christ" are to be drawn into the doxology, according to a not uncommon Greek idiom, or that originally the ᾧ was really before the διὰ, though in the single manuscript that remains this happens not to be the case. All the doxologies would then be in marked harmony with the prevailing presentation of Christ's relation to God, namely, that of the Representative of God, and Mediator between God and man. There is one other passage which has been adduced to disprove the truth of the words of Photius. It occurs in the second chapter: "Being content with the journey-supplies of God, and giving careful heed to his words, ye received them into your inmost soul, and his sufferings were before your eyes." His sufferings, according to this interpretation, are the sufferings of God; but God the Father did not suffer; therefore God the Son suffered. And here therefore Christ is represented as God. This explanation was common among our writers of the last century, but modern critics have for the most part given it up[v]. For if the words are to be taken to refer to God, there is not the least doubt that Clemens must be accused

[u] c. 59.
[v] Professor Lightfoot has defended it in an able note—but the four passages on which he has based his defence are liable to the charge of spuriousness or corruption. J. C. M. Laurent also adopts it, thinking that it is theologically quite correct to speak of Christ's sufferings as the sufferings of God.

of Patripassianism. The words would then be a direct statement that God suffered. Dorner, Bunsen, Ekker, and many others, suppose the αὐτοῦ to be indefinite, and its exact reference to Christ is to be inferred from the context. Instances of this indefinite use of αὐτοῦ occur in chapters 32, 34, and 59. It seems to me more likely that the text is corrupt, and that we should read μαθήματα 'instructions,' instead of παθήματα, as Junius proposed. The change of M into Π is frequent and natural[x], and in the present instance the upper stroke of the Pi has entirely vanished from the MS. This is also the case with the upper strokes in many of the Mus of the Alexandrian Codex, and the only difference between the Π in Παθήματα and the M above it in ἐστερνισμένοι is that the legs of the μ are farther apart than those of the π. The sense given by μαθήματα is unquestionably more suitable to the context than that given by παθήματα.

There are several expressions in the epistle from which some[y] have inferred that Clemens was acquainted in some measure with the so-called Alexandrian Logos-doctrine. Thus Clemens speaks, or seems to speak, of the "all-virtuous Wisdom" as a personality[z] (οὕτως λέγει ἡ πανάρετος σοφία); he mentions the holy Word in the same way (φησὶν γὰρ ὁ ἅγιος λόγος[a]); and he asserts that "God put together all things by the word of his greatness (ἐν λόγῳ τῆς μεγαλωσύνης), and by his word (ἐν λόγῳ) He can overturn them[b]." But we do not think these words warrant the inference. They contain no express declaration of the Logos-idea, and we have

---

[x] Παθητήν for μαθητήν occurs in the Letter of Ignatius to Polycarp, c. vii. One codex has the μαθητήν. See Dressel's note, p. 205, note 3.
[y] Lipsius, p. 103. [z] c. 57. [a] c. 13, 56. [b] c. 27.

no right to suppose that Clemens applied any of these terms to Christ. If he had formed a complete systematic idea of Christ, he might then have seen the necessity of identifying Christ with the Wisdom; but we must not assume that he did what he might have done [c].

Of the earthly life of Jesus Christ not much is said. His descent from Jacob is referred to [d]. Hilgenfeld has by a constrained interpretation of the passage fancied that Clemens represents Christ as descended from the Levites [e], and not from Judah. Clemens quotes some of Christ's words. His death and his resurrection are both mentioned. Everything that Christ does, He does in consequence of the will of God. He was sent into the world by God: "Christ was sent out from God, and the apostles from Christ; both missions took place in an orderly manner in consequence of a volition of God [f]." He is said to have been selected by God [g]. The resurrection of Christ was also the work of God, and it is declared to be the first-fruits of the coming resurrection [h].

We have no full exposition in Clemens of the work of Christ. Most of the statements with regard to Christ's death are indefinite. A unique and marvellous power is evidently ascribed to it; but the writer never

[c] This matter necessarily lies among uncertainties. Dorner assumes that Clemens must have known the Epistle to the Hebrews, and from this acquaintance infers that he knew the Logos-doctrine. See the long note on c. 27 in Dorner's Lehre von der Person Christi, p. 142. Baur also refers the words to Christ, though he remarks that in Clemens's words is contained no determined dogmatic meaning. (Das Christenthum, p. 329.)

[d] c. 32. [e] Apost. Väter, p. 65, note.
[f] c. 42. [g] c. 58. [h] c. 24.

speculates on the mode in which the results flowed from the death. In one passage the blood of Christ is looked on as affording to men an opportunity of changing their minds, and God is said to regard it as valuable on account of this service. "Let us look steadfastly to the blood of Christ, and consider how precious it is in the sight of God, because having been poured out on account of our salvation, it has presented to all the world the favour of a change of mind (μετάνοια)[i]." Clemens does not state here how the blood of Christ brought the grace of a change of mind, nor is the slightest mention of satisfaction in it, as Bull has fancied. On the contrary, the attention is here directed solely to the moral effects of Christ's death; to its putting within the reach of men a power which can change their hearts from the love of evil to the love of good. And indeed the emphasis seems to lie on the words 'to the whole world,' for the writer goes on to state how God had in former generations given room for a change of mind to those who wished to return to Him.

Oftener than once Christ is said to have died for us: "Let us reverence the Lord Jesus Christ, whose blood was given for us[k];" "Jesus Christ our salvation[l];" "On account of the love which He had to us, Jesus Christ our Lord gave his blood for us by the will of God, even flesh for our flesh and soul for our souls[m]." This latter passage has been insisted on by some as expressive of the vicarious sufferings of Christ; and some[o] have regarded it only as an approximation to

[i] c. 7. [k] c. 21. [l] c. 36. [m] c. 49.
[n] Dorner, Lehre, i. 138. Lechler: second ed. p. 480.
[o] Lipsius, p. 82.

that doctrine. Ritschl on the other hand, speaking generally of Clemens's statements of the death of Christ, says that the opinion of Clemens was that the death of Christ had occasioned repentance only as being an example of humility and as being a proof of God's love, " and had not therefore established as the apostles think a new relation of man to God, but had occasioned a new course of conduct of man to God[p]." Both parties seem to me wrong. The very way in which Clemens mentions the death of Christ shows that he attached a mysterious efficacy to it; but it seems to me that he does not attempt to explain the mystery. He simply says that the effect of Christ's death was to benefit our flesh and our souls. He gave up his own body for our sakes ($\overset{\cdot}{\upsilon}\pi\grave{\epsilon}\rho\ \overset{\cdot}{\eta}\mu\hat{\omega}\nu$), that we might have a glorious resurrection; and He gave up his own life or soul, that we might have life in Him. It is a statement of facts, not of explanations.

Nor is there any theory of redemption in the sentence, "They moreover gave her a sign, asking her to hang a scarlet rope out of her own house, thereby making it evident beforehand that there would be ransoming through the blood of the Lord to all who put their faith and hope in God[q]." For the ransoming here is not a thing accomplished, but prospective. And the meaning plainly is, that Rahab's sign was a pre-intimation that those who put their trust in God will be completely freed from the power and dominion of sin through the blood of Christ. How the blood of Christ is to accomplish this complete emancipation, Clemens does not say. These are all the references in Clemens to the

[p] Altkatholische Kirche, second edition, p. 281.   [q] c. 12.

death or blood of Christ; but as he applies some passages of the Old Testament to Christ, we may regard him as agreeing entirely with the sentiments therein expressed. These verses, taken from the fifty-third chapter of Isaiah, prove conclusively that Christ suffered for us, that it was on account of our sins that He was afflicted. " He bears our sins, and is in pangs for us . . He Himself was wounded on account of our sins, and was afflicted on account of our iniquities. The chastisement of our peace was upon Him; by his stripes we were healed. . . . . The Lord delivered Him up on account of our sins. . . . . He Himself will carry away their sins. . . He Himself carried away the sins of many, and on account of their sins He was delivered up [r]."

As little is said of the death of Christ, so little is said of his life and work. Closeness of union with Christ is continually implied and inculcated. The children of Christians are to be instructed in Christ [s]. Christians are called through God's will in Christ Jesus [t]. Our whole body is to be preserved in Christ Jesus [u]. Mention is made of piety in Christ [x], love in Christ [y], righteousness which is in Christ [z], and living in Christ [a]. The benefits which Christ works for us are thus spoken of. We are called and made holy in God's will through Christ [b]. Through Him peace is multiplied to the churches [c]. We are chosen through Christ by God for an especial people [d]. Through Him we look up into the heights of heaven, the eyes of our hearts are opened, and our darkness vanishes. Through Him the Lord has wished us to taste immortal knowledge [e]. He is our

[r] c. 16. [s] c. 21. [t] c. 32. [u] c. 38.
[x] c. 1. [y] c. 49. [z] c. 48. [a] c. 47.
[b] c. 1. [c] Ibid. [d] c. 58. [e] c. 36.

salvation, the defender and helper of our weakness [f], the high priest of our offerings [g]. Through Him God gives us faith, fear, peace, patience, long-suffering, self-restraint, chastity, and sobriety [h]. He is also our model (ὑπογραμμός) [i], and is adduced especially as a model of lowliness of mind, in a passage similar to that in the Epistle to the Philippians, ii. 6: "Our Lord Jesus Christ, the sceptre of God's greatness, came not in the pomp of vain glory or haughtiness, although He might have done so, but humbly [j]." And his death seems also to be referred to as an instance of obedience to the divine will [k]. Especial stress is also laid on our listening to his words [l]. Christ is thus represented as a teacher, as a dispenser of God's blessings, and as a model. Christians are said to be members of Christ, to be the flock of Christ [m], and Christ is said to belong to those who think humbly of themselves [n].

Of the second coming of Christ Clemens makes no direct mention, but he quotes a passage of Scripture which he would most probably refer to Christ, though he might also have applied it to God: "He will come quickly, and will not tarry, and suddenly will come the Lord into his shrine, even the Holy One whom ye look for [o]."

The Holy Spirit.—The Holy Spirit is spoken of in two connections, either as poured out on Christians, or as

---

[f] c. 36.   [g] c. 36 and 58.   [h] c. 58.   [i] c. 16.   [j] Ibid.

[k] Comp. c. 49, 7, and 21. The Corinthians are blamed for not living according to what is becoming to Christ; but the reading Χριστῷ has been suspected, and Junius proposed Χριστιανῷ, c. 3.

[l] c. 13 and 46.   [m] c. 54.   [n] c. 16.

[o] c. 23. Clemens's quotation is not in the exact words. See Isaiah xiii. 22 (Hab. ii. 3), and Mal. iii. 1.

speaking in the words of the Old Testament. In the first case it is scarcely possible to imagine that Clemens conceived the Holy Spirit a person, and in the second it is as impossible to imagine that he did not so look upon Him. "There was a full outpouring of the Holy Spirit ($\pi\nu\epsilon\acute{u}\mu\alpha\tau\sigma$ $\acute{\alpha}\gamma\acute{\iota}\sigma\upsilon$ without the article) upon all[p]," can only mean that there was some gift or grace richly distributed among all. It may be used, and most likely is used, for that gift or those gifts which the Holy Spirit is said to grant; but as Clemens never says that He does grant them, we cannot determine from his writings what was his belief on this point. In the statement that the apostles preached "with the full assurance of the Holy Spirit[q]," it is difficult to determine whether the writer means a full assurance of the efficacy of the proclamation produced by the Holy Spirit, or a full assurance that the Holy Spirit would be largely poured out on their hearers, or a full assurance resulting from a large measure of the Holy Spirit poured out on them. The passages which refer to the Holy Spirit as speaking through the prophets we shall discuss hereafter.

The Trinity.—There is only one passage in which God, Christ, and the Spirit, are placed together. It runs thus: "Have we not one God, and one Christ; and is there not one Spirit of grace which has been poured out upon us, and one calling in Christ[r]?"

Angels.—Angels are mentioned twice: in a passage already quoted as having a name inferior to Christ's; and in another he says, "Let us consider the whole multitude of angels, how standing near they attend on his will[s]." They are also introduced in a passage of

[p] c. 2.   [q] c. 42.   [r] c. 46.   [s] c. 34.

Scripture: "God placed the boundaries of the nations according to the number of the angels of God [t]."

The Devil is not once mentioned, but he was probably referred to in a passage which has been thus restored: "What sins we committed through some suggestion of the Adversary [u]." If Irenæus's description of the teaching of the letter is correct, mention must have been made of the Devil in the part that is lost. He thus sums up the teaching of the letter: "It announced one God, omnipotent, maker of heaven and earth, fashioner of man, who brought on the flood, and called Abraham, who led the people out of the land of Egypt, who spoke to Moses, who arranged the law and sent the prophets, who prepared fire for the Devil and his angels [x]."

Man: his original state.—Nothing is said of original sin, or of the state of man before conversion. The only remark that has any reference to the commencement of sin is that death came into the world through envy [y]; but here Clemens evidently refers to the first occasion of death, the jealousy between Cain and Abel.

Salvation.—Clemens's answer to the question, how a man is saved, is various in form, but fundamentally the same. Salvation is, according to his idea, dependent on good works. A holy life is salvation, or at least the reason of salvation; but as this holy life may be viewed in its sources as well as in its outward manifestations, faith and love are also spoken of as the causes of salvation, of the righteousness and perfection of the Christian.

---

[t] c. 29. This is the reading of the Septuagint in Deut. xxxii. 8. The reading was known to Philo De Plantat. Noë, § 14. i. p. 338, and is discussed by Justin Martyr, Dial. c. Tryph. c. 131. See Hilgenfeld, Apost. Väter, p. 64, note.

[u] c. 51.   [x] Contra Hær. lib. iii. c. 3. 3.   [y] c. 3.

At the same time, as already mentioned, God is always looked on as the source of moral excellence. Though Christ is once referred to as the Being in whom our salvation is found [z], yet He is never referred to as directly producing holiness; but, as we have already seen, his life and his death were both regarded as *means* by which man was to be brought to God. Accordingly the gate of righteousness through which the holy enter is said to be in Christ [a].

We may arrange what Clemens says on the subject of salvation under three heads: 1. The effects of the fear of God and obedience to his will. 2. Faith. 3. Love.

1. "The fear of God," he says, "saves all who live holily in it with pure mind [b]." "Blessed are we, beloved, if we do God's commandments in the concord of love, that our sins may be forgiven us through love [c]."

2. Faith in Christ is only once mentioned [d] and in a peculiar sense. It means a belief that Christ spoke through the prophets of the Old Testament. Mention is several times made of confidence in God [e] ($\pi i \sigma \tau \iota s$ $a \dot{v} \tau o \hat{v}$); and once the phrase occurs, "those who trust and hope in God." The remarks of Clemens refer therefore entirely to faith in God. The most striking passage with regard to this faith is in chapter xxxii. "We," he says, "are declared and made righteous ($\delta \iota \kappa a \iota o \dot{v} \mu \epsilon \theta a$), not by means of ourselves, nor through our own wisdom or understanding or piety or works which we did in holiness of heart, but through faith. Through which faith Almighty God has made and declared all men righteous from the be-

---

[z] c. 36.   [a] c. 48.   [b] c. 21.   [c] c. 50.   [d] c. 22.

[e] c. 3. 27. 35. In 35 the expression is, ἡ διάνοια ἡμῶν πίστεως πρὸς τὸν Θεόν, which some have been inclined to change, but which Lipsius justly retains.

ginning." We have a particular instance of the same truth when he says that it was through this confidence in God that Abraham wrought righteousness and truth[f]. This faith or confidence (πίστις) is an abiding continuous state of mind, in which the soul trusts all the promises of God, hopes in Him, and obeys His commandments. The transient action of this faith seems to be called πεποίθησις by Clemens. Thus we have the πεποίθησις πίστεως ἀγαθῆς, "the exercise of a good confidence;" and πίστις ἐν πεποιθήσει, "faith in activity." Some have thought that Clemens in some measure contradicts himself when he in another passage exhorts the Corinthians to clothe themselves with concord, "being proved to be righteous by deeds, not by words[g]." But the declaration or manifestation of righteousness here is not towards God, but towards men, and therefore the statement has no theological meaning; and the contrast is not between faith and works, but between words and works. Even if the statement had been made in a theological point of view, there would have been no contradiction. Clemens evidently regarded faith as the secret spring and true test of righteousness, and consequently thought of it always as manifested by good deeds. In one passage he directly joins faith and good works, as being of identical effect. We shall obtain God's promises, he says, if the disposition of our faith to God be fixed, if we accomplish what is agreeable to his blameless will, and follow the way of truth [h]. In like manner we find faith combined with hospitality: "Rahab was saved on account of her faith and hospitality[i];" and, as if corresponding to this, it is said that Lot was saved on account of his hospitality and piety[k].

[f] c. 31.   [g] c. 30.   [h] c. 35.   [i] c. 12.   [k] c. 11.

3. Love is referred to most frequently and enlarged on by Clemens. And here it is to be noticed that he speaks of "love in Christ:" "Let him that has love in Christ, keep the commands of Christ[1]." We have already seen that love is the means through which we obtain forgiveness of sins in conjunction with good works[m]. It is moreover said that love joins us to God. But especial stress is laid on love as the means of perfecting the Christian: "All the elect of God were perfected in love[n];" and the same expression occurs again[o].

Those who are thus saved are called brethren, the elect of God[p]. The blessedness of having sins forgiven falls only to those "who have been selected by God through Jesus Christ[q]." "Who is fit to be found in love except those whom God regards worthy[r]?" There can be no doubt from such passages that Clemens regarded the selection of Christians from the rest of the world as entirely dependent on the will of God. And he went farther than this; for he says that God "prepared his benefits before we were born[s]." In harmony with this idea, the Roman church speaks of itself and the Corinthian church as part of this selection[t].

The conduct of Christians thus dependent on God ought to be characterised by continual reference to Him. They obey God[u]. They love God as the merciful and beneficent Father[y]. They do all things in the fear of God[z]. They are bound to examine what is good and well-pleasing and acceptable in the sight of Him that made them[a]. Their boast and confidence is in

[1] c. 49. [m] c. 50. [n] c. 49. [o] c. 50. [p] c. 1. 46.
[q] c. 50. [r] Ibid. [s] c. 38. [t] cc. 29, 30. [u] c. 34.
[y] c. 29. [z] c. 2. [a] c. 7.

God [b]. They are to seek their praise in God [c]. They are to confess their sins to God, and to fall down before the Lord (Δεσπότῃ), and with tears to entreat Him to be mercifully reconciled to them, and to restore them to their holy and chaste life of brotherly love [d]. In one word, their whole life is said to be a life according to the directions of God (πολιτεία τοῦ Θεοῦ)[e].

Of the relation of Christians to Christ comparatively little is said. They are said to be members of Him; and evil speakings are brought upon his name when Christians behave foolishly and sinfully [f]. Christians are also described as having come under the yoke of his favour through Him [g].

The Church.—Christians are spoken of as members of each other, and as bound to help each other. Throughout the whole epistle the unity of a church of Christ is brought prominently forward [h]. A church is not a certain number of bishops or presbyters, but a company of those selected by God. Each is to be subject to his neighbour; and the mode of this subjection is to be determined by the gift God has given him. If he is rich, he is to help the poor; if he is strong, he is to help the weak; and so on; and thus the whole body is to be saved in Christ [i]. The church is not to be an irregular anarchical association. It is to have its rulers, even as an army has; to act in an orderly and obedient manner,

[b] c. 34.   [c] c. 30.   [d] c. 48.   [e] c. 54; cf. 22.   [f] c. 47.
[g] c. 16. Most probably the reading is corrupt, and early editions omitted "through him." The probable meaning is, that Christians receive God's favour through Christ; but as it stands, the passage means that they receive Christ's favour through Christ. Professor Lightfoot so takes the words and supposes them to mean "through His humiliation and condescension," in loc.
[h] c. 37.   [i] c. 38.

with humility and respect for each other[k]. And so intimate was the concern which these Christians felt in each other, that they hesitated not to admonish each other when necessary—a piece of disagreeable duty which they did not hand over to their presidents. "The admonition," says Clemens, in speaking of God chastising his children, "which we make to one another is good and exceedingly useful, for it joins us to the will of God[1]." The idea of the Church in this epistle is that of an assemblage composed of members of equal rights and privileges, all of whom are essential to each other as the parts of the body to the body, but some of whom, being more highly gifted, are to direct the less intelligent and the less gifted[m]. The letter itself is a letter from a church to a church. The church that writes does not say one word with regard to its rulers. The leaders of the church to which the letter is addressed are frequently mentioned, but they are spoken of in such a way that the right of the church itself to direct its own affairs is recognised. Some of the leaders of the Corinthian church are ill-treated by a few of the members, and divisions arise. The Roman church writes to the Corinthians to treat them better, urging them to do so by the most powerful arguments and appeals. It does not dictate to them in any way. It does not mention a bishop of the Corinthian church, much less appeal to him to settle the dispute. It recognises no body of men as having a right to control the church. It simply appeals to the church, the elect of God. It is to be observed too that there is only one church in Rome and one in Corinth. How many members composed the one or the other, how they met,

[k] c. 37.   [1] c. 56.   [m] c. 37.

and a great number of similar questions, are inquiries which the letter furnishes us with no means of answering.

The office-bearers of the church are particularly enumerated, and the mode of their appointment is clearly indicated. "The apostles," he says, "went forth proclaiming the good news that the kingdom of God was about to come. Preaching therefore in various country districts and cities, they appointed their firstfruits, having tested them by the Spirit, to be overseers (bishops) and servants (deacons) of those who were to believe[n]." We have in this passage the statement that there were overseers and servants in the churches, and that they were appointed by the apostles. This statement is given at greater length in another chapter: "Our apostles also knew through our Lord Jesus Christ that there would be strife on account[o] of the oversight. For this reason then the apostles having received full foreknowledge, appointed those already mentioned, [the overseers and servants,] and afterwards made an addition to them, in order that if they should fall asleep other approved men might succeed them in their service. Those then that were appointed by them [the apostles], or afterwards by other well-known men, the whole church giving their consent, and who have served the flock of Christ blamelessly, with humility, peacefulness, and generosity, who have also been borne witness to for a long time by all; these men we are of opinion cannot be justly dismissed from the service[p]."

---

[n] c. 42.

[o] ἐπὶ τοῦ ὀνόματος some translate "in regard to the dignity of overseers." So Bunsen, and many before him. See Jacobson's note.

[p] c. 44.

Before stating all that is implied in these sentences, we have to deal with a clause in it which has been tortured in a great variety of ways. The words are: καὶ μεταξὺ ἐπινομὴν δεδώκασιν ὅπως, ἐὰν κοιμηθῶσιν, διαδέξωνται ἕτεροι δεδοκιμασμένοι ἄνδρες τὴν λειτουργίαν αὐτῶν. The stone of offence in this sentence is the word ἐπινομή. It occurs rarely in Greek; and its only senses are, first, the rapid spreading of anything, such as fire or poison; and second, a bandage used by physicians in tying up wounds[q]. Neither of these meanings is suitable to the passage before us; and therefore any attempt to build any peculiar theory on the word is pure conjecture. The translation which I have given has not the slightest authority in itself. The word ἐπινομή, like ἐπινέμησις, may be supposed capable of the meaning of "a distribution;" and I conjecture that Clemens means that the apostles made a second choice of men, in order that if the first should die there would be others ready to take their place. Others have given to the word the meaning of "an additional law," "a precept added to former laws;" and the word has been also variously altered to suit this meaning. But whatever meaning be attached to it, no weight can be assigned to any inferences drawn from that meaning. Yet this word occupies a fundamental position in Rothe's exposition of the government of the church at this period. He found ἐπίνομοι· κληρονόμοι in Hesychius, and from this he forces out the meaning of a "testamentary direction." And then with this sense he forces the sentence to declare that "the apostles gave a testamentary direc-

[q] See Liddell and Scott for the two passages in which the first meaning occurs; the second meaning is found in Galen. See Lipsius, Disq. p. 20.

tion, in order that if they should die other justly esteemed men should succeed to their apostolic functions [r]." He felt himself compelled not merely to assign a new meaning to ἐπινομή, but to change the whole turn of the sentence. For the plain sense will admit only the προειρημένοι as the nominative to κοιμηθῶσιν [s], a point rendered incontestable by Clemens's insertion of ἕτεροι here. Bunsen proposed ἐπιμονήν [t], a conjecture in which he was anticipated by Turner, and supposes that what is here said is, that the apostles appointed the overseers for life, that the term of the office of oversight was to cease only with life. This interpretation is equally groundless as Rothe's, though perfectly consistent with the main tendency of the epistle.

From the important passage which we have quoted at length, we learn that the overseers and servants were appointed by apostles or by other well-known men, that the consent of the whole church to the appointment of its servants was in some way or other ascertained, and that a church claimed the right of expelling a servant if it saw fit. On this occasion the Roman church demurs to the Corinthian church using this right, because they would act unjustly if they were to expel well-tried men.

The following sentences of the same chapter prove the identity of the overseers and elders. " It will be no small sin in us if we remove from the oversight those who have offered their gifts blamelessly and holily.

---

[r] Anfänge, p. 389.

[s] See a full refutation of Rothe in Baur, Ursprung des Episkopats, p. 53 ff.

[t] Bunsen: Ignatius von Antiochien und seine Zeit, p. 98.

Blessed are those elders who, having journeyed through life before, had a fruitful and perfect dissolution; for they fear not lest any one should remove them from the place appointed to them [u]." Here we have proof as clear as we could wish that the elders were included among the overseers. The Roman letter implies that the Corinthians were intending to remove some, not one, from the oversight. The writer thinks of those who had had this service in the church before, and he naturally exclaims, "Blessed are they who are gone!" This would be an absurd exclamation if the persons called "blessed" did not occupy the same position as those who were on earth in the midst of trouble. Further proof is at hand. In the passage now quoted, the sin which the Corinthian church is supposed to be in danger of committing is the expulsion of holy men from their oversight. Elsewhere these same men are called "elders." "A most disgraceful report is it that the ancient church of the Corinthians should revolt against the elders on account of one or two persons [y]." These expressions do not force us to conclude the absolute identity of overseers and elders, but we are left to one of two conclusions: either elders and overseers were different names of the same office; or all elders were overseers, though all overseers were not necessarily elders. Their exact identity however is rendered extremely likely by the circumstance that only overseers and servants were formerly mentioned as the office-bearers of the churches. Now as the elders are declared to be office-bearers too, it is plain that the term either included both overseers and servants, or we must restrict it to one of them. We have no reason for applying

[u] c. 44.   [y] c. 47.

it to the servants, and consequently we must apply it to the overseers, and them alone. There is one passage that seems to point out the elders as the only servants: "Only let the flock of Christ be at peace with the appointed elders [z]." The omission of the servants however may be accounted for by the circumstances that the occasion of this letter was a revolt against elders, and that the deacons might perhaps more appropriately go with the flock, as they were not guides of the flock.

If we interpret the words which Clemens uses in regard to the Jewish Church as having a reference to the Christian Church, we get the same division of offices. He says: "To the high priest his own services are given, and to the priests their own place has been assigned, and on the Levites their own services are obligatory; the layman is bound by laic precepts." As Clemens gives us no key to the understanding of this passage, unless we accept his exposition of the offices of overseer and deacon as such, we can derive no authority from this passage for any theory. All that we have to do is to show that it harmonises; and if we regard Christ as the High Priest of the Christian Church, which Clemens himself calls Him, then the overseers or elders correspond to the priests, and the deacons to the Levites.

We have still to consider two passages which have been adduced as favouring the notion that there were three orders in the church—bishop or overseer, presbyters or elders, and deacons. The two passages are so alike that it will be sufficient to quote only one of them: "Let us respect those who rule over us (τοὺς προηγου-

[z] c. 54.

μένους ἡμῶν), let us honour our elders, let us instruct the young men with the instruction of the fear of God, let us direct our wives into what is good. .... Let your children have a share of the instruction which is in Christ[a]." Here a single glance will show that those " who rule over us" (ἡγούμενοι in the other chapter, ch. i.) are the office-bearers of the church; the elders are elderly men, the young men are young men, the women are women, and the children are children[b]. Some indeed take the elders to mean office-bearers in the church, while Burton has supposed that the rulers are civil rulers. Both of these interpretations seem to me contrary to the spirit of the context. If the rulers included the elders, why mention them again? Besides Clemens is discussing the propriety of acting worthily of God in all relations, and he could scarcely, in mentioning young men, women, and children, fail to take notice of the respect due to old men. The objection to Burton's notion is that Clemens is dealing entirely with the internal affairs of the Corinthian church. Both these interpretations are quite consistent with the opinions expressed in other parts of the epistle; but the same cannot be said of a variety of others which church zeal has excogitated. We give that of the Roman Catholic Thönnissen, who has published a separate dissertation on this passage. He wishes to show that there is one bishop, and that presbyters are different from bishops. He allows that the passages already quoted from chapters xl. xlii. and xliv. fail to do this; he lays his whole stress on the passages now before us[c]. Those who rule over us, he says, are bishops, the elders are the church presbyters, the young men are the laity;

[a] c. 21.
[b] So Bunsen: Ignatius und seine Zeit, p. 102.
[c] c. 1. and c. 21.

the women and children he does not include in his interpretation. He finds indeed a difficulty in Clemens's use of the plural "rulers." However, such a difficulty is a matter of slight moment. The rulers are the present bishop of Corinth and every bishop that is to succeed him. Clemens provides for futurity [d].

We have no intimation of the duties assigned to overseers and deacons. The work of the overseers is called a λειτουργία or service, and it is described as an offering of gifts (τὰ δῶρα προσφέρειν). Of the deacons nothing is said; and, so far as this epistle goes, it might be doubted whether they were a separate class at all. For in the passage already quoted "the overseers and servants" might perfectly well be the same persons; and in the only other two places in which the words occur, there is a possibility of regarding the two designations as merely different phases of the same office. "For long ago it was written of overseers and servants; for thus says the writing: I will appoint their overseers in righteousness and their servants in peace[e]." The church is urged to honour her elders[f], and to be in the subjection to them[g].

No mention is made of any of the rites of the church. Some have imagined an allusion to the Lord's Supper in the description of the overseers "bringing their gifts." But this is too limited a signification of the words. "Bringing their gifts," plainly means "doing

[d] Abhandlungen, p. 71. This is the second of the Abhandlungen, already mentioned. Thönnissen is remarkably candid in the first part of it, evidently with the hope of gaining greater favour for his new mode of proving the established doctrine. The treatise gives references to most of the literature on these passages.

[e] c. 42.   [f] c. 1.   [g] c. 57.

what service God has enabled them to perform for the church;" or, as W. Burton has it, "undergoing the duties of their episcopacy." The attempt that Cotelerius has made to prove that it refers to the Lord's Supper is unsuccessful, because he appeals for support to writers of a later date than Clemens. And even he includes more than the simple giving of thanks at the Lord's Supper; for he explains the δῶρα as "preces fidelium, sacrificia incruenta, sanctam Eucharistiam."

Future State.—Very little is said in Clemens of a future state. He devotes three chapters to the resurrection, but he speaks only of the resurrection "of those who serve the Maker of all in a holy manner[h]." His mode of proving the resurrection deserves notice. He appeals first to the resurrection of Christ as the firstfruits, and then he finds analogies of it in nature, in day and night, in fruits, and in the phœnix. He does not once utter a single remark about those who do not serve God. Perhaps something might be inferred from the statement that those who fear God will be protected from the coming judgments by his mercy[i]. But the expression "coming judgments" may possibly refer to anticipated calamities in this world, since this use of κρῖμα is quite common, and actually occurs in chapter xi. and in the previous chapter: "Let our souls be bound to Him, who is faithful in his promises and just in his judgments[k]."

The place to which the blessed go is called "the place of glory that is due," or "the holy place[l]." That Clemens means by this some region to which the pious immediately proceed, there can be no doubt; for he says

[h] c. 26. [i] c. 28. [k] c. 27. [l] c. 5.

expressly that "those who have been perfected in love, according to the favour of God, hold the place of the pious (ἔχουσιν χῶρον εὐσεβῶν), and will be manifested in the oversight of the kingdom of Christ [m];" that is, when Christ shall appear again to take a full view of his kingdom. These words were applied, moreover, not only to Christians, but to the generations of the faithful from the time of Adam.

The martyrs are spoken of as receiving their reward [n]. Of the greatness of this reward Clemens speaks in terms of the highest expectation. In reference to the passage, "Eye hath not seen, and ear hath not heard, and it hath not entered into the heart of man to conceive, how many things He has prepared for those that await Him," he exclaims, "How blessed and wonderful, beloved, are the gifts of God! life in immortality, brilliancy in righteousness, truth in boldness of speech, faith in confidence, self-restraint in holiness; and all these things have come under our power of apprehension. What then must the things be which are prepared for those who wait for him? The Fashioner and Father of the ages, the All-holy, alone knows their quantity and beauty [o]." These are "the great and glorious promises of God [p]," of which we may become partakers if we wait on God.

One passage in the epistle has been supposed by some to teach that the saints after death hear prayers. "Let us pray then," he says, "for those who are in any sin, that gentleness and humility may be granted to them, that they may yield not to us but to the will of God; for thus the mention of them to God and the saints, accompanied as it will be, with mercies, will

[m] c. 50.   [n] c. 6.   [o] c. 35.   [p] c. 34.

be fruitful and perfect q." The difficult words here are ἡ πρὸς τὸν Θεὸν καὶ τοὺς ἁγίους μετ' οἰκτιρμῶν μνεία, which have been understood in various ways. They have been taken to mean "prayers offered to God and the departed saints," "an entreaty for the restoration of the fallen one to God and the Church;" "the record of them before God and the Church r;" "the merciful remembrance of them by God and the Church;" and "the appeal for them to God and the angels." ἅγιοι is here taken in three senses: as saints in the Roman Catholic sense, as angels, and as the Church. There can be no doubt that it is most natural to take ἅγιοι here in the sense in which it occurs generally in the New Testament as the Christian brethren. This meaning also agrees best with the context.

We have already quoted the passage from Irenæus in which he mentions that Clemens spoke of the fire which God prepared for the devil and his angels.

The Scriptures.—Clemens quotes frequently from the Old Testament, and mentions or uses the following writers—Moses, David, Isaiah, Jeremiah, Ezekiel.

He speaks in the most decisive terms of the authority of the writers. The quotations are introduced by "It is written," "The holy word says," and such like. The books are expressly called the sacred books. "And what is wonderful, if those who in Christ were intrusted by God with this work, appointed those previously mentioned? when also the blessed Moses, a faithful servant in all his house, marked down in the sacred books all the things which had been commanded him. He was also followed by the other prophets, who bore witness to the laws which had been given by him s."

q c. 56.   r Lightfoot.   s c. 43.

The prophets were under the influence of the Holy Spirit, and so spake that the writers can quote their words as the words of the Holy Spirit: "Examine carefully the Scriptures, the true (sayings) of the Holy Spirit [t]." "The servants of the grace of God spoke through the Holy Spirit with regard to change of mind [u]." "Let us do what has been written, for the Holy Spirit says [x]," &c. "As the Holy Spirit has spoken with regard to him, for he says [y]." This being the case, the writer does not hesitate to attribute to God the words assigned Him in the Old Testament: "the Lord of all has Himself spoken with regard to a change of mind [z]." And such statements of God Himself are most probably what is meant by the τὰ λόγια τοῦ Θεοῦ, when mention is made of those who have received his oracles in fear and truth [a].

Notwithstanding this distinct assignment of the words of the prophets to the Holy Spirit, Clemens takes the liberty of misquoting the verses, changing the words, and joining together in a remarkable manner various passages culled from different authors. As an example we take the following from chapter xxix, placing beside it the translation of the Septuagint from which Clemens generally quotes:—

CLEMENS.	NUMBERS xviii. 27.
... And in another place it says: Lo, the Lord taketh to Himself a nation from the midst of nations, as a man taketh the firstfruits of his threshingfloor, and the holy of holies shall go forth from that nation.	And what is taken away from you shall be reckoned to you as wheat from the threshingfloor, and a taking away from the winepress.
	2 CHRON. xxxi. 14.
	And Core the son of Jemna the Levite, the gatekeeper at the east, had the charge of the gifts to give the firstfruits of the Lord and the holy of holies.

[t] c. 45.   [u] c. 8.   [x] c. 13.   [y] c. 16.   [z] c. 8.   [a] c. 19.

We have an instance of a very remarkable liberty which Clemens takes with the text of the Old Testament, in his speaking of overseers and deacons. Isaiah lx. 17 concludes with, "And I shall give thy rulers (ἄρχοντας) in peace and thy overseers in righteousness;" which Clemens thus quotes: "For thus the writing somewhere says, 'I will appoint their overseers in righteousness and their servants (deacons) in faith [b].'"

Clemens invariably quotes from the Septuagint version, and gives us readings found in it but not occurring in the Hebrew. The account of Cain and Abel, where the reason of the rejection of the sacrifice is given, and where the words Διέλθωμεν εἰς τὸ πεδίον are added, is an instance [c]. He also incorporates in his narratives taken from the Old Testament some incidents or opinions not found there. Thus he speaks of Isaac's willingness to be offered up; and in giving an account of the choice of the tribe of Levi for priestly offices, he introduces several circumstances which are found neither in the Old Testament nor in Josephus [d].

Clemens also quotes several passages which are now not to be found in the Old Testament. We give a list of them:—

1. The first quotation is tacked to two verses from Ezekiel, and the words are mentioned as being spoken by God. They are: "Say to the sons of my people, If your sins reach from the earth to the heaven, and if they be redder than scarlet, and blacker than sackcloth, and ye turn to me with the whole of your heart, and say, O Father; I will hear you as a holy people." The commentators, allowing that this passage is not in Scripture, bid us compare Jer. iii. 4, 19, Psalm ciii. 11, Isaiah i. 18, and Ezek. xviii. 30 [e].

[b] c. 42.   [c] c. 4.   [d] c. 43.   [e] c. 8.

2. "Moses again says: 'I am vapour from a pot [f].'" It would be useless to enumerate the conjectures which have been made with regard to this passage from the time of Chrysostom to the present day. They leave the reader where they find him.

3. "Far be from you this scripture (writing) where it says, Wretched are the double-souled, who waver in their souls; who say, These things we have heard even in the days of our fathers, and lo! we have grown old and none of them has happened to us. O fools, compare yourselves to a tree. Take the vine: first it sheds its leaves, then comes the bud, then the leaf, then the flower, and after that the unripe grape, then the ripe grape. See how in a short time the fruit of the tree reaches ripeness [g]." Wotton supposes this a combination of James i. 8 and 2 Pet. iii. 3, 4, but the variations are too great to admit of this explanation.

4. "For he says, (or, the Scripture says,) Eye hath not seen, and ear hath not heard, and it hath not gone up into the heart of man, how many things He hath prepared for them that wait for Him [h]." These words are the same as those quoted by Paul in 1 Cor. ii. 9. Origen and other fathers believed that this quotation was made from the Revelation of Elias, now lost, but in all probability it is a modification of Isaiah lxiv. 4, Sept.

5. "For it has been written: Be joined to the holy, for those that are joined to them shall be made holy [i]."

6. "For it has been written: Enter into thy chamber for a very little until my anger and wrath pass away, and I shall remember the good day, and I shall raise you from your tombs [j]." The first clause is taken from Isa. xxvi. 20. The last clause of this verse is found in

[f] c. 17.   [g] c. 23.   [h] c. 34.   [i] c. 46.   [j] c. 50.

4 Ezra ii. 16: "Et resuscitabo mortuos de locis suis." Lücke, in Die Offenbg. Joh. (i. 152), maintains that this cannot be the source of the quotation, the passage being a later Christian addition. Professor Lightfoot thinks that it is probably taken from Ezek. xxxvii. 12.

There is no theory of inspiration in Clemens; but some have supposed that the use of the word γραφεῖον [k] in reference to the Psalms indicates Clemens's adherence to the division of the books of the Old Testament into the Law, the Prophets, and the Hagiographa, the last of which was not equal in authority to the former. But this is building far too much on one word, especially when the earliest authorities that can be adduced for this use of γραφεῖον are Epiphanius and Jerome[1].

The New Testament.—There is no express reference to any book of the New Testament except to the letter of Paul to the Corinthians. The allusion to it suggests some difficulties: "Take up the letter of the blessed Paul the apostle. What first did he write to you in the beginning of the gospel? Of a truth he spiritually warned you through letter, in regard to himself and Cephas and Apollos, because even at that time you had formed parties[m]." Here it has been asked, Did Clemens know anything of the letter which Paul sent to the Corinthians before he sent the one which now stands as our first? or did he know anything of our second epistle, as he mentions simply *the* letter?

We cannot hesitate to answer, that Clemens's know-

---

[k] c. 28.

[1] See Epiph. Hær. 29, c. 7; and Hieron. in Prologo galeato and Præfatio ad Danielem; Philo de Vita Contemplativa, c. 3. ii. p. 475; Joseph. cont. Apionem, i. 8.   [m] c. 47.

ledge of both these unmentioned letters is perfectly consistent with the mode of speaking employed here. *The* letter does not mean *the only letter*, but it plainly means the letter in which reference is made to the subject of which I speak. Other passages show that Clemens was probably well acquainted with the writings of Paul; and we have already exhibited the remarkable correspondence of some parts of this epistle with the discourse addressed to the Hebrews. We cannot assert that Clemens quotes from any other part of the New Testament writings; but there is ample proof that he had access either to some oral source for the words of Christ, or some written source now lost. The words of Christ quoted may be divided into two classes. In one of these we range those words the like of which are found in our Gospels, though Clemens plainly does not quote from them. They are these:—

1. From the Sermon on the Mount we have the following: "Especially remembering the words of the Lord Jesus, which He spoke, teaching gentleness and patience; for thus He spoke: Pity, that ye may be pitied; forgive, that ye may be forgiven: as ye do, so shall it be done to you; as ye give, so shall it be given to you; as ye judge, so shall ye be judged; as ye are kind, so shall ye be treated kindly; with what measure ye measure, with the same shall it be measured to you[n]." Compare with this Matthew vi. 14; vii. 2, 12; Luke vi. 31, 37, 38. There is no reason for supposing that Clemens drew these words from the Gospel of the Nazarenes, as Wotton conjectures.

2. "Remember the words of Jesus our Lord, for He said: Woe to that man: well were it for him if he had

[n] c. 13.

not been born, rather than that he should cause one of those whom I have selected to stumble; better were it that a millstone were put round him and he were sunk into the sea, than that he should cause one of my little ones to stumble°." Compare Matt. xxvi. 24; Mark xiv. 21; Matt. xviii. 6; Mark ix. 42; Luke xvii. 2.

3. The next quotation has nothing similar to it in our Gospels. Clemens says[p] that the apostles through our Lord Jesus Christ knew that there would be strife on account of the office of overseer.

It is impossible to decide from what source Clemens made these quotations. From the way in which the sayings of Christ are introduced, we are led to believe that they were quite familiar to the Corinthians, or at least were accessible to them. The words "Remember the words" are perhaps understood most naturally, if we suppose that they were handed down by oral tradition. But we must suppose in the case of the second that it was either in a book or very soon afterwards found its way into one, as Clemens Alexandrinus quotes it almost word for word with our Clemens. Some have supposed that Clemens used the Gospel of Peter, or some such gospel; but it is impossible to be precise on such a point.

Some expressions or turns of thought have been appealed to as indicating Clemens's acquaintance with other sayings of Christ, or with the statements of the gospels. Clemens begins a sentence, "A sower went forth to sow;" which is regarded as proof that he knew the parable of the Sower. He uses the expression "giving more willingly than receiving," and hence he is supposed to have known the saying of Christ recorded

° c. 46.   p c. 44.

in Acts xx. 35; while Hilgenfeld puzzles himself with the expression, "The Lord Himself having adorned Himself with works, rejoiced [q];" which he thinks must be referred either to an uncanonical narrative, or to Matt. xi. 5, and Luke vii. 22; though the whole connection forces us to regard the writer as speaking of God and not of Christ.

Nothing is said of the authority of the New Testament writers. Some have taken the word "spiritually," applied to Paul, as meaning that he was divinely inspired. But Paul's own use of the word clearly demonstrates that it does not of itself imply extraordinary inspiration, that it is a word used of all Christians in whom the Spirit dwells and works. There are several passages which speak of the commission of the apostles, as the following: "The apostles were entrusted with the message of good news to us by Christ, Christ by God [r]." "They received commands, and being fully assured through the resurrection of our Lord Jesus Christ, and confirmed in their faith in God's Word, they went forth proclaiming the good news that the kingdom of God was about to come [s]."

Clemens mentions several facts of the lives of Peter and Paul, but in such a way that it has been inferred that he was not acquainted with the Acts of the Apostles. This perhaps is going too far, as none of his statements are contradictory to those in the Acts; and indeed most of them relate to a period of the lives of the apostles not falling within the range of that work. With regard to Peter he states that he endured several troubles on account of jealousy, and that having borne his testimony he went to the due place of glory. He

[q] c. 33.   [r] c. 42.   [s] c. 42.

remarks of Paul that he bore chains seven times, that he was put to flight, and was stoned, that he proclaimed the truth in the east and the west, that he taught the whole world righteousness, and that having come to the limit of the west and having borne his testimony before rulers, he was thus removed from the world and went into the holy place (c. v). Much discussion has arisen as to all that is implied in these statements. Whether does Clemens mean to state that Peter suffered martyrdom in Rome with Paul? What is meant by the τέρμα τῆς δύσεως, Rome or Spain? Now we have no means of determining precisely these questions. But from the way in which Peter and Paul are spoken of together, we should infer that Clemens was not aware that Peter had been in the west. Whether Spain is meant, is an insoluble question; but as Paul expresses a determination to visit Spain, we should regard it as probable from this expression that he did visit Spain. Some have brought together a number of passages in which Rome is called the west, and have hence wished us to believe that Rome was here mentioned. But the quotations are from Greek writers, to whom Rome certainly was the west; and even Clemens himself, in Rome, might call it the west. But would he call it the limit of the west? Or has any other writer so named it? Does Clemens then represent Paul as being martyred in Spain? He does not in fact say where he was martyred, and it is questionable whether he asserts that Peter and Paul were martyred at all. It cannot be proved that μαρτυρέω, 'to bear witness,' had acquired this meaning yet; and one can scarcely help applying μαρτυρήσας ἐπὶ τῶν ἡγουμένων (bearing witness before the rulers) to the various occasions on which Paul spoke before princes—some of which are mentioned in the Acts of the Apostles, and others of which must have taken place subsequently to any events recorded there[t].

Interpretation of Scripture.—Clemens regarded Christ as the centre of the Old Testament. This is manifest in the application of innumerable passages to Christ, such as the fifty-third chapter of Isaiah. Elijah and Elisha and Ezekiel are especially mentioned as proclaiming the coming of Christ[u]. In fact he expressly states[x] that Christ speaks through the Holy Spirit when he quotes the words of Psalm xxxiv. 11–18.

We find also in Clemens, as we have already seen, some instances of gnostic interpretation. In the fortieth chapter we have distinct enunciation of his belief that he was penetrating into the depths of divine knowledge. There is no hint however that the peculiar faculty required for this purpose was a $\gamma\nu\hat{\omega}\sigma\iota\varsigma$ or spiritual development; nor does he regard his interpretation as anything so singular as to require a full exhibition of it. He supposes his readers penetrating along with him into the depths of divine knowledge. We should be entirely wrong then if we were to maintain that Clemens had before his eyes a distinct theory of interpretation, but at the same time there are signs that the necessity of a pervasively Christian interpretation of the Old Testament was unconsciously forcing him to look for some mysterious intimations of Christian doctrine. The only conclusive instance of this however is where he discovers in the scarlet thread of Rahab[y] a prophetic intimation of the deliverance of men through the blood

---

[t] On the quotations from the Old and New Testament, see especially Hilgenfeld, Apost. Väter ; and Ekker, ch. iii.

[u] c. 17.   [x] c. 22.   [y] See Lips. p. 52.

of Christ[z]. But there are several other passages which probably must be so understood. Thus he speaks of Noah proclaiming a new birth to the world by his service, &c.[a] He interprets Psalm iii. 5, and Job xix. 25, 26, of the resurrection. Colomesius says he is the first to do so.

Morality.—Nothing need be said of the morality of this epistle. On the whole it bears testimony to a pure and noble code of morals—higher far than anything that can be found in heathenism. The most noticeable point in it is the attention the writer and the church pay to the conduct of women and young men, and to the Christian education of children. Perhaps in the case of women Clemens goes too far in self-denying injunctions, but we leave the reader to judge. He tells the women that they were to bestow their love ($\dot{a}\gamma\dot{a}\pi\eta$), not according to partiality ($\pi\rho o\sigma\kappa\lambda\iota\sigma\epsilon\iota s$), but they were to bestow it *equally* on all who feared God holily[b]. The $\dot{a}\gamma\dot{a}\pi\eta$ of course is that brotherly love which prevailed between members of Christ.

There is nothing like a system of morals. And accordingly those who have attempted to draw a system out of it have started from different points. Heyns looks on "love to God and to men" as the great principle of Clemens[c]; Jani van Gilse regards "union with God and Christ" as the main moral doctrine of the work[d]; while Junius wisely lays down faith, hope, and love, as his three principles, stating at the same time that Clemens nowhere calls them principles[e].

---

[z] c. 12.   [a] c. 9.

[b] c. 21. See on this subject and that of martyrdom, Van Gilse, Comment. p. 40.

[c] Comment. p. 12.   [d] Ibid. p. 34.   [e] Ibid. p. 11.

CHAPTER III.

POLYCARP.

Life.

THE knowledge which we have of Polycarp rests on two authorities—the writings of Irenæus, and a letter sent by the church in Smyrna to a neigbouring church. Various other notices occur in other writers, but all of these which have any foundation are founded on the statements of Irenæus. We shall therefore examine these first.

From a letter which Irenæus sent to Florinus on doctrinal points, and which Eusebius has preserved, we learn that he had access to the best sources of information with regard to Polycarp. " While I was yet a boy," he says, "I saw you in Lower Asia with Polycarp, pursuing a brilliant career in the royal court, and trying to be well pleasing to him. For I remember the occurrences of those days better than the more recent (for instructions which we receive in childhood grow up with our soul and become one with it); so that I can tell even the spot in which the blessed Polycarp sat and conversed, and his outgoings and incomings, and the character of his life, and the form of his body, and the conversations which he held with the multitude; and how he related his familiar intercourse with John and the rest who had seen the Lord, and how he rehearsed their sayings, and what things they were which he had heard from them with regard to the Lord and his miracles and teaching. All these things Polycarp related in harmony with the writings, as having received them from the eyewitnesses of the Word of life. These things then I was in the habit of eagerly hearing through the mercy given me by God, storing them up, not on paper but in my heart; and always I ruminate over them faithfully through the grace of God. And I can bear witness before God, that if that blessed and apostolic presbyter had heard any such thing [a], he would have cried out and stopped his ears, and according to his custom said, 'O good God, for what times hast thou preserved me that I should endure these things!'" and he would have fled the place in which sitting or standing he had heard such sayings [b]."

The second extract gives us more particular information with regard to Polycarp: " And Polycarp, who was not only instructed by apostles, and had intercourse with many who had seen Christ, but was also appointed for Asia by apostles, in the church that is in Smyrna, an overseer, whom also we have seen in the beginning of our life, for he remained a long time, and at an exceeding old age, having borne his testimony gloriously and most notably, departed this life, always taught these things, which also he learned from the apostles, which also he gave to the Church [c], and which alone are true. To these doctrines testimony is also borne by all the churches throughout Asia, and by those who have been up till this time the successors of Polycarp, who was a much more trustworthy and secure witness

---

[a] He refers to the heresies against which he is writing.
[b] Euseb. Hist. Eccl. v. 20; Iren. Stier. vol. i. p. 822.
[c] Different reading in Eusebius: "which the Church hands down."

of the truth than Valentinus and Marcion and the rest who held wicked opinions. He (Polycarp) also sojourning at Rome in the time of Anicetus, converted many from the previously mentioned heretics to the Church of God, having proclaimed that he had received from the apostles this as the one and only truth which he had delivered to the Church. And there are those who heard him say that John the disciple of the Lord having gone to bathe in Ephesus, on seeing Cerinthus inside, leaped from the bathing establishment without bathing, and exclaimed, 'Let us flee, lest the baths fall in, since Cerinthus the enemy of the truth is within.' And Polycarp himself, when Marcion one time met him and said, 'Do you recognise us?' answered, 'I recognise the firstborn of Satan.' Such was the caution which the apostles and their disciples took not to have even verbal communication with those who perverted the truth; as Paul also said, 'A heretical man avoid after a first and second [d] admonition, knowing that such a one has been turned away, and sins, being self condemned [e].'"

The third extract is from a letter which Irenæus wrote in the hope of quieting the exasperation caused by the controversies about the method of celebrating the Passover. "While the blessed Polycarp was sojourning in Rome in the time of Anicetus, they had slight disputes about some other matters, and immediately were reconciled. About this subject they did not show any liking for a quarrel. For neither was Anicetus able to persuade Polycarp not to observe [the fast], since he had always observed it with John the disciple of our

[d] The Latin here omits "second."
[e] Iren. adv. Hær. iii. 3 ; Euseb. iv. 14.

Lord and the other apostles with whom he stayed; nor did Polycarp persuade Anicetus to keep it, saying that he ought to retain the custom of those who were presbyters before him. And this being the case, they communicated with each other, and in the church Anicetus yielded up to Polycarp the giving of thanks, evidently by way of respect[f], and they separated from each other in peace, while all the church was at peace, both those who kept the fast and those who did not[g]."

These three extracts contain all the information which we derive from Irenæus. The information which he gives us is thoroughly to be relied on. It is that of one who knew Polycarp. There is indeed one portion of Irenæus's statements which has been questioned with the greatest justice. What he says about the apostle John has the appearance of being, to say the least, highly coloured. But then Irenæus says only that "there are some who heard from Polycarp the story." Whether Irenæus himself heard it from those who said that they had heard it from Polycarp, is left uncertain, and altogether the whole affair is not well authenticated. Moreover secondary traditions in the

---

[f] The words παρεχώρησεν εὐχαριστίαν can be translated in two ways. Either they mean that Anicetus simply permitted Polycarp to join his church in celebrating the Eucharist—but how this could be an ἐντροπή, such as adopt this meaning do not explain; or they must be translated as in the text. I take εὐχαριστίαν as having its original meaning, thanksgiving. And I suppose that Polycarp led the services on the occasion of the celebration of the thanksgiving or eucharist. For taking παραχωρεῖν εὐχαριστίαν in the sense of "to give the eucharist to Polycarp," εὐχαριστία being the bread of thanksgiving and the wine, see Le Moyne, Varia Sacra, vol. i. Prolegom. fol. 7. 3.

[g] Euseb. Hist. Eccl. v. 24. Iren. Stier. Frag. iii. p. 826.

hands of Irenæus, as we shall see, are not much to be trusted[h].

There are several points in the information of Irenæus to which special attention must be called. The reason for this is, that they have been misinterpreted by Eusebius and Jerome, who repeat his statements; and the assertions of Eusebius and Jerome have been regarded as historical by most modern scholars.

As far as the statements of Irenæus go, there is not the slightest reason for supposing that Polycarp was the only overseer in the church in Smyrna. Moreover, the application of the word Presbyter to him renders it likely that he was both a presbyter and an overseer at the same time, and that both terms meant the same office. The words of Irenæus are, ὑπὸ ἀποστόλων κατασταθεὶς εἰς τὴν Ἀσίαν ἐν τῇ ἐν Σμύρνῃ ἐκκλησίᾳ ἐπίσκοπος. If the clause be translated as I have rendered it, we have no warrant for saying that he was made an overseer by the apostles. The words εἰς Ἀσίαν κατασταθείς simply express the region to which the apostles appointed him. And the clause that follows is a separate and positive statement that he was an overseer in the church in Smyrna. Eusebius seems to have understood the words in this sense. Taking the words even in the sense in which the Latin translator of Irenæus took them,— " but also having been appointed by the apostles in Asia an overseer in that church which is at Smyrna"—we still retain the most essential point, that he was only one of the number. Eusebius thus paraphrases the information of Irenæus: " Polycarp, an associate of the apostles,

[h] The story has been repeated by Epiphanius and Theodoret, but the name of the heretic in the former is Ebion. See Lardner, Credib. part ii. c. 16.

entrusted with the oversight of the church in Smyrna by the eye-witnesses and servants of the Lord [i]." This may be perfectly correct, but the same cannot be said of Jerome's version of the information. "Polycarp," he says, "a disciple of the apostle John, and ordained by him bishop of Smyrna, was the chief of all Asia, inasmuch as he saw and had for masters some of the apostles and of those who had seen the Lord." Jerome, as far as we know, had not the slightest reason for associating Polycarp with John more than with some other apostles, except that John is the only apostle whom Irenæus mentions by name. Nor had he better reason for saying that he was ordained by John, though he has more show of it. For Tertullian relates that the church of the Smyrneans asserted that John appointed Polycarp [k]; but how he got his information, or whether he is as usual somewhat inaccurate, we cannot decide. Jerome's assertion, that he was chief of all Asia, has no meaning in it when we consider the mode of government of the churches in the time of Polycarp; and the reason he gives is as foolish as the assertion.

The other points to which we draw attention relate to the remarks of Irenæus in regard to Polycarp's visit to Rome and his observance of the Passover. We shall have to discuss them more fully in connection with Irenæus himself. In the meantime let it be remarked that Irenæus does not assign any reason for the visit of Polycarp to Rome. In the two passages in which he mentions it, he does it in the words "while Polycarp was sojourning in Rome." He does not even state at what time he went to Rome. He merely states that he was there in the time of Anicetus. Then

[i] Hist. Eccl. iii. 36.   [k] De Præscript. c. xxxii.

let it be observed that Irenæus states that while Polycarp and Anicetus did differ on some points, their difference as to the observance of the Passover was a point on which they did not give themselves any trouble. Their practice was different: their faith was one. And lastly let it be observed that Polycarp is represented as observing the Passover, and Anicetus and the Roman church as not observing it. At the first glance at least this representation is to the effect that the Roman church had no peculiar festival or fast at the time of the Passover. In a very short time after this things were completely changed, and the controversy that afterwards raged perverted Eusebius's interpretation of the words of Irenæus. He introduces our second extract from Irenæus in the following words, "That, while Anicetus ruled the church of the Romans, Polycarp yet surviving came to Rome and entered into a conversation with Anicetus on account of some discussion in reference to the day on which the Passover was to be observed, Irenæus relates[1]." Irenæus relates no such thing, as we have seen; and Hilgenfeld is therefore entirely wrong in appealing to this passage of Eusebius as proof that Polycarp came to Rome in order to have a conference with the bishop of the capital of the world in regard to the day of the Passover[m]. There is no reason to suppose that Eusebius had any other information than that to which he appeals and which he quotes. Even Baur's more moderate assertion, that Polycarp went to Rome "to converse with bishop Anicetus about different ecclesiastical subjects to which the question of the Pass-

---

[1] Hist. Eccl. iv. 14.

[m] Der Paschastreit der alten Kirche, von A. Hilgenfeld, p. 230 (Halle 1860).

over especially belonged[n]," is entirely without foundation. Jerome's account follows Eusebius: "He came to Rome on account of certain discussions relating to the day of the Passover, during the reign of the emperor Antoninus Pius, while Anicetus governed the church in the city[o]."

Later writers (Suidas and the authors of the Apostolical Constitutions) give us the succession of bishops in the Smyrnean church. Bucolus was the first, according to Suidas[p]. According to the authors of the Apostolical Constitutions, Ariston was the first, then Strataias the son of Lois, and then another Ariston[q]. No mention is made of Polycarp. The one account is as untrustworthy as the other.

Before we arrange the facts contained in our second authority we must examine the proofs of the genuineness of the letter—or, as it is called, the Martyrium of Polycarp. This Martyrium has only one external testimony worth notice with regard to it, namely Eusebius[r]; but this is not surprising, as the letter is not connected with the name of any remarkable person, and does not deal with such subjects as would induce subsequent writers to refer to it. Eusebius knew the work well. He has quoted the greater portion of it, and probably in his work on the Martyrs he had copied the whole of it. Yet he seems to have made no inquiries into the exact time at which it was written; all the information which he has given amounting to this, that the brethren in

[n] Das Christenthum, &c. p. 156.

[o] De Viris Illust. c. xvii.

[p] Sub voce Πολύκαρπος. He repeats the statements of Eusebius and Jerome in regard to the visit to Rome.

[q] Constit. Apostol. lib. vii. c. 46. 1.

[r] Hist. Eccl. iv. 15.

the church of the Smyrneans laid down the account contained in the letter. We have thus the certainty only that it was written before the time of Eusebius.

We are therefore left entirely to internal evidence. It is well to notice here the question which lies before us. The letter professes to be a letter from the church in Smyrna. The author of the letter is therefore some member of that church, acting simply as representative. Most think that we do not know who was this representative. If we take chapter xx. as genuine, the words μεμηνύκαμεν διὰ τοῦ ἀδελφοῦ ἡμῶν Μάρκου seem to me to point out Marcus as the author, though commentators generally regard Marcus as the person through whom the letter was conveyed, and Evarestus as the composer, not the mere penman, as I take it. Let Evarestus or Marcus be the author, we are equally in the dark with regard to the character and date of the composer. We cannot therefore discuss the authorship of the letter. Provided there is no glaring incongruity in the letter which would compel us to believe that it was not written in Asia Minor, we have no means of testing the pretensions of this letter to authorship by the known and well authenticated character and circumstances of the author. The author is unknown. We do not know what we ought to expect from him; and therefore we cannot discover by internal evidence whether any production assigned to him really was written by him or not.

The question therefore which we have to determine is, Is the letter what it professes to be? Is it a genuine letter sent from the Smyrneans to the church in Philomelium? when was it written? and what historical credit is to be attached to it? The difficulty of these questions lies in this circumstance, that the letter contains an account of several miracles, and that various inconsistencies and improbabilities are connected with these miracles. Now the letter might be written by the Smyrnean church, and yet contain the narrative of these miracles; for the Smyrneans might have been superstitious. Some of the miracles even are perfectly possible. Why should we deny their truth if there was sufficient evidence for them? What then are we to do with this miraculous element; and how, supposing it not to affect the question of authorship, is it to affect the historical credit of the epistle?

We turn to the letter itself, and seek for evidence as to its date and its historical value; but even here we are met with a difficulty. Along with the Greek form there has come down to us a Latin translation. This translation differs in some very important points from the Greek, and the critical question arises whether we have the original form of the production most clearly represented in the Greek or the Latin.

The letter itself, in its Greek form, claims to have been written by eye-witnesses of the martyrdom of Polycarp, and to have been composed before the conclusion of the year that followed that event [s]. We shall examine these claims. The writer mentions that the Smyrneans were eye-witnesses in three passages. In the first passage the writer states that "on Polycarp entering the stadium a voice came forth from heaven, saying, 'Be strong, and quit thyself manfully, O Polycarp.'" Then adds the writer, "And no one saw him who said it; but those of our number who were present heard the voice [t]." The plain and evident intention of

[s] c. 18. [t] c. 9.

the writer is to convey the notion that there was a real heavenly voice heard on this occasion. The improbability of such a miracle is at the least very great. The voice however may have been that of a Christian. But there is a great improbability about its being the voice of a Christian. Would a Christian dare to cry so loudly, in the midst of a tumult which was directed solely against Christians, that other men could hear the voice distinctly? And if the voice was that of a Christian, must he not have belonged to the church of the Smyrneans, and would he have been such a coward and deceiver as not to have told that it was he that cried aloud, and thus corrected the mistaken fancy of his brethren? We do not say that such a deception among Christians is impossible, but we must say that it is in the highest degree improbable. This way of accounting for the supposed miracle we reject; but still there may have been some sound, which the Christians there construed into the reported words. But then this other question meets us: What took the Christian brethren to the stadium? Were they going to glut their eyes with the sight of their aged pastor devoured by wild beasts? Was there not a strong feeling prevalent among Christians that it was sinful and cruel to attend these shows, even when slaves were the objects of the sport? Nay, would not the church itself have pronounced a strong condemnation against these very individuals, for thus being found in a place consecrated to the vilest exhibition of idolatrous worship? But perhaps it may be said that the games were over, and they expected that they would simply see Polycarp tried. This plea is invalid. The stadium was not the place for a trial. Polycarp was sought, according to the account, expressly at the request of the very people who were feasting their eyes with the death of martyrs by wild beasts. And though Polycarp came too late for the fight with wild beasts, the people in the stadium nevertheless expected to see a sight [u].

We have thus two improbabilities. It is not very probable that there was any voice from heaven; and it is improbable that there were Christians in the place to hear the voice. Besides this the writer affirms in the sentence preceding the mention of the heavenly voice, that there was "such a disturbance in the stadium that no one could be heard." The variations in the text of the chapter in which the narrative of the miracle is given are interesting. The Latin version, which on many accounts may be regarded as the best form, makes no mention of the impossibility of hearing. It says nothing of *Christians* hearing the voice. It says merely "those who were in the arena heard the voice: none of the others heard it." The Greek, as we have quoted it, says "those of our number who were present." Eusebius has "many of our number;" and Rufinus, his translator, has "very many."

The next passage in which the claim is made is perhaps still more remarkable. Polycarp, the writer relates, offered up a prayer, and then the firemen lighted the fire. Then the writer adds: "But a great flame flashing forth, we saw a great wonder to whom it was granted to see, who also were preserved to proclaim to the rest what took place." In Eusebius's copy the reading is more naive, and therefore more like the first attempt.

---

[u] The Latin form uses words from which the inference may be fairly drawn that no Christian was present: "populum qui in arena erat respexit universum impium et profanum." c. 9.

Instead of the οἱ being in the first person, it is in the third: "We saw a great wonder, and they were preserved to tell it." Then the writer relates the wonder: "For the fire making the form of a vault, as the sail of a ship filled with the wind, encircled like a wall the body of the martyr; and it was in the middle, not as flesh burning, but as bread toasted, or as gold and silver glowing in a furnace. And we also felt such a sweet smell, as if of frankincense or some other of the precious [spices] aromas. Then at length the iniquitous people, seeing that the body could not be consumed by the fire, ordered the confector [executioner] to go up to him and plunge his sword into him. And when he had done this, a dove and a great quantity of blood came out, so as to put out the fire ; and all the people wondered that there should be such a difference between the unbelieving and the elect, of whom he was one,—the most admirable martyr Polycarp having been an apostolic and prophetic teacher in our times, and an overseer [bishop] of the catholic church in Smyrna. For every word which he uttered both was accomplished and shall be accomplished [x]."

Almost every line of this extract bears marks of its being written at a period long subsequent to the death of Polycarp. Let us glance at the non-miraculous element in it. The writer assures us that the whole multitude on seeing the fire extinguished by the martyr's blood were astonished at the difference between the unbelieving and the elect. Now is this at all likely? What happened to an unbeliever which could in any way suggest a contrast? and how could they have regarded the putting out of the fire by the martyr's blood

[x] cc. 15, 16.

in any other light than that in which we must regard it—a most senseless divine interposition to make a display but to accomplish nothing at all? The martyr was not saved. If he was not burned, he was stabbed to death. And what good could the extinction of the fire do, when he was now dead? And then is it likely that the heathen would have looked upon the miracle in any such light as is here represented y? The remarkable circumstance about even the most authenticated of Christ's miracles was that they failed to produce on many the right impression with regard to his mission and character.

Then the part added to this is utterly out of place. One of the elect, the writer gravely tells the people to whom he writes, was Polycarp—as if they did not know, as if they had not written to ask more particularly about the martyrdom, having just heard the most general rumours. And not only so, but the writer goes into particulars. The church in Philomelium writes to the church in Smyrna, asking an account of the martyrdom of one of their overseers; and the church in Smyrna in its reply gravely informs its sister church that Polycarp was an overseer, not in *our* church, but in the catholic church in Smyrna. Then, as we shall see immediately, this letter is supposed to have been written before the end of the first year after the martyrdom; yet the church of Smyrna vouchsafes to the ignorant church in Philomelium the important information that he flourished in "our times," and was an apostolic teacher.

---

y Jortin (Remarks on Ecclesiastical History, p. 313, vol. i.) shows how the miracle would probably create an unfavourable opinion in the minds of the heathens.

Besides these objections, there are the other two objections which have been urged against the preceding. First, that it is extremely unlikely that there were any Christians in the stadium; and secondly, that if they had been there, they could never have seen what it is pretended they saw. It might indeed be alleged that some parts of the narrative may have been exaggerations of the fancy of the spectators—that a wind blowing may have turned the fire from Polycarp; that the fragrance came from the plants and shrubs which had been collected to cause the fire; that the herbs may have had some power in preserving the colour of the body fresh; and that, the wind still blowing, there was the remarkable coincidence of the extinction of the fire and the gush of blood from the martyr's body. This may be possible, and the eyes of the Christians may have been a little dazzled by the fire, and so stunned by seeing the sword enter the side of their pastor, that they twinkled; and the Christians regarded the twinkle as the flight of a dove [z] from the pierced body of Polycarp. If this then were the case—and we could resolve all the circumstances, narrated by the writer in such a way that there can be no doubt the Smyrneans regarded them as miraculous, into mere natural coincidences—we are perfectly sure of this, that the evidence of witnesses who so distorted the facts of sense is not worth much. We should

[z] Those who are inclined to trust the account of the martyrdom either refuse to contemplate each particular circumstance minutely (as Maurice?), or they have many ways of accounting for the statements. Thus Evans (in a note): "The original gives these circumstances a miraculous air. They are readily accounted for. I have omitted, with Eusebius, the story of the dove, which even if true will not appear wonderful to such as have seen those birds swoop towards a fire and out again." (p. 90.)

be compelled to an entire rejection of the historical character of the whole letter.

We may remark by the way that the whole of this passage, the dove alone being omitted, is to be found in Eusebius; and so the objections lie against his text as well as against the common text. The Latin translation however, though quite as fond of miracles as the Greek text, does not put forward its writer as an eye-witness here. Its words are cautious: "Those saw these wonders," it says, "which the Divine command had ordered to see it, that they might relate what they had seen to the rest."

The third passage[a], in which the writer mentions eye-witnesses, is a continuation of the preceding. Polycarp was dead. The history of his body now remains. The devil, it seems, jealous of the crown of martyrdom which Polycarp had received, resolved to make a last effort to injure him. He endeavoured to prevent his body from getting into the hands "of us, though many desired to have it and to communicate with his holy flesh[b]." "The devil therefore" (Eusebius says simply "some") "suggested to Nicetas, the father of Herod and the brother of Alce, to entreat the ruler not to give the body for burial, 'lest,' says he, 'leaving the crucified one, they begin to worship this one.' And they said these things at the suggestion and urgent entreaty of the Jews, who also watched, while we were about to take it out of the fire, being ignorant that we will not be able ever to leave Christ, who suffered for the salvation of the whole world of the saved [the blameless one for sinners], or even to worship any other. For Him, being Son of God, we worship; but the marytrs, as

[a] c. 17.   [b] Latin, "his holy ashes."

disciples and imitators of the Lord, we love worthily on account of their unsurpassable good will to their own king and teacher, whose fellow partakers and fellow disciples may it be granted to us to be. The centurion therefore, seeing the rivalry caused by the Jews, placed him in the midst of the fire and burned him. And thus we afterwards, gathering up his bones, more precious than precious stones and more tried than gold, laid them in a suitable place. And there, assembling in joy and gladness, according to our opportunities, God will grant us the privilege of celebrating the birthday of his martyrdom, both in memory of those who have wrestled before, and for the exercise and preparation of those who are hereafter to wrestle [c]." It is the last sentence from which critics have inferred that the letter was written in the course of the first year after the martyrdom. The Smyrnean church had not yet celebrated the birthday of the martyr, as the day of his death was called; and as it is supposed that they would do this on the very first recurrence of the day, the inference plainly is that the day had not yet recurred.

Here again we have to notice that the Latin version does not make the writers eye-witnesses. Instead of us it has got "our people," a term equivalent to Christians as it is here used.

Let us examine the particulars of this narrative. At the time of the martyrdom of Polycarp a fierce persecution was going on against the Christians. It was a persecution produced not by any edict of the emperor, but by the bitter hatred of all classes. The Christians too were accused of the most fearful crimes. Every kind of disgraceful deed and practice was imputed to them and

[c] c. 17.

credited by the people, so that it was sufficient for a man to confess himself a Christian to be condemned. And yet at this very time, according to our narrative, Jews and Christians openly quarrel about the body of a Christian, and at last the Christians have the better of the quarrel. Is this credible? How different are the statements in the so-called Second Apology of Justin Martyr! Urbicus condemns a man for being a Christian. Lucius, a Christian, interferes in his behalf. He also is condemned. Another bold Christian shared a like fate. And Vettius Epagathus, in the persecution at Lyons, was in like manner condemned. Is it likely that a mob would be more considerate [d]?

Then the reason assigned for the anxiety either of heathens or Jews to prevent the Christians getting the body, is astonishing. What did a heathen care whom the Christians worshipped, if they only worshipped Cæsar along with his god or gods? Refuse to acknowledge that the civil power of the emperor extended to religion, and then the heathen by his creed was bound to punish to death. But otherwise the worship of Christ or Polycarp was all the same. Still more absurd is it to attribute such a reason to the Jews. The Jews would let the Christians worship any one, provided their law was not insulted by representing the crucified one as their promised Messiah, and they would rather have had Christians worship Polycarp than Christ. And then, to crown the absurdity, the centurion, to settle the dispute between the Jews and Christians, burns the body in the fire which the blood of Polycarp had already extinguished. Of course it is possible to imagine that another fire was lighted for the purpose; but the narrative intimates no such

[d] Euseb. Hist. Eccl. v. i.; and in Routh, Rel. Sacr. vol. i. p. 297.

thing, and by the use of the article τοῦ πυρός leaves the reader to understand that it was the fire previously mentioned.

Besides these insuperable objections there are other reasons for regarding the whole of this passage as the work of an age much later than that of Polycarp. In a production of which the age is known, our only method of testing its statements is comparison with and authentication by contemporary documents. Now in the passage quoted, the following things cannot be paralleled from any contemporary writer. 1. We have no instance of any one collecting relics at this time, still less of communicating with holy flesh. This last expression, I suppose, means taking the eucharist in the company of the bones, and thus as it were taking it in company of the martyr[e]. Such a practice is not described in any writing contemporary with, or a considerable time subsequent to, the age of Polycarp. 2. We have no instance from a contemporary writing of the day of martyrdom being called the birthday of the martyrs, or of any church celebrating that day[f]. This custom unquestionably began at a period not very long after this, but there is not the slightest proof that it had yet begun.

The result of the examination of these three passages is, the most decided doubt as to the claims made. This doubt is confirmed by the readings of the Latin version. The Latin version is in many respects much more satisfactory and reliable than the Greek. Several of the objectionable passages which we shall subsequently notice are not found in it. In this case the writer of it does not claim to be an eye-witness, and the insertion of such a claim at a later period is a far more likely occurrence than

[e] See note of Valesius in Eus. Hein.   [f] Ibid.

the omission of it in the course of its being translated. And if this be the case, we must suppose the writing either to be a forgery in the name of the church, or that the church wrote the letter long after the death of Polycarp, or that the epistle was written soon after his death, but was considerably interpolated afterwards.

The only other indication of a date has been found by Valesius in the sentence, "You have requested a more particular account of what took place," from which he infers that the members of the church in Philomelium had merely heard of the martyrdom, and consequently that some time had elapsed before they received the written account.

The hypothesis by which we can give the most probable account of this production is, that it really was, as it professes to be, a letter from the church in Smyrna: that it was a short summary of the principal circumstances of the martyrdom; and that as this letter went down to posterity it gathered length and absurdities. The reason for such an hypothesis is, that there are statements in the narrative so contradictory that it is scarcely possible for the same writer to have composed the whole. We have already had a remarkable instance. We have seen the writer describe the performance of a miracle to prevent the martyr from being put to death by burning; then immediately after he was put to death by stabbing, no miracle now interfering; and at last the body that was committed to the flames in vain is described, when dead, as put into a fire which had been extinguished, and then really burned. We need not insist on more of these. One alone will suffice. From the extracts we have given, it will be remarked that the writer describes the most minute particulars of the martyrdom; yet towards the close of the martyrdom we learn that the members of the Philomeliensian church were anxious to have the particulars, but the brethren in Smyrna say to them, "We *for the present* have pointed out the occurrences summarily (ἐπὶ κεφα-λαίῳ) through our brother Mark [g]."

In our hypothesis we have fixed on no date; but as such a description would naturally be written not very long after the event, we may reckon a few years after the death of Polycarp as the most probable period of its production. This is rendered likely by the circumstance mentioned in the end of the letter, that there was a copy of it belonging to Irenæus; a statement which is likely to be true. It is moreover natural that the account should be written shortly after the event, and the words appealed to by Valesius certainly bear out this supposition. If this assumption be correct, the following statements in it are clear marks of interpolation.

1. The inscription is interpolated. It runs thus: "The church of God which sojourns in Smyrna, to the church of God which sojourns in Philomelium, and to all the parishes of the holy and catholic church in every place," &c. The last clause is one of the most absurd that could be well conceived. Here is a letter addressed especially to one small church, and in general to all the churches in all the world. The phraseology also is posterior to the date which we have assumed as the most probable. Eusebius seems to have read something else, or there is something wrong in his text; for though he quotes the clause which has now been translated, yet he says that it was addressed to the sojourners throughout Pontus. Philomelium, according to our best information, was not

[g] c. 20.

in Pontus; and how Eusebius got hold of this notion it is impossible to say. The adoption of such an insignificant town as Philomelium for the residence of the addressed church, is a point distinctly in favour of such a letter being written. Some indeed read Philadelphia, but the weight of evidence goes with Philomelium.

2. In chap. ii. the doctrine that man merits redemption by his own suffering is mentioned: " Buying back eternal punishment through one hour." Such a doctrine is unknown among writers contemporary with Polycarp, though we find it upwards of half a century after in Tertullian.

3. In the same chapter the writer says: "The martyrs saw with the eyes of the heart what good things are reserved for those who suffer, which neither ear hath heard nor eye seen, nor have entered into the heart of man; but the Lord pointed them to them (the martyrs), *who were no longer men, but already angels.*" This surely smells of a later age.

4. In the fourteenth chapter occurs a prayer which Polycarp offered up when tied to the pile. It runs thus: "O Lord God Almighty, the Father of thy beloved and blessed child Jesus Christ, through whom we have received the full knowledge of Thee, the God of angels and powers [h], and of the whole creation, and of the whole race of the just who live before Thee, I bless Thee that Thou hast thought me worthy of this day and hour to take my part in the number of thy witnesses, in the cup of thy Christ, for the resurrection of eternal life, both of soul and body, in the

[h] The Latin begins the prayer, "O God of angels, O God of archangels."

incorruption of a holy spirit, in which [or, among whom] may I be accepted before Thee this day in a rich and acceptable sacrifice, even as Thou the unerring and true God hast previously prepared, manifested, and fulfilled. Wherefore also I praise Thee for all; I bless Thee, I glorify Thee with the eternal and heavenly Jesus Christ, thy beloved child, with whom to Thee and the Holy Spirit be the glory now and for the ages to come. Amen." As might be expected, Eusebius's version of this prayer differs in some points—but especially in the last sentence, which is as follows in the historian: "I glorify Thee through the eternal High Priest Jesus Christ, thy beloved child, through whom and along with Him in the Holy Spirit be glory," &c. The Latin version differs greatly from both Greek texts, agreeing more nearly with Eusebius. Who were the reporters of this prayer? Not the Christians, as we have seen, and surely not the heathens. If the writers had informed us on what authorty they had regarded the prayer as the prayer of Polycarp, we might have been satisfied; but in the want of such information it looks more like the work of another person, or at least the expansion of some utterance of the martyr. At all events the difference between Eusebius, the Latin translation, and the Greek text, prevents us from regarding any one as completely correct. Some of them must be incorrect, and we have no means of determining if any of them is correct.

5. Chapter twenty-first, which gives a particular account of the date of the martyrdom, is open to serious objections. We translate it: "Now the blessed Polycarp bore his testimony on the second day of the first part of the month Xanthicus, the seventh day before

the calends of May, on the great Sabbath, at eight o'clock. But he was captured by Herod in the high-priesthood of Philip the Trallian and the proconsulship of Statius Quadratus, and in the eternal kingship of Jesus Christ, to whom be glory, honour, greatness, eternal throne, from generation to generation. Amen." It is a serious objection against this chapter that Eusebius makes no mention of it. This of all chapters would have caught the eye of the historian and chronologist; and when we find that he takes no notice of it, we are led to infer that it was not in his copy, or, as is more likely, that he distrusted it. Besides, the particularity of the date is out of character with its being a contemporary writing. Then we must suppose that the writers mention the month Xanthicus for the benefit of the church in Philomelium, and the seventh before the calends of May for the parishes throughout the whole world. Moreover we can scarcely conceive the people of Philomelium to have been ignorant who was proconsul during their own days; and yet, if the letter was written soon after the death of Polycarp, the writer evidently presumed them ignorant of such a fact. Perhaps this also was for the benefit of the whole world. Then, "in the eternal kingship of Jesus Christ" is a mode of dating which, as far as I can trace, meets us first in the martyrdom of Pionios, the transcriber of this letter, and indeed may have been invented by him. We may remark too, that notwithstanding the particularity of the chronology we are left in doubt or difficulty with regard to some points. Thus the second day of the month Xanthicus is, according to Usher, the twenty-sixth of March. The seventh before the calends of May is the twenty-fifth of April. Therefore some adopt the reading 'Απριλλίων found in a writer of Sicilian Fasti. Then we are ignorant whether the writer meant "at eight o'clock" for Philomelium or for the whole world. If for the first, then it is our eight o'clock in the morning, according to Jacobson. If it is for the whole world, then it is our two o'clock p.m. Taking all these things into consideration, and we might add a few more, we reject this chapter unhesitatingly as being the work of an interpolator. It was most probably inserted when the church began the celebration of the day of Polycarp's martyrdom, or shortly after this.

The concluding sentences of the Martyrium throw some light on the interpolations. The names of the transcribers are there recorded. Each one seems to have written his name after his predecessors on copying the letter, Irenæus excepted. "Gaius transcribed the letter from the copy of Irenæus, the disciple of Polycarp, who also lived in the same society as Irenæus; and I Socrates in Corinth, transcribed it from the copy of Gaius. Grace be with all. But I again, Pionios, wrote it from the preceding, after having sought them out again, the blessed Polycarp having made them manifest to me in a revelation, even as I shall make plain in what follows, having collected them when already they had almost faded away through time."

The writer does not say what he meant by *them*, but there can be little doubt that he means the whole narrative. Here then is the source of the interpolations. The text was improved as it went through the hands of transcribers, and Pionios claims the credit of re-discovering the old copy by means of personal communications with Polycarp. Many of the wonderful parts of the narrative would no doubt receive embellishments from the revelation of Polycarp to Pionios. Hefele is inclined to cut off this part as spurious. Of course it is. The writer of it does not pretend that it is part of the letter. He tells us that he is a transcriber and re-fashioner. Besides this, Hefele supposes the clause about revelation has been inserted to give weight to a spurious Martyrium of Polycarp ascribed to Pionios. But his reasoning is not sound. He depends upon the words 'as I shall show in what follows;' but what Pionios is to show, is not, as Hefele supposes, the substance of the revelation, but the mode in which Polycarp made the revelation, and the reality of the martyr's appearance to him.

Eusebius makes a statement with regard to this letter which also deserves notice in this connection. He says that "in the same writing with regard to Polycarp were also conjoined other martyrdoms which took place in the same Smyrna about the same time as the martyrdom of Polycarp[i];" and he mentions especially the martyrdom of one Pionios, who, he says was distinguished among the martyrs of those days. Some critics have taken this passage as implying that the martyrdoms of those persons were described in the letter of the Smyrnean church. There certainly seems some reason for this supposition, for it is not likely that the Smyrnean church would omit an account, or at least a brief allusion to occurrences, of so deeply interesting a nature. Yet the word συνῆπτο, tied together, is so unusual, and designates so exactly an external connection, that one is strongly impelled to the belief that the historian refers to some writing in which various martyrdoms were collected, and perhaps connected by a few

[i] Hist. Eccl. iv. 15.

sentences from the collector. In favour of this too is the absence of any such notices in our letter, as it has come down to us.

We thus reach the knowledge of the circumstance, that at an early period some of the Christians began to feel an interest in these martyrdoms, and collected them. It is easy to see, that with the loose notions about authorship and historical authority then prevalent, and through an anxiety to make his book complete, an editor would set down into his work all the narratives or anecdotes which he could collect about his martyrs. Supposing that he had just notions of discriminating what belonged to one author and what to another, he would have simply then placed his additions at the side, as we place them in footnotes; but the next transcriber would without hesitation have incorporated these notes with the text. So the circumstances of the case and the character of the letter as it now stands both compel us to believe that it has received many additions and undergone changes. And indeed we may perceive in this letter how the imagination of an editor acted in the expansion of his theme. One of the interpolators plainly had in his mind the crucifixion of Christ in making his additions. The circumstances are necessarily different, but the resemblances are nevertheless so close that we cannot account for them in any other way. We have first Polycarp prophesying that he must be burned alive, three days before his capture[k]. Then we find the Irenarch's name to be Herod. Then the horsemen and persecutors (διωγμῖται) came out against him running, as against a robber. The day on which they did so was the preparation day (τῇ παρασκευῇ), Friday; and the day on

[k] Matt. xxvi. 2.

which he was led to the city was the great Sabbath, that is, the sabbath preceding the Passover. In coming into the city he rides part of the way on an ass. Perhaps also we should notice here, that when he cannot be burned he is stabbed, and blood gushes out[1].

The question then comes, How do these interpolations and changes affect the historical character of the work? In our opinion they completely damage it. We have no security for any one fact in it, because we have no means of eliminating what was written by the church in Smyrna from what was fabricated by Pionios and other transcribers. The only help is from internal evidence. And yet it is scarcely conceivable that all which was interpolated should outrage probability, and thus manifest its authorship. Such writers as these martyrologists would insert occasionally what is very probable, simply because giving reins to their fancy they might occasionally stumble upon probabilities. If they were base forgers and intentionally introduced downright lies, they would be still more certain to give a colour of truth to the miraculous by sober narratives. We therefore decline to say what is true in the Martyrium of Polycarp, nor do we pretend to define the exact position even of the church in Smyrna as an historical authority. Ignorant entirely of the exact period at which the church wrote, and sure that this first letter was swelled by large additions from various hands, we think that we have no security for the truth of any one of the statements contained in it.

---

[1] Hilgenfeld has remarked this resemblance (Paschastreit, pp. 245, 246), to show that the writer followed the Synoptic Gospels; but the piercing of the side and the gushing out of blood are mentioned only in John, a circumstance which Baur has noticed: Christenthum, p. 526.

And we are confirmed in this, when we see the attempts made by Tillemont, Jortin, and others, to reconcile the various statements or elicit the truth.

This Martyrium has been praised above all the others as a splendid monument of antiquity [m]. We cannot assign it this high place. There is a certain simplicity in it, a straight-forwardness of narrative, and on the whole a rather pious feeling; but its great merit lies in its being so widely different from most of the martyria. There is comparatively little of the miraculous in it. There is much less of nonsense. There is an air of greater probability about the most part of the narrative, and especially the circumstances of the flight and capture of Polycarp are so unusual and so naively related, that one does not like to doubt their truth. There is occasionally a touch of pathos in the relation which we can scarcely imagine to have come from the pen of a man given to revelations from his overheated fancy. We leave the reader however to judge for himself. As we have said, not one of the facts has proper historical authority for it, but each reader may judge for himself what is likely to have happened, and what not. We give the main points of the narrative, which have not yet been detailed [n].

[m] Bull remarks on this letter, " De qua Epistola nemo doctus hucusque dubitavit, nemo cum ratione dubitare poterit." (Def. Fid. Nicæn. ii. 3, 9.) Scaliger praises it in extravagant language. Notwithstanding, its genuineness was called in question by Milton, and more recently by Semler, (Baumgarten's Untersuchung Theologischer Streitigkeiten, zweiter Band, herausgegeben von D. Johann Salomo Semler, p. 18,) and several of its statements have been doubted by Walch (Bibliotheca Patristica, p. 25); Kortholt, mentioned by Walch; Jortin in his Remarks on Ecclesiastical History, vol. i. p. 304; and Middleton, Inquiry into the Miraculous Powers, &c., p. 124.

[n] Neander in his Church History admirably narrates the most important parts of the narrative.

The letter, after describing shortly the terrible tortures to which some of the Christians had to submit, details more particularly the constancy and firmness of one Germanicus. The whole multitude, assembled to witness his fight with the wild beasts, were astonished at his courage, and cried out, "Away with the atheists. Let Polycarp be sought." Polycarp on hearing of this was inclined to remain in the city, but his friends urged him to withdraw. He then withdrew to a small farm at no great distance from the city, where he spent the day and night in praying for the churches. "This," says the writer, "was his habit. And praying, he had a vision three days before he was captured. He saw his pillow on fire. And turning, he said, to those who were with him, prophetically, 'It behoves me to be burnt alive[o].'" People went immediately in search of the aged Christian, and came so near that the martyr had to retire to another farm. They tracked him out there, but could not find his person. They got hold, however, of two boy-servants, one of whom they tortured till he told where Polycarp was to be found. On this troops were sent to take the Christian. "They went out on the preparation-day, at the hour of supper." Arriving late in the evening, they found Polycarp in an upper room lying. He might indeed have escaped to another farm, but he did not wish, saying, "God's will be done." He therefore received his captors in a friendly manner, asked that food and drink should be given them, and requested permission from them to spend an hour in undisturbed prayer. This being granted, "he stood and prayed, being full of the grace of God, so that he could not be silent for two hours, and those who heard

---

[o] c. 5.

were astonished, and many repented that they had gone forth against such an aged, God-honoured old man." This prayer over, they set him on an ass and brought him to the city on the Saturday called the great Sabbath. On his way he was met by the Irenarch Herod, who was anxious to bring him to the stadium, and Nicetas the father of the Irenarch. They removed him from the ass and took him up into their own conveyance, in the hope of making him yield up his religion to the civil power. "What is the harm," said they, " of calling Cæsar lord, and sacrificing and doing suchlike things, and being saved?" Polycarp at first gave no reply, but at last said, "I am not to do what ye counsel me." Then they had recourse to threats, and hurled him down from the chariot, spraining his ankle in their violent efforts. Polycarp heeded not, but went eagerly onwards until he was brought into the stadium, where the confusion was so great that no one could be heard. Then was heard the heavenly voice previously mentioned. And after that the proconsul asked him if he was Polycarp. He replied that he was. Then he urged him to deny Christ, and to swear by the fortune of Cæsar, and to cry out, "Take away the atheists!" and he strengthened his entreaties by begging him to respect his own age. Polycarp then first looked on the great masses assembled with a serious countenance, shook his head, and then groaning and looking up to heaven, he said, "Take away the atheists." The proconsul continued his entreaties: "Swear, and I release thee. Revile Christ." "Eighty and six years," said the firm Christian, "have I served Him, and He has done me no ill, and how can I blaspheme my King who has saved me?" The proconsul still persevered, until Polycarp said boldly, "I am a Christian. If you wish to hear what Christianity [p] is, grant me a day." The proconsul replied, "Persuade the people;" but Polycarp refused to have anything to do with the people. Then the proconsul threatened him with wild beasts—and the writer details the various answers and questions which were bandied between him and the Christian. The face of Polycarp all the time, so far from falling, was full of joy, and the proconsul in astonishment sent the herald to proclaim: "Polycarp has confessed that he is a Christian." Then all the multitude of Gentiles and Jews that dwelt in Smyrna yelled out in uncontrollable anger, "This is the teacher of impiety, the father of the Christians, the destroyer of our gods, who teaches many not to sacrifice, nor worship the gods." On this they asked the Asiarch Philip to set a lion on Polycarp, but he informed them that he was not at liberty to do this, since the hunt was over. "Then it seemed good to them to cry out with one accord so that Polycarp must be burnt alive. For it behoved that the vision about the pillow which had been made to him should be fulfilled, when seeing it burning in his prayer, he said, turning to the faithful with him, prophetically, 'I must be burned alive.'" Then the Jews and Gentiles collected sticks from the prisons and baths—the pyre was prepared, he took off his garments, and he was bound to the stake. But the fire refused to burn his body, and he was stabbed by the confector, as has been more fully narrated already. Then are described the dispute about his body, the burning of it, the collecting of the bones, and finally we have a chapter devoted to the prayer of

[p] That this passage is an interpolation may be inferred from the use of the word χριστιανισμός, which occurs first in Clemens Alexandrinus.

the martyr. The rest of the letter gives directions to transmit the letter to other brethren [q]; fixes exactly the day and the year of the martyrdom [r]; and concludes with a salutation and the names of the transcribers [s].

We have now examined the whole of the information which pretends to be based on historical evidence. We have not yet said a word about the precise date of Polycarp. If we believe the Martyrium, Polycarp had served Christ eighty-six years. Some take this expression to mean that he was at that time eighty-six years of age. The former is the most likely interpretation. Irenæus mentions that he was exceedingly old. Now we know that he was at Rome in the time of Anicetus, and Eusebius expressly states that he suffered martyrdom in the reign of Verus, that is, of Marcus Antoninus. Marcus Antoninus began to reign in 161, and we must therefore place the martyrdom some time after this. But that we must make this time very short, is evident from the circumstance that he had had intercourse with some of the apostles. Supposing him one hundred at his death, he would then have been born between the years 60 and 70, but he could scarcely have been said to have had intercourse with the apostles if he was only an infant. His intercourse with them must then have taken place between 70 and 80 A.D. If on the other hand we suppose him eighty-six at his death, he must have been born between 70 and 80 A.D., and had the intercourse between 80 and 90 A.D. In any way we are startled either at the great age of the man, or at the possibility of his having intercourse with the apostles. Hence writers have not been satisfied with the date of Eusebius and Jerome—and his martyrdom

[q] c. 20.   [r] c. 21.   [s] c. 22.

has been variously placed at 147, 155, 161, 166, 169, 175, and 178 A.D., all without the slightest authority. The statement of Eusebius is in harmony with the statements of Irenæus; and, if any reliance can be placed on the Martyrium, and commentators be right in their identification of the proconsul Statius Quadratus [t], Polycarp must have perished about the time of Marcus Antoninus.

II. THE WRITINGS OF POLYCARP.

Irenæus mentions the writings of Polycarp twice. The letter to Florinus, already quoted, concludes with this sentence: "This also can be proved from his letters which he sent either to the neighbouring churches confirming them, or to some of the brethren warning them and urging them on [u]." And in his work against heretics he says, "There is also a letter of Polycarp's written to the Philippians of a most satisfactory nature, from which also those who are willing and have a care about their salvation can learn the character of his faith, and the proclamation of the truth [x]." Eusebius himself refers twice to the letter addressed to the Philippians, once in speaking of Ignatius, and on the other occasion he mentions that Polycarp in the letter quotes from the First Epistle of Peter [y]. Jerome farther mentions that this letter was publicly read in his day in Asia. His words are: "Quæ usque hodie in Asiæ conventu legitur." What is meant exactly by the "conventu Asiæ" no one knows. He probably means

---

[t] See Usher's note on c. 21.   [u] In Eus. Hist. Eccl. v. 20.
[x] Iren. adv. Hæres. iii. 3; Eus. Hist. Eccl. iv. 14.
[y] Eus. Hist. Eccl. iv. 14.

simply that the letter was read in the public assemblies of the Asiatic churches.

The genuineness of the letter has been frequently attacked, mostly, however, by writers of the Tübingen school. Schwegler regards it as "a shadow of the pastoral letters written at the same time, (about A.D. 169,) under the same relations and doubtless in the same church circles." He characterises the letter itself as "an extraordinarily poor, weak, unconnected compilation of Old and New Testament passages, a trivial stringing together of commonplaces, liturgical formulas, and moral admonitions; a letter without occasion and object, without individuality and prominent character, without idiosyncrasy in language and ideas, entirely unworthy of the great chief of the churches of Asia Minor[z]."

The circumstances which he and Hilgenfeld have adduced in favour of their opinion, besides the character of the letter, are the frequent mention of heretics in the epistle, the nature of the heresies mentioned, and the number of the heretics. Thus in chapter second Polycarp mentions "the empty vain talk and the error of many," and in chapter seventh the "vanity of many" is again spoken of. These statements indicate a strong direction of the time, according to Schwegler and Hilgenfeld. Then there are clear indications that Polycarp had to deal with decided Docetes and Marcionites. "Whoever," he says, "does not confess that Jesus Christ has come in the flesh, is anti-Christ; and whosoever does not confess the testimony of the cross, is of the Devil; and whosoever treats deceitfully the words of the Lord to suit his own desires, and says there is no

[z] Nachapostolisches Zeitalter, vol. ii. p. 154.

resurrection nor judgment, he is the firstborn of Satan[a]." These last words are supposed to have a personal reference to Marcion, for we know from Irenæus that Polycarp did actually apply the term "firstborn of Satan" to Marcion.

Besides the notices of heresies, appeal is made to the references to Ignatius in chapter thirteenth. There the letters of that martyr are expressly mentioned, and as a late date is assigned to them, any notice of them must be somewhat later.

The only passage which is supposed to give something like a real clue to the date, is one resembling a passage in the First Epistle to Timothy, ch. ii. 2. In runs thus, "Pray for all saints; pray also for the kings (regibus) and powers and princes, and for those who persecute and hate you." Hilgenfeld maintains that the title "kings" could have been used only after there were two emperors on the throne, consequently for the first time only in the reign of Marcus Antoninus [b].

These objections are of no real force against the genuineness of the letter. They are of considerable force against the date generally assigned to its composition. Mention is made of Ignatius in the thirteenth chapter, and the mention is of such a nature that it is plain the letter was written shortly after the martyrdom of that man. But the date commonly assigned to that event is based entirely on a Martyrium which is full of improbabilities; and when we come to examine it, we shall see how utterly unworthy of credit it is in this very particular. There is nothing then to prevent us supposing that the letter was written after Polycarp had visited Rome, and had had interviews with the Marcionites. Hilgenfeld's argu-

[a] c. 7.   [b] See Hilgenfeld's note 4, Apost. Väter, p. 273.

ment, however, from the words "Pray for kings," for assigning this letter to the time of Marcus Antoninus, is entirely destroyed by the circumstance that Justin Martyr not only uses the words ἄρχοντες, as he acknowledges in reference to Antoninus Pius and Marcus Aurelius, but the word βασιλεῖς [c].

Many, while admitting the genuineness of the letter, have taken strong exception to chapter thirteenth. The first that brought forward objections prominently was Daillé [d], in his work on the writings attributed to Dionysius the Areopagite and Ignatius. His objections are two : first, that the chapter is an evident break in the epistle, that it either ought to end with the twelfth chapter, or that chapter thirteenth should be omitted, and chapter fourteenth joined to the twelfth. Second, that in chapter ninth Ignatius is held forth as a martyr in the words, "I exhort you all to obey the word of righteousness, and to practice all patience, which also you saw before your eyes, not only in the blessed Ignatius, Zosimus and Rufus, but also in others of your number, and in Paul himself, and the rest of the apostles, being persuaded that all these did not run in vain, but in faith and righteousness and that they are in the place due to them with the Lord with whom they also suffered. For they did not love the present age, but Him who died for them." While in chapter thirteenth he is spoken of as alive: "With regard to Ignatius himself and those who are with him, give us more certain information if you have got it."

We think Daillé's objections are irrefragable. The first one indeed is not of much consequence; for though there is no connection between chapters twelfth and

[c] Apol. Prim. c. 17. [d] Daillé, p. 427.

thirteenth, yet it is certainly not impossible that Polycarp may not have been able to strike up a connection between the various things which he wished to say. But the second is of a totally different nature. In the ninth chapter Ignatius is spoken of as a martyr—an example to the Philippians of patience. Nay more, he seems to be reckoned among those who came out of the Philippians, and therefore it is likely that the Ignatius known to the Philippians was connected with the Philippian church. In the thirteenth chapter Polycarp requests information with regard to "Ignatius and those with him." These words occur only in the Latin translation of the epistle. To get rid of the difficulty which they present, it has been supposed that the words "de his qui cum eo sunt" are a wrong rendering of the Greek περὶ τῶν μετ' αὐτοῦ. And then the words are supposed to mean "concerning Ignatius (of whose death I heard, but of which I wish particulars) and those who *were* with him." But even the Greek could not be forced into such a meaning as this; and moreover, there is no reason to impugn the Latin translation, except the peculiar difficulty presented by a comparison with the ninth chapter [e].

Ritschl has attempted to show that the letter has been largely interpolated, but his reasons are purely subjective. He maintains that chapter third and parts of chapters eleventh and twelfth are interpolated. He rejects also the passage in chapter ninth, already referred to, and the passage in chapter thirteenth, which we have now discussed. "The interpolations," he informs us, "proceed from the same man who partly interpolated, partly composed,

[e] See Bunsen, Ignatius und seine Zeit, p. 108, who shows very clearly the force of Daillé's objections.

the Ignatian letters." He allows the references to gnosis to remain, and in consequence of them makes the date of the letter lie somewhere between 140 and 168 A.D [f].

Of his other letters no trace has been left. Some indeed suppose that a few extracts from them have come down to us in the Catena of Victor of Capua. But as he quotes them from the Responsiones of Polycarp, and as Irenæus says nothing of this work, we may set them down as spurious. At the best they are entirely unauthenticated, though there is nothing in them greatly opposed to their being the work of Polycarp. Later writers speak of various other productions of Polycarp. Suidas mentions a letter to Dionysius the Areopagite, Maximus a letter to the church of Athens, and a work called $\Delta\iota\delta\alpha\chi\eta$. Pionius, the writer of a Martyrium of Polycarp, attributes other works to him [g]. No one supposes any of these works to have been genuine.

The letter has no express object. Polycarp tells the Philippians that he would not have written of his own accord regarding righteousness, but they had requested him. Polycarp at the same time however refers to a circumstance which had probably considerable influence in leading the Philippians to ask him to write. We gather from the brief exhortations in the letter, that Valens, one of the presbyters in the church at Philippi, had been guilty of adultery. His wife had probably come to the knowledge of the fact, had been examined by the church, and had told lies to save the character of her husband. The knowledge of these circumstances is based however on very little. Polycarp, in the pas-

[f] Die Entstehung der altkath. Kirche, p. 584. Ritschl devotes an appendix to the exhibition of his opinions on the letter of Polycarp.

[g] See Cave's Historia Literaria, vol. i. p. 29.

sage where he refers to this case, urges the Philippians to be chaste and truthful. "I am very sorry," he says, "for Valens, who was made a presbyter among you some time ago, that he is so ignorant of the place which has been given him. I warn you therefore to abstain from adultery, and that ye be chaste and truthful. Abstain from every evil. For he who cannot govern himself in these things, how does he proclaim the truth to another? If any one abstain not from adultery, he will be polluted by idolatry and judged as among Gentiles." Then a little after he says, "I am very sorry for him and his wife. May God give them true repentance." The Latin text has "avaritia" for what we have translated "adultery." It is not impossible that avarice may have been his crime; but the probability is, as has been suggested, that the Greek had πλεονεξία, and that the Latin translator took this word in its usual sense, forgetting that it could also mean adultery, and how appropriate such a use of the word would be in circumstances where the utmost delicacy was necessary, and where Polycarp would feel an anxiety not to be a stumbling-block to a brother who might yet return to the paths of righteousness.

There is no trace of a date in the letter, except in the chapter which we have rejected as an interpolation. How far the mention of the heresies to which we have alluded determines its date, may be questioned; but the great probability is, that it was written after Polycarp had engaged in the work of converting the Marcionites, as we have noticed already. He speaks of the church in Philippi as having existed in early times, as having known God before the Smyrneans knew Him [h],

[h] c. 11.

and as having had Paul for their teacher. We gather, however, that the generation whom Paul had taught had passed away. He preached "to the men who then were."

The letter is of great importance in regard to the history of the New Testament. Polycarp has made several most distinct quotations from Peter and Paul. The subject is discussed hereafter. There is also a most striking resemblance between some parts of the letter of Polycarp and that of Clemens to the Corinthians. The resemblance however does not warrant us in supposing either that Polycarp knew Clemens's letter, or the converse. This resemblance occurs in passages which relate to the common thoughts and precepts of the early Christians.

The letter has not much literary merit, but it has much that is really noble, and it is pervaded by a true Christian spirit. It is remarkably simple and earnest. We have already quoted the criticism of Schwegler, and we only remark now in regard to it, that it is akin to that of his master Baur, who speaks in the most depreciating terms of one of the noblest of Paul's letters, the letter to the Philippians, so full of deep love and glowing devotion to Christ and his Church, and so touching in the kind words which flow from the bold, determined, unflinching preacher of righteousness and liberty.

There is not much to be said of the theology of Polycarp. Those who suppose different schools of early Christianity are as usual divided in their opinions as to which Polycarp should belong. Some compare his epistle with that of Clemens, and set him down in the same school. Others attempt, with entire want of success, to show that its theology is akin to that of the Ignatian letters, for they are forced to confess that there are great and striking differences[i].

III. ABSTRACT OF THE LETTER.

The letter opens thus: " Polycarp and the elders with him to the Church of God which sojourns in Philippi, mercy to you and peace from Almighty God and the Lord Jesus Christ our Saviour be multiplied." Polycarp expresses his joy in them because they had received those who were in bonds for Christ, and because the firm root of their faith bore fruit for Jesus Christ[k]. He therefore urges them to serve God with fear, believing on Him who raised Christ from the dead, and who will raise them also if they walk in his commandments. He at the same time describes to them the course of conduct acceptable to God[l]. He does not take it upon him to write these exhortations of his own accord; they had urged him. He could not attain to the wisdom of the blessed and glorious Paul, who taught them personally the word of truth, and in his absence from them wrote to them letters, in which if they were to look eagerly, they might be built up in faith, hope, and love[m]. The love of money is the beginning of evils. We must therefore arm ourselves with the weapons of righteousness, teaching ourselves first to walk in the commandment of the Lord, our wives to be content with their husbands and to train their children in the fear of the Lord, and widows to be free from evil-speaking and other vices[n]. He then describes what

---

[i] See Hilgenfeld, Apost. Väter, p. 273. [k] c. 1.
[l] c. 2.   [m] c. 3   [n] c. 4.

ought to be the character of deacons and of the younger men [o], and of presbyters. Then he urges the duty of forgiveness of sins, but cautions them against false brethren, who lead astray vain men [p]; "for every one that does not confess that Jesus Christ has come in the flesh is anti-Christ." He mentions other forms of false teaching which they were to avoid, and he exhorts them to fast and to pray to God not to lead them into temptation [q]. Then he advises them to cling to Jesus Christ, who endured all things that we might live in Him; He is to be our pattern [r]. They were therefore to be patient, according to the example which they had received, not only from Ignatius and Zosimus and Rufus, but also from Paul and the rest of the apostles, for they did not love the present age, but Him who died for them [s]. They were then to follow the example of the Lord, to love one another and do good, so that the Lord might not be evil spoken of among them [t]. Polycarp expresses his great sorrow for Valens, that had been made a presbyter among the Philippians. He warns them all to be on their guard against adultery, and to be chaste and truthful; he had found no such vice among the Philippians. He hopes God will give Valens and his wife true repentance, and that they will look on them as erring members, not as enemies [u]. He hopes that they are well exercised in the sacred writings, and he prays that God may build them up in faith and truth. Then he mentions for whom they ought to pray [x]; then he mentions more particularly their letter, and that of Ignatius to him, promises to do what they ask him,

[o] c. 5. [p] c. 6. [q] c. 7. [r] c. 8. [s] c. 9. [t] c. 10. [u] c. 11. [x] c. 12.

and requests more particular information regarding Ignatius[y]. He mentions that he writes the letter through Crescens, and recommends him and his sister to the Philippians. The letter concludes: "Grace be with you all. Amen."

IV. THE DOCTRINES OF THE LETTER.

God.—The teaching of Polycarp with regard to God is entirely of a practical nature, and occurs only in a practical connection. He calls God almighty when wishing that the church in Philippi might have mercy and peace multiplied to them from Him[z]. He states that nothing escapes the notice of God—neither reasonings, nor thoughts, nor any of the concealed things of the heart—in order to urge the widows to be free from every evil[a]. God also is not mocked, and therefore men ought to walk worthily of God's commandment and glory[b]. "We are before the eyes of God" is also given as a reason for the performance of duty[c]; and he urges them to pray to the all-seeing God not to lead them into temptation[d]; his omniscience thus being a security for their spiritual safety. God's will also is spoken of as the cause of salvation to men, and men are to put their trust in Him[e]. It was He who raised Christ, and will raise those who walk in his commandments[f]; He will also punish the disobedient[g].

Christ.—There is no direct statement of the divinity of Christ. Routh has fancied that in one passage there is an express declaration, but he does not attri-

[y] c. 13. [z] c. 1. [a] c. 4. [b] c. 5. [c] c. 6.
[d] c. 7. [e] c. 1. [f] c. 2. [g] Ibid.

bute certainty to his rendering [h]. The passage is, "For we are before the eyes of the Lord and God [i];" he evidently translates it, "For we are before the eyes of the Lord, even God [k]." If this were the correct translation, then the word 'Lord' would unquestionably refer only to God, as in the usual phrase 'the Lord God,' and we should have no reference at all to Christ. The probability is, however, that the word 'Lord' indicates Christ, and 'God' God the Father. This coupling of God and Christ together is frequent in this epistle: "Mercy from God and the Lord Jesus Christ [l];" Christians are "chosen by God and our Lord [m];" "Men are to put their faith in the Lord Jesus Christ and his Father [n];" "Deacons of God and Christ [o];" "Obedient to presbyters and deacons as to God and Christ [p]." It will be noticed too that in this coupling Christ is sometimes indicated by the word 'Lord.' This word occurs several times, but on every occasion we may apply it to Christ, and on most we must so apply it. The ambiguous cases are two—where mention is made of walking in the commandment of the Lord, and where Polycarp hopes the Lord may give a change of mind to the erring Valens and his wife [q]. In the first instance we most naturally think of God as Lord, in the latter we think most naturally of Christ as being Lord of the Church in a peculiar sense.

[h] He says simply, "Christ alone seems to be meant by these words." Script. Eccl. Opusc. vol. i. p. 26.

[i] The Latin translator omits 'Dei' altogether, and one has 'Dei' alone.

[k] c. 6.   [l] c. 1.   [m] Ibid.   [n] c. 12.   [o] c. 5.

[p] Ibid. This coupling occurs so frequently, that we doubt whether the hand of an interpolator has not been at work.

[q] c. 11.

Of Christ's peculiar relation to the Father only one passage speaks. He is called Jesus Christ the Son of God[r]. Nothing is said of his pre-existence, but it is asserted that the prophets foretold his coming, and that the apostles preached it[s]. With regard to the honour due to Him, we shall speak in mentioning the relation in which He stands to Christians.

His coming to earth is maintained as real, and the man who denies his real humanity is pronounced anti-Christ[t]; and He is said to have become the servant of all. Nothing is said of his life on earth, but a quotation is made from the New Testament in which his sinlessness is asserted[u]. Frequent mention is made of his death. It is spoken of as a wonderful instance of patient endurance, and as such worthy of our imitation[x]. They are said to glorify Him who suffer on account of his name[y]. The object which He had in dying is expressed in various ways. It is represented as the taking away of sins: "He bore to go up even to death, on account of our sins[z];" "He carried away our sins in his own body up to the tree[a]." It is also represented as the source of life: "He endured all things that we might live through Him[b]." The same idea is really implied in the statement that Christ is the earnest of our righteousness[c]. There is also a more general expression of the object of his death, when He is described as having died on our behalf ($\dot{\upsilon}\pi\grave{\epsilon}\rho$ $\dot{\eta}\mu\hat{\omega}\nu$), and having been raised on our account[d] ($\delta\iota'$ $\dot{\eta}\mu\hat{a}s$). The cross is referred to in the puzzling assertion, that "whosoever shall not confess the testimony of the cross is from the devil[e]." The testimony of the cross most

[r] c. 12. [s] c. 6. [t] c. 7. [u] c. 8. [x] Ibid. [y] Ibid.
[z] c. 1. [a] c. 8. [b] Ibid. [c] Ibid. [d] c. 9. [e] c. 7.

probably means the witness borne by Christ to the utter vanity of this sinful age, and the necessity of righteousness and obedience to God. It has been most variously interpreted—the truth of the cross[f], Christ's sufferings on the cross, &c.

The resurrection of Christ is mentioned several times, and is always attributed to God's power: "Whom God raised, loosing the pangs of death[g];" "He who raised Christ from the dead[h]." The honours and universal sway awarded Him after his resurrection are also mentioned: "Him who raised our Lord Jesus Christ from the dead, and gave Him glory and a throne on his right hand, to whom all heavenly and earthly things are subjected, whom every breath serves[i]." Of his action in heaven, apart from his present influence on men, nothing is said unless it be implied in the designation "eternal priest[k]." These words apply far more probably, however, to the purifying influence which He continually exercises on his people, cleansing them from their sins, and presenting them pure to God.

With regard to his action on men now, it has been already noticed that mercy and peace and election to salvation are spoken of as coming from God and Christ. A change of mind we also saw attributed to his power, and He is alluded to as forgiving sins[l]. His future action is consonant with these powers; He is to be the judge of the living and dead[m]. We must stand before the judgment-seat of Christ[n]; we are therefore bound at

---

[f] See note on the passage in Jacobson.
[g] c. 1.   [h] cc. 2, 12.   [i] c. 2.   [k] c. 12.
[l] c. 6. The word 'Lord' is here used, so that there may be some uncertainty with regard to the application of the passage to Christ, but the context is decidedly in favour of this view.
[m] c. 2.   [n] c. 6.

present to follow his example, to serve Him, to put our confidence in Him and God, and our confidence must bear fruit to Him [o]. If we thus obey Him, and please Him in this age, we shall receive the age to come [p]. He has promised to raise us from the dead, and if we live in a manner worthily of Him, and place our faith in Him, we shall yet reign with Him [q].

Throughout the whole letter there is not a single allusion to Christ's rescuing us from any suffering or penalty of sin. Salvation of such a nature may be implied in the statements of Polycarp, but there is no reason to suppose that he for a moment thought of the relief from pain. His mind glows with the thought of being relieved from sin. The only occasions on which the idea of suffering comes to the mind of the writer, are when he denounces those who refuse to put their faith in Christ: "God will seek Christ's blood from those who disobey Him [r];" and when a woe is pronounced on those through whom the name of the Lord is evil spoken of [s].

Spirit.—Polycarp does not mention the Holy Spirit. He quotes from Peter's First Epistle the words "Every lust wars against the spirit," but spirit there clearly means the spiritual nature of man, and Peter has actually ψυχή.

Angels.—No mention is made of angels. The devil is mentioned, as we have seen, under the name of devil and Satan, and as having a first-born and other children.

Sin.—No mention is made of original sin, but the universal sinfulness of man is to be inferred from the statement, "We are all debtors of sin [t]." He of course means the Smyrnean Church and the Philippian; but

[o] c. 1.   [p] c. 5.   [q] Ibid.   [r] c. 2.   [s] c. 10.   [t] c. 6.

the remark could not have been made, except on the hypothesis of universal sinfulness.

Salvation.—Rescue from this state of sin is the result of God's willing it through Jesus Christ. "Knowing that ye are saved by favour, not from works but by the will of God through Jesus Christ [u]." The condition of one who is saved is one of confidence in God and Christ. Those who believe in Christ rejoice with joy inexpressible [x], while he urges them to serve God with fear and truth, leaving their vain talk and trusting in Him who raised our Lord from the dead [y]. We have a still more exact description of faith and love. "Through the letters of Paul," says Polycarp, "you will be able to be built up into the faith given you, which is the mother of us all, hope following and love going before, love towards God and Christ and one's neighbour. If any one be within these, he has fulfilled the law of righteousness, for he that has love is far from every sin [z]." In various passages he describes what the Christian should avoid, giving particular counsel to presbyters and deacons, young men, wives, widows, and virgins—all presenting a noble picture of that life which had been revealed from heaven.

The Church.—The overseer of a church is not mentioned in this letter, and as Polycarp directs his counsels to presbyters and deacons and almost every conceivable class in the church, the inference is very probable that either there was no overseer or that the overseers were identical with one of the classes mentioned. There is not much to identify any of the classes mentioned with the overseers, but since we know that the overseers

[u] c. 1.   [x] Ibid.   [y] c. 2.   [z] c. 3.

and the presbyters are the same in Clemens's letter and the same in the New Testament, there is an extreme probability that they are the same here too. The evidence for their identity in this letter is that the duties assigned to the presbyters are exactly the duties assigned in other writings to the overseers, and that oversight is one of these. The presbyters are to be "compassionate," merciful to all, turning back those who have strayed, taking the oversight of all the sick, not neglecting the widow, or the orphan, or the needy[a]."

Besides this, we must regard Polycarp himself as a presbyter. The commencement of the letter leads us to infer this: "Polycarp and those who with him are elders." It might possibly mean "Polycarp and elders who are with him," but this is not a likely translation of the words[b], and certainly disagrees with the Latin translation. Then, in the chapter quoted, Polycarp passes from addressing the presbyters in the third person to the first: "Not stern in judgment, knowing that we are all debtors of sin." Of course the overseers might be included among or along with the presbyters and yet not be the same, but when we have no intimation of a difference, the presumption is that there is identity. Nor is any inference to be drawn from the circumstances that Polycarp's name appears at the head of the letter. Polycarp's advice was asked, not that of the church[c].

The reason urged for Polycarp's not describing himself as overseer, and not alluding to the duties of the over-

[a] c. 6.

[b] The Greek is, Πολύκαρπος καὶ οἱ σὺν αὐτῷ πρεσβύτεροι: the Latin, "Polycarpus et qui cum eo sunt presbyteri."

[c] Dorner's opinion on this subject I take to be unwarranted. Die Lehre von der Person Christi, vol. i. p. 173, note.

seer, is drawn from the modesty of the man[d]. He would not persume to give directions as to what the overseer should do. But this reason surely will not hold in that passage where he urges the young men to refrain from all vices, and to be "subject to presbyters and deacons as to God and Christ[e]." Surely the modesty of the man would not have prevented him from asking the young men to be subject to the bishop. In fact, if ever there was opportunity for introducing with honour a bishop, this was the occasion. Indeed, the passage sounds like one of those hierarchical revelations which we have in the pseudo-Ignatius. It merely sounds like it, however, for the meaning of it plainly is that the young men were to listen to the counsels and advices of the wise and holy presbyters and deacons, as being based upon God's law and being a duty to God and Christ. There is no more attribution of dignity to the presbyters and deacons in this passage than there is to masters in Eph. vi. 5: "Servants, obey your masters in the flesh as Christ, with fear and trembling in the simplicity of your heart."

Presbyters and deacons are the only office-bearers spoken of in the church. We do not learn what were the duties of the deacons, nor are we at all to regard the summary of the duties of the presbyters as exhaustive. It is worthy of remark that no notice is taken of preaching.

No mention by name is made of any of the office-bearers in the church of Philippi, with the exception of Valens. The letter is written at the request of the church, and Polycarp recommends to the brethren

---

[d] Rothe, Anfänge, p. 410; Hefele in loc.   [e] c. 5.

Crescens through whom he sends the epistle, and his sister. In dealing also with the case of Valens he does not address any one in particular, but trusts they will act gently towards him in hopes of winning back their erring brother.

No light is thrown on any of the customs of the early church. Fasts are alluded to[f], but they are entirely private and at the will of the individual. We discover the existence of false brethren—men who bear the name of the Lord in hypocrisy and mislead vain men[g].

Future State.—We have already quoted a few of the passages that refer to the future state, the judgment-seat of Christ, God's raising up of those who obey Him, and His vengeance on those who disobey Him. It is further stated that fornicators will not inherit the kingdom of God[h]; while it is said of Paul and others "that they are in the place due to them, with the Lord, with whom also they suffered[i]." Polycarp quotes Paul's assertion that the saints shall judge the world[k].

Scriptures.—Polycarp speaks of the sacred writings, but in such a way that no information is given with regard to the books that were meant by the term. "I trust," he says, "that you are exercised in the sacred writings." He regards the prophets as really foretelling future events[l]. He quotes the Psalms twice, but does not introduce his extracts as quotations. Once indeed the words as they stand now do intimate that the passages adduced are Scriptures. The passage occurs only in the Latin translation, and has been variously read and variously construed. It is as follows: "Confido

---

[f] c. 7. See Heyns's Commentatio, p. 69.
[g] c. 6.   [h] c. 5.   [i] c. 9.   [k] c. 11.   [l] c. 6.

enim vos bene exercitatos esse in sacris literis, et nihil vos latet ; mihi autem non est concessum. Modo, ut his Scripturis dictum est, Irascimini et nolite peccare, et sol non occidat super iracundiam vestram :" " For I trust that ye are well exercised in sacred literature, and that nothing escapes you, but to me it has not been granted. Only, as has been said in these writings, 'Be angry and sin not,' and 'Let not the sun go down upon your wrath.'" The first quotation is from Ps. iv. 5, and the second from Eph. iv. 26. The plain inference from this reading is that Eph. iv. 26 forms part of the Scriptures; but such an application of the word Scripture as meaning the Old Testament and part of the New looks like a corruption or an interpolation. One of the MSS. thus exhibits the words : " Non est concessum uti his Scripturis dictum est enim :" " It is not permitted to use these Scriptures, for it has been said,"—which does not make a whit better sense than the other. Many expedients have been devised to throw light upon this passage, all of them unsatisfactory, and perhaps the same may justly be said of the following method. I should be inclined to suppose "ut dictum est his Scripturis" an addition of the Latin translator, and I should read " Confido autem—nihil enim non concessum est ;—modo irascimini :" " I trust you know the Scriptures and nothing escapes you—for there is nothing which God has not granted. (Comp. 1 John ii. 20, 'Ye know all things.') Only take care of your frame of mind—Be angry and sin not."

These are all the allusions to the Old Testament. He quotes also from an apocryphal book, Tobit, as usual without mentioning that it is a quotation[m].

[m] c. 10.

Pertaining to the New we have the following circumstances. Polycarp quotes the words of the Lord, twice in close agreement with Matthew, and once in exact agreement with Matthew and Mark.

Acts.—There is an exact quotation from the speech of Peter as given in Acts ii. 24.

Peter's Letters.—There is a nearly exact quotation from 1 Pet. i. 8, and exact quotations from 1 Pet. i. 21, 1 Pet. ii. 12, 22, 24, 1 Pet. iii. 9; and 1 Pet. i. 13 and 1 Pet. ii. 11 are also most probably quoted.

Some have supposed an allusion in ch. iii. to the Second Epistle of Peter, but the points of resemblance are too distant and common-place.

Letters of Paul.—We have already found an exact quotation from Eph. iv. 26, and we have a nearly exact quotation from Eph. ii. 8, 9. Polycarp quotes 1 Cor. vi. 2 exactly, and we have a maimed quotation from the same Epistle, 1 Cor. vi. 9, 10. There is a probable reference to Gal. i. 1, and Gal. iv. 26 is quoted but applied to faith. Gal. vi. 7 is also exactly quoted.

A resemblance to 1 Tim. vi. 10 occurs, and we have an exact quotation from 1 Tim. vi. 7. There is a probable allusion to 2 Tim. ii. 12.

We have probable references to Rom. xii. 17 or 2 Cor. viii. 21, and to Rom. xiv. 10, 12.

An almost exact quotation is made from 2 Thess. iii. 15.

Most probably 1 John iv. 3 is quoted. None of these quotations are proof of any authority being ascribed to the New Testament books. Indeed, as Polycarp does not mention the sources from which he derives his information, and as he had access to apostles and men who had heard and seen Christ, we are not warranted in supposing that he derived his knowledge from our

Gospels or that he knew the words of Peter's speech from the Acts. But these quotations prove conclusively that he was well acquainted with the First Epistle of Peter, and we have strong probability that he knew the second letter of Paul to the Thessalonians, the first letter to the Corinthians, the letter to the Ephesians, to the Galatians, to the Romans, and the first letter to Timothy. There is also probability, though not nearly so great, that he knew the second letter to Timothy and the First Epistle of John.

In making a quotation from the sayings of Jesus, Polycarp introduces it with the words, "As the Lord said," or "As the Lord said teaching." The only exception to this is where he welds a part of the Lord's Prayer into one of his sentences. In the case of all other quotations he goes on as if they were not quotations. They seem to come spontaneously and suitably, and he adds no authority to their truth. There is one apparent exception. In quoting 1 Cor. vi. 2 the writer adds, "as Paul teaches." But as this occurs in the Latin translation [n], and as it is the only instance of an author's name being mentioned, Credner has justly suspected it to be the addition of the translator.

Polycarp, however, makes an express reference to the letters of Paul. He declares that he is not able "to follow the wisdom of the blessed and glorious Paul, who when among you taught accurately and securely the reason with regard to the truth face to face with the men then living; who also when absent wrote letters to you, which if you study ye will be able to be built up into the faith given to you, which is the mother of us all [o]."

[n] c. 11.   [o] c. 3.

This expression 'letters' has caused a good deal of discussion. The most natural interpretation is that Paul wrote several letters, and the immense probability is that he did write oftener than once to a church so much beloved. At the same time clear proof has been adduced that ἐπιστολαί has been used even by the best Greek writers when speaking only of one letter [p].

Morality.—We have already spoken of the morality contained in these letters. We remark one thing only, the exhortation similar to one already noticed in Clemens, to wives to be content with their own husbands, and to love all others equally in continence (ἀγαπώσας πάντας ἐξ ἴσου ἐν πάσῃ ἐγκρατείᾳ [q]). The letter is from beginning to end moral; and if we were to exhibit its morality fully, we should have to translate the whole of it. It is far too much to say, however, as Rössler and Balthasar have said, that Polycarp has given an exposition of the whole of Christian doctrine, theoretical and practical [r].

V. LITERATURE.

Most of the codices in which the Epistle of Polycarp occurs will be noticed in the references to the Epistle of Barnabas. They are Cod. Vat. 859, Ottobonianus 348, Codex Casanatensis, G. v. 14, Codex Mediceus, Plut. vii. num. 21, and MS. Barberinum [s]. There are also two manuscripts of the Latin translation in the Vatican:

[p] See Jacobson's note on the passage.   [q] c. 4.

[r] Junius, Comment, p. 82.

[s] Besides these, Jacobson has collated Cod. Bibl. Reg. Paris (formerly Colbertinus), which is said to be of the fourteenth century. Dressel marks it Codex Parisinus 937, and as of the sixteenth century. (Prolegg. xxxvii.)

one Cod. Reg. 81, reckoned to belong to the ninth century; the other is the Codex Palatinus 150, from which Dressel obtained a new translation of the Pastor of Hermas. It belongs to the fourteenth century. There is also a Latin translation in the Medicean Library, called by Jacobson, who collated it, Cod. 20, Plut. xxiii. Bibl. Mediceo-Laurentianæ. It is attributed by Bandinius to the fifteenth century.

EDITIONS.

The epistle of Polycarp was first printed in the Latin translation only by Jacobus Faber (Stapulensis), Paris 1498, fol. The Latin translation was after that frequently reprinted. The first Greek copy did not appear till 1633, when it was edited by Halloix from the copy of Sirmond in his Illustrium Orientalis Ecclesiæ Scriptorum Vitæ et Documenta. Usher published a new edition (London 1647) from the copy of Andreas Schottus, which Vossius had compared with the edition of Halloix. It appeared after that in the collections of Cotelerius, Le Moyne, Ittigius, Frey, Russel, and Gallandi. Both the letters and the Martyrium appeared in the editions of the Ignatian letters published by Aldrich, Oxford 1708, and Thomas Smith (1709.)

It has appeared in more modern times in the collections of Hefele, Reithmayr, Lindner, Jacobson, and Dressel. And Routh has edited it with notes in his Scriptorum Ecclesiasticorum Opuscula. The best edition is that of Jacobson. Dressel's text is furnished with the most careful critical apparatus, and a good recension of the ancient Latin version from the two Vatican codices.

CHAPTER IV.

THE EPISTLE OF BARNABAS.

I. THE AUTHORSHIP.

THE Epistle of Barnabas has always been reckoned among the writings of the Apostolical Fathers: but how far it deserves to be placed among the earliest writings of the Christian Church, has been and still is subject of much discussion. The most important point to be determined is its authorship. The production itself bears no name and gives no clue to its writer. The Latin translation of it contains no inscription. A few of the Greek manuscripts have either in their inscription or subscription, "The Letter of the Apostle Barnabas;" the Greek of Tischendorf has simply, "The Epistle of Barnabas."

The external evidence is unanimous in ascribing it to Barnabas, the companion of Paul. The letter is first mentioned by Clemens Alexandrinus, who expressly refers to it seven times [a], and quotes largely from it. The writer is called the Apostle Barnabas, and he is described as the person "who preached along with Paul the gospel in the service of the Gentiles," κατὰ τὴν διακονίαν τῶν ἐθνῶν). The next writer who quotes the letter is Origen,

---

[a] Strom. ii. 6. p. 445; 7. p. 447; 15. p. 464; 18. p. 472; 20. p. 489; v. 8. p. 677; 10. p. 683. The passages are quoted in Hefele, Prolegomena.

who calls it "a catholic epistle [b]." He says nothing about Barnabas himself. These two are the principal witnesses. But in noticing the early testimonies we have to consider statements of Eusebius and Jerome. The words of Eusebius are, "Among the spurious (νόθοις) let there be set down the writings of the Acts of Paul, and the so-called Shepherd, and the revelation of Peter, and in addition to these the well-known letter of Barnabas, and the so-called teachings of the apostles [c]." The word νόθος [d] suggests the idea that Eusebius held the production not to be the genuine work of Barnabas: but there can be no doubt that Eusebius did not mean this. In the next sentence but one he expressly declares these writings to belong to the ἀντιλεγόμενα, works for which some claimed inspiration, but which were generally regarded as not inspired. Jerome says the same thing: "Barnabas the Cyprian, the same as Joseph the Levite, ordained an apostle to the Gentiles along with Paul, composed one letter tending to the edification of the Church, which is read among apocryphal writings [e]." Whether Eusebius and Jerome regarded the letter of Barnabas as genuine is not expressly stated. From the decided way in which Jerome speaks, "Barnabas composed a letter," it is most probable that he regarded that person as its real author. There is no obstacle to this opinion in an accidental mistake which Jerome has made in attributing a passage

[b] Contr. Cels. i. 63; De Princip. iii. c. 2.

[c] Euseb. Hist. Eccl. iii. 25.

[d] Henke, p. 19 ff.

[e] De Viris Illustr. ch. 6. On the use of the term apocryphus here see Ernestus Henke, De Epistolæ quæ Barnabæ tribuitur authentia commentatio (Jenæ 1827), p. 12 ff., and the authorities quoted there, especially Pearson.

from the letters of Barnabas to Ignatius: Hieron. adv. Pelag. iii. 2. p. 783. The name Ignatius is blank in the Vatican MS.

This is the external evidence. Clemens Alexandrinus is the only writer that expressly identifies the author of the epistle with Barnabas the companion of Paul. Origen and Jerome were most probably of the same opinion. And nowhere is a contrary opinion expressed. But that there were doubts with regard to its genuineness, or at least that the early Christians felt that the genuineness was not established by good evidence, we may justly infer from its position among apocryphal writings. It is difficult to believe that the early Christians would have rejected as uninspired the production of a man who was recognized by the Apostles as a God-inspired man, who had received a special mission along with Paul to the Gentiles, and who stood forward so prominently among the apostles of the Lord. There must have been some strong reasons for doubting the genuineness of the work, though these reasons have not been recorded.

Another circumstance must be noted in weighing the external evidence. Clemens Alexandrinus quotes several works as if they were genuine, though when discussing them he allows they were spurious. Thus he speaks of Peter in his revelation saying such and such a thing, though he must have believed that the Apostle Peter was not the author [f]. This circumstance permits us to suppose that Clemens may have used the name Barnabas merely as a convenience for quotation; but when we consider that he not merely uses the name Barnabas,

[f] Eclogæ Proph. 41, 48, 49.

but describes him as the companion of Paul, and seems to attach weight to the statement, we are forced to the conviction that Clemens unquestionably believed the apostolical Barnabas to be the real author.

Some indeed have supposed that Clemens varied in his opinion with regard to the genuineness of the work. They ground this idea on the supposition that they find in the works of Clemens a want of that respect for the opinion of Barnabas which we should expect he would pay to the work of an apostle[g]. The two passages which are adduced in proof of this want of respect are Pædag. II. x. 84. p. 221. Pott., and Strom. II. xv. 67. p. 464. Pott. In the first, Clemens censures some inaccuracies in natural history which occur in the epistle of Barnabas. But as he does not mention Barnabas by name, we cannot say expressly that he intentionally accuses Barnabas of error. And besides this, Clemens held that an apostle might go wrong in mere outward things, such as natural history facts, without his authority as a spiritual guide being in the slightest degree impaired. Clemens in this very instance agrees with the spiritual interpretation of Barnabas while rejecting his facts. In the second passage Clemens gives three allegorical interpretations of the first psalm, one of them being found in Barnabas. Some have supposed Clemens to shew a want of respect for Barnabas in preferring another interpretation to his. But the inference is groundless. Clemens would allow

---

[g] Cotelerius, Patres Apost. i. p. 6; Hug as referred to by Hefele in his Sendschreiben des Apostels Barnabas aufs neue untersucht, übersetzt und erklärt, Tübingen 1840, p, 151. This work contains an admirable exposition and examination of all the interesting points with regard to Barnabas, his life, and his letter.

the possibility of the three interpretations being correct, and he therefore is very far from impugning the authority of Barnabas in mentioning another interpretation which seemed to penetrate more completely into the spiritual idea of the psalm [h].

The external evidence is then decidedly in favour of the authorship by the Apostle Barnabas, yet it is scanty and not that of contemporaries.

The internal evidence is conclusive against the authorship of Barnabas. The few facts which are related of Barnabas are just such as make it next to impossible that Barnabas could have written this letter. Barnabas, we are told in the Acts, was a Levite; we are told also that he was sent to reconcile the Jewish Christians and the heathen Christians; we know also that he was an intimate friend and companion of Paul, and must have known and agreed with Paul's opinions regarding Judaism. And we know also that in the only difference he had with Paul on the subject of Judaism, he erred in too great attachment to the Jewish party [i]. We thus ascertain pretty clearly that Barnabas as a Levite must have been intimately acquainted with the rites of Judaism; we know also that he did not despise these rites, but looked upon them as preliminary to the freer dispensation of Christ; that he sympathized alike with the adherence of the Jewish Christians to the Jewish rites, and with the desire of the Gentiles to be free from the burden of the law; and we cannot but deem it as certain, even should it not be true that he was one of the Seventy, that he knew well that Christ had submitted to the performance of the Jewish rites, that

[h] Hilgenfeld, Apost. Väter, p. 44. [i] Gal. ii. 13.

some of the best apostles had done the same, and we also rest assured that he had himself as a Jewish Christian still kept up his attendance at the temple when in Jerusalem. Now the writer of the epistle before us snaps all historical connexion between Judaism and Christianity. The performance of the Jewish rites, according to him, was not introductory and educatory, but a gross sin, a misconception of the true meaning of the law, a carnal instead of a spiritual interpretation of the Divine will. The Jews might have been partakers of God's covenant, but even at the law-giving they showed themselves unworthy, and ever after that the covenant belonged not to them, but was reserved for Christians. There were a few brilliant exceptions to the general mass of Jews—Moses, and David, and the prophets, who saw into the Divine meaning and spiritual force of the law; but the Jews never understood the law aright. Therefore Christ came to consummate their sins, and to give the covenant to others. Here is a fundamental difference between Barnabas and the writer of this epistle—a difference which pervades the whole of the epistle, and which shows itself in every chapter and particular head of the subject, in the writer's views of the offerings of the temple, of the sabbath, and of the temple itself. This difference seems to me quite sufficient to settle the whole matter. It is just possible that Barnabas may have changed his opinions, and lost all his knowledge of Judaism, and sympathy with its better side; and it is just possible that he may have written this letter in his dotage; but the possibility is one of which the highest degree of improbability may be safely predicated. Here then the external and internal evidence is at variance, but the external is so worthless that we cannot for a moment hesitate to follow the internal.

We have now set forth the main point. But the evidence against the authorship of Barnabas, as might be expected, lies thick in every page. We shall set down the principal of the objections which have been urged.

First and most remarkable are the numerous mistakes and inaccuracies that characterize the writer's statements with regard to the facts of Judaism. 1. He thus describes the ceremonies on the great Day of Atonement: "What then says he in the prophet? 'And let them eat of the goat which is offered in the fast for all the sins.' Attend carefully: 'And let all the priests alone eat the entrails unwashed with vinegar[j].'" And he quotes another passage thus: "'Take two goats, good and like, and offer them, and let the priests take the one as a burnt-offering for sins.' What then are they to do with the other? 'Cursed is this one,' says he. Notice how the type of Jesus is here presented: 'And all ye spit upon it, and pierce it, and put scarlet wool around its head, and thus let it be sent into the wilderness.' And when this has been done, he who bears the goat drives it into the wilderness, and takes away the wool, and places it on an herb called rachie[k]." Then Barnabas goes on to show how these goats are a type of Christ, the one led to the altar a type of Christ crucified, and the other sent into the wilderness a type of Christ destined to return to the world in glory, and like goats were chosen that the identity of the crucified Jesus with the risen Jesus might be recognized. Now if the reader turns to Leviticus, chapters xvi. and xxiii., where the

[j] c. 7.   [k] Ibid.

ceremonies of the Day of Atonement are prescribed, he will fail to find most of the passages which the writer has quoted, and he will find some statements contradictory of them. Thus no one was allowed to eat on the Day of Atonement, neither people nor priests. Lev. xxiii. 29. Then in Lev. xvi. 27 we are told that every part of the goat was burned; no portions were excepted. Again, nothing is said of the similarity of the goats, or of the spitting upon and pricking of the scape-goat. And on all these points the Talmud speaks only more conclusively against Barnabas, because condescending to more minute particulars. According to it, the priests had not only to fast on the Day of Atonement but on the day before, and the scape-goat was not merely not spit upon and pricked, but very special injunctions are given not to let the slightest injury come near it. In Leviticus nothing is said of a man carrying the goat, or of wool being wound round its head. The Talmud, however, expressly mentions the red wool, but the wool was not taken off the goat. One part of it was put round the goat, the other was to be laid on the rock over which the goat was precipitated. The writer of this letter knows nothing of such a termination to the goat [1]. Now the argument from this mistake is surely a strong one. Here is a rite described in Leviticus, with which description Barnabas must have been well acquainted; he had no doubt compared the statements in the law with the actual performance of the rite according to Pharisaic tradition, which he had witnessed often in Jerusalem. He must have known very well both the biblical mode and the traditional mode. How then

[1] See Hefele, Sendschreiben, &c., p. 67, for a full exposition of the mistakes.

could he be the author of a production in which statements contradictory and divergent from both are given? In fact, we may go farther and affirm that the writer was neither accurately acquainted with the text of the law nor had ever seen the celebration of the Day of Atonement.

2. In an exposition of the red cow as a type of Christ, the writer makes the following statements[m]:—That men in whom sins are complete, were ordered to offer up a heifer and burn it, that three children were then to lift the ashes and put them into vessels, then twine purple wool and hyssop round a rod, and that thus the children were to sprinkle the people one by one, that they might be purified from their sins. If Numb. xix. be examined, we find that the ashes of a red heifer were used, not to purify the people in general, but only those who had become impure by touching dead bodies; that there is not a word of men who were great sinners presenting the animal, but, on the contrary, that it was presented by men who, being clean, became unclean simply by performing this ceremony; and it was not children but a clean person that was to sprinkle with the ashes of the heifer the unclean person and everything connected with him; and that Barnabas omits all notice of the principal ceremony—the priest taking of her blood with his finger and sprinkling it directly before the tabernacle of the congregation seven times. It is scarcely possible to conceive such mistakes to have been committed by a person like Barnabas, so thoroughly acquainted with the law; and we may safely affirm it to be most improbable. Indeed, the account could not have been written by any one who had seen the cere-

[m] c. 8.

mony, for it is not merely at variance with the Bible, but at utter variance with the Talmud, which directs expressly that priests only take part in the ceremony, that they be kept clean for seven days previous, and excepts boys who have not reached the age of intelligence taking any part even in the sprinkling [n].

3. The other mistake is of a different nature. The writer remarks [o]: "The Scripture says, Abraham circumcised of his house 318 men." The passage is nowhere to be found. But there is unquestionably a mistake in the statement, for Abraham had 318 slaves born in his own house when he went against the five kings to rescue Lot, and as it is also stated that he circumcised not only the men born in his house, but also those bought with money of the stranger, the number he circumcised must have been greater. This is not the only blunder which the writer commits here; he has made an oversight which is far more decisive against the authorship of Barnabas than a mere lapse of memory. The writer allegorizes on this number as if the Old Testament had been written in Greek. The Greek letters being used for numbers, he finds in 318 the name of Jesus and an intimation of the Cross, a piece of gnosis which he would scarcely have perpetrated had he not been so much accustomed to the Scriptures in Greek as to have forgotten that Hebrew letters had been originally used in indicating the number.

4. We might add among such mistakes as Barnabas would have probably avoided a slip in the history of Joshua, and a very frequent quoting of passages as from Scripture which are not to be found in our Bibles. We do not feel inclined to lay stress on such mis-statements;

[n] Hefele, Sendschreiben, &c., p. 75. [o] c. 9.

they have some weight in them taken along with the others, but they could not overpower strong external evidence, as we have no right to determine beforehand the limits even of an apostle's fallibility in such matters.

II. The epistle was probably written after the death of Barnabas. The destruction of Jerusalem is mentioned in the letter. Now we know that John Mark was associated with Paul before that event, that Paul mentions John Mark oftener than once, but that he does not say anything of Barnabas, except in so far as he describes him to be the uncle of Mark; and the inference is that Barnabas had died before Paul wrote, and therefore before the destruction of Jerusalem [p]. The inference is not an inevitable one, but it may be taken as a considerable help amidst an utter want of positive statement.

III. The writer asserts that every Syrian, Arabian, and all the priests of idols are circumcised [q]. Josephus [r] asserts that the only Syrians that were subjected to circumcision were the Syrians of Palestine. We have here therefore an unquestionable mistake. Now is it likely that Barnabas, who had been for so long a time resident in Antioch, the capital of uncircumcised Syria, as we may call it, would be so misinformed as to commit such a mistake?

IV. The absurd statements with regard to the habits of animals have seemed to some inconsistent with the character which we must assign to Barnabas as an apostle. I cannot regard this argument as strong,

---

[p] Hefele, Sendschreiben, &c., p. 37.   [q] c. 9.

[r] Contra Apion. I. xxii., Bekker, vol. vi. p. 200; and Archæol., lib. viii. 10. 3.

for we have no reason to believe that the apostles were well acquainted with the habits of animals, and still less reason have we for fancying that any Divine interposition would take place to prevent their minds from accepting as truth what now appears to us ridiculous fictions.

V. The tasteless allegorizings and the writer's evident delight in discovering hidden meanings in Scripture are unworthy of an apostle. This argument goes for something, but I do not think that of itself it could at all stand out against good external evidence. There is more force in it, however, if we reflect that no work of the first century, putting out of sight this letter, contains such an immoderate amount of allegory, and lays such stress on γνῶσις, that intelligence which sees beneath the carnal of the Old Testament deep spiritual truths. The tone of the work is entirely out of keeping, if we rank the book among apostolic writings, while it stands as a fit companion to many works of the second century. Even this argument, however, is not one that could be urged very strongly. For why should not one man have anticipated the tone of an age subsequent to him— nay, in some measure have given rise to it? Or might not other books of a similar nature have perished?

VI. The writer speaks of the apostles as having before their conversion been guilty of the grossest sins[s], (ὑπὲρ πᾶσαν ἁμαρτίαν ἀνομώτεροι). Such an expression is regarded as unworthy of Barnabas, the statement being untrue, and more like that of a rhetorician of the second century than that of an apostle of the first. That the statement as applied to some is untrue, we know from the gospels; that it is true of any but Paul, who was

[s] c. 5.

guilty of the most merciless cruelty, and perhaps of Matthew, we cannot affirm from the New Testament. Yet there may have been some truth in it. There is certainly nothing unlikely in it, but, on the contrary, a probability in its favour, as Christ took up with publicans and sinners for the most part; and, consequently, we cannot attach any weight to this argument.

These are the arguments which have been adduced to prove that Barnabas was not the author of the epistle. Some of them are not satisfactory, others would never establish the point, but form a portion of cumulative evidence, while the first we cannot but deem as settling the question conclusively. In fact, there is no way of getting over the difficulty. An attempt has been made by Schenkel to obviate the force of these objections. He has tried to show that a large portion of the epistle is spurious, and that the main design of the epistle was not to attack Judaism, but to explain the object of Christ's coming to earth. His attempt, however, is an utter failure, not worthy of present consideration. Hefele[t] has once for all completely demolished the theory, and it need now only be mentioned as a warning for future speculators, not as contributing to any insight into the subject in hand.

There is nothing to prevent us believing that Barnabas was really the name of the writer — but of this Barnabas we know nothing. There is no end of conjectures with regard to the authorship. Le Moyne went so far as to suppose Polycarp to be the writer[u].

The question which we have next to discuss is, who

[t] Das Sendschreiben, pp. 203 ff.

[u] Var. Sacr., vol. i. Prolegg. p. 22. On the various conjectures see especially Fabricius, Bibl. Eccl., pp. 41, 42; Henke, p. 53.

were the persons to whom the letter was addressed. Origen calls the letter a catholic letter, (ἐπιστολὴ καθολική). Modern scholars have supposed that Origen so called it because he found no special description of the readers. Origen, however, uses the term exactly as it is applicable to the catholic epistles of the New Testament. There is no reason for supposing that the letter was addressed to one single church. It was written for a much wider circle of readers. The writer, it is true, speaks of their progress in the divine life, and therefore we must suppose that he was to a certain extent cognizant of the affairs of his readers; but we find similar statements in the Second Epistle of Peter and the First Epistle of John, and it is expressly affirmed in I Peter and James that the letters were intended for only a certain class. The writer again informs his readers that, while he speaks to them, many good things have gone well with him in the way of the equity of God, "dum ad vos adloquor, multa mihi bona successerunt in via æquitatis Domini." These words, viewed in their connexion, have been taken to mean that the writer had much success in proclaiming the gospel among his readers in previous periods. They certainly may mean this, but they may mean, that not only have his readers the Spirit of God in them by his help and that of others, but he himself is fully persuaded that, while in the act of addressing them, the Spirit has suggested to him new and deep conceptions of the dealings and words of God [v]. The writer further tells his readers that he

[v] Tischendorf's text is in favour of the second meaning. It is, συνιδὼν ἐμαυτῷ ὅτι ἐν ὑμῖν λαλήσας πολλὰ ἐπίσταμαι ὅτι ἐμοὶ συνώδευσεν ἐν ὁδῷ δικαιοσύνης κύριος: 'Being conscious to myself that having spoken among you I know many things because the Lord journeyed with me in the way of righteousness.'

is always ready to give them a share of what wisdom he himself has received; and in one passage he assures them that no one had received from him a truer saying than what he gave them in the immediate context, but that they were worthy of it. These expressions have been adduced by Hefele as qualifying the statement of Origen, but a glance at the Catholic epistles of the New Testament will show that this one is as worthy of the title as any of them. Nor can we go the length of feeling assured that the writer was either a missionary or regular preacher among the people whom he addresses. He may have been, but we cannot affirm that he must have been. The persons addressed are most generally called children, sons and daughters; but he also speaks of them as brothers[x], and oftener than once he assures them that he does not wish to lay claim to any superiority, but to address them as one of themselves.

We know nothing of the locality in which the readers or writer of the letter dwelt. An early critic attempted to determine the place, fixing on Alexandria[y]; but his attempt is a series of baseless conjectures. The only question with reference both to the readers and writer on which we can with some chance of success reflect is whether they were Jewish or heathen Christians. That they were Jewish Christians has been inferred from the whole tenor of the work. What would be the use, it is said, of showing that the law was not obligatory, that Jews were no longer required to offer sacrifices, to keep the sabbath or to worship in the temple, if the readers

---

[x] cc. 3, 6. The word 'brothers' occurs also in c. 1, but the reading is doubtful in Latin, and Tischendorf's text omits it.

[y] Tentzel in Fabric. Bibl. Eccles. p. 42.

had been originally heathens? And then an appeal is made to the style of reasoning as calculated to satisfy only those who had once been Jews. We cannot but think that there is a radical mistake in these arguments. It is entirely forgotten that all Christians regarded the Jewish scriptures as sacred, that all of them had therefore an infinite interest in understanding them, and that consequently they had to grapple with the very difficulty which the writer here tries to overcome. Were they to take the law literally? If not, is it possible that God could have commanded once what was now obsolete and to be neglected? Or was there beneath all the outward rites enjoined a meaning which enlightenment could make visible to the Christian mind? These are inquiries which must have been suggested to all Christians, Jews or not Jews, and therefore there is nothing in the subject-matter compelling us to believe that either the readers or the writer were originally Jewish. Beyond this general tenor, there is no single passage which gives the shadow of support to the notion that they were Jewish Christians[z]. On the contrary, there are indications that the great majority of the readers had originally been heathen. We cannot make an express affirmation with regard to the writer, because it is natural for a writer to identify himself with his readers. Yet even with regard to him is it likely that, if he had

[z] Appeal is made to such passages as we have already noticed in Clemens Romanus, where Jews are spoken of as 'our fathers.' Hefele has brought together all the arguments for the Jewish origin of the writer: Sendschreiben, &c., pp. 129 ff. Weizsäcker, in a programme Zur Kritik des Barnabasbriefes aus dem Codex Sinaiticus, Tübingen, 1863, tries to show that the epistle is directed against Jews, and that there is great similarity between its arguments and those of Justin Martyr's Dialogue with Trypho.

been trained in the Jewish faith and had been much accustomed to the Jewish Scriptures, he would have so frequently misquoted Scripture, misrepresented Jewish customs, and argued as if the Bible had been written in Greek? We do not mean to set it down as an unquestionable fact that the writer had been converted from heathenism: but the extraordinary number of his misrepresentations of Scripture and Jewish practices, and the vehemence of his denunciation of Judaism, may be taken to weigh rather against his Jewish origin than for it. In fact, one of the mistakes, the appeal to the Greek letters as numbers, is conclusive proof of the writer's habitual use of the Greek Scriptures. The theory of Neander, however, that the writer was an Alexandrian Jew, obviates the force of any inferences that might be drawn from this mistake. Others besides him have thought that both the writer and readers belonged to Alexandria. They account in this way for the extraordinary phenomenon which the letter presents —the complete separation of ritualistic Judaism from Christianity. Schenkel especially has tried to show that the persons to whom that portion of the letter which he regards as alone genuine was addressed were Alexandrian Jews[a]. But his arguments are of a flimsy nature. The most weighty is adduced from a passage where the writer says, "Ye ought not to separate yourselves as if justified[b]." Schenkel supposes an allusion here to the Therapeutæ[c] of Alexandria, but the supposition is groundless; for there is nothing in the state-

---

[a] Studien und Kritiken von Ullmann und Umbreit, Jahrgang 1837, drittes Heft: Ueber den Brief des Barnabas. Ein kritischer Versuch von Daniel Schenkel, pp. 652-686.
[b] c. 4. [c] Schenkel, p. 680.

ment of Barnabas at all characteristic. There is a great deal more weight in the arguments adduced by Hilgenfeld for the Alexandrian origin of the letter. The extraordinary development and extension of allegorical interpretation, he thinks, can be accounted for in no way but by supposing that the writer was influenced by the Alexandrian philosophy. And he farther finds traces of this philosophy in the expressions γῆ πάσχουσα [d] and δόγματα [e]. The inference goes on the supposition that a man who was influenced by the Alexandrian Religious-Philosophy was a resident in Alexandria[f]. The evidence that the readers also had in the main been heathens, is not strong, but still decisive enough in the midst of an utter want of evidence on the other side. It consists of three passages [g]. 1. The writer says, "We ought therefore to inquire, brethren, concerning our salvation, that the devil may at no time have entrance into us and turn us away from our life[h]." Now is it likely that the writer would so speak to his readers had they at one time before this been sunk in the carnality of Judaism? Would he not have spoken of their returning to Judaism, or being led astray again into it? 2. "God hath shown to all of us beforehand that we may not run as proselytes into the observance of the law of the Jews[i]." How would the writer speak of them becoming proselytes had they been one time Jews, and how could he represent the danger as a novel one if they had formerly been under

[d] c. 6.   [e] cc. 9, 10.

[f] Hilgenfeld, Apost. Väter, p. 43; comp. 18, note 14; and see Neander's Church Hist. vol. ii. p. 406, and p. 22, note (Bohn's edition).

[g] Dr. Joh. Kayser, Ueber den sogenannten Barnabasbrief (Paderborn, 1866), has adduced a few additional passages which he thinks point in the same direction, from chapters second, fourth, and fourteenth.

[h] c. 2.   [i] c. 3.

the law[k]? 3. "Before we put our confidence in God, the habitation of our heart was corruptible and weak, as being in truth a shrine built with hands: for it was full of idolatry and the house of demons, because we did what was contrary to God's will[m]." These words are certainly a more exact description of the conversion of heathens than of the conversion of Jews. One would have expected a different turn of expression if the readers had at one time been Jews[n]. It is indeed not absolutely inapplicable to Jews, but it is more applicable to heathens. We regard it then as very probable that the readers were mostly heathens. But at the same time we cannot fancy that at the time the letter was written an accurate distinction was drawn between Jewish and heathen Christians. At a very early period the apostles turned from the Jews to preach the gospel to others, and throughout the whole of the Christian churches the heathens must have formed by far the most numerous class, though Jews may have been more or less mixed with them. The difficulty of making an exact distinction as to the class of readers would be vastly increased if the letter was addressed not to one church but to Christians throughout a large district. We thus come to the conclusion that the letter was addressed to Christians as Christians, whatever they had been before, and we deem it most probable that the great

---

[k] The Sinaitic Codex reads ἐπίλυτοι, and Weizsäcker by amending it into ἐπιλύτῳ has tried to give an entirely different turn to the sentence. But his emendation is unnecessary, and in reality does not serve his argument.

[m] c. 16.

[n] Schenkel adduced this and other passages to prove that there were traces in the letter of a Christian interpolator who had been a heathen. See also Hilgenfeld, Apost. Väter, p. 32.

mass of those addressed had been at one time given to the worship of idols.

The date of the letter next claims our attention. We have already seen that it could not have been written before A.D. 70. The destruction of Jerusalem is expressly mentioned. This is the earliest date that can possibly be assigned to it. Then, on the other hand, it must have been written at least several years before the work in which Clemens Alexandrinus quotes it was written, and this forms the limit on the other hand. And here we think we must let the matter rest. There is nothing in the letter to bring us nearer to the exact date. As some, however, have ventured to fix almost the exact year, we must examine their arguments. 1. The sentence in which the destruction of Jerusalem is mentioned runs thus: "For on account of their warring the temple was destroyed by enemies. Now also those very servants of the enemies shall build it up º." Gallandi changes the punctuation and reads, "For on account of their warring the temple has been destroyed now:" that is, a year or two ago: and accordingly he fixes on the years between 71 and 73 as the period in the course of which it was written. The objection to this plan is that the punctuation is bad and made for the theory, and that no slighter basis for a theory could possibly be imagined. 2. In the passage already quoted with regard to the destruction of Jerusalem it is said that the enemies of the Jews would rebuild it. The writer mentions this prophecy oftener than once, and speaks of it as in the course of fulfilment. The fulfilment of it is made to consist in the heathen building up a spiritual temple to God in their hearts. Now, says Hefele, the writer in

º c. 16.

speaking of the reconstruction of the temple could scarcely have been silent in regard to the rebuilding of the city, had Ælia Capitolina been really founded. Therefore the letter was written before the founding of Ælia Capitolina by Hadrian in A.D. 119[p]. But this argument is wholly wrong. The writer has nothing to do with the city: it is entirely with the temple. And it would be a digression to introduce Ælia Capitolina. The writer mentions a prophecy that the city and people as well as the temple would be delivered up, to add force to the utter abolition of Judaism, but this he does merely incidentally. And even had it been part of his subject, no one would have fancied the existence of a Roman city on the ruins of the Jewish as standing in the way of his statement. Hilgenfeld[q] appeals to another passage which he takes to refer to the destruction of Jerusalem. The words are, "Ye understand that, since ye have seen (cum videritis) so great signs and prodigies (monstra) in the people of the Jews, and thus God has left them[r]." He lays especial stress on the words "since ye have seen," which he regards as proof that the destruction of Jerusalem took place in the lifetime of the readers. But he has laid far too much weight on the words. For first he has to give good reason why these signs mean the destruction of Jerusalem and nothing else; for the words can apply as well to the final expulsion of the Jews from their own land after the war of Barcochba as to the destruction of Jerusalem, and could certainly include both events. Then the argument has no force unless the words "since

[p] Hefele adopts the date of the Chronicon Paschale. See Clinton, Fasti Romani, vol. i. p. 118.
[q] Apost. Väter, p. 36.   [r] c. 4.

ye have seen" be taken in their literal sense. But no one would have any right to maintain that Barnabas's argument was good only if the persons addressed saw with their own eyes the signs and wonders. Then if he means "seeing with the mind," they might see the signs and wonders long after the events had happened. The Greek of Tischendorf does not admit of the application made by Hilgenfeld. Translated it is, "when ye see that after so great signs and wonders having taken place in Israel even thus they have been abandoned, let us give heed lest," &c. This is most probably the correct form. The τηλικαῦτα τέρατα and σημεῖα, the great signs and wonders, are the miracles of Christ, as is proved by the following chapter, where it is said that Christ, "teaching Israel and performing so great wonders and signs, preached the gospel." 3. Hefele remarks, on the authority of Sulpicius Severus, that with the termination of the second Jewish war terminated the strifes of the Jewish Christians, and therefore the letter must have been written before the year 137. We have already replied to this by showing that there is no reason for regarding the letter as addressed to Jewish Christians, and we may add that the authority of Sulpicius Severus could not go for much if we had to weigh it. 4. Hefele takes the statement, "the enemies will rebuild the temple," as applying to the Romans exclusively: and as in the passage the enemies are represented as beginning to do the work, he infers the letter was written in the beginning of the Roman Church. This is pressing the words too closely. The writer evidently takes the servants of the enemies to mean the heathen in general, and has no thought of the Romans especially, who were not the servants but the enemies themselves[s]. The enemies include both servants and masters: and therefore the prophecy that those who destroyed the temple would rebuild it, finds its accomplishment in the spread of the gospel among the heathen Romans and all the nations subject to them. We have therefore here no clue to the date. 5. Origen tells us that Celsus spoke of the apostles as having been men of bad character, and he supposes that Celsus must have grounded his statement on the words of this letter already quoted, ὑπὲρ πᾶσαν ἁμαρτίαν ἀνομωτέρους, and therefore it is inferred that this letter was written before the work of Celsus, that is, before the middle of the second century. Here we have simply a conjecture of Origen's, but how we are to judge of the probability of this conjecture we have no means of determining. Origen may have had good reasons for thinking so, but we do not know. And yet we take this to be about the strongest hint that we have. 6. It has also been remarked that in some MSS. the letter of Barnabas is placed after the letter of Polycarp, and it is inferred therefore that the person who put it in that place must have regarded it as shortly posterior to the letter of Polycarp, and consequently the date of the writing is placed between A.D. 107 and 120. But the inference here is purely gratuitous, as might be shown by innumerable instances of productions of different eras being sewed together without respect of date. And even if it were certain, the opinion of the person who put them together could not count for much, unless we knew a good deal more about him. And then we should have to make ourselves sure about the date of

[s] Hilgenfeld reads with the Sinaitic Codex " they themselves and the servants of the enemies."

the letter of Polycarp. 7. Hefele finds allusions to the Ebionites and Docetes in the letter, and therefore he supposes it must have been written at the same time as the letters of Ignatius which make mention of the same classes of heretics. But the allusions are too remote for us to build any satisfactory conclusion on them. Those to the Ebionites consist entirely in the general tenor of the letter, and especially in the writer's accusation of the Jews that they honoured the temple as being the house of God[t], and in his rebutting the inference that Christ was man drawn from the appellation given Him of "the Son of David[u]." The allusions to the Docetes are found only in the emphatic manner in which the writer several times affirms that Christ had appeared in the flesh[x]. 8. An argument has been based on a passage in c. 4, in which Barnabas quotes from Daniel the words, "And I beheld the fourth beast, wicked and powerful, and more savage than all the beasts of the earth, and how from it sprang up ten horns, and out of them a little budding horn, and how it subdued under one three of the great horns." But Barnabas gives no interpretation of this prophecy, and it is very difficult to come to any satisfactory conclusion as to what his interpretation would have been. Hilgenfeld supposes that Domitian was the last of the ten emperors according to the calculation of Barnabas, that Nerva is the little horn, and that the epistle was written in his reign, before he adopted Trajan, either in the end of 96 A.D. or beginning of 97 A.D. Weizsäcker thinks that Vespasian is the little horn, and Volkmar thinks that Barnabas expected that Domitian would come to life again, and destroy the dynasty of Nerva,

[t] c. 16. See Irenæus, Adv. Hær. i. 26.   [u] c. 12.   [x] cc. 5, 6.

Trajan, and Hadrian. These various opinions show how uncertain any interpretation of the passage is [y]. 9. The writer quotes a passage which is now found in the Fourth Book of Esdras (c. 12 [z]). The Fourth Book of Esdras, it is said, must have been written about thirty years after the destruction of Jerusalem; the letter of Barnabas must have been written after the appearance of the Fourth Book of Esdras, and therefore it was composed about the beginning of the second century. But the writer does not mention the Fourth Book of Esdras. It is uncertain whether he took his quotation from it or not, and the date of the Fourth Book of Esdras is also a matter of uncertainty. 10. The coincidence of the writer with Justin Martyr and Tertullian in the mistakes already noticed with regard to some Jewish rites, is thought to indicate that the date of the letter must be placed somewhere in the second century. The coincidence is all the more striking that Justin Martyr makes no mention of Barnabas, and from the single remark which Tertullian makes with regard to that apostle, we conjecture that he mistook the epistle to the Hebrews for the letter of Barnabas [a]. The coincidence is rendered more puzzling by some considerable differences [b].

[y] Hilgenfeld, Novum Testamentum, note in loc.; Weizsäcker, p. 30: Volkmar, Programme on Barnabas, p. 10; and J. G. Müller's Erklärung des Barnabasbriefes, p. 107.

[z] Kayser, p. 34.

[a] Tertull. De Pudic. c. 20. See also Hieron. De Viris Illust. 4, 5; "*Epistola autem, quæ fertur ad Hebræos non ejus* (Pauli) *creditur propter styli sermonisque dissonantiam sed vel Barnabæ juxta Tertullianum, vel Lucæ.*" Comp. Philastrius de Hær. c. 89; and the notes of Fabricius on it in Oehler's Corpus Hæreseologicum, vol. i. p. 84.

[b] See this whole subject admirably discussed in Hefele, Sendschreiben, &c., pp. 184-192.

A few other points have been adduced as indicating the date, but of a kind totally unsatisfactory. We therefore come to the conclusion that it must have been written after the destruction of Jerusalem, that it could not have been written after the close of the second century, but that there is no certain way of fixing on any intervening date as the period of its composition. Most have been inclined to place it not later than the first quarter of the second century, and all the indications of a date, though very slight, point to this period.

The object of the letter is stated in the first chapter to be that the readers "might have their knowledge perfect along with their faith." In other words, Barnabas wished especially to disclose to his readers the discoveries of his γνῶσις. And here and there in the letter he speaks with very great satisfaction of his accomplishments in this way. Thus after giving one of the most trifling and contemptible of his allegorical interpretations, he adds, "No one ever learned a truer piece of reason (γνησιώτερον λόγον). But I know that ye are worthy."

As we have seen, it may well be doubted whether Barnabas had any Christian heretics in his mind while writing. All that he says of them would apply as strongly to Jews as to Ebionites. The most remarkable passage is that referred to already, which runs as follows: "When they are going to say that Christ is the son of David, fearing and understanding the error of sinners, he says[c]." The Jews might in opposition to Christians maintain that the Messiah was the Son of David merely, and some of them seem to have been

[c] c. 12.

of this opinion, at least in the time of Christ, and we shall find the same opinion in Justin's "Dialogue with Trypho." There is no sufficient evidence for supposing that Barnabas alludes to the Docetes or to Gnosticism [d]. His only wish is to prevent his readers from falling into a mere carnal Jewish interpretation of the Old Testament.

The words, " Ye ought not to draw yourselves apart as if already made righteous, but coming together into the same place, inquire what is for the common good and advantage of the beloved [e]," are too indefinite to warrant any inference as to the class meant. Perhaps it was not a class at all, but some individuals here and there, as in Heb. x. 25, who *acted* as if they required no exhortation to goodness. They may not have definitely supposed that their righteousness was complete.

The only other question which remains to be discussed is the integrity of the epistle. We have already mentioned that Schenkel has attempted to show that many chapters are interpolations [f]. He bases his opinion on the want of continuity, on the different treatment of the Old Testament and the New, and on the different mode of quoting the Septuagint. But his arguments have no foundation in fact, and external evidence is entirely against him. Clemens Alexandrinus quotes several of the chapters which he has marked out as spurious. More rational objection has been taken to the second part [g], because its style is more clear, exact and accurate

---

[d] See Dorner, Entwicklungsgeschichte, vol. i. p. 167.   [e] c. 4.

[f] Several scholars before him were of this opinion: Clericus, H. E. p. 474; Cotta, K. H. vol. i. p. 643.

[g] By Vitringa, Hypotyp. H. S. p. 228; Le Moyne, Varia Sacra, vol. ii. p. 929.

than that of the first, and because the second part is not given in the Latin translation.

The second part, however, is expressly referred to by Origen [h], part of it is quoted by Clemens Alexandrinus (Strom. ii. c. 18. p. 472), words in it are alluded to by Jerome (Interpret. Verb. Hebr.), and it occurs in all the Greek manuscripts. External evidence is therefore decisive in its favour, and the difference of style is well accounted for by the change of subject. In the second part the writer deals with plain moral precepts, of which he must have had a clear conception, and which are expressed in short sentences. The first part, on the other hand, deals with subjects difficult of explanation, which were not completely seen on all sides by the writer, and which he did not expect his readers to understand without some thought and study. That there may have been interpolations in the work is most likely, but that they must have been inconsiderable we cannot doubt. To us, parts of the nineteenth chapter seem to have been interpolated. The writer repeats frequently the same idea, most unnecessarily, though this is rather like himself as he appears in the first part. The subject admits of indefinite extension without detriment to the connexion. Many of the precepts found their way into other books. Almost the whole of chapters xviii, xix, and xx, are incorporated in the Seventh Book of the Apostolical Constitutions. And thus the text in the extracted copy may have been mixed up with the text of the letter itself. And there are two commands which appear to me more worthy of a later age than of the second century. They are these: 1. "By thy hands thou shalt

[h] De Princip. iii. 2, 4.

work for the redemption of sins." Such an exhortation can be paralleled from no contemporary writer. 2. "Thou shalt hate the wicked man to the last." In direct contrariety to this Christ said, "Thou shalt love thy enemy;" and no hatred was permitted. The sentence might mean, according to the common text, "Thou shalt hate the wicked one to the last," but even thus it does not sound like a precept of the second century of Christianity[k]. The Sinaitic Greek, as it omits the article, might mean, "Thou shalt hate wickedness."

Of the religious character of the letter almost nothing need be said here. Some of those who trace the different styles of the apostles, discover in this letter Paulinism, but Paulinism in its negative character, and already tending towards the Gnosticism of the second century[l]. How far this assertion is true with regard to Paulinism, we leave the reader to judge for himself. With regard to Gnosticism, we see no point of similarity in this letter, except in the snapping entirely of the historical connexion between Judaic ritual and Christianity. There is no denial of the authority of the Old Testament, no contempt of its assertions, and no absurd theory with regard to its God. The work is completely Christian. Aug. Kayser thinks he can prove that it is neither Pauline nor Ebionitic, and that there is no trace of a spirit of conciliation in it[m]. Dorner maintains that its doctrine stands nearer to the type of Peter than to those of Paul and John. "With the

---

[k] A similar precept is found in the longer Greek form of Ign. ad Phil. c. 3, "You ought to hate those who hate God;" but the context shows that real hatred is not meant, but, on the contrary, love.

[l] Hilgenfeld, Apost. Väter, p. 43.

[m] Revue de Théologie, Strasbourg, 1851, p. 215.

fundamental thoughts of Peter he combats Judaism within Christianity[n]."

The epistle of Barnabas was written in Greek. The first four chapters and part of the fifth, however, came down to us in a Latin translation only, until the Greek of the Sinaitic Codex was found by Tischendorf. The Latin translation does not contain the second part. There is one interpolation in some of the MSS., inserted before chapter xii, but it is so notoriously out of place that no critic has ever regarded it as possibly a part of the letter. The Greek of the epistle is studded with Hebraisms, such as πρόsωπον λαμβάνειν, περιπατεῖν used to designate a mode of life, κολλᾶσθαι μετὰ τῶν φοβουμένων, &c. The language is stiff, awkward, and occasionally ungrammatical. Participles are sometimes used where we should expect finite verbs. The author seems to write with difficulty; he struggles to express his thoughts, and succeeds but imperfectly. He is awkward in connecting his sentences, and travels backwards and forwards in laying before his readers any train of thought. We should be inclined to regard the work as the production of a man who was not cultivated, and who had derived most of his information and thoughts from the exhortations and conversations of his Christian brethren and from the reading of the Septuagint.

II. ABSTRACT.

The letter begins, " Hail, sons and daughters, in the name of our Lord Jesus Christ, who has loved us, in peace." He expresses the delight he feels in their spiritual prosperity, and congratulates himself on the

[n] Entwicklungsgeschichte, p. 168, note.

success that had attended his addresses to them, especially in regard to his own soul. He assures them that he loves them beyond his own life, and now he hastens to write to them, that along with their faith they might have their knowledge (γνῶσις) complete. There were three stages in the evolution of life, the hope of it, the beginning of it, and the completion of it [o]. The Lord through the prophets had made known the past, in which was the hope of life; now they had the beginning of the life itself, and he hoped in his letter to show them a few things which would increase their happiness, not as a teacher but as one of themselves. II. Since the days then are evil, and the devil has power over this age, they ought to give particular heed to the laws or kind purposes of God, having the fear of God and patience to aid their faith; and with these and other virtues must be conjoined wisdom, understanding, science (ἐπιστήμη), and knowledge (γνῶσις). God [p] then teaches us through the prophets that He does not care for sacrifices and suchlike services. In proof of this he appeals to Isaiah i. 11–14, and Jer. vii. 22, 23, and remarks that these rites are condemned in order to open up a way for the new law of Christ, which has a human offering [q], (that is, requires a man to sacrifice himself spiritually). These passages also teach us, who are inclined to err like the Jews, how we ought to come to

[o] The Greek of Tischendorf differs much from this, but is not so good.

[p] The connexion here appears to be: Let us apply our γνῶσις. The Jews seem to be commanded to offer up sacrifices once and again, but if we look at the Old Testament with true insight, we shall find that these commands were mere types of a worship, which even through the prophets he has more fully explained, as in the passages which he quotes.

[q] "Which is not to have a man-made offering."—Tischendorf.

God; and we must take care that the devil do not turn us away from our salvation. III. The writer continues the subject, and appeals to Isaiah lviii. 4, 5, in which God speaks to the Jews, and shows how their fasts were vain. In verses 6-10 He addresses us, telling us in what a proper fast consisted. In thus instructing us God was provident and merciful, showing beforehand how we ought not, "like proselytes, to rush into the law of the Jews." IV. We ought therefore to examine into suchlike matters: for these are the things that can cure us. We ought to flee from all iniquity and hate the error of this time [r]. For the time of trial foretold by Daniel was at hand, when the predictions in Daniel vii. 7, 8, 24 would be fulfilled. We ought to understand these things, and take no part with those who heap up sins and say that the Testament was equally theirs (the Jews') and ours [s]. It was only ours. For the Jews had lost their testament, because Moses on account of their idolatry broke the tablets, intimating thereby that we should be privileged to have our hope in faith in Christ. Wherefore we should hate iniquity. We should not give up meeting together, as if we were already perfectly righteous (tanquam justificati), but we should all meet to consult for the common good. We shall all be judged according to our deeds, and therefore we should take care that the wicked one do not exclude us from the kingdom of the Lord. What a terrible fate awaits us, if we are so beguiled, is plainly shown us in the calamities that have come upon the Jewish people.

[r] The error of this time, as Hefele remarks, is principally Judaism, but includes also the prevailing vices and heresies of the age.

[s] Some read, "was theirs and not ours," see Dressel. Reithmayr says that *non* is in the Corbie MS. Tischendorf's Greek has simply, "the covenant is ours indeed."

V. The writer now draws special attention to the sufferings of Christ. The object of the Lord's suffering, he says, is that we might be sanctified. And in proof of this he quotes Isaiah liii. 5, 7, remarking that certain things were said to the Jews regarding Him, and certain things "to us." We ought to be thankful to God for showing us the past and future, but at the same time we should remember Proverbs i. 17[t], and keep out of the way of darkness. The reason of the Lord's suffering indignities from men is partly found in the circumstance that the prophets who were the servants of Christ so prophesied of Him. He came to redeem his promise to them, and to show by his life here that He would rise again and judge the world. If He had not come in the flesh, then man could not have looked on his transcendent glory and lived. Another purpose which his coming served was to consummate the sins of the Jews, just as it was prophesied, "When I shall smite the shepherd, the sheep of the flock shall be scattered." And He suffered on the cross according to prophecy: Ps. cxviii. [cxix.] 120. VI. "When Christ did what He was ordered, what says He?" To this question an answer is given in Isaiah l. 8, 9, and viii. 14. When a stone is there spoken of, it is plain that we are not ordered to place our confidence in a mere stone. But it is so said because "the Lord placed his flesh in strength[u]." The sufferings of Christ were foretold in

---

[t] Hefele takes these words to refer to the Jews; Hilgenfeld shows that they refer to the Christians, Apost. Väter, p. 16, note.

[u] The exact meaning of these words it is difficult to determine. The word 'strength' is an explanation of 'stone.' Hefele gives two meanings. Strength is mentioned because Sion was to be built on his flesh, or the word strength refers to the firmness with which He endured suffering. Hilgenfeld supposes it to mean the powerful

Psalms xxi. [xxii.] 17, cxvii. [cxviii.] 12, 22. Moses also says to them, "Behold, the Lord God says these things: Enter ye into the good land which the Lord sware to give to Abraham and Isaac and Jacob, and inherit it, a land flowing with milk and honey." Now the true meaning of this is given by γνῶσις. In substance it is, "Put your hope in Jesus who is about to be manifested in the flesh." The more copious explanation of it is: Man is simply earth fashioned under a plastic hand, for Adam was made from earth. Now the Lord has made *us* after a new model, when He re-formed us so that we should have the souls of children. This re-fashioning is what is meant when God spoke to his son about us (not about the human race in general), "Let us make man in our image and likeness, and let them rule over the beasts of the earth," &c. This really then is our entering into a good land, that is, into a new state or formation. The prophet describes this new creation when he says, "I will take away the stony hearts and give them hearts of flesh." This refers to Christ, who was to appear in the flesh and to dwell in us so as to re-form us. And the prophet alludes in other places to the Lord's dwelling in our hearts, as in Ps. xli. 3. It is to us then that Moses really referred when he said, "Enter into the good land," for we are the persons whom the Lord has led into it. But what is the meaning of the milk and the honey? Honey means faith in the Lord's promise, and milk his word, and as children are fed by honey and milk, so are we by faith and his word. The promise that we "shall increase and rule the fishes" has not been fulfilled yet, but will

working of his earthly appearance. Perhaps it is meant to show the strong reality of Christ's appearance and suffering.

be fulfilled when we have become perfect so as to be heirs of the Lord's covenant[x]. VII. All things therefore have been made plain to us already in the prophets by the good Lord. Even with regard to the peculiar circumstances of his suffering we have distinct notices. Thus, his drinking gall and vinegar was foreshadowed in the drinking of vinegar and gall on the Jewish fasts—and there is a minute type of his sufferings in the sufferings to which the goat sent forth into the wilderness was exposed. VIII. We have another type of Christ in the red heifer mentioned in Num. xix. 2. The explanation of these types is plain to us. They are obscure to the Jews. The reason is that they have not listened to the voice of the Lord. IX. For the true circumcision is a circumcision of the ears and the heart. Jer. iv. 4. The Lord has declared circumcision not to be a mere effect on flesh, but the Jews have missed the true meaning of circumcision because a wicked angel cheated them, (ἐσόφισεν αὐτούς[y]). Jer. vii. 26, &c. But some may say that circumcision was given for a seal. This cannot be the case, as not only the Jews, but Syrians, Arabians, all priests of idols, and Egyptians are circumcised. Besides, even if you look at the first circumcision, the circumcision in Abraham's house, you will see Jesus in it. There were three hundred and

---

[x] Hefele supposes that Barnabas gives three Gnostic interpretations of the passage in Moses. He makes γὴ πάσχουσα mean, 1. the incarnation of Christ; 2. the new creation in Christians; and 3. the Church. The first depends solely on laying an undue stress on γάρ, and for the third there is no authority, as Barnabas does not mention the Church. Besides, the application of the three meanings destroys the connexion of the passage, and Hefele has not taken into account Barnabas's lumbering way of stating his opinions.

[y] Tischendorf has ἔσφαξεν, 'slew them.'

eighteen men circumcised. Now ten in Greek is represented by the letter I, and eight by the letter H. These are the two first letters of the name Jesus ('Ιησοῦς). And the letter for three hundred is T, which plainly is the shape of a cross, and foreshadowed it here[z]. X. The writer applies his gnosis to the directions of Moses in regard to food, showing that they really contained δόγματα[a], or principles, which at first sight are not apparent but are really concealed within them. Moses did not mean to prohibit our actual eating of the animals. He spoke in spirit. "Eat not swine" means consort not with men who, like swine, forget their master when their belly is full, and remember him only when it is empty. The prohibition to eat other animals is to be explained in like manner, the character of the animals indicating the character of the men to be avoided. And so when Moses says, "Eat those that have two claws and who ruminate," he means, "Be joined to those who fear the Lord and ruminate on his word." And by double-clawed, Moses means the righteous man, who lives in this world but looks for the holy age to come. These were the real laws of Moses, though the Jews did not understand him. XI. Let us examine whether the Lord has not said something about the water and the cross. Now we find Israel blamed for not accepting the true baptism and building up other and false baptisms for themselves, Jer. ii. 12, 13, and Christ is mentioned as a living fountain, Isaiah xvi. 1, 2; xlv. 2, 3; xxxiii. 16. And we have in another

[z] We omit here notice of the mistakes in the quotation of the Old Testament, and of the additions to it, that occur in these Gnostic interpretations, as we have noticed them elsewhere.

[a] On the peculiar use of δόγμα here see Hilgenfeld, Apost. Väter, p. 23, note 21.

prophet (Psalm i.) the combination of water and wood: "The man who does these things shall be as the wood planted by the outgoings of the waters," &c. The cross is meant here, and the true intent of the passage is, "Blessed are those who, placing their hope upon the cross, went down into the water." And again, Christ's body [b] is meant by the good land in Zeph. iii. 19, and the meaning of Ezek. xlvii. 12 is, "Whoever listens to Christ shall be saved for ever." XII. In like manner the Lord speaks about the cross in another prophet, saying, "And when shall these things be ended?" And the Lord says, "When wood shall be bent and arise, and when blood shall drip from wood [c]." Again, we have a type of the cross in the stretching out by Moses of his hand in order that the Israelites might prevail over the Amalekites. And in another prophet, Isaiah lxv. 2, he speaks of stretching out his hands. In another place Moses gives a type of Christ when he erected the brazen serpent. Jesus the son of Nave (Joshua) was also a type of Christ. Some wicked people say that Christ is the son of David, but David himself called him Lord (Ps. cx. 1), and so did Isaiah (xlv. 1).

XIII. Let us now inquire whether the Jews or Christians are the true heirs of the covenant. The history of the patriarchs gives us insight into this matter. The Lord told Rebecca that she had two nations in her womb, and that the elder should serve the younger. Gen. xxv. 23. Then, again, Jacob declared this still more plainly to Joseph when he gave

---

[b] This interpretation is by no means a certain one. Christ's name is not mentioned, but simply τὸ σκεῦος τοῦ πνεύματος αὐτοῦ. See Hefele and Hilgenfeld on the passage.

[c] From an apocryphal book. Comp. 4 Esdras v. 5.

the greater blessing to the younger in preference to the elder. Gen. xlviii. 11. And we have perfect security in our Gnostic interpretation when we consider what God said to Abraham: "That thou hast believed, has been set down to thee as righteousness: lo! I have made thee the father of nations that in uncircumcision trust on the Lord[d]." Gen. xv. 6, &c. For the Christians therefore the covenant was designed. XIV. Then it is a question—Did God ever give the covenant to the Jews which He swore to the fathers He would give? Yes, He gave it, but they were not worthy to receive it. For God gave two tables of stone written with his own finger, but to be understood only by means of spiritual enlightenment[e]. And Moses was just taking them down when the Lord told him of the idolatry of his people. Moses, understanding this, cast away the tables and they were broken. Moses therefore did receive the covenant; but the people were not worthy to keep it. Then we received it. For the Lord Himself gave it to us, having suffered on our account. He was manifested that He might ransom us from darkness and place his covenant in us by his word. See Isaiah xlii. 6, 7; xlix. 6; lxi. 1, 2. XV. The Jews also do not celebrate the right Sabbath. With regard to it, the Scripture says (Exod. xx. 8, Deut. v. 12), "Sanctify the Sabbath of the Lord with

[d] Hilgenfeld regards the last clause as an expansion by Barnabas of the idea contained in the first.

[e] καὶ ἔλαβε παρὰ κυρίου τὰς δύο πλάκας γεγραμμένας τῷ δακτύλῳ τῆς χειρὸς κυρίου ἐν πνεύματι. I have adopted Hefele's mode of understanding the passage. Hilgenfeld connects the words with Moses' reception of the tables—that he received them in an inspired state. The context and the peculiar order of the words are both against Hilgenfeld.

pure hands and a pure heart." This Sabbath is mentioned in connexion with the creation, Gen. ii. 2. But the meaning of the whole depends on the meaning of the words "He ended on the seventh day." Now a day with the Lord is a thousand years. The Lord therefore will end all things in six thousand years. Then the time of rest will come, when the Son of God shall appear and destroy the time of the lawless one (the devil). The expression "Sanctify the Sabbath with pure hands," &c., plainly implies that it will be completely sanctified when we have all become perfectly righteous, that is, when Christ comes back to reign. And the Lord declares his rejection of the Jewish new-moons and sabbaths. The true Sabbath therefore is the seventh of the thousand years, and as this commences with the eighth day, the day of Christ's resurrection and ascension, we celebrate it in gladness.

XVI. The Jews made an equally gross mistake in regard to the temple. They placed their hopes not on God Himself but on the temple, as if it had been God's house. But the Lord Himself shows the folly of trusting in a building; see Isaiah xl. 12; lxvi. 1. The hope of the Jews is utterly vain. For in Isaiah xlix. 17 it is said, "Lo! those who have taken down the temple shall themselves build it." This is now taking place spiritually. But the Lord has revealed how the temple and the city and the people of Israel were to be delivered, for the writer says, "And it shall come to pass in the last days that the Lord will deliver up the sheep of his pasture, and the sheep-stall and their tower for destruction." Is there then a temple of God now existing? There is. Our hearts are God's temple. The word of God's faith, the calling of his promise, the wisdom of his decrees, the commandments of his teaching are in us. He is Himself prophesying in us, dwelling in us. We have become new creatures, a spiritual shrine to the Lord. XVII. Barnabas hopes he has explained every question of the present time that relates to salvation. He does not intend to speak of things to come, as they lie in darkness.

Part II.

XVIII. Let us now go to another kind of knowledge ($\gamma\nu\hat{\omega}\sigma\iota\nu$) and teaching. There are two ways of teaching. Over one of these, the way of light, angels of God are appointed. Over the other, which is the way of darkness, angels of Satan preside. XIX. Barnabas describes the way of light. You must love God, be simple in heart and rich in spirit, do what is pleasing to God, be humble, be pure, love your neighbour, be liberal, and make no schism. XX. The way of darkness is crooked and full of curses. In it are those things that destroy the soul, idolatry, pride in power, hypocrisy, double-heartedness, pride, and want of the fear of God. Those in it do not associate with the good but persecute them. They have no pity on the needy. They afflict the afflicted, defend the rich, and judge the poor contrary to law. XXI. It is good to walk in the commandments which have been mentioned. For those who do them shall be glorified in the kingdom of God, but those who choose the other way shall perish with their works. Men who are exalted in this life should never lose sight of those to whom they have once done a good turn. For the Lord and his reward are near. And may God who is Lord of all the world grant you wisdom, discernment, intelligence, and knowledge of his commandments. Remember me also. Be ye saved, children of love and peace. The Lord of glory and of all grace be with your spirit. Amen.

III. THE DOCTRINES OF BARNABAS.

God.—Barnabas is entirely free from speculations on the nature and character of God. He knows Him always as the source of spiritual life and of holiness, and when he refers to his natural attributes, it is to deepen the impression of his moral. He speaks of God as having created men[f], and as being Lord for ever and ever[g]. It is obedience to God's commandments that constitutes morality, and so he speaks of the equity and equities (δικαιώματα) of God[h]. Whether God created morality or was Himself eternally moral, the writer does not trouble himself with determining, but of this he is always sure, that we are bound to do what is pleasing in God's sight[i]. We are "to practise the fear of the Lord and to keep his commandments[k]." We are "to love Him that made us," and not take his name in vain[l]. We are to trust Him and hope in Him[m]. The power to do this comes from God Himself. It is his spirit infused into man that can make him truly righteous, and Christians are urged to become taught of God (θεοδίδακτοι)[n]. In fact, conversion is just putting confidence in God, and then God dwells in the heart of his people, after He has changed their minds[o]. God is thus at once the author of conversion and the new aim introduced into the converted man's life. He is also the governor of the

[f] cc. 16, 20.   [g] c. 18.   [h] cc. 1, 2.   [i] c. 19.   [k] c. 4.
[l] c. 19.   [m] c. 16.   [n] c. 21.   [o] c. 16.

world, especially showing Himself kind to Christians in the spiritual revelation He made through the prophets [p]. He is also judge of the world [q], rewards the liberal [r], will not regard the person of any, and ought to be feared as having power over all [s].

Christ.—The writer of the letter speaks of Christ frequently as the Son of God [t]. That he meant by the term 'Son of God' more than what could be properly affirmed of any man, is certain. For he tells us that "He is Lord of the world [u]," and that the sun was the work of his hands [x]. He calls Him Lord again and again, and declares that in the creation God spoke to his son and said, "Let us make man [y];" and that He will come to judge the world [z], or, as in another passage, He will destroy the time of the lawless and judge the ungodly [a]. He is said to have manifested Himself the Son of God in that He came not to call the righteous but sinners to a change of mind [b]. In these statements we have proof that the writer believed in the pre-existence of Christ, in his peculiar character as Son, and in his future glory. We have also the statement that "all things are in Christ and for Him [c]." But though we cannot doubt that the writer, like Paul, would have applied these words absolutely to Christ, yet in the connexion in which they occur they have a narrower force, and mean that all the Jewish prophecies and rites found their fulfilment and solution in Christ, and were meant to turn the eyes of the Jews to Him. There is one passage also in which probably reference is made to the worship

[p] cc. 3, 4. [q] c. 4. [r] c. 19. [s] Ibid. [t] cc. 5, 6, 7, 12, 15.
[u] c. 5. [x] Ibid. [y] Ibid. [z] c. 7. [a] c. 15. [b] c. 5.
[c] c. 12.

of Christ: "Thou shalt love Him who made thee, thou shalt glorify Him who ransomed thee from death [d]." The latter clause, in which alone reference to Christ may be supposed to be made, can also refer to God, especially as God is said elsewhere to ransom from death. We have no express declaration of the divinity of Christ. In the chapter, however, which we have suspected as interpolated, there is one sentence which bears on the point: "Thou shalt not command thy female slave or thy male slave in bitterness, who hope in the same [God], lest perchance thou fear not God who is over both: for He came not to call according to person, but those whom the Spirit has prepared [e]." The grammatical construction here represents God as coming to call. That this may be said in a figurative way is possible, but by far the most likely interpretation would refer it to Christ's coming. If it refers to Christ's coming, then Christ's coming must be taken to be equivalent to God's coming. This renders it likely that Christ and God are the same, but it does not render it absolutely necessary; for it is merely actions that are said to be equivalent. The writer may have regarded Christ's coming as really the coming of God, simply because He brought God's message and came God-commissioned and God-possessed, just as in the Epistle to Titus the appearance of God is identified with the appearance of Christ; and compare also Matt. xxiv. We cannot therefore from this passage affirm that the writer would have spoken of Christ as God, or as equal to God. Besides this, it is possible that the writer may have been careless in his expression, leaving his readers to infer the subject from the nature of the

[d] c. 19.   [e] Ibid.

verbal action. Such a slip is not usual in the writings of Barnabas, but it does occur[f]. Alongside of these statements of Christ's high position occur also statements implying his dependence on God. His coming into the world and his suffering were done in consequence of the commandment of God, and God is said to prepare a people for Him and to have ransomed Him[g]. Whether this last expression may not be a slip, which is corrected in the Sinaitic Greek, or whether it refers to God's rescuing Him from the hands of wicked men, raising Him from the dead, and giving Him a place above every name in heaven, it is difficult to say[h]. The writer speaks most positively of the human nature of Christ. He affirms that He really did manifest Himself in flesh. He again and again repeats the affirmation, and declares that that appearance was rendered necessary by the work which He wished to perform, as how could men look on Him if He had appeared in all his glory, when they could not gaze upon the sun the work of his hand[i]. Of his life, however, he tells us nothing except that He selected Apostles[k], but of his death he makes frequent mention. He affirms the historical fact that "Christ rose from the dead, and after having manifested Himself He went up into the heavens[l]." We hear nothing of Christ's life as an example, and, in fact, he does not give us any description of his character. The writer's subject did not permit him to treat this matter. Of the purpose of his death, on the other hand, he speaks most explicitly. We should rather say of the purposes, for he mentions several. Christ died

---

[f] In ch. xvi. αὐτῶν is used indefinitely.   [g] c. 14.
[h] Hefele understands it of his being saved from death.
[i] c. 5.   [k] c. 5.   [l] c. 15.

on account of our sins[m]. He died that we might be healed, "that his wound might give us life[n]," that "we might be sanctified[o]," "that He might make death void[p]," exhibit the truth of a resurrection, and demonstrate that He would yet come to judge the world[q]. He died also to fulfil the promise He had given to the fathers in the Old Testament[r], and "He came in the flesh that He might complete the sins of those who had persecuted the prophets[s]," take away from them the covenant entirely, and bestow it on the new people whom God had prepared for Him[t]. Of the mode in which the death of Christ was to accomplish all these objects the writer says nothing. He asserts that we are sanctified by the remission of sins, by the sprinkling of Christ's blood[u]; and he also remarks that on account of our sins He Himself was to present the vessel of his spirit as a sacrifice[x]. We have therefore a direct comparison of Christ's death with the sacrifice of Isaac and the Jewish sacrifices; but how the writer thought a sacrifice operated to the taking away of sins, we have no means of knowing. This the letter positively asserts, that Christ would not have suffered had He not suffered on our account. "Let us believe that the Son could not have suffered, except on our account[y]."

Of the second coming of Christ the writer speaks distinctly. He will come to destroy the time of the lawless and to judge the ungodly[z]; and it is affirmed that the Lord is at hand[a]. We have no hint, however, whether the writer expected a personal reign of Christ on earth; and though he speaks positively of a mil-

[m] c. 7. [n] cc. 7, 12. [o] c. 5. [p] Ibid. [q] Ibid. [r] Ibid.
[s] c. 5. [t] c. 14. [u] c. 5. [x] c. 7. [y] Ibid. [z] c. 15.
[a] c. 21.

lennium, he introduces no earthly notions into it, but regards it as a rest which only the holy and the righteous will enjoy[b].

The Holy Spirit.—There is no express declaration with regard to the Holy Spirit. The writer speaks of the spirit infused from the honourable fountain of God[c]; where the expression must apply not to a person but to a thing. Then he urges his readers to be rich in spirit[d], where also the word has an impersonal meaning. The word "spirit" seems to be applied to the higher nature of man in the expression "Having hope in Jesus in the Spirit[e]." The Spirit is spoken of as preparing men for holiness[f], and as speaking into the heart of Moses[g]; in both of which cases there is good reason to infer the writer's belief in the personal existence of the Spirit: and we must also say the same of an expression which occurs twice, "The Spirit of the Lord foresaw," referring to the predictions in the Old Testament[h].

Angels.—All that the writer says of good angels is that there are some set over the way of light to guide men to the truth[i].

Devil.—The devil and his angels are more frequently spoken of. The devil is called the Dark One (ὁ μέλας) in two passages, c. 4, and c. 20. He is said to have the power of this age[k], to be the ruler of the season of iniquity[l]; and the writer is anxious that his readers should be on their guard against him, lest he find entrance into their hearts[m], and exclude them from the kingdom of the Lord[n]. The coming of Antichrist is also spoken of as having been foretold by Daniel[o]. The

[b] c. 15. [c] c. 1. Tischendorf's Greek has, "poured out from the Lord rich in love." [d] c. 19. [e] c. 11. [f] c. 19. [g] c. 12. [h] cc. 6, 9. [i] c. 18. [k] c. 2. [l] c. 18. [m] c. 2. [n] c. 4. [o] Ibid.

action of the devil through angels is also referred to. It is the "angels of Satan" that are set over the way of darkness to lead men to ruin[p]. The fatal errors of the Jews are ascribed to the misleading and bewitching power of an evil angel[q], and the heart of man before his conversion is described as a habitation of demons[r]. It is said also that all the wicked shall be destroyed with the wicked ones[s].

Man.—No deliverance is given with regard either to the nature or origin of sin. The writer says that transgression took place in Eve through the serpent[t]. This statement is all that is given with regard to our first parents. Nor is there any statement with regard to the general depravity of the race. But the writer unequivocally recognises in himself and his hearers a mighty change which had taken place in them, and which we now call conversion. Before this change he describes their hearts as corrupt and weak, because they were in the habit of doing what was displeasing to God. The state of mind produced by the change is summed up by calling it confidence in God. The effects of the change are thus described: "Having received remission of sins and having put our hope in the name of the Lord, we became new, being fashioned again from the beginning. Wherefore in us, in our habitation, God truly dwells. How? The word of his faith, the calling of his promise, the wisdom of his laws ($\delta\iota\kappa\alpha\iota\omega\mu\dot{\alpha}\tau\omega\nu$), the commandments of his teaching, He Himself prophesying in us, He Himself dwelling in us, opening to us enslaved to death the doors of the shrine, that is, the mouth, giving a change of mind to us, He has led us into the

[p] c. 18.   [q] c. 9.   [r] c. 16.   [s] c. 21. This may mean, "along with wickedness."   [t] c. 12.

imperishable shrine [u]." A man who undergoes such a change is said to be saved, to be made alive, while in his previous state he is described as being enslaved to death. It is sometimes also represented as a ransoming from darkness, and Christ and God are both said to effect this ransom. "Moses," he says in speaking of the covenant, "being a servant received it, but the Lord Himself granted unto us to be the people of inheritance, having suffered on our account. For He was manifested that they (the Jews) might be perfected in their sins, but that we inheriting through Him might receive the covenant of the Lord Jesus, who was prepared for this, that He Himself appearing and rescuing from darkness our hearts, which had been consumed by death and delivered over to the lawlessness of error, might place his covenant in us by his word. For it is written how the Father, rescuing us from darkness, commands Him to prepare for Himself a holy people [x]." It is well to observe that this change is always looked on as a moral change; that ulterior consequences, such as a rescue from any amount of suffering, are never thought of, nor are once mentioned. If we wish to be saved or cured, our way is to flee from all iniquity, and to have no similarity to the wicked [y]. The Apostles "preached the good tidings of the remission of sins and purification of heart [z]." And the moral results of the change are still more largely set forth in the description of the way of light. (See Abstract.) At the bottom of all this change and moral purity is trust in Christ, or, as the writer more frequently puts it, hope in Christ. He is the head corner-stone. It is He that renews us in the forgiveness of sins: all things are made new by Him.

[u] c. 16.   [x] c. 14.   [y] c. 4.   [z] c. 8.

It is He that has introduced the new law by which it is demanded of a man that he offer himself up a spiritual sacrifice. And of those who place their hope in Him, it is said that they will live for ever[a]. The only way by which the Israelites could be saved was by trusting the cross of Christ[b]: and mention is elsewhere made of putting one's hope in the cross[c].

The writer is not inconsistent with himself and this doctrine of trust in Christ when he urges his readers to search into the will of the Lord, and to do what is pleasing to Him, that they may be saved in the day of judgment[d]. For they knew well that the only possible way at once to learn the will of the Lord, and to be able to do it, was by means of this trust, and therefore his exhortation simply urges them to put their trust in God, and bases the exhortation on a great blessing that will be vouchsafed to them in consequence. The matter is entirely different, however, with the other passage which we have already quoted and discussed (p. 276); for by the common interpretation, work is not merely a condition of forgiveness, but a something that deserves and produces forgiveness. We ought here to remark that another phase of the way of salvation, as exhibited in this letter, has yet to be discussed when we notice the views of the writer on baptism.

Of the divine life in Christians not much is said. The readers are described as having an abundance of virtues given them by God, as having received implanted grace[e]. He urges them also to be God-taught[f]. There is one passage on this part of our subject which deserves attention, in regard to the doctrine of the perseverance of

[a] c. 8. [b] c. 12. [c] c. 11.
[d] c. 21. [e] c. 1. [f] c. 21.

saints. It runs as follows : " Give heed lest at any time reposing, although already called, we slumber in our sins, and the wicked one receiving power over us, stir us up and exclude us from the kingdom of the Lord[g]." He gives also but few hints of the outward manifestations of this divine life. We gather from him that some Christians were in the habit of neglecting the assembling of themselves together, as if they thought that they required no spiritual aid from their fellows, but were already made righteous. We know also that Christians had to undergo trials, for he says that the purple wool is the type of the Church, and in the type Christ speaks to us thus, "Those who wish to see me and touch my kingdom, must afflicted and suffering receive me[h]." We learn also that the Christians were in the habit of celebrating the first day of the week as a day of gladness[i]. Of the mode of celebration no hint is given. Two reasons are assigned for the celebration of that day. One, dependent on a mystical interpretation of Gen. ii. 2, is that the new world, after the six thousand years of this age have passed away, will begin with the first day of the week. The other was the more rational one, that Christ rose from the dead on that day. It is important to remark that the writer does not refer it to any command; but regards it simply as an institution (if we may use so strong a word) established by custom and dependent on the feelings of Christians. Barnabas did not regard it as a substitute for the Jewish Sabbath. On the contrary, he believed the celebration of the Jewish Sabbath to be an utter mistake, for the Sabbath meant was a period of one thousand years. And he evidently opposes the cele-

[g] c. 4.   [h] c. 7.   [i] c. 15.

bration of the Lord's day, as being voluntary and joyful, to the Jewish Sabbath[k].

Baptism also seems to be mentioned by the writer—but only seems, for he refers entirely to a spiritual baptism. He speaks of the water and the cross entirely in a spiritual sense, and blames the Jews for not having caught their spiritual meaning. He accordingly finds baptism in any allusion to water in the Old Testament. Baptism is therefore equivalent with him to conversion. Explaining a passage in the Old Testament[l], he says: "It means this: We go down into the water full of sins and filth, and come up bearing fear as fruit in our hearts, and having hope in Jesus in the Spirit[m]." That the word baptism as used by the writer has not the slightest reference to any Christian ceremony, may be seen at a glance from the eleventh chapter in the Abstract.

Future State.—The writer speaks most distinctly of a future state. We have already mentioned that he called Christ the judge, and that he speaks of his coming. "The righteous man waits for a holy age[n];" "He who does the commandments shall be glorified in the kingdom of God[o]." He will also rise again. The wicked, on the other hand, "will be destroyed with his works;" "The day is at hand in which all things will be destroyed along with the wicked one[p]." It may be doubted, however, whether the writer means by this expression that the wicked will cease to exist, for he portrays the way of darkness as "the way of eternal ($αἰωνίου$) death with punishment[q]." It is indeed possible that eternal death may with him mean eternal destruction, and the punishment consequently would have reference to this life and

---

[k] See Hilgenfeld, Apost. Vät., p. 28, note 36.   [l] Exek. xlvii. 12.
[m] c. 11.   [n] c. 10.   [o] c. 21.   [p] Ibid.   [q] c. 20.

the final punishment of destruction; but is this the likely meaning? It deserves notice that the writer sums up the blessedness of those who do God's will in the one word "resurrection[r];" while he sums up what awaits the disobedient in the one word "retribution" (ἀνταπόδοσις). This would lead us to infer that the writer believed the wicked would not be raised again, but we should be very rash indeed if we were to regard this as by any means an inevitable conclusion. Indeed, the writer's views on the particulars of this doctrine are not distinctly apprehensible by us; for he looked not on them as dogmas which he was bound to explain minutely, but as terrible realities, sufficiently well known to himself and his readers for all practical purposes. Most of the passages which have been quoted in regard to a future state have been taken from the second part. Those in the first part relate more precisely either to the establishment of the future and holy age by Christ, or to the Judgment. Those relating to the future age have been noticed already. In regard to the Judgment it is said, "The Lord judges the world without respect of persons. Every one shall receive according to what he does. If he has been good, his goodness goes before him; if wicked, the reward of iniquity follows him[s]." He speaks of men who are impious and "condemned to death[t]," and he asserts that the man shall justly perish who knows the way of truth and yet does not keep from the way of darkness[u]. The Judgment is also mentioned in the second part: "Remember the day of judgment day and night[x]."

The Scriptures.—Barnabas quotes frequently from the Old Testament, but seldom mentions the name of the

[r] c. 21.   [s] c. 4.   [t] c. 10.   [u] c. 5.   [x] c. 19.

writer, and only once informs us of the exact place in which the passage is to be found. The books from which he quotes are the Pentateuch, the Psalms, Proverbs, Zephaniah, Haggai, Zechariah, Isaiah, Jeremiah, Lamentations, and Daniel, and from the apocryphal books, Sirach, Esdras, and possibly Enoch[y]. The text from which the quotations have been made is identified without question as the Septuagint. The only instance in which the writer of the letter adopts a reading different from that of the Septuagint, and accordant with the Hebrew text, is in the celebrated passage, "God ended on the seventh day," where the Septuagint reads "God ended on the sixth day." This does not at all prove that the writer used the Hebrew, for such a remarkable difference must have been matter of notoriety to the Christian Church, and, consequently, any Christian, however unlearned, would know of the different readings, and would feel himself at liberty to use that which he thought the most correct. Some writers have appealed to two other passages as being taken from the Hebrew, but certainly without good reason. In one—Isaiah viii. 14—the Septuagint has a negative; Barnabas and the Hebrew happen to agree in not having it. In the other instance—Isaiah xxviii. 16—Barnabas reads, "who hopes on Him shall live for ever;" the Septuagint, "who hopes on Him shall not be put to shame;" the Hebrew, "who trusts Him will not make haste," *i.e.* need to flee. Barnabas is unlike both in words, but his meaning really agrees with both. From the New Testament there is but one express quotation. It is of a passage in Matthew xx. 16 and xxii. 14, "Many are called, but few are chosen." Besides this,

[y] See Hefele, Sendschreiben, &c., pp. 215 ff.

however, a considerable number of passages have been adduced in which some resemblance is traced to the books of the New Testament. These resemblances do not argue any knowledge of the New Testament, as they are sufficiently well accounted for by the nature of the subject demanding them, and by their being so general as to belong to no Christian writer exclusively[z]. The only instance that can for a moment detain the reader's attention is what looks like a quotation from Revelation. In the letter of Barnabas occur the words, "The Lord is near and His reward;" in Revelation xxii. 12, "Lo, I come quickly, and my reward is with me." We could not, however, argue from this that the book of Revelation was known to the writer[a]. In the Latin translation occurs a saying of Christ's not found in the New Testament, "As the Son says, let us resist all iniquity and hate it[b]." It is not given in the Sinaitic Greek.

There is one passage which is thought to throw light on the relation of Barnabas to our gospels. It is as follows[c]: "Wherefore we pass the eighth day in gladness in which Jesus also rose from the dead, and having manifested himself ascended into the heavens." Some suppose that Barnabas asserts here that Jesus rose again and ascended to heaven on one and the same day. He therefore must have been ignorant of the gospel of Matthew. But the words cannot mean more than that it was on the same day (the eighth, or Sunday) that Jesus rose again and ascended into heaven; for the point of identity required is not that the two events should occur in *one* day, but on an eighth day. It is not likely that the writer had no knowledge of the

[z] See Weizsäcker, p. 33. [a] See Lardner's Credibility, part ii. c. 1.
[b] c. 4. [c] c. 15.

various appearances of Christ, especially since the First Epistle to the Corinthians is on all hands allowed to be genuine. Some have put a period instead of a comma at "dead": but this desperate expedient is unnecessary: for if we had no other resource, we might fairly suppose that Barnabas forgot the connexion of the relative with the second clause of his sentence.

The writer of the letter unquestionably regarded the books of the Old Testament which we have mentioned as containing the sayings of God. He announces no theory of inspiration. We could not be sure that he would have affirmed that everything in these books came from God, nor can we expressly affirm what the writer meant by God speaking through the prophet, whether he meant that every word spoken by the prophet had the authority of God for its truth, or whether the prophet was urged on by God in some mysterious way to speak out what was in him. In fact we have no explanations. But this only is plain, that he believed that God did speak in the Old Testament. Thus he introduces a quotation from Isaiah by "God says[d]." In other instances the quotation is introduced by "The Scripture says[e]," or, "It has been written[f]." Of Moses it is said that "he spoke in spirit[g]," and that the Spirit spoke into his heart[h]; and many of the other writers are called prophets, Daniel among the number[i].

The most prevalent representation of the origin of the Old Testament is that it was a work of Christ's, or, as He is almost invariably called in this connexion, of the Lord's through the prophets. Thus a passage is introduced with the phrase "The Lord says in the

[d] c. 5.   [e] cc. 6, 13.   [f] c. 16.
[g] c. 10.   [h] c. 12.   [i] c. 4.

prophet[k]." There are several passages in which the Lord is represented as speaking or making things known through the prophets[1], and it is expressly affirmed that the prophets derived their gift of prophecy from Him, and accordingly prophesied of Him[m]. So entirely was prophecy the work of Christ, that an intimation in the Old Testament is looked upon as a definite promise of Christ's, and one reason assigned for Christ's coming into the world was that He might fulfil the promises He had given through the prophets.

Along with this reverence for the Old Testament we find what must seem to our times a most puzzling phenomenon. It is this. The writer very frequently misquotes and alters the Old Testament, jumbles passages together most unwarrantably, appeals to apocryphal books using the same introductory formulas as he uses in introducing the canonical books of the Old Testament, and not unfrequently quotes as Scripture passages that cannot now be recognized as similar to any in our Bibles. We shall adduce instances of these peculiarities. Of the way in which he occasionally deals with the Old Testament we give the following instances, all selected from one chapter (xii.):—

BARNABAS.	SEPTUAGINT.
Moses said to them, When, says he, any one of you is bitten, let him come to the serpent that lies upon the wood, and let him hope in faith that, though dead, it can make alive, and immediately he will be saved.	Num. xxi. 9. And Moses made a brazen serpent, and set it up on a sign, and it came to pass when the serpent bit a man, and he looked upon the brazen serpent, he lived.

[k] c. 9.
[1] cc. 1, 2, 3, 5. These passages might refer simply to God, but the probability is that Christ is meant. [m] c. 5.

And laying this name upon him [viz. Joshua] when he sent him as a spy of the land, he said, Take a book into your hands and write what things the Lord says, because the son of God at the last days will cut off by the roots all the house of Amalek.	Exod. xvii. 14. And the Lord said to Moses, Write down this for remembrance into a book; and give it to the ears of Joshua, that I shall utterly wipe the remembrance of Amalek from beneath the sky.
And again thus says Isaiah, the Lord said to my Christ the Lord.	Isa. xlv. 1. Thus says the Lord God to my anointed Cyrus.

The Septuagint is word for word the same in the remaining portion which Barnabas quotes from Isaiah, but different from our English translation.

Now in the first passage adduced we have words which are not found in the Old Testament, but which are simply based on it. We have much the same also in the second. It indeed may be conceived that the writer did not regard them as quotations, but wishing to present the narrative in a dramatic way, he feigns speeches, as Livy and other historians did before him. But such a supposition has not much likelihood in it. In the third passage, κυρίῳ is put in the place of κύρῳ, and the whole application of the words is thus altered. The passages from the apocryphal books and the passages alleged to be in the Old Testament, but not now found there, deserve a fuller notice. The following is a list of them:—

1. "The final stumbling-block has drawn nigh with regard to which it has been written as Enoch says:— 'For for this purpose has the Lord cut short the times and the days that His beloved may hasten and come to His inheritance.[n]'" It is doubtful whether the quotation

[n] c. 4.

made from Enoch is "The final stumbling-block. ——— has drawn nigh," or whether it is the sentence commencing "For for this purpose." The passage is not to be found now in the book of Enoch, though Hilgenfeld thinks that he has discovered something corresponding to it. It is even doubtful whether the book of Enoch is referred to at all, for the Latin gives Daniel instead of Enoch, and Volkmar has tried to show, in the belief that Enoch is the right reading, that another book of Enoch and not that known to us, is the one from which the quotation is made.

2. "In like manner he defines with regard to the cross in another prophet who says, 'And when shall these things be concluded?' And the Lord says, 'When wood shall be bent and rise up again, and when blood shall drip from wood[o].'" The book from which the first part is taken is unknown; the latter part, "blood will drip from wood," is found in 4 Esdras v. 5, but it may be questioned whether it has been taken from this. Some suppose that the whole passage was taken from an early apocryphal work, now lost[p].

3. "For the writing says, 'And it shall come to pass in the last days that the Lord will deliver the sheep of the pasture and their stalls and tower to destruction[q].'" Some have supposed this to be an agglomeration of ideas taken from Jeremiah xxv. 36, and Isaiah v. 5; others derive it from the book of Enoch.

4. "Do not be a person stretching forth thy hands to receive, and drawing them close to give[r]." This is taken from the Wisdom of Sirach iv. 31, which runs thus, "Let not thy hand be stretched out to receive, and contracted in giving."

[o] c. 12.   [p] See Müller in loc.   [q] c. 16.   [r] c. 19.

5. "Confess your sins [s];" with which is compared Sirach iv. 26, "Be not ashamed to confess your sins." There is a remarkable similarity of Greek expression, the phrase ἐξομολογεῖν ἐπὶ ἁμαρτίαις occurring in both.

The two last quotations seem taken from the book of Sirach, the first we may say indubitably. We should not have quoted them however as relating in any way to the question of inspiration, had they not been already quoted in this connexion by others. For, as they are introduced by no formula, the writer gives no hint of his opinion with regard to their authority. He quotes them without stating the fact; but a simple quotation proves nothing at all.

The letter gives no information with regard to the authority of the New Testament, except in the single passage to which we have already referred. That passage is introduced with the formula, "As it has been written[t]," and hence it has been inferred that the Gospel of Matthew was ranked with the books of the Old Testament in authority. The words "It is written" are prefixed only to quotations from canonical works, and consequently in this new application of it we must admit a recognition on the part of the writer of the sacred character of the work from which he quotes. The argument is good, but unfortunately the expression on which it is based is not entirely free from suspicion. For this would be the only instance in which the phrase would be used to introduce a saying of Christ's within the first two centuries of the Christian era. His sayings are peculiarly marked out as his own, and referred to always as possessing the authority of Him who was Lord of the Church.

[s] c. 19.   [t] c. 4.

The interpretation of the Old Testament next deserves our attention. The letter seems to have been mainly written to cast light on this subject. The difficulty that presented itself was this—Here are God's words, how are we Christians to understand them? The solution was at once demanded and furthered by the belief that these words were in fact the words of Jesus Christ, the Saviour and Lord of Christians, and that consequently they must have a bearing upon Christians. The writer of the letter believes that some parts of the Old Testament were written for the Jews, some parts for the Christians[u]. This he states several times in the most express language, and if we may judge from the instances of both which he adduces, the denunciations were designed for the Jews, the promises and exhortations to spiritual improvement for the Christians. The reason of this lay in the circumstance that the Jews could not comprehend the spiritual nature of the messages delivered to them. They took the words literally, they obeyed them literally, and so at the very first they were excluded from God's covenant. The fact of their exclusion is intimated several times. "The Jews lost for ever that testament which Moses received[x];" "Moses cast down the tables of stone, and their testament was broken[y];" "And Moses understood that they had again made molten images, and he cast the tables from his hands, and the tables of the covenant of the Lord were broken to pieces. For Moses indeed received them, but they were not worthy[z]." The consequence of this was that they entirely failed to recognize Christ in the words of the prophets, and the books of the Old Testament were thus from the beginning sealed

[u] c. 5.   [x] c. 4.   [y] c. 4.   [z] c. 14.

to them. They formed carnal and outward conceptions of the sacrifices, of the regulations about animals, of circumcision, of the sabbaths and the temple, and so they went on heaping sin upon sin. How then are these matters to be understood? The fact that the Lord must be recognized as the real spokesman in the Old Testament is the fundamental principle, and then a true enlightenment, a gnosis, a power to perceive what is spiritual, will give the rest. And so the author, in this letter, affords us many specimens of his Gnostic power to explain the Scriptures, never taking them to mean what they seem to mean, but developing from them some hidden and spiritual idea. In doing so he proceeds on no principle but that of finding something either about the Lord, or in harmony with the moral or spiritual aspects of Christianity. Provided he does this, he feels secure that his gnosis is leading him right. A question arises here:—Did the writer believe that the Jews ought not to have taken the literal meaning of the precepts given them, or that they ought to have obeyed them literally, but at the same time with a clear and full understanding of their typical meaning? We cannot help thinking that he went so far as to pronounce the Jews wrong in at all regarding them as literal. We base this conclusion on two passages. In speaking of circumcision he says, "Therefore He has circumcised our ears, that hearing the word we might believe; for the circumcision in which they have trusted has been destroyed. For He has said that the circumcision is not a circumcision of the flesh; but they transgressed, for an evil angel deceived them[a]." Now here at first sight we might imagine from the use of the perfects that the

[a] c. 9.

writer referred to the abrogation of circumcision by Christ after his appearance on earth; but then the writer nowhere refers to such an abrogation, while, as we have seen, he distinctly states that the Jews lost the covenant when Moses broke the tables. Besides this, the meaning of the first sentence may possibly be, The circumcision in which they have trusted has been brought to nought, that is, Jerusalem has been destroyed, the covenant of which the Jews thought circumcision was a seal was lost long ago, and now their very hopes in the direction of a conquest are completely frustrated. But whatever be the meaning of this sentence, of the next there can scarcely be a doubt. It plainly refers to the Jews of all times, and it states as distinctly as we can expect, that the Jews made an utter mistake in supposing the circumcision of the flesh to be what was meant by Moses, and their mistake was the work of an evil angel [b]. The second passage admits of a double translation. It runs, "Why has Moses said, 'Ye shall not eat the pig, &c.?' He had in his spiritual meaning three propositions ($\delta \acute{o} \gamma \mu \alpha \tau \alpha$) under that command. Finally, He says to them in Deuteronomy, 'And I will place my just laws before this people.' Accordingly, then, it is not God's commandment not to eat. But Moses spoke in spirit [c]." The other translation is, "Is it not God's commandment then not to eat? Yes; but Moses commanded it in spirit." We adopt the first translation for the following reasons. 1. By making $\mathring{α}ρα$ "accordingly" we find a reason for the writer's quotation from Deuteronomy. God gave his people

[b] See Neander's Church History, vol. ii. p. 407. Bohn's ed.
[c] c. 10.

δικαιώματα, not mere arbitrary laws, such as a prohibition to eat what could in itself do no harm. 2. The δὲ is more satisfactorily accounted for. The mere not-eating was not a commandment of God's, but there was a spiritual commandment—Moses was giving a spiritual commandment. And so the writer goes on to explain this spiritual commandment. But even taking the sentence the other way we come to the same conclusion. "Was it not a commandment not to eat?" "Yes; but Moses spoke spiritually." What does this mean but that the writer does not deny the existence of a commandment, but he refuses to take it in a literal sense. It was a commandment, but still only a spiritual commandment. So that from both interpretations we gather that the writer believed that the Jews were wrong in refusing to eat, and wrong in not perceiving the spiritual purport of the commandments. It is of consequence to remark too, that the explanation of the writer is a general explanation of the passage, not an historical one. He does not say, Did God command the Jews not to eat? but, Is it now a commandment, lying upon us in the Old Testament, not to eat? He was determining a practical question, but though doing so, the determination implies a solution of the historical question. From these two passages we infer then that the writer regarded the literal observance of the Jewish laws at any time as a mistake. How then, one may reasonably ask, did he view the Christian practice of baptizing? On this subject we have no light. The writer speaks of baptism, but he refers solely to the baptism or purification of the Jews. He speaks of water, but he evidently no more means by water simple water than he means by the cross a simple piece of wood. He has not condescended to such externals. Though thus absolutely given to spiritual meanings, and though tied hand and foot to the habit of spiritualizing every thing, he must sometimes have felt twinges about his theory. For, unfortunately, facts occasionally stood in his way. Abraham circumcised his household; many of the best men of Israel went through all the rites commanded, and Jesus Himself submitted at least to some of them. How did he reconcile these with his theory? The most probable explanation is that he did not attempt to reconcile them, that in fact he had formed no distinct theory of the matter; that he was not a profound thinker, and could quite easily hold to things that are irreconcilable by us, and that as his interpretation was a practice, and his gnosis a glory, he rushed on in his Gnostic interpretation, careless to what it might lead him, but sure of this only, that it would lead him to something great and good. Unfortunately, he gloried in his weakness. And it is really refreshing to turn from the consideration of the absurdities that run though his whole interpretation to a glance at the morality which his work displays. However weak and misdirected his intellectual powers may be, and however light his head occasionally may seem, his heart always beats right. There is not one expression contrary to the soundest morality, and much that stands out in magnificent contrast to the morality of his age, even of its highest philosophers. Few especial points, however, demand notice. He distinctly forbids the heathen customs of procuring abortions, and exposing or killing children. He inculcates the care of one's family, love to one's neighbour, and a universal liberality. He forbids schism; he urges confession of sin, and he tells Christians that they were not to go to prayer with a bad conscience [d].

At the same time it is to be remarked that he did not deem it his duty to speak against slavery. In a passage quoted already from c. 19, both male and female slaves are mentioned. The proprietor is not ordered to dismiss them, but he is urged "not to command them in bitterness." And probably the exhortation which precedes this passage, "Thou shalt be subject to masters as the image of God" ($\tau \acute{u} \pi \omega\ \Theta \epsilon o \hat{u}$), was especially intended for slaves. In the same chapter, too, it deserves notice that while he adduces nearly all the commandments, he never mentions the observance of Sunday as a duty.

IV. LITERATURE.

Dressel mentions five manuscripts of the epistle of Barnabas; two in the Vatican, two in other libraries at Rome, which he calls MS. Barberinum and Cod. Casanatensis, and one in the Medicean Library at Florence. Notices of these manuscripts come out in the notice of the editions.

The first news we have of the letter of Barnabas in modern times is from Jacob Sirmond, who obtained a copy of Polycarp's letter from the Jesuit Turrianus, and in transcribing found that it contained also the letter of Barnabas. Sirmond sent a copy of the epistle of Polycarp

---

[d] A full exposition of the duties to God and Christ, to men, and to oneself, is given in the three commentationes mentioned above.

to Halloix, who noticed that it contained something extraneous, as did another copy of Polycarp's letter which he had received from Andreas Schottus, a Jesuit. Both Sirmond and Halloix then sent a request to Cresollius, who was at that time living at Rome, to examine all the manuscripts of the letter of Polycarp which he could fall in with. Cresollius examined two. The one of these is that which Dressel calls Codex Vaticanus 859, and which he infers, from an inscription on it, cannot have been written later than the year 1173. The other is the Cod. Ottobonianus 348, which Dressel takes to belong to the fourteenth century. It belonged to the Duke of Altaemps, formerly Cardinal Columna, and is accordingly called by Cresollius Codex Columneus. Cresollius was told that it was the most ancient. Dressel believes that both codices are derived from the same source. In both, the letter of Barnabas was joined with the letter of Polycarp. Neither Sirmond nor Halloix published the letter. Salmasius took a copy of the manuscript of Schottus already mentioned, and gave it to Vossius, along with a copy of a Latin translation, which had been found by Hugo Menardus in the monastery of Corbie. Vossius willingly gave his copy to Archbishop Usher, who was at that time preparing his edition of the Ignatian letters, and the letter of Barnabas was for the first time printed in Usher's edition of the Ignatian letters at Oxford, 1643. All the copies, however, were burnt in a fire that broke out in Oxford in 1644. Meantime Hugo Menardus had been preparing an edition of the letter from the copy which he had received from Sirmond, but he did not live to see it finished. It was published at Paris, 1645, after his death, under the editorship of Luc Dachery, and contained, besides the Greek text, the Latin translation, found in the Corbie monastery [e]. The text of this edition, as might be expected, was very unsatisfactory. Vossius felt this, and resolved to prepare a better edition. For this purpose he examined three manuscripts, one in the Medicean Library at Florence, and the other two in Rome, one in the Vatican, and the other belonging to the Theatini. The use of these latter, he says, he owed to Lucas Holstenius. His edition of the letter of Barnabas appeared along with his letters of Ignatius, Amsterdam 1646; second edition, London 1680. Vossius gives no description of the manuscripts, his notes are exceedingly few, and he does not set down the various readings of the codices. The Florentine manuscript is that called Cod. Mediceus (Plut. vii. num. 21) by Dressel (p. lxii.), and said to belong to the fifteenth century. The manuscript of the Theatine library is not to be found now. And the codex from the Vatican Library is that mentioned already as 859.

The letter of Barnabas was subsequently edited by Mader (Helmstadt 1655), and in the collections of Cotelerius, Russel, Gallandi, Hefele, Reithmayr, and Muralto. It was published separately by Fell (Oxford 1685, 12mo.), and by Le Moyne in his Varia Sacra. Dressel has examined all the manuscripts to which he

---

[e] ἡ φερομένη τοῦ ἁγίου Βαρνάβα ἀποστόλου ἐπιστολὴ καθολική. Sancti Barnabæ Apostoli (ut fertur) epistola Catholica. Ab antiquis olim Ecclesiæ Patribus, sub ejusdem nomine laudata et usurpata. Hanc primum e tenebris eruit, Notisque et Observationibus illustravit R. P. domnus Hugo Menardus monachus Congregationis Sancti Mauri in Gallia. Opus Posthumum. Parisiis 1645. The Preface and introduction are by Dachery. The notes are considerable.

could get access, viz., the five mentioned above, and has given an accurate register of the results. The two manuscripts which we have not yet noticed are marked by him MS. Barberinum 7, and Cod. Casanatensis G. V. 14. The Barberine manuscript is a copy by Lucas Holstenius from a codex which has disappeared. The Codex Casanatensis contains the epistles of Ignatius, and agrees with the Medicean previously noticed in very many points, so much so that at first sight the Medicean seems to be the source of the Casanatensis. But Dressel observed decided differences. The letters of Polycarp and Barnabas are written by a different hand. The codex belongs to the fifteenth century.

It is remarkable that the letter of Barnabas is joined to that of Polycarp in all the manuscripts. And all of them also agree in omitting the first four chapters found in the Latin translation.

A copy of the Greek original of Barnabas was found by Tischendorf, in the Codex Sinaiticus, and was published in two forms; in the Bibliorum Codex Sinaiticus Petropolitanus and in the Novum Testamentum Sinaiticum, and the various readings with the new portion of Greek are given in the second edition of Dressel's Patrum Apostolicorum Opera. Volkmar edited the first five chapters in a programme. (Turici 1864). Hilgenfeld used the whole of the Sinaitic readings in his edition in the Novum Testamentum extra Canonem receptum, 1866; and the same has been done by Müller, in his Erklärung des Barnabasbriefes (Leipzig 1869). Simonides also printed an edition of the entire text, as found in the Sinaitic, with notes; on the title-page of which the date is 1843, and the place of publication Smyrna.

The Greek of the first four chapters and a half, differs considerably from the Latin, but the differences are not of great moment as far as the sentiments of Barnabas are concerned. In the other chapters the verbal variations are exceedingly numerous, but unimportant. Sometimes its readings are decidedly superior to those found in the other MSS., and it contains many of the conjectural emendations previously proposed by scholars. Sometimes, on the other hand, its readings are unintelligible and perplexing.

The Greek of the first four chapters exhibits some peculiar phenomena. Several words of unusual formation such as ἀκριβεύεσθαι, ἀνθρωποποίητος, and παρείσδυσις, are found nowhere else. One word ἐκσφενδονᾶν, occurring in c. 2, is found in Suidas, without any meaning attached to it except in one MS., notorious for additions of its own. It is also found in Eustathius or Eumathius an erotic writer as late at least as the twelfth century, who uses the word when describing how a girl was hurled from a ship (p. 261). The Greek of Tischendorf uses it in the sense of "turning away," a sense unknown to antiquity, but now common among the people of Greece. The Greek also contains two or three additions to the Latin translation, which seem to us out of place and bewildering. And the quotations which Clemens Alexandrinus makes from Barnabas do not agree in some points with the Tischendorf Greek. Thus Clemens has συλλήπτορες where the Tischendorf Greek has βοηθοί. Clemens has also πέμψαι, according to the Greek idiom which requires the aorist for a single act, where the Tischendorf Greek has the present infinitive, as if misled by the Latin. These peculiarities lead one to suspect that we have in the Sinaitic Greek either a very corrupt MS. of Barnabas, or a translation based on the Latin.

An English translation is given in Wake's Genuine Epistles of the Apostolical Fathers, and in the first volume of the Ante-Nicene Library.

CHAPTER V.

THE PASTOR OF HERMAS.

I. AUTHORSHIP.

THE Pastor of Hermas has been assigned by some to Hermas the contemporary of the Apostle Paul, and by others to Hermas the brother of Pius II. As nothing more is known of these men than what comes out in the discussion of the authorship of this work, we proceed to this part of our subject at once.

The external testimony commences with Irenæus. He simply quotes from the book, introducing the quotation with these words, "Well then declared the Scripture which says [a]," It is not absolutely necessary to suppose that Irenæus regarded the work as inspired from the mere application of the word "writing" or "scripture" to it. He applies the same word occasionally to apocryphal books and to uninspired writings, and he may also have made a mistake, fancying that the passage he quoted was Scripture. Yet still it would be only in a case of necessity where we should refuse to the word its common application.

The next witness is Clemens Alexandrinus. He refers to the work several times, appealing to it and quoting

[a] Contra Hæres. iv. 20. 2.

CHAP. V.] *THE PASTOR OF HERMAS.* 319

it as a credited and inspired book. "The shepherd, the messenger of conversion, says to Hermas with regard to the false prophet[b];" "The power which appeared to Hermas says to him in the vision[c]." More fully in these words: "Divinely therefore does the power that speaks to Hermas by revelation say that the visions and revelations are on account of the doubtful, who reason in their hearts if these things are really so or not[d]." Besides this, he quotes largely from the epistle, generally with the words, "As says the Pastor:" lib. ii. pp. 452, 458; iv. p. 596; vi. p. 764.

The next witness is Origen, in whose works frequent references to the book occur. The substance of what he has to tell us is contained in the following sentences: "'Salute Asyncritus, Phlegon, Hermas, Patrobas, Hermes, and any brethren that may be with them.' In regard to these the salutation is simple, nor is any mark of praise added to them. I think, however, that that Hermas [the person saluted in the verse commented on] is the writer of that book which is called Pastor, which writing seems to me to be very useful, and, as I think, divinely inspired[e]." It is plain from this that Origen knew absolutely nothing of Hermas, that tradition entirely failed him on the subject, that he judged the book a very useful book, and from internal evidence regarded it as divinely inspired, and that, inferring from the character of the book, he regarded it likely that the apostolical Hermas was the author. The whole is a matter of mere conjecture. All the other quotations of Origen are in harmony with the opinions here ex-

[b] Strom. I. c. xvii § 85. p. 369.   [c] Strom. II. c. i. § 3. p. 430.
[d] Strom. I. xxix. § 181. p. 426.   [e] Comment. in Rom. [xvi. 14.] lib. x. 31.

pressed. In one passage[f] he appeals to it as Scripture: "Now that we may believe on the authority of the Scriptures that these things are so,"—and then he quotes, in proof, passages from the Maccabees, "the book of the Pastor in the first commandment," and the Psalms. In another passage he gives an allegorical interpretation of a very literal statement in the work, just as if it were Scripture. He mentions that the book "seems to be despised by some[g]," but in such a way that it is plain he was very far from sharing in the contempt. Hefele, indeed, has adduced another passage from Origen to prove that he has spoken slightingly of the book. The quotation, however, he has made is a mistake which it would not be worth noticing, had it not been so frequently copied. Hefele applies the words "if it pleases any one to receive such a scripture" to the Pastor of Hermas. A glance of the passage will show that he is wrong: "We read—if however it pleases any one to receive such a scripture—that the angels of justice and iniquity contended about the salvation and destruction of Abraham, while both troops wish to claim him for their assembly. If any one is displeased with this, let him turn to the volume which is entitled the Pastor, and he will find that all men have two angels, a bad one who exhorts to wickedness, and a good one who persuades all that is best[h]." Origen here turns away from a doubtful scripture to the trustworthy statement of the Pastor. In two other passages, indeed, Hom. viii. on Numbers, and Hom. i. on Psalm xxxvii., Origen appends the words "si cui tamen scriptura illa recipienda videtur," "si cui tamen libellus ille recipiendus videtur,"

[f] De Principiis, lib. II. i. 5.   [g] Ibid. lib. IV. xi. p. 168 (Greek).
[h] Hom. xxxv. in Luc.

to quotations from the Pastor, but even if these words do not owe their origin to the Latin translator or some annotator, they merely indicate that Origen allowed the possibility of the rejection of the inspired character of the work. They say nothing of the personal opinion of Origen himself.

The next witness is Eusebius, whose words are to the following effect: " Since the same apostle, in his salutations at the end of the Epistle to the Romans, has made mention among others of Hermas, who is said to be the author of the book of the Shepherd, it ought to be known that this book also has been spoken against by some, on account of whom it cannot be placed among the undisputed scriptures, but by others it has been judged most necessary for those who are in need of introductory grounding in the elements. Whence also we know that it has been already publicly read in the churches, and I have noticed that some of the most ancient writers have used it[i]." Eusebius does not expressly state his opinion, but it is clear that he is strongly inclined at least to place it among inspired books. In another place he quotes the passage of Irenæus adduced above, as proof that that early writer regarded it as inspired[k]. In a third[l], he seems by placing it among the spurious writings ($\dot{\epsilon}\nu$ $\tau o \hat{\imath}\varsigma$ $\nu \acute{o} \theta o \iota\varsigma$) to declare against it. But the context plainly shows that we must take "spurious" in a modified sense, as equivalent to "antilegomena."

We need not go farther in our evidence. The sum and substance of what we learn is that Origen and Eusebius knew nothing of Hermas or the author of the book, and

[i] Euseb. Hist. Eccl. iii. 3.   [k] Ibid. v. 8.
[l] Ibid. iii. 25.

if this were the case, it is not likely that the uncritical, uninquiring age that followed, would present new facts. Jerome simply repeats the statements of Origen and Eusebius, and adds that in his time also the book was read in certain churches of Greece, but was almost unknown among the Latins. He himself places it alongside of the Wisdom of Solomon, the Book of Jesus the Son of Sirach, Judith and Tobias, as uncanonical[m]. So did Rufinus and councils of the Church. Athanasius[n] speaks of it as a most useful book, and quotes it very much, as Origen did before him, but says that it was not part of the canon[o].

The early witnesses adduced without a single exception were inclined to regard the book as divine. We have already seen that the only evidence which, as far as we know, they had was internal, and we have seen also that there were some who opposed its inspiration. Tertullian was one of these, and from the way in which he speaks we gather that the only evidence which he had was also internal. He notices the book three times. The most characteristic passage is the following. He is arguing in favour of the Montanist opinion that a Christian who has committed adultery cannot by repentance become a Christian again. "But I would give in to you if the writing of the Pastor, which alone loves adulterers, had deserved to be reckoned a divine book[p]; if it were not judged by every council even of your [catholic or orthodox] churches as apocryphal and spurious[q]." In the same treatise he alludes to the work as "that apocryphal Shepherd of adulterers," and affirms

[m] In Prologo Galeato.   [n] De Incarnatione Verbi.
[o] De Decretis Synodi Nicænæ ; in Epistola Paschali.
[p] "Divino *instrumento* meruisset incidi."   [q] De Pudicit. c. x.

that the epistle of Barnabas (he means the Epistle to the Hebrews) "was more received in the churches than it[r]." The other reference to the work is much more indefinite. In discussing the position of the body which should follow prayer, he puts the question "What if that Hermas, whose writing is generally entitled Pastor, on concluding prayer had not sat upon the couch but done something else, should we set that also down as a practice to be observed? Certainly not[s]." Some have thought that Tertullian held a higher opinion of the Pastor when he wrote his treatise De Oratione than when he wrote the one De Pudicitia. But such a supposition is entirely unwarranted. He did not require to appeal to the apocryphal character of the book in this instance. And though the "ille" of itself might have little particular force, yet when we know his opinion, as expressed in De Pudicitia, there is good reason for regarding it here as an expression of contempt. From Tertullian then we gather that the Pastor was rejected as spurious by the councils of some churches. He himself when a Montanist also unhesitatingly rejected it, and makes known the grounds of his rejection in calling it the Pastor of adulterers. He knew nothing of the authorship, but the book itself did not deserve to be reckoned an inspired one.

These are all the testimonies that speak of the apostolical Hermas as author. The other Hermas is maintained to be the author on three authorities—a fragment found by Muratori, and attributed by Bunsen to Hegesippus, a passage in the Catalogus Liberianus, and three verses in a poem falsely ascribed to Tertullian. The Muratori fragment is to this effect: "The Pastor was

[r] De Pudicit. c. xx.   [s] De Oratione, c. xvi.

written very lately in our times in the city of Rome by Hermas, while Bishop Pius his brother sat in the chair of the church of the city of Rome." The Catalogus says, " Under his (Pius) episcopacy his brother Ermes wrote the book in which is committed and contained what the angel commanded him when he came to him in the garb of a Shepherd [u]." The poem informs us, "That now in the ninth place Hyginus got the chair, and then after him Pius, whose brother Hermas was the Angelic Pastor, because he spoke words given to him." This is all the evidence. An unauthenticated fragment which claims to have been written near the time of Hermas, a catalogue of bishops of the Church of Rome, of late date and liable to interpolations, and a poem which is anonymous and stupid, are the sole authorities, if we can give them such a name, for this opinion. Some indeed add a fourth, one of the letters forged in the name of Pius, where one Hermas is mentioned as the author ; and it is stated that in his book a commandment was given through an angel to observe the Passover on a Sunday [x]. But this letter is allowed on all hands to be unhistorical. Notwithstanding this worthlessness of the testimony, we should have given the statement at least some consideration, had it not been indirectly contradicted by all other witnesses. There is nothing known of Hermas the brother of Pius which should prevent us from regarding it as his production, for we know absolutely nothing of him, not even that there was such a man. But it is not [y] likely that the book would

[u] Lipsius, Chronologie der Römischen Bischöfe (Kiel 1869), p. 266.

[x] The same statement is made in a Catalogue published by Lipsius, p. 273.

[y] Zahn, Der Hirt des Hermas (Gotha 1868), rejects the authorship

v.] *THE PASTOR OF HERMAS.* 325

have passed as Scripture in the time of Irenæus and Clemens Alexandrinus if it had been written about 140 A.D. by a person known to be the brother of the Roman Bishop. And it is plain that if Origen, or Eusebius, or Tertullian had known anything about this Hermas, or had ever heard him mentioned in connection with the authorship of the Pastor, they could have had no difficulty in settling the inspiration. The work could not for a moment have been placed by them even among the antilegomena. The arguments they use for or against the inspiration go on the supposition either that the writer was the apostolical Hermas, or some one who pretended to be that person. They were entirely ignorant of any other author, and it is not likely that the authors of this fragment, catalogue, and poem, would know better than Origen or Eusebius. It is far more likely that after councils, especially of the Latin-speaking churches, had pronounced the book uninspired, the story was got up, that the real writer was Hermas, a brother of Pope Pius [z].

Perhaps, too, there is some weight in what Bellarmine [a] says in regard to Jerome's statement that the work was almost unknown among the Latins: "At si auctor libri fuisset homo Latinus et Romani pontificis frater, debuisset liber ipsius notior Latinis esse quam Græcis." Notwithstanding, the internal evidence goes to show that the work was written in Italy.

of Hermas the brother of Pius (p. 27). He thinks that the notice of Hermas as the brother of Pius in the Catalogus Liberianus is taken from the forged letter of Pius.

[z] See Gaâb, Der Hirte des Hermas (Basel 1866), pp. 5 ff, who discusses very thoroughly the reasons for rejecting the statement of the Muratorian Canon.

[a] De Script. Eccles. p. 48; Paris ed. 1617.

On applying to the work itself for information as to its author, we are involved in still greater difficulties. The author says that he was carried away by angels, sometimes to a lofty rock, sometimes to a mountain, and indeed to places of all kinds. He meets with angels and talks of them, and he sees rare and marvellous visions. Are we to believe that he fancied all this was real? Origen and others fancied this, because they regarded the book as inspired. But their opinion, as we have seen, was based on an unsupported guess. If it was not inspired, then either the writer fancied that he had seen these visions, or tried to make other people fancy this, or he clothed the work in a fictitious form designedly and undisguisedly. If he did the first he must have been silly [c]. If he did the second he must have been an impostor. If he did the third, he has done only what multitudes of others have done after him, with John Bunyan at their head. And there is by far the greatest likelihood that he was an honest, upright, and thoughtful man, one who would scorn a deception. Now if the work is fictitious in its angels, its towers, its beasts, its women representing the churches and virtues, and its localities, what good reason have we for supposing that the single man introduced as the narrator is not also a fictitious character? On the contrary, the statements made in the work with regard to Hermas and his family seem to us to force the conclusion that they are fictitious. Is it likely, for instance, that a man would in one part praise

---

[c] Jani van Gilse has tried to show that Hermas was a mystic, Comment. pp. 85 ff.; but his arguments would prove John Bunyan also to be a mystic. The Irvingite Thiersch finds in them almost the only remains of uncanonical prophecy; p. 353.

himself in the most extravagant terms, and in another hold himself up as having been a deliberate liar his whole life? Is it likely that a man would describe his wife as having a malicious tongue and his children as profligate? Yet these things, and a good deal more, does Hermas do. That the reader may judge for himself, however, we lay before him what is said of Hermas and his family.

The name Hermas occurs only twice or thrice in the work, in the commencement of the first book. His visions began thus. He tells us that the man who had brought him up sold him to a woman of the name of Rhoda, in Rome. After a long time he began to love her as a sister, and wished in his heart he had such a beautiful and good woman for his wife. Then as he is walking and thinking about the beauty of God's creation, the Spirit carries him away, and the woman whom he had desired for his wife looks down from heaven and accuses him of sinful thought. Hermas cannot understand how he has committed sin, but at last a woman appears to him and tells him that thought causes sin, but that God is angry with him not on account of his own sins, but on account of the sins of his family. They are said to have committed "wickedness against the Lord and their parents." Hermas is blamed because out of too great love to them he had not warned them, but allowed them to lead a dissolute life, and because on account of their sins he had been so engrossed in secular business as to forget God [d]. The crime of the family is pointed out elsewhere in these terms: "Thy seed, O Hermas, has sinned against God, and they have

[d] Vis. i. 3; Zahn, p. 81, takes the passage to mean that Hermas lost his worldly property; but the Latin is against him, and the use of καταφθείρω a few lines above.

blasphemed against the Lord, and in their great wickedness they have betrayed their parents. And they passed as traitors of their parents, and by their treachery they did not reap profit. And even now they have added to their sins lusts and iniquitous pollutions: and thus their iniquities have been filled up [e]." Their extravagance, it would seem, had run away with the property of Hermas; his foolish indulgence of his children had led him to devote himself to business, and sorrow and vexation had come upon him. He had once been rich, but now his riches had been greatly diminished, and he was more fit in consequence of this diminution for the service of God [f]. A change had come over him, and he is now commissioned to teach his family. He is to speak to his sons and his wife. His wife, it is said, "restrains not her tongue with which she acts maliciously [g]." He is to forget the injuries which his sons have done him, and "to take care that they be purged from their sins [h]."

With regard to himself Hermas says, "I have never spoken a true word in my life, but I have always lived in pretence, and have affirmed a lie for the truth to all [i]." And in another passage the Pastor says to him, "Your folly is persistent, and you do not wish to purify your heart and serve God [k]." On the other hand, he is described as "patient and temperate, and always smiling;" as "abstaining from every evil lust, and full of all simplicity and great innocence [l]." And in another passage it is said that he will be saved, "because thou hast not departed from the living God. And thy simplicity and singular self-restraint will render thee safe, if thou abide in them [m]."

[e] Vis. ii. 2. [f] Ibid. iii. 6. [g] Ibid. ii. 2. [h] Ibid. ii. 3.
[i] Mand. iii. [k] Sim. vi. 5. [l] Vis. i. 2. [m] Ibid. ii. 3.

Assuming Hermas to be the author, writers have keenly discussed whether he was a clergyman or a layman. We have seen that he was taken up with secular employments, and such words as "you have been involved in your wicked transactions [n]," scarcely admit of a doubt that Hermas at one time was a merchant of some kind or other. Nor have we any reason to believe that he gave up his business. The work does not urge to the utter rejection of business or riches, but to the adherence to one business and the circumscribing of riches. There cannot also be any doubt that Hermas was a teacher in the church. He is commissioned to exhort men to repent [o], and he is promised the remission of his great offence if he teach the word daily [p]. It will be seen that it is possible, as far as the statements of the text go, that Hermas may have been no longer a merchant when he became a teacher, but the probability is that he was both at the same time, and that churches in his day were very ready to be instructed by any one, whatever his profession, who could instruct them. There is no reason, however, to suppose that Hermas was either a presbyter or deacon. The right of teaching in those days belonged to him who had the gift. The inference has been drawn from the words, "Thou wilt read in this city along with the elders who are over the church [q]," that he was one of the elders, but the inference is unwarranted, and indeed, if the Greek of Origen here represented the original, Hermas is appointed to teach the elders what they are to do, at least in the one matter referred to. "Thou wilt proclaim," are the

[n] Vis. ii. 3.   [o] Mand. xii. 3; Sim. viii. 11.
[p] Vis. i. 3, according to the Vatican; but different in Palatine and Greek.   [q] Ibid. ii. 4.

words "to the elders of the church," (σὺ δὲ ἀναγγελεῖς τοῖς πρεσβυτέροις τῆς ἐκκλησίας).

The date of this composition is matter of considerable difficulty, for there is no very precise indication. Some have supposed that several passages afford warrant for inferring that it was written soon after the death of the apostles. Mention, they fancy, is made of those who were contemporary with apostles as still surviving [r]. But supposing the interpretation correct, we are left to a very wide margin, for a man who was a contemporary of apostles, especially of John, who died about the beginning of the second century, might live far into the second century. Another passage adduced speaks of Clemens and Grapte. Clemens was to send one book to foreign nations, and Grapte, whom modern commentators take to have been a deaconess, was to admonish the widows and orphans [s]. This Clemens, it is maintained, can be no other than the Clemens known to us by his letter; and here he is spoken of as alive. Hence the Pastor must have been written before his death. Why he should be no other than the Roman Clemens, why he should not be fictitious, or why he should not be some other one of the many who bore that name, we are not informed. The supposition has not a whit more authority than the idea of Origen that Clemens means the spiritual man and Grapte the literal.

Some also have found a proof of the lateness of the work in a supposed reference to the *subintroductæ*; but this can be regarded as a proof only on the supposition that the custom of having *subintroductæ* was a custom of late origin. Besides this, it may be questioned whether there is a distinct reference to a well-recognized

[r] Vis. iii. 5.   [s] Ibid. ii. 4.

class, or rather an accidental similarity arising from the peculiar turn of the narrative. Hermas is left to the care of the virgins who represent the virtues. They ask him to spend the night with them, and sleep with him. "You will sleep with us," say they, "but as a brother, not as a husband; for you are our brother [t]." The making of Hermas a brother is natural enough in the circumstances of the allegory, and might therefore have happened in any age.

The two ascertained limits of a date which we have, are the death of the apostles, which is affirmed oftener than once, (Vis. iii. 5; Sim. ix. 15, 16, 25,) and the time of Irenæus. The mode in which mention is made of the apostles leads us to believe that a succession of teachers had passed away; so that some time must have elapsed since the death of the apostles. Other assertions tend towards the same conclusion. The gospel is spoken of as preached in the whole world. "All nations which are under heaven have heard and believed [u]." No great stress can be laid on such an hyperbolical expression as this; for such an assertion was made at a much earlier period. But considerable stress may be laid on the representation given us in the work of the character and circumstances of the Christian Church. Evils and corruption are described as having invaded it. Many of the Christians had lost themselves in worldly pursuits; many had become deserters in the hour of trial; and the work is written especially for the purpose of calling back to repentance those Christians who had left the right path. The references to the persecutions of Christians are also clear indications of the comparative

[t] Sim. ix. 11.   [u] Ibid. ix. 17.

lateness of the work. The martyrs are described as enduring wild beasts, scourges, prisons, crosses, for His name's sake [v]. The mode of procedure with regard to them is deliberate: "They are led to the powers and interrogated [x]." Such a description as this is scarcely applicable to the outbursts against the Christians in the reigns of Nero and Domitian, but refers us to a time when the proceedings against them were judicial. We thus cannot go farther back than the rescript of Trajan; and taking all the circumstances into consideration, and noting the respect paid to martyrs, we incline to the opinion that it was written either towards the end of the reign of Hadrian or in the reign of Antoninus Pius [y].

The place in which the Pastor of Hermas was written is also matter of doubt. The whole scenery of the visions leads to the conclusion that it was written in Italy. The writer mentions Rome, Ostia, and Cumæ [z]. He also refers to the Italian custom of fixing vines to elms. The only foreign place he mentions is Arcadia [a]. As the work is also professedly addressed to a church in a city, the city can scarcely be any other than Rome. Whether Hermas was originally a Jew, or indeed what he was at all, it is useless to debate.

Many writers think they can trace in the work a strong Judaistic element [b]; though one scholar, Ritschl [c], sees in it a tendency towards Paulinism. The principal marks of the supposed Judaistic element are the following.

[v] Vis. iii. 2.
[x] Sim. ix. 28.
[y] Hilgenfeld, Apost. Väter, p. 160.
[z] See Abstract.
[a] Zahn would amend this into Aricia.
[b] Schwegler, Nachapostolisches Zeitalter, vol. i. p. 333; Hilgenfeld, p. 166.
[c] Altkatholische Kirche, p. 290.

The writer lays great stress on the doctrine that there is one God who has made all things. This is his first and fundamental article of belief; and proof is adduced to show that it was also the first and fundamental article of the Ebionitic belief. This correspondence is fancied to arise from the Judaistic element in the writer. The writer's views with regard to Christ are especially supposed to be Ebionitic. The Holy Spirit, according to Baur and others, is represented here as not only the higher being of Christ, but as identical with the pre-existence of the Son; while Hilgenfeld supposes the writer to mean by the Holy Ghost "the only power which immediately proceeds from God," and this power is represented as first working in the body of Christ. Both Baur and Hilgenfeld suppose these notions to arise from the Judaistic desire to keep the unity of the Godhead intact—the Holy Spirit being identical with the divine nature of God, and Christ as such being not properly and fully divine, though elevated above man. Hilgenfeld even supposes that Hermas regarded Christ as in some way the chief of angels, and an angel Himself. He grounds this supposition on an arbitrary reference of the word "angel" to Christ in several passages; and then he finds a similarity between Hermas, who speaks of six superior angels, and the later Jewish teaching, which recognised seven superior angels, Hermas, according to Hilgenfeld, evidently meaning Christ for the seventh and chief of the angels. Besides this, he regards the whole angel-system as Judaistic [d]. He recognizes traces

[d] On the thoroughly anti-Ebionitic opinions of Hermas with regard to Christ, see a very able discussion in Dorner's Entwicklungslehre, vol. i. pp. 186 ff.; Wescott's History of the Canon, p. 176, and Gaâb, pp. 80 ff.

of Judaism in the doctrine of Hermas with regard to the Church and the work of salvation. Such are the principal proofs of the Judaistic element. We cannot help thinking that we have here a baseless fabric. As we shall see in our discussion of his theology, there is nothing in the teaching of Hermas with regard to God, Christ, the Church, or the work of salvation, which is contrary to the truths or spirit of Christianity. He does not enter largely into some of these subjects, it is true; but we have no right to infer from his silence that he differed from the Christian Church, or that his mind was peculiarly open to Judaic or Ebionitic teachers.

Where he got his angels, and what previous works he imitated in his Visions and Similitudes, are questions of a totally different nature; for a man may get many of his beliefs and his machinery from sources from which he might differ in all that is essential.

Hilgenfeld finds another sign of Jewish tendency in the blame attached to "those who lived with foreign nations [e];" words which he thinks "call to mind the μετὰ τῶν ἐθνῶν συνήσθιεν, which Peter first permitted himself, and afterwards, from fear of the Judaists, shrank from [f]." If there were any real similarity here, there would be good reason for suspecting Hermas of Judaistic tendencies; but there is no real similarity. Hermas here blames Christians—Jewish and heathen Christians—for living with foreign nations, not because foreign nations were "common," but because habitual intercourse with them, and continual absence from the society of Christians, led Christians into a heathenish

[e] Sim. viii. 9.
[f] Gal. ii. 12. Hilgenfeld, Apostolische Väter, p. 175.

and worldly life. Some indeed, even of them, are represented as retaining the faith in their hearts, but, surrounded by the vanities of this life, they did not, and could not, carry out their faith into full practice, in the comforting and helping of their brethren and the spread of the truth.

Earlier commentators have found in Hermas all manner of heresies. Blondellus speaks of him as an "impure dogmatist, the fountain of Novatians and Pelagians, a whirlpool of Montanistic opinions [g]." The Count de Gasparin has repeated these foolish accusations. He says that " Hermas reproduces all the false doctrines of his predecessors—clerical authority, materialised unity, baptismal regeneration, salvation by penance, meritorious indigence." And then he gives "two of the errors which are his own [h]." Some, on the other hand, have supposed him to attack false opinions. Cotelerius thought the work a defence of Christianity against Montanism. Some modern critics, especially Ritschl and Lipsius [i], have traced tendencies similar to, and contemporary with, Montanism, in its ideas of fasting, repentance, and second marriage ; and the opinion has been adopted by Westcott [k]. Westcott adds to this that " the book is of the highest value as showing in what way Christianity was endangered by the influence of Jewish principles as distinguished from Jewish forms." And Hilgenfeld supposes he can discover particular reference to Gnostic teachers [l]. The exact state of the

[g] Apol. pp. 16, 17, quoted by Bull, who defends Hermas against Blondellus and others : Defens. Fid. Nicæn. i. 2. 3.

[h] Christianity in the First Three Centuries, p. 91. See also Doctrinal Errors of the Apostolical and Early Fathers, by William Osburn, Jun., p. 120.   [i] Altkath. Kirche, p. 529.

[k] History of the Canon, p. 173.   [l] Apost. Väter, p. 177.

matter we shall leave our readers to judge from the exposition which we give of his theology.

Perhaps nothing could more completely show the immense difference between ancient Christian feeling and modern than the respect in which ancient and a large number of modern Christians hold this work. We have seen that Irenæus, Clemens Alexandrinus, Origen, Eusebius, and Jerome thought very highly of the work; the three earliest speaking of it as inspired, and the two latter evidently much inclined to that opinion. We have not room for the many depreciatory opinions which have been expressed in modern times. We take one of the latest. Stoughton says of it that it conveys an impression anything but favourable to the churches that adopted it. "It has some poetry, but more childishness." "Compare Bunyan with Hermas, and the manliness of popular puritan thought in the seventeenth century appears in enviable contrast with the puerility of popular catholic thought in the second and third [m]." Bunsen [n], on the other hand, has well shown its true religious spirit and its high value as a help to the Christian, though he seems to me to have gone too far in comparing it with Dante's Divina Commedia and Bunyan's Pilgrim's Progress, as he had formerly been too niggardly of praise in calling it "a good but dull novel [o]."

The Pastor of Hermas has generally been reckoned among apocalyptic works. It differs, however, entirely in this respect, that it does not profess to reveal the future. All its visions and similitudes are expounded; and, in fact, its visions are generally similitudes: so

---

[m] Ages of Christendom, pp. 132, 133.
[n] Christianity and Mankind, vol. i. pp. 182, 183.
[o] Hippolytus, first edit. vol. i. p. 315.

that the book is, properly speaking, a book of parables. So far is the writer from making pretence to oracular wisdom, that oftener than once he expresses his doubts. He says, for instance, that he does not know whether a person who denies the Lord from his heart will obtain life[p]. At the same time, the machinery of the work is apocalyptic, and Jachmann [q] has endeavoured to trace some of the conceptions of Hermas to other apocalyptic literature. He fails entirely in substantiating any imitation of Daniel or the Apocalypse of John, but is successful in establishing some points of similarity between it and the fourth book of Ezra.

The object of the Pastor of Hermas is to urge those Christians who had turned away from God to return and repent. Some have supposed that Hermas desired especially to fortify the Christians for the coming persecution or tribulation which he mentions, and no doubt the prospect of such an event would be an urgent reason for writing. But there is no proof that this was *the* circumstance that gave rise to the work.

Dorner sees also in the work an ethical representation of the church in opposition to the liturgical and episcopal [r], but the proofs he adduces are unsatisfactory. There is no reason to suppose that Hermas thought of the church in any other way than as it is thought of in the New Testament—the aggregate of those who love Christ, the body of Christ. No doubt in the time of Hermas as well as in the time of the apostles there were men too eager to have the pre-eminence, and there must

[p] Sim. ix. 26.

[q] Der Hirte des Hermas, von Dr. K. K. Jachmann, Königsberg 1835. p. 56.

[r] Entwicklungslehre, vol. i. p. 186.

have been some overseers who did not attend to themselves and their flock as they ought to have done. But there is no hint that the church had in any degree turned from Christ to place faith in its own officers. The passages appealed to by Dorner are, one in which those who hold the first seats are mentioned, and several in which the chair is mentioned. The first is as follows: "Now I say to you who preside over the church and love the first seats [s], Be not like to drug-mixers: for the drug-mixers carry their drugs in boxes, but ye carry your drug and poison in your heart [t]." Here Hermas simply urges presidents of the churches to be holy men, men full of instruction and at peace with each other, but there is not the faintest hint of hierarchical practices. Of the other set of passages the following will suffice: "Since every infirm person sits on a chair on account of his infirmity [u]." Here Dorner supposes an attack upon the chair of the elder, and draws his inferences accordingly. It would be easy to show how strongly the context of several of these passages speaks against the notion of hierarchy in the church, but the abstract of the work will suffice for this purpose.

The book is a very interesting one. It has indeed been pronounced by many a very silly and worthless production. And this much may be allowed, that its artistic merit is not great. But even in this respect it is not so utterly contemptible as it has been declared to be. Bunyan's Pilgrim's Progress would no doubt look a very absurd affair if it had been written in Greek and criticised by Greek critics. Every allegory must have a good deal of useless matter in it, as a large part of it

---

[s] The Greek has πρωτοκαθεδρίταις. [t] Vis. iii. 9. [u] Ibid. 11.

is illustration and not statement, and so it would be disagreeable to the tastes of some critics. In the Pastor the allegories and visions are on the whole well conducted; they are occasionally perhaps too minute. But this is the only objection that can be brought against them. And apart from this merely allegorical wrapping, the matter is full of true thought and deep religious feeling. Its morality is always right, and it presses its views with an earnestness that would fix the attention and engage the heart of the man of the second century. And it did fix his attention, as we have seen in looking at our ancient authorities.

The book ought to derive a peculiar interest from its being the first work extant, the main effort of which is to direct the soul to God. The other religious books relate to internal workings in the Church—this alone specially deals with the great change requisite to living to God. It is indeed intended for the servant of God who has grown cold in his attachment to his master, but its representations of truth are applicable to all living to God. It may disappoint the modern theologian. Its creed is a very short and simple one. Its great object is to exhibit the morality implied in conversion. And in the Similitudes it exhibits the dangers which lie in wait for those who are urged to put their faith in God. It discriminates character and circumstances successfully, and it is well calculated to awaken the Christian to a true sense of the spiritual foes that are ever ready to assail him.

The whole style and tone of the book are directly opposed to modern theology. The writer's doctrine with regard to angels and demons, and his great freedom from dogmatic exposition, are perhaps the most marked features of the work. And even his sentiments would fail sometimes to awaken a response in some modern Christians. He pronounces sadness a sin, a most dangerous foe to the Christian. He speaks of the sad man in terms of the strongest reprobation. He allows indeed that some people have just reason to be sad; but then this sadness is to be viewed as a temporary evil, the temporary scaffolding while the work of upbuilding is going on. As a persistent thing he condemns it utterly.

II. ABSTRACT.

The Pastor of Hermas is now divided into three books—Visions, Commands, and Similitudes. The manuscripts are not divided at all.

Vision 1. The person who brought Hermas up sold him in Rome to a woman called Rhoda. After a long time he became well acquainted with her, and loved her as a sister[y]. And one time when she was bathing in the river Tiber, he stretched out his hand to her and took her out. Then he began to think of her beauty and goodness, and wished she were his wife. As he was thus thinking, he came to Ostia, and while walking fell asleep. Then the Spirit carried him away over an impassable road, and then he crossed a river, got to even ground, and began to pray. At his prayer the heavens were opened, and he saw the woman whom he loved saluting him from heaven. She told him she was there to accuse him of his sins before God. He did not know

[y] The first few sentences leave much to the reader's powers of conjecture. Both Hilgenfeld and Bunsen try to fill up the story. See their abstracts, Apostolische Väter, p. 129, and Christianity and Mankind, vol. i. p. 185.

what sin it was, but she tells him that he had conceived a desire for her, and that this was sinful. Then the heavens were shut again; and Hermas was sad at heart, and asked himself how he could be saved. While in this state he is accosted by an elderly woman in a splendid robe, seated in a snow-white chair. She tells him that God is angry with him, not on account of his own sin, but on account of the sins which his sons have committed, and because he himself, on account of their follies, has become involved in worldly affairs. Then she read to him out of a book, some things in it being terrible, and the conclusion more agreeable. Four young men then take the chair to the east, and two men appear and carry the old woman to the chair in the east, after the woman has explained to Hermas that the terrible things are for deserters and Gentiles, and the agreeable things for the just.

Vision II. While journeying in the district of Cumæ, Hermas remembers the vision he had a year before. Then the Spirit carries him away to the same place as that to which the Spirit had formerly conveyed him. And then he sees the old woman reading a book. He asks permission to transcribe it, on getting which he copies it, letter by letter, but without making out a single word of it. Then it is snatched from him by some one, he does not know who. Fifteen days after the meaning is explained to him. The writing informs him of the sins of his children and wife, and of their opportunity of repentance, and asks him to tell the presidents of the church to persevere in acting righteously. Then a beautiful young man appears to him, and tells him that the old woman who gave him the book was the Church. Then in his own house the elderly woman appears to him, and asks him to write two books, one for Clement and another for Grapte. And he himself is to announce the contents of the book to the elders of the Church.

Vision III. presented to Hermas "a great tower built upon water, with shining squared stones." The tower was built square by the six young men who had come along with the elderly woman that made the revelations to Hermas. Another multitude of men were transferring stones, some from the lowest depths of the foundations, others from the earth, and were handing them to the six men, who on receiving them continued to build with them. The strong stones and those that were taken out from the foundation, were put just as they were into the building, for they all fitted each other, and the building made from them looked like one stone. Of the stones that were taken from the earth some were rejected, some were put into the building, and some were cut down and cast away far from the tower. Some of them also lay round the tower unused, because they had cracks or were otherwise unsuitable. Some of the stones cast away far from the tower were rolled into a desert place, others fell into the fire, but could not be rolled into the water.

The elderly woman explains the meaning of this vision. The tower is the Church. The tower is built on water, because "your life has been and will be saved through water." The six young men are six angels who were created first, and those engaged in transferring the stones were also angels, but of an inferior grade. The stones are human beings. The exactly-fitting stones are apostles and teachers who have lived or live blameless holy lives. Those taken from the foundations are the sufferers for Christ. The other stones are explained in a similar way. When he is satisfied with the explanation of these, the elderly woman presents to his view seven women. These are Faith, Self-restraint, Simplicity, Innocence, Moderation, Knowledge, and Love. She points out to him the connexion between these, and commissions him to proclaim to the saints certain words which she speaks to him. He then asks how she had appeared to him in three different forms— in the first vision as an old woman; in the second with the face of a young woman, but with the body and hair of an old woman; in the third, entirely as a young woman with the exception of her hair. He is informed by a young man that these various appearances corresponded to the state of mind in which he and his fellow-Christians were; that the first vision came to him when they were vexed by worldly affairs, the second came after they had been gladdened by the first, and the last when their joy was still fuller.

Vision IV. Hermas sees an immense animal, from whose mouth fiery locusts proceeded, and which had on its head four colours. Through faith in God he is enabled to meet this monster without fear. The Church comes to him in the shape of a virgin in bridal dress, and tells him that the beast means great coming tribulation, and that only those whose faith is wavering have any cause to fear. The Church also explains the meaning of the four colours. The black is the world; the ruddy and bloody intimate that the world must perish by blood and fire; the golden are the faithful who have fled from this age; and the white is the pure world in which the elect of God shall dwell after they have been purified through the trials and fire of this age.

This vision concludes book first. Book second contains twelve commandments or commissions which Hermas receives from a pastor of repentance. After he had prayed and sat on his couch, a man of reverend look, dressed like a shepherd, clothed with a white skin, carrying a wallet on his shoulders and a staff in his hand, came up to him and saluted him. This is the angel or messenger of repentance appointed to Hermas.

The first command he gives is to believe in one God. The second command inculcates childlike simplicity of heart, and forbids most strongly the listening to or believing any one who slanders another. It also inculcates liberality. The liberality it inculcates seems almost to be indiscriminate; for, according to it, a person cannot be wrong in giving. If the recipient takes charity compelled by necessity, he is free from all crime; but if a person gets it on false pretences, he will have to account for it to God. The giver has nothing to do with the matter.

Command third inculcates the love of truth, and the obligation to speak the truth. God is truthful in everything, and God gave man a spirit free from all lying. They therefore who make this spirit a lying spirit are answerable to God for such a deed.

Command fourth inculcates chastity and the avoidance of even the thought or mention of adultery. Hermas takes occasion to ask the angel about certain difficult questions relating to marriage: as, whether a man ought to keep a wife convicted of adultery? if he is permitted to marry while the other dismissed wife is alive? if he ought ever to receive the wife back on her exhibiting signs of repentance? This leads to a discussion with regard to the possibility of repentance in Christians, and the command concludes with an answer to the question, Whether, when a husband or a wife has died, the survivor can marry without sin?

Command fifth urges the necessity of patience and abstinence from all anger. If a man is patient and long-suffering, then the Holy Spirit which is within him will not be darkened by any evil spirit; but if he gives way to anger, the Holy Spirit, being tender, will go away, while evil spirits will enter in great numbers.

Command sixth states that there are two ways open for a man, the way of righteousness and the way of wickedness; and that each man has two angels with him, an angel of righteousness and an angel of wickedness. If he feels inclined to be holy, he may know then that the angel of goodness is with him; if he has evil suggestions, then the angel of wickedness is in him. He is to avoid the latter, and to repose in the good angel, and walk in the way of righteousness.

Command seventh inculcates the fear of God. The devil is not to be feared. His works are to be feared and avoided. All nature fears God, and they who fear Him will live for ever.

Command eighth affirms that we must abstain from some things and not abstain from others. We must abstain from evil. Then the writer names expressly what evils he means. And we must not abstain from good, but do it. And then the writer points out what good things ought to be done.

Command ninth urges the necessity of faith to him who prays. Doubt is the daughter of the devil, and accomplishes nothing; faith comes from God, and has great power.

Command tenth affirms that sadness is the sister of doubt, mistrust, and wrath; that it is worse than all other wicked spirits, and grieves the Holy Spirit. It is therefore to be completely driven away, and instead of it we are to put on cheerfulness, which is pleasing to God. " Every cheerful man works well, and always thinks those things which are good, and despises sadness. The sad man, on the other hand, is always bad."

Command the eleventh describes the true prophet and the false; the Holy Spirit that is within the one, and the empty, earthly, reward-loving spirit which is within the other. It urges adhesion to the Holy Spirit, and avoidance of the earthly, and sets down as a criterion the acts and company of each.

Command twelfth commands Hermas to abstain from every evil desire. It explains what is included under the term *evil desire*, and asserts that evil desires come from the devil. He is therefore to resist them, armed with the fear of the Lord, and to clothe himself with the desire of justice.

The twelve commands being concluded, the angel of repentance exhorts Hermas to walk in them. He however rejoins, that this is impossible. The angel replies, that such a notion must be driven away; that those who are full of faith and purify their hearts need have no fear of the devil, and will without fail keep these commands. The devil gets the victory only over those who are wavering in their faith.

The third book consists of ten similitudes.

Simil. I. gives no comparison. It states that the servants of God are pilgrims in this world, and it exhibits the folly of those who spend their time in adding to their riches and lands, and giving themselves up to the laws of this world, when they ought to be doing the work of God and obeying the law of that heavenly city to which they profess to be bound.

Simil. II. While Hermas was walking in the fields he began thinking of the vine and the elm. The pastor came to him and showed that the junction of these two was like the junction of the rich and the poor in the Church. The elm does not bear fruit, but it supports the vine, which, thus supported, produces abundant fruit. So the rich man is needy towards God, but he helps the necessities of the poor man who is rich in grace, and whose prayers are powerful in behalf of his rich helper.

Simil. III. As in winter living trees and dead trees cannot be distinguished, so in this age, which is the winter to the just, the just cannot be distinguished from the unjust.

Simil. IV. As in summer there are trees which are seen to bear fruit and other trees which are withered and fruitless, so in the age to come the fruits of the just man will be manifested, and all the just will be glad, but sinners will be burned.

Simil. V. While Hermas is fasting, the pastor asks him why he has come so early in the morning. Hermas replies that he is fasting. The pastor informs him that he is not keeping a right fast, and adds the following similitude. A certain possessor of vineyards went away for a time from his possessions, leaving them in charge of a servant, to whom he gave the one injunction to attach the vines to stakes. The servant did this, but seeing the vines like to be choked with weeds, he also pulled them out. When the master returned he was much gratified to see that the servant had done more than he had been ordered to do, and so he called together his son and friends, and proposed to them to make the servant fellow-heir with his son. They assented. A few days after the proprietor held a feast, and sent a large supply of food to the trusty servant. He divided it among his fellow-servants. On this the proprietor again called his son and friends together, and they still more urgently entreated that he should be made a fellow-heir. The explanation is: the proprietor is God. The servant is the Son of God. The vineyard is the people. The stakes are angels appointed to restrain the people of God. The weeds are the sins of God's servants. The food sent from the table is God's commands. The friends are the angels that were first created.

Simil. VI. Hermas goes along with the shepherd of repentance into a field, where he sees a youthful shepherd taking care of numerous cattle that sported in great delight. There were two classes of cattle; the one very joyful, and the other simply feeding. On advancing a little he saw another shepherd, tall and fierce, with a whip in his hand. He led the second class of cattle into a steep place full of thorns and briars, where they were greatly tormented. The youthful shepherd is the angel of pleasure. The cattle are the lovers of pleasure; the first class being those who are wholly given over to death, and for whom there is no hope of repentance; the second, those who have been led astray into pleasure, but who are brought back by the stern angel of punishment through the providential dealings of God with them. Then they are delivered over to the angel of repentance, with whom Hermas was walking.

Simil. VII. A few days after Hermas meets the pastor

in the same plain in which he had seen the other shepherds, and asks him to order the shepherd that presided over punishment to depart from his house. He is told that the shepherd of punishment cannot yet depart; that he remains for the sake of the family of Hermas, who are afflicted in his affliction, but that the affliction will not be severe. Meantime he and they are to walk in God's commandments.

Simil. VIII. The pastor shows Hermas a large willow, covering plains and hills, under the shadow of which came all who were called in the name of the Lord. Then a mighty angel cut down with a pruning-hook branches from the tree, and the people under the shadow received little twigs. Notwithstanding the cuttings the tree remained whole. Then the angel demanded the twigs back again, and examined them. Some were utterly rotten, some were dry, some were green but had cracks, some were half-dry; in fact, there was every variety. The people were then arranged into classes according to their twigs, and those who had green and fruit-bearing twigs were crowned. Then the pastor of repentance took the twigs of the others and planted them, and after several days he found some of the dry had become green, and changes, either for the better or worse, had come over all. The willow-tree is the law of God; namely, the Son of God, who has been preached over the whole earth. The angel is Michael. The people under the shadow are those who hear the good news, and the twigs represent the effects produced by the preaching and the characters of the individuals.

Simil. IX. The ninth similitude is a fuller description of the Church. Bunsen makes it the commencement of the third book; the second book consisting of the

Mandates and the other Similitudes. The pastor comes to Hermas again and takes him up to the summit of a mountain in Arcadia. There he saw a great plain surrounded by twelve mountains of various characters. One was black as smoke, the second had no vegetation, the third was full of thorns, and the others were equally characteristic; the twelfth being all white, and most delightful to look at. Then a large white rock was shown him, rising from the plain, square and higher than the mountains. This rock had a new gate, around which stood twelve virgins, four of whom seemed to be higher in dignity than the others. Then he saw six men come and call a great multitude of men to build upon the rock, and the virgins handed the stones to them through the gate. The Similitude enters into numerous details with regard to the various kinds of stones and their approbation or rejection. Then came a man of great size and examined the stones; rejecting some, and handing them over to the pastor of repentance. After a short time the pastor goes round with Hermas, and finds the whole structure as of one stone and all right, then leaves Hermas behind him with the virgins. The rock and the gate are the Son of God; the virgins are holy spirits, such as Faith and Self-restraint; the six men are angels. The tower is the Church. And the mountains are the various classes of men who compose the Church. The Similitude enters fully into a description of these various classes. The man of great size is the Son of God, who comes to look after the building of the Church.

Simil. x. The angel who had handed him over to the pastor of repentance comes to him along with the pastor, and addresses earnest exhortations to him to keep the commandments of the pastor, and to proclaim them to all. He urges him also to keep the virgins ever in his house, a thing which he can do only by keeping his house pure. After a few remarks of a similar nature, he rose from the couch, and went away with the pastor and the virgins, saying that he would send them back again to his house.

III. THE DOCTRINES OF HERMAS.

Almost all the dogmatic statements in the Pastor of Hermas are made in connexion with their moral effect on man. There is, however, more of the speculative, and at least more of the distinctly-pronounced dogma in it than in the other writings of the same age.

God.—The first Command commands us to "believe first of all that there is one God, who created and perfected all things, and made all things out of nothing. He alone contains the whole of things, but Himself cannot be contained [z]." He is frequently spoken of as the God who made all things out of nothing, and as possessed of all power and all knowledge [a]. It is He that has communicated to all things the virtues they possess [b]. Man is bound to fear Him, for He can save and destroy [c]. But Hermas advances far beyond the mere physical idea of infinite power. He describes God's character. He is the God of truth [d]; He is full of mercy [e]; He is kind as well to the wicked as to the good [f]; He is faithful in his promises [g]; forgetful of injuries [h]; ready to hear and answer prayer: and so his

[z] Mand. i.   [a] Vis. i. 1, 3; iii. 3; Mand. iv. 3; Sim. v. 7; ix. 23.
[b] Sim. v. 5.   [c] Mand. xii. 6.   [d] Ibid. iii.
[e] Vis. i. 3; iii. 9.   [f] Mand. ii.   [g] Proem. Mand.   [h] Mand. ix.

servants are bound to fear Him; to walk justly; to love the truth; to love their enemies; to put their faith in Him [i]; to ask Him unhesitatingly for spiritual blessings [k]; and, in one word, to live to God. This "living to God" is a mode of expression continually used in the work as equivalent to a completely holy life.

God is represented, however, as angry with sin; but then the statement is made that "God who rules all things, and has power over all His creation, does not remember offences against those who confess their sins, but becomes propitious [l];" or as the common Latin translation has it, is easily appeased. And, accordingly, the readers are urged to turn to the Lord with all their heart, and serve Him according to His will, and then He will give a remedy to their souls, placing behind Him all their sins, and they will have power to rule over the works of the devil [m].' The Lord is, consequently, ever ready to pardon sins, to purge away sins [n], and to turn His anger away from those who trust Him [o]. This trust comes from Himself. Faith is his gift [p]; so is repentance [q]. The people of God are chosen by Him [r]. He dwells in them, and they will know all things [s]. If they have God in their hearts, they will keep His commandments and do His works, and be uninjured by evil [t]. But God is sometimes angry with them, and He sends them temporal calamities as punishments for their forgetfulness of Him [u]. The writer attempts no conciliation of the diverse statements which he makes with regard to God.

[i] Mand. xii. 3.
[k] Ibid. ix.
[l] Sim. ix. 23.
[m] Mand. xii. 6.
[n] Vis. i, 1, 3.
[o] Ibid. iv. 2.
[p] Mand. ix.
[q] Vis. iv. 1; Sim. ix. 14.
[r] Vis. i. 3; ii. 1, 2.
[s] Mand. x. 1.
[t] Ibid. xii. 4.
[u] Vis. iii. 5, 6; i. 1; Sim. vi. 3.

Christ.—The name "Christ" does not once occur in the book, and little is said of Him at all. He is always spoken of as the Son of God[x]. He is "more ancient than the whole creation; so that He was present in counsel with his Father in his act of creation[y]." "The name of the Son of God is great and immeasurable, and sustains the whole world[z]." He appeared in the world, and endured great suffering that He might do away with the sins of his people[a]. He at the same time pointed out to them the ways of life, and gave them the law which He had received from his Father[b]. He is therefore Lord of his people, having received all power from his Father[c]. He is the rock on which the Church is built, and the only gate by which one can enter into the Church[d]. No one can enter into the kingdom of God but through the name of His beloved Son. Accordingly, the Son of God is preached to the ends of the earth[e]. Those who deny Him in this world shall be denied by Him in the next[f]. On the completion of the Church the Son of God will rejoice, because he has received his people pure[g]. It will be observed that these passages give us no insight into the writer's notion of the relation of the Son of God as pre-existent to the Son of God as incarnate. Hermas speaks of Him as one and the same being; and there is nothing to indicate that he felt any particular difficulty in so thinking of Him.

The relation of Christ to the Holy Spirit, as set forth by Hermas, has been matter of keen discussion. In Sim. ix. 1 the messenger of repentance comes to Hermas, and

[x] Vis. ii. 2; Sim. v. 5, 6; viii. 3; ix. 1, &c. [y] Sim. ix. 12.
[z] Ibid. ix. 14. [a] Ibid. v. 6. [b] Ibid. [c] Ibid.
[d] Ibid. ix. 12. [e] Ibid. viii. 3; ix. 17. [f] Vis. ii. 2. [g] Sim. ix. 18.

says, "I wish to show thee what the Holy[h] Spirit, that spoke to thee in the image of the Church, showed thee. For that Spirit is the Son of God." Here we have simply the assertion that Christ is a holy spirit—a statement made in the New Testament[i], and which is in perfect harmony with Hermas's use of the word "spirit," as we shall see. Nor is there any thing unusual in the passage "All your seed shall dwell with the Son of God, for ye have received of his spirit[k]." The "spirit of Christ" is also a New Testament expression. The only remaining passage is one of great difficulty; partly because the subject itself is difficult, partly because the text is corrupt, partly because the language is indefinite, and partly because, as it occurs in the midst of an allegory, we are left to guess some portions of the explanation. The passage is contained in the fifth Similitude, an abstract of which has been given above. In the explanation of the Similitude we have in the common translation, but not in the Palatine or Simonides, the words, "The Son is the Holy Spirit[l]." This can mean nothing more than that the "son" of the Similitude is the Holy Spirit. There is no identification here of the Son of God with the Holy Spirit. On the contrary, it is expressly stated that the Son of God is the servant: and hence Hermas must have regarded the Spirit and the Son of God as two distinct beings. But then, what is the spirit, and what is his relation to the son? Hermas's words are: "Hear now, why God employed the son and the good angels in His counsels in regard to the inheritance. That holy spirit which

---

[h] "Holy" is omitted in the common translation. [i] 2 Cor. iii. 17, 18.
[k] Sim. ix. 24. The Latin translations have: "for ye are all of his spirit."
[l] Ibid. v. 5.

was infused first of all, God placed in a body in which it might dwell; namely, in a chosen body, as seemed good to Him. This body then into which the holy spirit was led, obeyed that spirit, walking righteously in sobriety and chastity, and did not in any respect stain that spirit. Since, therefore, that body had always obeyed the holy spirit, and had laboured with him righteously and chastely, and had never given way, but had lived bravely with the spirit, it was approved of by God, and received [as a partaker, Gr.] with the holy spirit. For the passage of this body (i. e. its mode of living) pleased God, in that it was not stained on earth, possessing the holy spirit in itself. He therefore called the son and good angels into his counsels, that some place of habitation might be given to this body, because it had served the holy spirit without complaint, lest it should seem to have lost the reward of its service. For every body will receive a reward which is found pure and without stain, in which the holy spirit may have been placed to dwell." Then the similitude is applied to Hermas in the advice, " Keep thy body pure and clean, that that spirit which dwells in it may render testimony to it, and thy body be saved (justified, Gr.)ᵐ." Now it will be noticed that Hermas does not once speak of the body

ᵐ All the forms of this passage are corrupt. I have translated from the common translation, amended somewhat by help of the Palatine and Vatican, which are substantially the same as my version, except in the first sentence. The Vatican has " created" for " infused " and the Palatine has, " The Spirit which was created pure of all" (qui creatus est omnium purus), evidently for " first of all." The Greek differs considerably. It has παρὰ "from" by mistake for περὶ, "in regard to;" it adds, " of the slave " to " inheritance ;" and some words have fallen out in the sentence next to the last. The last sentence appears only in the common translation and Vatican. The Palatine and Vatican have nuntios honestos corresponding to the ἀγγέλους ἐνδόξους of the Greek. We give a translation of the Greek. "I shall tell you why the Lord took his son or the flesh mentioned here as Christ's body; and if he had intended this, some hint of it would have been given. On the contrary, he speaks of the reward coming to every pure body. The doctrine which Hermas seems to teach appears to be somewhat allied to that of Tatian. God planted within man's flesh the Holy Spirit. If that Spirit be retained, then man, who was made neither mortal nor immortal, but capable of both, becomes immortal. And this spirit is retained by purity of life, especially by chastity. But then, how does this fit in with the rest of the parable? There is unquestionably a difficulty here, but a difficulty which we are not bound to solve. Hermas's words evidently mean what I have stated, and as he has not deemed it necessary to show the connexion between his explanation and the rest of the parable, perhaps it was because he had no definite idea of a connexion. If, however, we apply the doctrine to the body of Christ, as representative of humanity, the connexion might be—Christ's body was kept absolutely pure. Therefore the spirit was called in to testify to his merits, and every other body that is kept pure will have similar testimony borne to it. Another explanation

as counsellor and his glorious angels from the inheritance of the slave. The Holy pre-existent Spirit, which created the whole creation, God made to dwell in flesh which he chose. This flesh then, in which the Holy Spirit dwelt, was nobly subject to the Spirit, walking in holiness and chastity, and in no way polluting the Spirit. Since then it had lived nobly and chastely, and had laboured and toiled along with the Spirit, and had behaved vigorously and courageously along with the Holy Spirit in every deed, He took it as a partner; for the conduct of this flesh pleased him because it was not defiled on the earth, while it had the Holy Spirit. He therefore took as fellow counsellors His son and the glorious angels, in order that this flesh, which had served the Spirit blamelessly might have some place of tabernacle and that it might not seem * * * [Something evidently lost here] the reward, having been found spotless and blameless in which the Holy Spirit dwelt."

seems to me more likely. The object of Christ's mission, as it is stated in the sixth chapter, is to preserve the people whom God had given to Him. Who could best bear witness to this fact? The Holy Spirit who dwelt in the bodies of those who were pure in heart, and the good angels who attended on those who walked in the way of righteousness. They are the proper witnesses to the facts of Christ's work, and therefore they are called in to give their advice with regard to the reward of Christ and his people. It deserves notice, however, that the writer does not say what is meant by the inheritance. And the only reward assigned to purity of body is a locality for the body; or, in other words, Hermas probably meant to affirm that all who remained pure would rise again to glory.

It would be impossible to give anything like an idea of the doctrines which have been supposed to be hid in this obscure passage. Bull regarded the words " the Son is the Spirit," as applicable to Christ in respect of his divine nature, while the " body" and the servant indicated his human[n]. Jachmann applies the words " holy spirit " to the third person of the Trinitarian doctrine, justly remarking that the times of Hermas knew nothing of a distinction of natures. The Tübingen school suppose that Hermas regarded the Holy Spirit as the higher being of Christ, and that he knew nothing of Christ's pre-existence but "as a holy spirit[o]." Bunsen has given the following explanation: "This 'Son of God' is distinguished as the 'Holy Ghost,' the 'first created,' from the man Jesus, who is the servant of God[p].

[n] Defens. Fid. Nicæn. i. 2. 5; ii. 2. 3. So does Zahn, who defines the σάρξ, 'der ganze Mensch Jesus,' p. 255.

[o] See Hilgenfeld, Apost. Väter, p. 166; Dorner, Entwicklungslehre, vol. i. pp. 195 ff; Jachmann, p. 70.   [p] Sim. v. 6.

The Holy Spirit lived in Him, and it was in consequence of his holy life and death that the 'servant of God' was made partaker of God's nature. So, to a certain degree, is every faithful believer. But that holy servant of God, the man Jesus, is most unequivocally and emphatically called in that same passage the 'Son of God.'. The Son of God is the Holy Ghost, and that servant is the Son of God [q]." He expresses the idea of Hermas in his own words, thus: "The difference established by him between the Eternal Spirit and the man Jesus is, that the one is the infinite consciousness of God, of Himself, and of the world; and the other, the identical image of that consciousness under the limitations of the finite within the bonds of humanity[r]."

Holy Spirit.—It may be matter of question whether Hermas makes any reference to the Holy Spirit. He speaks several times of the holy spirit, but his mode of speaking is so different from ours that we are at a loss to determine whether we are entitled to identify his opinion with any modern opinion. His work abounds in the application of the word "spirit," used with the notion of personality to the passions and emotions of the mind. Thus evil speaking is said to be "an evil spirit, and an inconstant demon (πονηρὸν γὰρ πνεῦμά ἐστιν ἡ καταλαλιὰ, καὶ ἀκατάστατον δαιμόνιον), never at peace, but always dwelling in quarrels[s]." And in like manner "doubt" is said to be "an earthly spirit proceeding from the devil[t]." This hypostatizing of the passions into spirits is still farther illustrated by a passage in Sim. ix. 13-15. There certain virgins are introduced, ex-

---

[q] Bunsen, Christianity and Mankind, vol. i. p. 211. In a note he enters more fully into an explanation of the passage.

[r] p. 213.   [s] Mand. ii.   [t] Ibid. ix.

plained to be the powers of the Son of God, and affirmed to be holy spirits. Women also in black dress form a part of the allegory. When this part of the allegory is explained, the names of the virgins or holy spirits are, Faith, Self-restraint, Power, and Patience. The women in black are explained to be Unbelief, Intemperance, Disobedience, Deceit, Sadness, Malice, Lust, Wrath, Lying, Folly, Slander, and Hatred. And the interpreter adds, " The servant of God who carries these spirits [u], shall indeed see the kingdom of God, but shall not enter it." It will be noticed that when the passion is bad the word " spirit " then becomes equal to demon. So it is said that " boldness and vain confidence is a great demon" (magnum dæmonium [x]).

This method of hypostatizing must be kept in mind, if we are to understand the references to the holy spirit, for the writer speaks of it in a way that he could not have done had he regarded the holy spirit as one of the persons of the Deity, or as gifted with full and complete personality. Thus " the holy spirit " is identified with goodness in man, and is spoken of as expelled by wickedness. " Be patient," he says, " and thou wilt work all righteousness. But if thou art patient, the holy spirit which dwells in thee will be pure, and will not be darkened by another wicked spirit, but delighting it will be enlarged.... But if any anger shall come upon thee, then forthwith the holy spirit which is in thee will be straightened, and will seek to depart; for it is suffocated by the wicked spirit [y]." In like manner man is said to be left by the holy spirit, when

---

[u] The Greek has "names": but the reading of the translations is evidently the correct one.

[x] Sim. ix. 22.   [y] Mand. v. 1.

evil spirits come in and he is blinded by evil thoughts[z]; and sadness, more wicked than all spirits, is described as crushing out the holy spirit, and again saving. Hermas is warned to take away sadness, and not crush the holy spirit which dwells in him, "lest it entreat God[a] against thee and depart from thee." This holy spirit is given by God, and though its personality seems so distinctly marked out in these passages, yet in the context occur the words "sadness mixed with the holy spirit[b]." The holy spirit is spoken of as being introduced into the body of man, and commanding obedience; and it is declared that if a person defiles this body, he defiles the holy spirit[c]. Hermas is also warned not to join a bad conscience with the spirit of truth, nor cause sorrow to the holy and true spirit[d].

All these passages connect the holy spirit with moral goodness. There are some that do not so easily identify themselves with this notion. Thus it is said that a Spirit carried Hermas away[e]. There is also a whole commandment devoted to the distinguishing of true prophets and false, where at first sight the holy spirit seems to mean the prophetic gift. But then, as the prophetic gift plainly means, not the power of foretelling but the power of giving out God's message, the holy spirit is seen to be identical with holiness. The holy spirit is there said to be given by God, and to come from Him. It is also called the "divine" spirit and the spirit of divinity. The prophet "has the divine spirit from above." The holy spirit is also identified with the

[z] Mand. v. 2.   [a] Ibid. x. 2. The Vat. reads Lord.   [b] Ibid. x. 1.
[c] Sim. v. 6, 7.   [d] Mand. iii. "of God" is added in the common translation and Vatican.
[e] Vis i. 1; ii. 2.

prophetic spirit. By the agency of an angel of the prophetic spirit the prophet is said to be filled with the holy spirit, and then the spirit speaks and is manifested. Holy men too, into whose assembly the prophet enters, are described as having faith in the divine spirit, and as having themselves a spirit of divinity. On the other hand, the false prophet has no virtue of the divine spirit in him. On the contrary, it is said that "the devil fills him with his spirit." The spirit which is in the false prophet is earthly, empty, powerless, and full of folly [f].

Angels.—The references to angels are more frequent than in contemporary works, because the allegory required their aid. It is difficult, however, to determine how far we ought to regard the statements with respect to angels as the beliefs of the writer, and not as mere conjectures. As he does not hint that he is merely conjecturing, and as his statements with regard to angels are made in the same way as his other statements, the immense probability is, that however he reached his beliefs, he really did believe in what he would call his facts with regard to angels. Angels by the writer are generally mentioned as employed in some work; good angels in works of goodness, and wicked angels in evil deeds. The writer mentions six angels who were created first, and to whom the Lord entrusted the whole creation, to increase and rule over it. Six other holy angels are also mentioned, who are not so excellent as the first class [g]. Those who were created first were also called by God into his counsel in regard to the salvation of man [h].

Several special angels are introduced, and two are

[f] Mand. xi.   [g] Vis. iii. 4.   [h] Sim. v. 5.

named. One is Michael, the magnificent and good, or, as the Greek has it, great and glorious, who governs the people of Christ, inserts the law in the hearts of those who believe, and watches if they keep the law[i]. The other name is uncertain, the readings being various and not easily explicable. "The Lord sent his angel who is over the beasts, whose name is Thegri[k]." The Palatine writes the name Tegri, the Vatican Hegrin; and Jerome has been supposed by some to allude to this angel by the name Tyrus. But Cotelerius is unquestionably right in supposing that Jerome referred to an apocryphal book now lost. Most probably the name Tegrin, as Dressel supposes, is connected with ἄγριον, but commentators have not settled and cannot settle the meaning[l]. Besides these named, angels keep the people of Christ within bounds[m], angels warn to well-doing[n], an angel called "the Pastor" presides over repentance[o], "and all who repent are justified (made righteous) by a most holy angel[p]." Every man has two angels; one of righteousness and the other of iniquity. The one speaks to him of righteousness, chastity, kindness, pardon, love and piety, and is to be obeyed; the other whispers all evil to him, and is to be discarded[q]. Besides these angels, the writer mentions an angel who presides over pleasure, and who allures men away from the right path[r]; and a just angel, who presides over punishment[s].

In two passages good men are said to have their life

[i] Sim. viii. 3. Cotelerius in loc. quotes Nicephorus, who calls Michael ὁ τῆς Χριστιανῶν πίστεως ἔφορος. Lib. vii. c. 50.

[k] Vis. iv. 2. [l] See the notes of Cotelerius and Oxon. in the edition of Clericus. [m] Sim. v. 5. [n] Vis. iii. 5. [o] Lib. ii. (Proem.) Mand. iv. 2, 3. [p] Mand. v. 1. [q] Ibid. vi. 2.
[r] Sim. vi. 2. [s] Ibid. vi. 3.

with the angels, and as these statements are given as promises, they have been taken to refer to the blessings of the future state. The words are peculiar. Unfortunately they differ in the different manuscripts. The first passage is, "Continue steadfast, ye who work righteousness, and doubt not, that your passage may be with holy angels[t]." The Greek has πάροδος, the Vatican *transitus vester*. The Palatine reads "ut fiat iter vestrum." The Greek and Vatican unquestionably point to a future state, or rather to the passing from this life into the next, but the words might possibly refer to the passing through this life under the protection and in company of holy angels. The Palatine seems to intimate the latter more distinctly. The second passage is: "Of such the passage is with angels[u]." The writer is explaining a similitude, and "these" are men who have walked in truth. The Palatine reads, "Talium ergo traditio cum angelis erit." The Vatican has "these then have their passage among angels." As the writer is describing the reward of those who had walked in truth, the words must refer to the future state.

The Devil.—The devil is mentioned especially as the enemy of Christians. Christians are represented as in a pilgrimage. The state through which they pass is not the state of their Lord. They ought not to buy fields or indulge in delicacies, for all these things belong to another, and are under his power[x]. The Christian's bounden duty is therefore to "leave the devil and his pleasures, which are wicked, bitter, and impure[y]." The devil tempts Christians, plans mischief against them, and lies in wait for them[z]. But for all that, Christians

[t] Vis. ii. 2.   [u] Sim. ix. 25.   [x] Ibid. i. 1.   [y] Mand. xii. 4.
[z] Ibid. iv. 3.

are not to fear him; he has no virtue in him[a]. God knows the weakness of men, and the manifold wickedness of the devil[b]. If men then put their trust in God, and resist the devil, he will give way. He is hard, indeed, and sure to wrestle, but he must yield. Only those who waver fear the devil[c]. Christians are to fear the deeds of the devil[d]. All doubt comes from him[e]; evil desire comes from him[f]; false prophets are filled with his spirit, which is an earthly spirit[g]; and he is a most wicked (nequissimus) devil[h].

Man.—Hermas says little of the nature of man. He makes no mention of original sin, and one passage can scarcely be reconciled with it. He says that a man ought always to speak the truth, that the spirit which God gave him might be found true with all men. " Those therefore who lie deny the Lord and rob Him, not rendering back to Him the deposit which they received. For they received from Him a spirit free from falsehood. If they give Him back this spirit untruthful they pollute the command of the Lord[i]." At the same time Hermas is most precise on the evil effects of sin. It produces death and captivity[k], and man needs to be saved from it, to be renovated and restored to God. This is done without in any way impairing man's free will. There is a statement in Hermas so precise on this point that it has frequently been quoted in proof of his adherence to the doctrine of free-will[1], as opposed to God's determination of man's salvation. The passage runs thus : " To those whose heart the Lord saw would

[a] Mand. vii.; xii. 6 [b] Ibid. iv. 3. [c] Ibid. xii. 5. [d] Ibid. 7.
[e] Ibid. ix. [f] Ibid. xii. 1. [g] Ibid. xi. 1. [h] Sim. ix. 31.
[i] Mand. iii. [k] Vis. i. 1.

[1] For a short account of how modern writers have viewed Hermas in relation to the doctrine of free grace, see Jachmann, p. 78.

be pure and would serve Him, He gave repentance with the whole heart; but to those whose deceitfulness and wickedness He saw, and who He perceived would repent deceitfully, He did not give repentance, lest they should again profane His name [m]." Something to the same effect is also stated in Sim. ix. 33 : " When the Lord had seen that their repentance was good and pure, and that they could remain in it, he ordered their former sins to be blotted out." Other passages have also been adduced not so precise, where Hermas simply says that those who purify themselves will receive from the Lord a remedy for their former sins [n], and if a man resists the devil, he will flee in disgrace from him [o].

There are also some passages [p] in which Hermas makes mention of the elect, and these have been adduced to show that Hermas was not consistent in his expression of thought. It is most probable, however, that Hermas used the word " elect" without any other meaning than that they were at present selected from the world to be the Church of God; and the word thus becomes synonymous in its use to " the holy" or to " the brethren." Such at least must be its meaning in one of the passages in which it is used: " For the Lord has sworn by his glory in regard to his elect, that if any one of them sin beyond the appointed day, he shall not have salvation [q]." For, according to this, even some of the elect may not be saved. Another passage of a similar nature occurs in Vis. i. 3. At the same time it has to be borne in mind that Hermas declares that repentance and faith come from God, and our whole salvation is thus radically ascribed to God. Whether Hermas felt any difficulty in

[m] Sim. viii. 6. [n] Ibid. viii. 11. [o] Mand. xii. 5; Jachmann, p. 77.
[p] Vis. iii. 5 ; iv. 2. [q] Ibid. ii. 2.

reconciling man's free will with God's gift of faith we do not know; but, as he has not expressed it anywhere so we may regard it as most probable that he never felt it.

Man's Salvation.—The salvation of man is spoken of in various ways. It is sometimes called repentance, or change of mind. Sometimes the words "to live to God," are plainly used as equivalent to "to be saved [r]." Sometimes the idea is expressed by the word "life." And the words "safe" and "salvation" are themselves frequently employed.

The doctrine of repentance is involved in some difficulty; for the word μετάνοια is applied in two ways. It is used to express that complete change of the inner being, feelings, and thoughts of man which we now term conversion; or it may mean repentance for sins committed after conversion has taken place. In fact the word simply means change of mind, or of the purpose of the soul, and though in the New Testament it always implies a change from worse to better, it may be correctly applied to cases where the change is from the better to the worse, as is done in one passage in Hermas. (Vis. iii. 7.) In most passages, however, we can clearly ascertain the meaning from the context.

Forgiveness of sins is granted at once on repentance. "Whosoever with his whole heart repents and purifies himself from all the iniquity mentioned above, and adds no more to his sins, will receive from the Lord a cure for his former sins, if he doubt not with regard to these commandments, and will live to God[s]." This declaration is prefaced with the information that repentance is announced to all, even to those who do not deserve

[r] See Mand. iii. and viii.
[s] Sim. viii. 11. The Greek omits the words "repents and."

salvation on account of their deeds, because God is merciful and patient, and wishes to save the invitation [t] made through his Son. In another passage repentance is described as a turning from wretchedness to goodness, a putting on of all virtue and justice [u]. In a third passage there is a more minute description of a change of mind; but it is possible that the description is meant to apply to the repentance of the Christian, and not to the conversion of the sinner. "It behoves him who repents to torture his own soul, and to show a humble mind in every deed, and endure many and various afflictions; and if he endure the afflictions which come upon him, then assuredly He who created all things and endued them with power, will be moved with mercy towards him, and will give him some remedy, especially if he see the heart of the repentant pure from every wicked work [x]."

This change of life is expressly connected with water, which in baptism was the great symbol of purification of the whole man, and it is described as a great and holy calling, the Palatine adding, "with which the Lord has called his own to perpetual life [y]."

"The elect of God," it is said, "will be saved through faith." Faith has this work assigned to it as the first of virtues, and as producing the rest. It is the mother of self-restraint. From self-restraint arises simplicity; from simplicity guilelessness, from guilelessness chas-

---

[t] The reading of this passage is extremely doubtful. The Greek has κλῆσις, the common translation "invitatio," and the Vatican "mutationem." The Palatine reads quite differently:—"et vult ecclesiam suam quæ est filii sui, salvare." This seems to give the meaning, κλῆσις being used for κλητοὶ, "wishes those who were called by His Son to be saved." [u] Sim. vi. 1.

[x] Ibid. vii. Instead of "assuredly" both Latin forms read "perhaps."
[y] Mand. iv. 3.

tity; from chastity intelligence, from intelligence love, Whoever retains the works of these virtues "shall have his habitation with the saints of God [z]." This and another [a] are the only passages in which faith is spoken of as producing salvation. In all the others, and in fact in Mand. viii., faith and its concomitants are ushered in with the words, according to the common translation, "Hear the virtue of good works which you ought to work, that you may be able to be safe." The Greek has the same meaning, but differs in form. "Tell me," says Hermas, "the nature of the good deeds that I may walk in them and wait on them, so that doing them I can be saved." The activity of man in procuring his salvation is often spoken of by Hermas; and for the most part he urges men to one or two particular things which will save them. So, in speaking of sin, he says that "the memory of injuries works death," and the Vatican adds "the forgetfulness of injuries works eternal life [b]." Again, Hermas is said to be saved by his simplicity and singular continence, and all who have the same character will attain to eternal life [c]. If one abstains from all concupiscence he will be an heir of eternal life [d]. "If you keep the truth you will be able to obtain life [e]." "Through patience and humility of soul men will obtain life [f]." Several times the performance of the commandments given by the angel of repentance is said to be rewarded with life, or living to God [g]; and the commandments themselves are said to

[z] Vis. iii. 8.   [a] Mand. viii.   [b] Vis. ii. 3.
[c] Ibid.   [d] Ibid. iii. 8.   [e] Mand. iii.
[f] Sim. viii. 7. The Greek is somewhat different in form, but has the same meaning. It has the following sentence not found in the translations: "Life is the possession of all who keep the Commandments of the Lord."   [g] Mand. viii. Sim. vi. 1.

be able to bring salvation to men [i]. In addition to these explanations of the way of life, we have oftener than once the assertion, "life is made safe through water." A notice of these expressions will fall under the subject of Baptism. Hermas speaks also of God being propitiated. Thus he says, " When he thinks justly he will have the Lord propitious to him [k];" and salvation and propitiation are plainly identical in the question of Hermas, " How shall I be able to be saved, or how shall I propitiate God in regard to my great sins, or with what words ask the Lord that He may be propitious to me [l]?"

Hermas never speaks of regeneration: and the only two instances in which δικαιῶ, to justify, is used, have no idea in them similar to the modern theory of justification. The one runs: " All were justified by the most holy angel;" that is, all were declared righteous by the angel [m]. The other is: " The Lord who has dropped His righteousness down upon you, that ye may be justified and sanctified from all your iniquity "—or that ye may be made righteous and holy from all your iniquity [n]. Here by the justification is meant the real purification of the soul from iniquity [o]. Christians are called saints, the elect, the called, the righteous.

Conduct of Christians.—Hermas is more precise on certain points of Christian conduct than his contemporaries, and several unusual subjects thus turn up in the course of his work. There is one passage which has been adduced to show that Hermas hints at the doctrine of the merit of works of supererogation. The passage runs thus: " If you do anything good beyond what

[i] Sim. vi. 1. [k] Vis. i. 1. [l] Ibid. i. 2.
[m] Mand. v. 1. [n] Vis. iii. 9. [o] See Zahn, p. 167, note.

God has commanded, you will acquire for yourself more abundant glory, and you will be more honoured with God than you would have been. If therefore in keeping the commandments of the Lord, you do in addition these services, you will rejoice [p]." The nature of this fast is, that he keep himself pure from the world, and then that he live on the day of the fast on bread and water, and give what else he would have eaten to the widow and the needy.

It will be seen that unquestionably there is a false idea propounded here in supposing that any external deed will gain a man greater honour, or make him more acceptable to God. But at the same time the deed urged is such that it might make a man holier, and thus bring him nearer to God, and make him more acceptable.

The subject of repentance is one that occurs frequently in the works of Hermas. How often will a renewed man fall back into his old state, and renew himself again? Hermas answers positively that there is but one change of mind for such a man, and no hope after that. Most commentators have supposed that Hermas means that if a Christian once sins greatly after his conversion, he may repent and God or the Church will forgive him; but if he repent a second time, his repentance is not to be accepted, and he perishes or is expelled from the Church. We lay the passages before the reader, premising that the introduction of the Church is purely gratuitous. We shall

---

[p] Sim. v. 3. The text is somewhat different in the Palatine and Vulgate translations. The Vulgate reads: "If therefore you keep the commandments of the Lord and add these stations to them, you will rejoice."

attempt to show that Hermas's doctrine is purely spiritual, and is a psychological problem, not a matter of doctrine at all.

In discussing adultery, he says that the husband ought to receive the guilty wife back; "but not often; for to the servants of God there is but one repentance [q]." In the third chapter Hermas refers to the teaching of some, that there was only one repentance; namely, that which takes place at baptism, and which is accompanied by remission of sins. The angel tells him that this was true doctrine, and that the man who receives remission of his sins should sin no more. But he farther adds that God, knowing the wiles of the devil, extended his mercy; and if a man who had experienced the great change, shall be tempted by the devil and sin, he can repent once again. But if he sin after that, and then repent, such conduct will do the man no good, for he will with difficulty live to God. I take it that Hermas here means that a man can have the great change of mind only once, because it is only once that a man can be called from death into life. It is possible, however, for a man who has thus been called to relapse into a condition as bad as ever. Hermas thinks he may possibly recover from this relapse once; but if he falls into his evil ways again, his case becomes hopeless. God leaves him to his hardness of heart, and the man after that will find it difficult to live to God, however greatly he may change his convictions on the point. He goes farther even than this. He gives it as his opinion that, while Gentiles may undergo the great change of mind at any time up to the last day, there is a certain fixed time appointed by God within which if

[q] Mand. iv. 1. The reading of the Palatine is considerably different.

a saint do not return from his relapse he will not be saved. "For the repentance of the righteous has limits. Filled up are the days of repentance to all saints [r]." Accordingly, Hermas describes certain classes of Christians to which repentance is impossible. "This (angel of pleasure)," he says, speaking of one of these classes, "corrupts the minds of the servants of God, and turns them away from the truth, deceiving them with pleasures; and they perish." These he divides into two classes. To one of them "there is no return to life through repentance. . . . They are destined for death [s]." Another class of Christians he describes as dead to God, and not changing their minds [t]. And another class still he mentions, for whom he says, "death is set forth, and no change of mind [u]." The doctrine of Hermas on this subject of repentance has been censured as Montanistic. We have seen that Hermas does not once speak of it as a church matter: and his words are nowhere so decided and positive as those of the Epistle to the Hebrews [x]. In several passages it is shown how earthly calamities are intended to produce a turning to God in Christians (especially Sim. vi.). One of these passages has been absurdly supposed by some to countenance the doctrine of purgatory [y]. Hermas speaks in reference to a vision, and says of a certain class, "Repentance is yet possible, but they cannot find a suitable place in this tower, but they will find a suitable place much lower; and, that too, only when they have been tormented and fulfilled the days of their sins; and on this account they will be transferred, because they have

---

[r] Vis. ii. 2. Comp. Vis. iii. 5.   [s] Sim. vi. 2.   [t] Ibid. viii. 6.
[u] Ibid. ix. 19.   [x] Heb. vi. 4-6.
[y] Scultetus and Rivetus. See Bull's Defens. Fid. Nic. i. 2. 4.

partaken of the righteous word [z]." The lower place is a part simply of the allegory: the whole takes place in this world; and the sentiment is, that if a man sins, he may be tormented by the ills of this life, recognise in them the just sentence of God, and return to holiness. But if punishment has not this effect on men, "then they will not be saved, on account of the hardness of their hearts."

One of the points of the Christian life which is brought prominently forward in the Pastor of Hermas is the renunciation of the world. The world, as we have seen already, he regards as being under the power of the devil, and, accordingly, Christians are urged to purify their hearts "from all the vanities of this age [a]." The acquisition of riches is emphatically forbidden. "Look to it, therefore," says the Pastor, "as one dwelling in a foreign land make no more preparation for thyself than such is merely sufficient for thee [b]." "Instead of the fields, therefore, redeem souls from necessities, as each of you can; look after widows and orphans, and do not neglect them, and spend your riches and all your means on such lands and houses." "Do not desire the riches of the Gentiles, for they are destructive to the servants of God; but with the riches which you have of your own do those things by which ye can gain joy [c]." He goes farther even than this, and asserts that those who have riches must lose part of them before they themselves can become useful to God, as on account of their riches and their business they are tempted to deny

[z] Vis. iii. 7. [a] Mand. ix. [b] Sim. i.
[c] Ibid. I have translated from the Vulgate. The Greek is quite peculiar, but may be rendered: "Do not practise the lavish expenditure of the Gentiles: for it is disadvantageous to you the servants of God; but practise your own lavish expenditure in which you can rejoice."

God [d]. And he regards those who love this world and glory in their riches as peculiarly liable to death and captivity, since they act only for the present, and forget the glories of the future [e]. The rich are therefore urgently entreated to help the poor [f], and a similitude [g] is devoted to show how the help of the rich man does as much good to himself as to the poor man; and another similitude [h] is employed to show how this age is winter to the righteous. The Pastor of Hermas seems the more urgent on this topic, that Hermas himself is represented as having been carried away by his worldly business [i].

Another subject which engaged the Christian mind is that of marriage. The decisions of the Pastor on this subject are—that if a woman commit adultery, the religious husband is not to remain with her. He is not allowed however to marry, because she may possibly repent. If she repents, she is to be taken back once; not oftener. But in no case is the man to marry. So also is the wife to act if the husband commit adultery [k]. If a husband or wife dies, the survivor may marry, but he who remains unmarried " gains greater honour and glory with the Lord [l]."

In regard to prayer, Jachmann [m] inaccurately accuses Hermas of a false material representation. The Pastor simply says, that if a man purify his heart from all doubt, and put on faith, and trust God, he will receive whatever he ask [n]. But there is not a word to intimate that the Pastor refers to temporal blessings. On the contrary, the whole tenor of the work forces us to believe that he had no reference to anything but spiritual

---

[d] Vis. iii. 6.   [e] Ibid. i. 1.   [f] Ibid. iii. 9.   [g] Sim. ii.
[h] Ibid. iii.   [i] Vis. i. 3.   [k] Mand. iv. 1.   [l] Ibid. iv.
[m] p. 84.   [n] Mand. ix.

desires and the spiritual life. Nor is there anything peculiarly wrong in the Pastor's reference to the martyrs. He assigns a special place of honour to them, but in words that would include a great number more than those who suffered death, and exclude many who did suffer death. "The place which is at the right hand," he says, "belongs to others who have already pleased God [o] and have suffered for his name's sake [p];" and this place will be given to those who do like deeds and suffer like sufferings.

One other point in the religious life as exhibited by the Pastor of Hermas deserves notice. It is its cheerfulness. Sadness is spoken of as most disastrous to the servants of God, and they are urged to clothe themselves with joyfulness. "Every cheerful man does what is good, and always thinks on those things which are good [q]."

Church.—The references of the Pastor of Hermas to the constitution of the Church are few. He unquestionably means by the Church the whole body of good men in all ages, and it is curious that he speaks of the unity of the Church as realized only when at last it has been purified from all the wicked. "As the tower became as if it had been made of one stone after it had been purified; so the Church of God, after its purification and the rejection of the wicked, and the hypocritical, and blasphemers, and the wavering, and those who have acted wickedly in various ways, shall be one body, one mind, one thought, one faith, one love, and then shall the Son of God rejoice among them, and receive his people pure [r]." The Church in this sense is regarded as the prime object of God's attention. "It was created first of all,"

[o] The Vulgate reads: "Qui meruerunt Deum."
[p] Vis. iii. 1.   [q] Mand. x. 3.   [r] Sim. ix. 18.

says the Pastor, "and on its account the world was made [s]." The exact meaning of this assertion has been doubted: Rothe [t] supposing that Hermas made the Church a kind of æon, and a heavenly person the first creature of God; as if, like Clemens Alexandrinus, he had made a distinction between the heavenly and earthly Church. But there is far more likelihood in the opinion of Dressel [u], that the idea is, that God formed the notion of the Church first, and made the creation of other things have a reference to it. Little is said of the history of the Church, but in speaking of baptism we shall have to notice the admission of the good men of the Old Testament into it. The time at which the book was written was believed not to be far distant from the period when the Church would be completed [x].

With regard to the management of the churches, there can be little doubt that in the time of Hermas presbyters and overseers were identical. The evidence for this is as follows: The Church orders Hermas to give a book to the presbyters, and these elders are described as being "those who preside over the Church [y]." In Sim. ix. 27 the overseers are mentioned, and, as if to explain the title, it is added in the Vulgate, "that is, presidents of the churches." The common text in the same chapter speaks of a different class, the præsides ministeriorum, who protected the needy and widows, and who have been identified with deacons. These passages are not decisive, for several reasons. In the first passage Origen reads simply $\pi\rho\epsilon\sigma\beta\upsilon\tau\acute{\epsilon}\rho o\iota s$ in giving the Greek. In the second, the Greek and the Palatine differ considerably from the common text, and give no ex-

[s] Vis. ii. 4. Comp. Vis. i. 1, 3.   [t] Anfänge, p. 612, note 42.
[u] See Dressel, note in loc.   [x] Vis. iii. 8.   [y] Ibid. ii. 4.

planation of the word 'overseer,' and make the episcopi protect the needy and widows. The probability however of their identity is rendered greater by the only other references to the managers of the churches. They are never spoken of in the singular. It is always "those who preside over the Church [z];" and these words plainly refer, not to all those who have rule in the Church universal, but to those individuals who had the government of the Church in the city in which Hermas was [a]. There is one passage indeed from which Cotelerius had inferred that Hermas knew three orders of managers, but the words warrant no such inference. "Those stones," he says, "are apostles, and overseers, and teachers, and deacons, who have walked in godly purity, and have acted as overseers and teachers and deacons to the elect of God chastely and reverently [b]." The apostles and overseers, Cotelerius says, carry on the oversight, the teachers are elders teaching, and the servants are deacons. For this identification however of the teachers and elders there is not the slightest authority in Hermas, and accordingly Oxon. finds it only in Cyprian. On the contrary, the Pastor speaks of these teachers oftener than once [c], and it is perfectly plain that he did not think of them as, nor identify them with, any class of Church governors, but he spoke of them simply as teachers.

The only rite of the Church to which Hermas refers is that of baptism; but his references are few and obscure. The obscurity arises from the habit prevalent in the early writers of using the word denoting the mere symbol or external instrument for all that was

[z] Vis. ii. 4; iii. 9.   [a] Ibid. ii. 4.   [b] Ibid. iii. 5.
[c] Sim. ix. 15, 16, 25.

symbolized. We have already seen this in the Epistle of Barnabas. This circumstance frequently makes it difficult, sometimes impossible, to determine whether the writer had any reference to an external rite at all. The rite of baptism is expressly referred to in Vis. iii. 7, where it is said, "These are they who have heard the word, and wish to be baptized in the name of the Lord; but when the chastity demanded by the truth comes into their recollection, they draw back and again walk after their own wicked desires." In another passage there is unquestionably a reference only to the symbolized truths of baptism. The Church (tower) is said to be built on waters, and the reason assigned is, "For your life was saved by water, and will be saved [d]." The meaning of this cannot be that the external rite of baptism is the means of salvation to a man, and that at last he will be saved through it. For, not to take into consideration that the whole tenor of the teaching of Hermas is opposed to such a notion, the few references made to baptism afford sufficient evidence to contradict such an interpretation. For Hermas expressly says that some, after receiving this seal, and after having received faith and love, "have stained themselves and been cast forth from the class of the righteous, and have returned to their former state and become even worse than they were before [e]." The meaning must therefore be, that men are saved by the purifying power shadowed forth in the water, and that they will be saved by the same means. The identification of the symbol and the thing symbolized is seen in a passage where there is unquestionably a reference both to the external rite and the internal state. "I have heard from some teachers,"

[d] Vis. iii. 3.   [e] Sim. ix. 17.

he says, "that there is no other repentance than that which takes place when we descend into the water and receive remission of our former sins[f]." It is easy to account for this identification of symbol and truth. The fact was, that when a man felt a change come over him through the preaching of the truth, he felt at the same time an impulse to profess the truth, and baptism was his outward confession of his acceptance of Christianity, his recognition of the process of change of mind which had been going on within him. Though therefore the rite had in itself no power, yet he felt impelled and commanded to go through it, and consequently he marked the date of his forgiveness from the solemn outward act by which he professed himself washed from sins and renewed to God. In Sim ix. 16 Hermas speaks of the effect of baptism in words slightly different. He says: "Before a man bears the name of the Son of God he is dead, but when he receives the seal he lays aside his deadness and resumes life. Now the seal is water; into water therefore they descend dead, but they ascend alive." These words are introduced to show how the Old Testament saints required that the apostles should come and preach to them before they could enter the kingdom of God. They had lived in a holy manner, but they had not received the full blessings which were bestowed in baptism. The apostles and teachers, therefore, "after falling asleep in the power and faith of the Son of God, preached the name of the Son of God also to those who had fallen asleep, and themselves gave them the seal of the preaching. They descended therefore into the water with them, and again ascended. But these descended alive and again ascended alive; but the

[f] Mand. iv. 3.

others, who had fallen asleep before, descended dead but ascended alive." There is extreme improbability in the supposition which Jachmann and others make, that Hermas here refers to a literal baptism in the other world. In fact, most of the ancient Jews had probably undergone many baptisms, being baptized with Moses and others; but it was the peculiar truths and power which Christ revealed and conveyed that were necessary to render the Old Testament saints fit for the kingdom of God. Cotelerius is therefore fully justified in saying that Hermas speaks of a baptism metaphorical and mystical, meaning the blessings which God grants in the baptism [g].

We have already seen that Hermas mentions the practice of fasting with especial praise [h]. This practice was confined, however, entirely to individuals. It was not, in fact, enjoined at all, even by the Lord, as Hermas remarks, and he gives a similitude to show that the Lord feels peculiar delight in a servant who, without being ordered to fast, practises fasting. In another passage answer to prayer is the reward of fasting. "Fast therefore and you will receive from the Lord that which you ask [i]."

Future State.—The teaching of Hermas with regard to a future state is exceedingly indefinite. We have already noticed some expressions with regard to angels and the opinion of Hermas with regard to the Old Testament saints. Hermas's doctrine of the future state comes out most prominently in contrasting it with this world. This age is winter to the just, the future or coming age is summer. The elect of God will dwell in the future age and remain pure and unstained to

[g] Not. in loc. [h] Sim. v. 3. [i] Vis. iii. 10.

eternal life [k]. They will all be joyful then. Those who do good now will have fruit then [l]. Hermas speaks of the blessings of the life to come [m], and he says that, according to God's promise, all things will become smooth to the elect if they keep his commandments [n]. On the other hand, this age is to be destroyed through fire and blood [o]. Evil desire puts to death the servants of God, and whosoever is subject to it will die for ever [p]. Those who sin and do not repent of their sins will be burned, as will also the Gentiles, because they did not recognise their Creator. But the most fearful punishment awaits those who have known the Lord and done iniquity. Those who sin in ignorance are destined to death, but those who have known the Lord and seen his wonderful works, if they live wickedly, will be doubly punished, and will die for ever [q].

Scriptures.—There is not one express quotation from the Old or New Testament, and only one that can be identified. This occurs in Vis. ii. 2, where the words of Matthew x. 33 are or seem to be quoted. The quotation is more distinct in the common text, and nearly vanishes in the Greek and the Palatine. Some have fancied a reference to an uncanonical gospel in Sim. ix. 16, but there is no foundation for such a conjecture. There is a more unquestionable reference to an apocryphal work in Vis. ii. 3: "The Lord is near to those who turn to Him, as it is written in Heldam and Modal, who prophesied in the wilderness to the people." Eldad and Medad, of which the names Heldam and Modal (Heldat and Modat in the Palatine) are modifications, are mentioned in Numbers xi. 26, 27, and

[k] Vis. iv. 3.   [l] Sim. iv.   [m] Vis. i. 1.   [n] Ibid. i. 3.
[o] Ibid. iv. 3.   [p] Mand. xii. 2.   [q] Sim. ix. 18.

an apocryphal book under their name is referred to in a work falsely attributed to Athanasius (Synopsis) and in the Stichometria of Nicephorus.

IV. LITERATURE.

MANUSCRIPTS.

The Pastor of Hermas was known for a long time only in the Latin translation. The codices of this translation are divided into two great classes. At the head of the first is the Codex Vaticanus 3848, written at the end of the fourteenth century[r]. Cotelerius mentions three manuscripts used by him; one belonging to the library of St. Germain de Prés (S. Germani), with a trustworthy text but unfortunately mutilated, now in the National Library at Paris, 11,553; another more recent, and so different from the common text that he was inclined to think that the Latin translation was a different one. It belonged to the library of St. Victor[s], now 14,656 in the National Library. A third he met with in the library of the Barefoot Carmelites in the neighbourhood of Paris (apud Carmelitas Excalceatos Suburbii Parisiensis[t]). Clericus says that he gave the readings of the Lambeth MS. more fully and accurately than Fell. Fell used two manuscripts—a Bodleian and a Lambeth. Bunsen thus speaks of the manuscripts: "We possess it only in a rather barbarous Latin translation, and all our five manuscripts represent but one original. In the three Paris manuscripts the Latin of the translation is corrected, which is also the case, although in a far less degree, in one of the two English

[r] Dressel, Prolegomena, p. lviii.
[s] S. Victor, 292.   [t] In Præf.

copies, that of the Bodleian Library. The MS. at Lambeth Palace is the only one which is free from a manifest interpolation common to all the others [u]."

Anger also mentions a Dresden codex. He says it is a manuscript of the Vulgate in the Royal Library of Dresden (marked A 47 fol.), in which between the Psalms and the Proverbs he found the Pastor of Hermas. It belongs to the fifteenth century [x].

The second class includes but one codex—Codex Palatinus 150, in the Vatican Library. It belongs to the fourteenth century. As has been remarked already, it was first published by Dressel. Its merits have been discussed.

In 1856 appeared the first edition of a Greek text of the Pastor of Hermas, under the care of Anger and Dindorf. The manuscript from which it was taken was furnished by Simonides. Simonides had brought with him three leaves of a codex lately found in Mount Athos, and a copy of all the rest except a small portion. Anger discovered that Simonides had not sold to the Leipzig University Library the original three leaves and the first copy of the rest but a second copy deliberately altered by himself in many places. On acquiring the first manuscript he published the results of a comparison in his Nachträgliche Bemerkungen. In a short time, however, considerable doubts were thrown on the genuineness of all the MSS, through a revelation of Simonides's forging practices made by a companion [y]. Tischendorf's suspicions had also been aroused. On examining the manuscript, however, he believed the three leaves to be

[u] Christianity and Mankind, vol. i. p. 184.

[x] Pastor of Hermas by Anger, Praef. p. viii.

[y] Enthüllungen über den Simonides-Dindorfischen Uranios von Alexander Lycurgus. Leipzig 1856.

genuine and the copy to be a copy of a genuine manuscript, and he gave a new recension of them in Dressel's Apostolical Fathers. He also wrote a dissertation, showing that the Greek, though not forged, must have been a re-translation from the Latin. His arguments seemed to himself to be most convincing, and he remarks at the conclusion of his essay: "Non deerunt quidem qui etiam tot argumentorum conjunctorum vim subterfugiant: nimirum sunt qui probabilitatis certique sensum aut natura non habent aut studiis amiserunt, quique verum tamquam adversarium malunt convincere quam integro animo invenire [z]." "There will no doubt be individuals who will be able to elude the force of even so many arguments joined together, to wit, those who have naturally no perception of what can be proved and is certain, or who have lost this perception by their party-feelings, and who prefer refuting the truth as if it were an adversary to finding it out with unbiassed mind."

The aspect of the question was greatly changed by the discovery of the Sinaitic manuscript. The history of this manuscript borders on the miraculous. In 1844 Tischendorf visited the Monastery of St. Catherine at the foot of Mount Sinai. He found there a large basket full of old parchments destined for the fire and in rummaging amongst these he fell in with a considerable number of sheets of a copy of the Old Testament in Greek. "The authorities," Tischendorf says, "of the convent allowed me to possess myself of a third of these parchments or about forty-three sheets, all the more readily as they were destined for the fire. But I could not get them to yield up possession of the remainder. The too lively satisfaction which I had displayed aroused

[z] p. liv.

their suspicions as to the value of this manuscript. I transcribed a page of the text of Isaiah and Jeremiah, and enjoined on the monks to take religious care of all such remains which might fall in their way [a]." On his return to Saxony he published these leaves under the title Codex Frederico-Augustanus, but, says he, "I did not divulge the name of the place where I had found it, in the hopes of returning and recovering the rest of the manuscript." Not able to go to Sinai himself, he wrote to a friend in regard to the manuscripts. "But," wrote the friend, "the monks have, since your departure, learned the value of these sheets of parchment and will not part with them at any price." In 1853 Tischendorf set out for the east "to copy this priceless manuscript;" but singularly enough Tischendorf could hear nothing of the document which was so highly valued and which he had urged the monks to preserve with the utmost care. "I was not able," he says, "to discover any further traces of the treasure of 1844. I forget: I found in a roll of papers a little fragment which, written over on both sides, contained eleven short lines of Genesis, which convince me that the manuscript contained the entire Old Testament, but that the greater part had been long since destroyed. On my return I reproduced in the first volume of a collection of ancient Christian documents, the page of the Sinaitic manuscript which I had transcribed in 1844, without divulging the secret of where I had found

---

[a] When were our Gospels written? an argument by Constantine Tischendorf, with a narrative of the discovery of the Sinaitic manuscript. Fourth edition. London: The Religious Tract Society 1869. Tischendorf has told the story of the discovery in very many books: such as his Notitia, his N. T. Sinaiticum, his Travels, and in special pamphlets.

it [b]." In 1859 Tischendorf again set out for the east. And this time he was successful. The torn and scattered fragments, which had been cast into the large basket to feed the fire had come forth, they had all united and now constituted a complete whole, a whole so complete that the like of it does not exist. Not only were the other parts of the Old Testament found: but the only complete uncial manuscript of the New Testament was contained in it, and added to this was the complete Greek of the Epistle of Barnabas and nearly as much of the Greek of the Pastor of Hermas as had been given in the Simonides manuscripts. And the circumstances in which the discovery was made are of a singularly surprising nature. Tischendorf says: "After having devoted a few days in turning over the manuscripts of the convent, not without alighting here and there on some precious parchment or other, I told my Bedouins on the 4th February, to hold themselves in readiness to set out with their dromedaries for Cairo on the 7th, when an entirely fortuitous circumstance carried me at once to the goal of all my desires. On the afternoon of this day I was taking a walk with the steward of the convent in the neighbourhood, and as we returned towards sunset he begged me to take some refreshment with him in his cell. Scarcely had he entered the room, when, resuming our former subject of conversation, he said, 'And I, too, have read a Septuagint, *i.e.* a copy of the Greek translation made by the Seventy [c],' and so saying he took down from the corner of the room a bulky kind of volume wrapped up in a red cloth and laid it before me. I unrolled the cover and discovered, to my great surprise, not only

[b] p. 26.   [c] The marks of quotation are Tischendorf's.

those very fragments which fifteen years before I had taken out of the basket, but also other parts of the Old Testament, the New Testament complete, and, in addition, the Epistle of Barnabas and a part of the Pastor of Hermas. Full of joy which this time I had the self-command to conceal from the steward and the rest of the community, I asked, as if in a careless way, for permission to take the manuscript into my sleeping chamber to look over it more at leisure [d]." It is plain that by this time the monks had forgotten their priceless treasure and that they had allowed the steward to gather the scattered leaves and to keep them for his own delectation in his cell. Tischendorf asked leave to transcribe the whole and soon obtained it. He then asked the manuscript for the Emperor of Russia, and again he seems to have had no difficulty in persuading the monks to make a present of their priceless treasure to the Emperor. There are many circumstances in this narrative calculated to awaken suspicion, and there are other circumstances of an equally suspicious nature which I have not mentioned. But those who are most competent to judge, have allowed that it seems a genuine ancient manuscript.

Tischendorf assigns this manuscript to the fourth century: but the data on which dates are assigned to uncials are exceedingly unsatisfactory and entirely negative. The utmost that can be based on the data in this case is that it may have been written in the fourth century. There is therefore ample room for discussing the age and value of the manuscript from internal evidence, that is, from the inflections and grammatical peculiarities that appear in the manuscript and from

[d] p. 29.

the state of the language as indicated by the errors of the transcriber or transcribers.

Now we find that the text of the Pastor of Hermas found in the Sinaitic codex is substantially the same as that given in the Athos manuscript. The variations are comparatively slight. And almost all the arguments that were adduced against the Athos manuscript are adducible against the Sinaitic. Tischendorf's opinion, however, changed on his finding the agreement between the two texts. In his Notitia, p. 45, he wrote: "I am glad to be able to communicate that the Leipzig text is derived not from middle-age studies but from the old original text. My opposite opinion is proved correct in so far as that the Leipzig text is disfigured by many corruptions, such as without doubt proceed from middle-age use of Latin." And he repeats his belief that the Leipzig text is genuine in the Prolegomena to the Novum Testamentum Sinaiticum[e]. The discovery of this manuscript does not however impair the force of the arguments which he employed; and as they are in the main applicable to the Sinaitic codex, they compel us to doubt the purity of the Greek text of Hermas given there.

The arguments may be divided into two classes; those which indicate that the Greek is of late origin, and those which tend to prove that the Greek text is derived from some Latin translation.

The late origin of the Greek is indicated by the occurrence of a great number of words unknown to the classical period, but common in later or modern Greek. Such are $βουνός$[f], $σύμβιος$ (as wife)[g], $μέ$ (for $μετά$[h]),

[e] p. xl. and note.
[f] Vis. i. 3.
[g] Ibid. ii. 2,
[h] Ibid. iii. 3.

πρωτοκαθεδρεῖς, ἰσχυροποιῶ, κατεπιθυμῶ [i], ἀσυγκρασία [k], κατάχυμα [l], ἐξακριβάζομαι [m], and such like. The lateness of the Greek appears also from late forms; such as ἀγαθωτάτης [n], μεθιστάνει [o], οἶδας, ἀφίουσιν [p], (ἀφίνουσιν in Sim. Greek), κατέκοπταν [q], ἐνεσκιρωμένοι [r], ἐπεδίδουν [s], ἐτίθουν [t], beside ἐτίθεσαν [u], ἔσχαν [x], λήμψῃ [y], ἐλπίδαν [z], τιθῶ [a], ἐπέριψας and ἤνοιξας [b], εἰπᾶσα [c], χεῖραν [d], ἁπλότηταν [e], σάρκαν [f], συνιῶ [g], συνίει [h]; and some modern Greek forms, such as κρατάουσα for κρατοῦσα [i], have been corrected by the writer of the manuscript. The lateness of the Greek appears also in the absence of the optative and the frequent use of ἵνα after ἐρωτᾶν, ἀξιῶ, αἰτοῦμαι, ἐντέλλομαι, ἄξιος, &c., generally with the subjunctive, never with the optative. We also find ἐάν joined with the indicative [k]. Εἰς is continually used for ἐν [l], as ἔχουσιν τόπον εἰς τὸν πυργόν [m]. We have also παρὰ after comparatives [n], and peculiar constructions, as περιχαρὴς τοῦ ἰδεῖν [o], σπουδαῖος εἰς τὸ γνῶναι [p], ἀπεγνωρίσθαι ἀπό [q]. And we have a neuter plural joined with a plural verb, κτήνη ἔρχονται [r]. Most, if not all, of these peculiarities now mentioned, may be found in Hellenistic writings, especially the New Testament; and some of them may be paralleled even in classical writers. But if we consider that the portion which has now been examined is small, and that every page is filled with these peculiarities, the only conclusion to which we can come is,

[i] Vis. iii. 2. [k] Ibid. 9. [l] Ibid. [m] Mand. iv. 2.
[n] Vis. i. 2. [o] Ibid. 3. [p] Ibid. iii. 7. [q] Ibid. 2.
[r] Ibid. iii. 9. [s] Ibid. 2. [t] Ibid. [u] Ibid.
[x] Ibid. iii. 5. [y] Ibid. 10. [z] Ibid. 11. [a] Ibid. i. 1; ii. 1.
[b] Ibid. iv. 2. [c] Ibid. 3. [d] Ibid. v. [e] Mand. ii.
[f] Ibid. iv. 1. [g] Ibid. 2. [h] Ibid. [i] Vis. iii. 8.
[k] Ibid. iii. 5. [l] Ibid. i. 1, 2, 4; iii. 7, 9. [m] Ibid. iii. 9.
[n] Ibid. 12. [o] Ibid. iii. 8. [p] Ibid. iii. 1. [q] Ibid. ii. 2.
[r] Ibid. iv. 1.

that the Greek is not the Greek of the at least first five centuries of the Christian era. There is no document written within that period which has half so many neo-Hellenic forms, taken page by page, as this Greek of the Pastor of Hermas.

The peculiarities which point out a Latin origin are the following:—

There are, first, a number of Latin words where you would naturally expect Greek. Such are συμψέλλιον, κερβικάριον, λέντιον, καρπάσινον.

Then there is a considerable number of passages preserved to us in Greek by Origen and other writers. The Sinaitic Greek differs often from this Greek, and agrees with the Latin translation, especially the Palatine. There is every, especially internal, probability that the Greek of the ancient writers is nearer the original than the Sinaitic.

Then there occurs this passage, ἐρεῖς δὲ Μαξίμῳ· ἰδοὺ θλίψις ἔρχεται[s]. The common Latin translation is: "Dices autem ; ecce magna tribulatio venit." Now here there is no trace of the Μαξίμῳ. But we find it in the Palatine, "Dicis autem maximo : ecce tribulatio," which Dressel changes into "Dicis autem ; maxima ecce tribulatio." The Palatine accounts well for the origin of Μαξίμῳ in the Sinaitic Greek, but it is difficult to account for the common "magna," if Μαξίμῳ had been originally in the Greek. The Aethiopic may be supposed by some to solve the difficulty, for it has both "maximus," and "magna." "Say to Maximus : Behold great affliction cometh."

All these examples have been taken from the Sinaitic

[s] Vis. ii. 3.

Greek. But the arguments become tenfold stronger if the Sinaitic Greek is to stand or fall with the Athos Greek. And this must be, for they are substantially the same. No doubt some allowance must be made for the carelessness of transcribers, but after every allowance is made, there is enough to convict both texts of a late origin, and to make it extremely probable that both are translations from the Latin.

EDITIONS.

The first edition of the Pastor of Hermas appeared at Paris 1513, fol., under the care of Jacobus Faber (Stapulensis). Dressel praises it for the correctness of the text. It was reprinted in most of the subsequent collections of the Fathers. It was also edited by Barth in 1655. Cotelerius, as we have seen, inserted a new recension of it in his collection. It was after that edited by Fell, Oxford 1685, and Fabricius made it part of his Codex Apocryphus Nov. Test. tom. iii. Hamburg 1719. It appeared also in Russel, Gallandi and Migne. Since that time it has been published by Hefele, Dressel, and Hilgenfeld. Hilgenfeld has also edited the Latin translation by itself (Lipsiæ 1873). An Ethiopic translation of the Pastor of Hermas has appeared: "Hermæ Pastor Æthiopice primum edidit et Æthiopica Latine vertit Antonius d'Abbadie. Leipzig 1860." The conclusion maintains that Hermas is Paul; in other words, that the prophet Hermas is no other than the apostle Paul. He adduces several reasons for this opinion; among others the words of the Acts, "They called Silas Zeus, and Paul Hermes." In two of the similitudes several chapters are condensed. This happens in regard to the famous passage on the Son being the Spirit.

A translation is given in Wake's Genuine Epistles of the Apostolical Fathers, and in the First volume of the Ante-Nicene Library. More recently a translation by Hoole has appeared.

CHAPTER VI.

PAPIAS.

I. LIFE.

THE only reliable sources from which we derive information with regard to Papias are the works of Irenæus and Eusebius. Irenæus mentions him as "a hearer of John," "a companion of Polycarp," and calls him "an ancient man [a]." There has been much dispute as to whether the John here mentioned was the apostle John; for Eusebius is decidedly of opinion that he was not a hearer of John the apostle. The historian has supplied us with his evidence. He appeals to a passage at the commencement of the work of Papias which runs thus: "But I shall not be slow to put down along with my interpretations those things which I learned well from the elders and remembered well, assuring you of the truth with regard to them [b]. For I did not, like the many, delight in those who spoke much, but in those who taught the truth; not in those who rehearsed the commands of others [c], but in those who rehearsed the commands given by the Lord to faith, and proceeding from truth itself.

---

[a] Adv. Hæres. v. 33, 4 ; also in Euseb. Hist. Eccl. iii. 39.

[b] For the inferences which may be drawn in regard to our gospels from this passage, see Westcott, Hist. of Can. p. 78.

[c] Valesius translates ἀλλοτρίας ἐντολάς, "nova quædam et inusitata præcepta." Something new and strange is implied in the very contrast between these commands and those of Christ.

If then any one who had attended on the elders came, I inquired diligently as to the words of the elders; what Andrew or what Peter said, or Philip or Thomas, or James, or John, or Matthew, or any other of the disciples of the Lord; and what things Aristion and the elder John, the disciples of the Lord, say. For I was of opinion that what could be got in books would not profit me so much as what I could get from the living and abiding voice [d]." Eusebius infers from the double mention of the name of John that two Johns existed, and that the latter mentioned John, called the elder or presbyter, was the instructor of Papias. We think Eusebius is right in his inference. As Eusebius well remarks, Papias makes a clear distinction between what Peter and John and the other apostles said, and what Aristion and the elder or presbyter John were still saying. He plainly confessed too that his information was derived not from the apostles themselves, but from those who had been in the company of the apostles. And Eusebius further informs us that Papias made frequent mention of Aristion and John the elder in his work, quoting their traditions. We scarcely think that Eusebius could have been mistaken on such a point as this, for the traditions of John the elder must have been easily distinguishable from those of the apostle. At the same time we are inclined to think that Irenæus meant the apostle John in his statement [e], but even this is by no means certain. For in mentioning John before, he simply calls him a disciple of the Lord, which John the

---

[d] Euseb. Hist. Eccl. iii. 39.

[e] Köstlin (Zur Geschichte des Urchristenthums; Theologische Jahrbücher. Tübingen 1850) shows well the tendency of Irenæus to convert post-Apostolic men into Apostolic, p. 14.

presbyter was; while, if he had meant the apostle John, he would probably have called him apostle. Besides, there is nothing impossible in the supposition that Papias should in his boyhood have listened to the Christian veteran, have failed to remember much of his discourse, and been therefore dependent on those who were older than himself. In fact, if he had met many of those who had conversed with the other apostles, who all left this world a considerable time before John, he must have been born before the death of John [f].

Of his life and death we know nothing on good authority, except that he was overseer of the church sojourning in Hierapolis [g], a city of Phrygia and the birthplace of the great Stoic philosopher Epictetus. Later writers have described his martyrdom [h]; some [i] saying that he suffered with Onesimus at Rome, others [k] that Pergamus was the scene of his death, and that the event happened at the same time as the martyrdom of Polycarp.

II. WRITINGS AND TEACHING.

Irenæus [l] mentions that Papias wrote five books, and Eusebius informs us that the name of the book was "An Exposition of the Lord's sayings [m]." Of the nature of this work we can form no exact idea, as all the extracts, except one, which have come down to us are of an historical nature. This much we know from the passage

[f] The literature on this subject is extensive. See Steitz in Herzog's Real-Encyclopædie and Studien und Kritiken, 1868, p. 63.
[g] Euseb. Hist. Eccl. iii. 36.   [h] Gobarus in Phot. Bibl. 232.
[i] Halloix from the Acts of Onesimus: but see Permaneder, Patrol. Spec. p. 59, note 18.   [k] Chron. Pasch. ad. ann. 163.
[l] Adv. Hæres. v. 33, 34.   [m] Hist. Eccl. iii. 39.

already quoted, that it was based on unwritten tradition, and Eusebius also asserts that it contained some strange parables and teachings of the Lord and other things of a somewhat fabulous nature ($\mu\nu\theta\iota\kappa\omega\tau\epsilon\rho\alpha$). Eusebius describes Papias as a man "most learned in all things, and well acquainted with the Scriptures[n]." In another place, however, he estimates him from his work as having an exceedingly small mind[o]. Various efforts have been made to reconcile these apparently discrepant statements, and some have entirely rejected the first, partly on account of the supposed discrepancy, and partly because the passage is not found in several manuscripts. It seems to me most likely that there is a real discrepancy, but that that discrepancy existed in the original work of Eusebius; that when mentioning him first in company with others he spoke of him as he ought to have done, but in coming suddenly upon a dogma which he disliked, he rashly pronounced the propounder of it a man of small capacity. At the same time there can be no doubt that the praise and the blame might justly fall on the same man; that a man might be $\lambda o\gamma\iota\omega\tau\alpha\tau o\varsigma$, a very great reader, and yet a very poor thinker.

The only point of doctrine on which we have the opinion of Papias is that of the millennium. He held, according to Eusebius[p], "that there would be some millennium after the resurrection of the dead, when the personal reign of Christ would be established upon this earth." Eusebius was probably mistaken. Papias and most, perhaps all, early Christians believed, if they had a belief on the matter, that after the resurrection the

[n] Hist. Eccl. iii. 36. [o] Ibid. 39.
[p] Ibid.

just would dwell upon this earth renewed and beautified. It is likely that Eusebius identified this opinion with the belief in a millennium. Even modern critics have found a reference to the millennium in a speech which Papias set down as Christ's on the authority of the elders. We get our information from Irenæus, who says that the "elders who had seen John, the disciple of Christ, remembered that they heard from him how the Lord taught with regard to those days, and said, "The days will come in which vines shall grow having each ten thousand branches, and in each branch ten thousand twigs, and in each real twig ten thousand shoots, and in each shoot ten thousand clusters, and in each cluster ten thousand grapes, and each grape when pressed will give five-and-twenty metretes of wine. And when one of the saints shall lay hold of a cluster, another shall cry out, 'I am a better cluster, take me, bless the Lord through me.' In like manner he said that a grain of wheat would produce ten thousand ears, and each ear would have ten thousand grains, and each grain would yield ten pounds of clear, pure, fine flour; and that apples, and seeds, and grass would produce in similar proportions; and that all animals using as food what is received from the earth would become peaceable and harmonious, being subject to men in all subjection." Irenæus says that these words of Christ were given in the fourth book of Papias. "And he [Papias] added, saying, 'These things can be believed by those who believe.' And Judas the traitor not believing and asking, how shall such growths be accomplished by the Lord? the Lord said, 'They shall see who shall come to them.'" There is nothing improbable in the statement that the Lord spoke in some such way, and it is

not at all improbable that Papias took literally what
was meant for allegory. We have no express quotation from Papias which showed that he referred these
statements to a millennium, or that he took them
literally. Irenæus unquestionably did both.

The most important of the traditions of Papias which
have reached us is that which relates to Matthew and
Mark. With regard to Matthew he says that "he wrote
the sayings in the Hebrew language, and each one
interpreted them as best he could [q]." The word λόγια
'sayings,' is, as Schleiermacher [r] has shown, applied
to oracular utterances, words of divine origin; but
considerable discussion has taken place as to whether it
can mean here only the sayings of Christ or whether it
might not include such narrative as we have in Matthew. The natural force of the word would unquestionably confine it to the 'sayings,' but it would be rash to
base upon this the assertion that Papias meant to say
that Matthew gave no connecting narrative [s]. How did
Papias get this information? He has already told us
the general sources of his information. In this instance
we cannot be far wrong in ascribing it to John the
elder, as in the information with regard to Mark, John
is expressly quoted. The extract runs thus: "And the
elder said this. Mark having become the interpreter of
Peter, wrote accurately what things he remembered.
He did not, however, relate in exact order the things
which were spoken or done by Christ. For he neither

[q] Eus. Hist. Eccl. iii. 39.

[r] Schleiermacher, Studien und Kritiken, 1832, p. 735.

[s] See Davidson's Introduction to the New Test., vol. i. p. 65;
Westcott, p. 79. Davidson, Introduction to the Study of the New Test.,
vol. i. p. 467, and Zahn in Studien und Kritiken, 1866, p. 475.

heard the Lord nor accompanied him. But afterwards, as I said, he accompanied Peter, who gave forth his teachings to suit the wants of the people, and not as putting together a full account of the sayings of the Lord; so that Mark, thus writing some things just as he himself recollected them, made no mistake. For of this one thing he took especial care, to omit nothing of what he heard or to put nothing fictitious into them." Eusebius also informs us that he made quotations from the first Epistle of John and the first Epistle of Peter, and that he gave another story, that of a woman who was accused of many sins before the Lord; "which story," he adds, " is now contained in the gospel according to the Hebrews." This is, no doubt, the story which found its way into many manuscripts of John's gospel; though the expression 'another story' makes it perfectly possible that Papias gave a different version, or rather additional particulars, with regard to the woman there mentioned.

The other traditions of Papias have no dogmatic reference. He relates two miracles. The first of these was the resurrection of a dead man. The words of Papias do not imply that this was a miracle wrought by a man, but simply that it took place in the time of the apostle Philip, whose daughters were under the pastoral charge of Papias and told him the story. The other story seems also to have been authenticated by them. It was that Justus, surnamed Barsabas, mentioned in the Acts of the Apostles, drank deadly poison without being in the least injured. There are other two fragments, which have been attributed to Papias. One, as quoted by Œcumenius, relates that the death of Judas was caused by a carriage running over him and crushing out his intestines. Theophylact adds many absurd particulars to this statement, apparently as if he had found them in the work of Papias, but the best critics regard them as the fabrications of a later age[t]. The other gives an account of the four Maries mentioned in the New Testament. It runs thus:—" Mary, the mother of the Lord; Mary, the wife of Cleophas or Alpheus, who was the mother of James, overseer and apostle, and of Simon and Thaddeus and of one Joseph; Mary Salome, the wife of Zebedee, mother of John the evangelist and of James; and Mary Magdalene. These four are found in the Gospel. James and Judas and Joseph were sons of the aunt of the Lord. James also and John were sons of the other aunt of the Lord. Mary, the mother of James the Less and Joseph, wife of Alpheus, was the sister of Mary the mother of the Lord, whom John names Cleophæ, either from the father or the family of the clan or some other cause. Mary Salome is called Salome either from her husband or her village; some say that she was the same as the wife of Cleophas, because she had two husbands." The information of this fragment, first published by Grabe, Spic. tom. i. p. 34, is interesting, if we could but depend on it. Unfortunately, there is no testimony to its genuineness but the inscription "Papia." The statements made here, as Routh remarks, differ from those of Epiphanius, Hæres. 78. num. et 8, and the Chronicle of Hippolytus Thebanus in a Bodleian MS.

The collectors of the fragments of Papias adduce several other very questionable quotations from Papias—

[t] See Casaub. Exercitat. xvi. adv. Baronium sect. 69; Routh, Reliquiæ Sacræ, vol, i. p. 25. Some reject even the passage from Œcumenius, as spurious; but the matter is not worth discussing.

one especially from Andreas Cæsariensis, who says that Papias knew the Revelation of John. The date of this Andreas is unknown; Pearson supposes him to have flourished in the fifth century [q]; but even were he better known, his assertion is not to be relied on, though not unlikely in itself.

Many scholars have thought that Papias was often the source from which Irenæus derived the sayings of elders which he quotes anonymously. Nothing positive can be made of such a guess, and the matter, besides, belongs more to our discussion of Irenæus than of Papias.

There is nothing in the fragments of Papias to enable us to speak with regard to his theology [r]. He may have been a Jewish-Christian, but there is not the slightest proof. The only two circumstances which can be adduced to give a colour to this supposition are, that he concerns himself with the details of Christ's earthly life, and that he does not seem to have mentioned Paul's writings. He may, however, have quoted Paul for all that we know, and even if he did not, his subject was Christ's sayings. And surely it was no mean curiosity that concentrated itself on the truths to which the Son of God had given utterance. Nor would it be any disparagement to Papias if he had deemed them of far greater importance than those of Paul.

The work of Papias was extant in the time of Jerome [s]. Perhaps it may yet be recovered, for some work with the name of Papias is mentioned thrice in the Catalogue of

[q] Vind. Ign. Pars I. c. 10.

[r] On Papias's testimony to the New Testament there is a very able chapter in Westcott's History of the Canon, p. 76 ff.

[s] Epistol. ad Licin. 28, p. 196, tom. i., ed. Frob. Basil. 1526.

the Library of the Benedictine Monastery of Christ Church, Canterbury, contained in a Cottonian MS. written in the end of the thirteenth or beginning of the fourteenth century[t]; and, according to Menard, the words, "I found the book of Papias on the Words of the Lord" are contained in an inventory of the property of the Church of Nismes, prepared about 1218[u].

The fragments of Papias are given in Halloix, Grabe, Gallandi, Migne, and Routh.

[t] Memoirs of Libraries, by Edward Edwards, Lond. 1859, vol. i. pp. 122–235. The catalogue gives nothing but the name Papias. The numbers are 234, 267, and 556.

[u] See Fabricii Bibl. Græc. vol. vii. p. 153, Harless; and Migne, Patrolog. Curs. Græc. Ser., vol. v. p. 1254.

INDEX.

A.

ABORTIONS, procuring of, 311.
Adultery, 371, 374; story of woman taken in, 399.
Ælia Capitolina, 268.
Africanus, Julius, 22.
Alce, 206.
Aldrich, 247.
Alexander, Dr. W. L., 74.
Allegorical interpretation, 103.
Alzog, 38.
Anastasius Bibliothecarius, 25.
Anastasius Sinaita, 25.
Anaxagoras, 103.
Andreas, Cæsariensis, 401.
Andrew, St., 394.
Anencletus, 115.
Anger, 383.
Angels: in Clemens Romanus, 164; Barnabas, 293; Hermas, 361.
Anicetus, 193, 223.
Annegarn, 38.
Ante-Nicene Christian Library, 44, 392.
Anti-Christ, 233.
Antoninus Pius, 332.
Antonius d'Abbadie, 391.
Apion, Dialogues of Peter and, 148.
Apostles, the, 187; character of, 259.
Apostolical Fathers, 103.
Aristarchus, 15.
Aristion, 394.
Aristobulus, 104.
Ariston, 198.

Atonement, doctrine of, 79; see death of *Christ;* day of, 255.
Athanasius, 322, 382.
Athenagoras, not noticed by Eusebius, 17.
Aucher, 22.
Augustine, 76.
Aurelius, Marcus, 223.

B.

Balthasar, 246.
Baptism, 298, 310, 367, 377.
Barbeyrac, 90.
Barcochba, 268.
Barecroft, 42.
Barnabas the Apostle, 252, 258.
Barnabas, Epistle of: its authorship, 248; ascribed to Barnabas the Apostle, 249; internal evidence, 252; for whom written, 261; the place of the writer, 262; the date, 267; the object of the letter, 273; theology of the letter, 276; abstract, 277; its doctrines, 288; literature, 312.
Barth, 391.
Baumgarten, 219.
Baur, Ferdinand Christian, 45, 68, 127, 159, 173, 197, 218, 231, 333.
Bekker, 23, 24.
Bellarmine, 35, 325.
Bennet, Dr. James, 77.
Bernardus, 126.
Bernays, Jacob, 20.

Bickersteth, Rev. E., 44.
Bignonius, 128.
Biographia Ecclesiastica, 41.
Bishops, or overseers appointed by the Apostles, 171; same as presbyters in Clemens Romanus, 173; their work, 177; not mentioned in Polycarp's letter, 239; probably the same as presbyters in Hermas, 376.
Blondellus, 335.
Blunt, Professor, 30, 84, 87.
Boehringer, 41.
Boisius, 151.
Bottsacus, 41.
Bucolus, 198.
Bull, Bishop, 85, 219, 357, 372.
Bunsen, Baron, 73, 93, 158, 173, 176, 228, 336, 340, 357, 382.
Burton, Dr., 87.
Burton, W., 176, 178.
Busse, 38.

C.

Caillau, 43.
Calvinists regarded as heretical on the Trinity by Petavius, 86.
Canisius, 43.
Casaubon, 400.
Cassiodorus, 20.
Catholic letter, 261.
Catholics, Roman, 29; writers on the Fathers, 38, 67.
Cave, 40.
Cedrenus, Georgius, 23.
Ceillier, 36.
Celsus, 270.
Cerdo, 105.
Cerinthus, 193.
Charpentier, 38.
Chevallier, Temple, 152.
Christ, opinions of Fathers in regard to, 68; opinions of Clemens Romanus, 155; Clemens does not call him God, 155; questionable whether Clemens thought of him as the Logos, 158; his subordination to God, 159; his death as represented by Clemens, 160; life and work of Christ in Clemens, 162; second coming, 163; his words, 185; the centre of the Old Testament, 189; as presented in the Epistle of Barnabas, 289; the purpose of his death, 292; as presented in the Epistle of Polycarp, 234; as presented in the Pastor of Hermas, 353.
Χριστιανισμός, 222.
Christianity, its first form, 60; unspeculative, 62, 63, 102.
Chrysostom, 183.
Church, its nature according to Clemens Romanus, 169; according to Polycarp, 239; Hermas, 375.
Clarke, Dr., 88.
Clarke, Dr. Adam, 42.
Clemens, 330.
Clemens Alexandrinus, 10, 15, 116, 126, 129, 130, 186, 222, 248, 250, 267, 274, 275, 376.
Clemens Flavius, 133.
Clemens Romanus, 18; bishop of Rome, date of his holding office, 114; diversity of position assigned to him, 115; was he the person mentioned in the Epistle to the Philippians? 119; his death, 120; was he a Jew? 121; was he a Roman? 121; his writings, 124; Epistle to the Corinthians, 125; genuine, 126; incomplete, 127; not interpolated, 128; inspired, 130; date, 130; occasion of the letter, 137; character of the letter, 138; his theology, 140; abstract of the letter, 143; writings ascribed to him, 148; relation of the Epistle to the Corinthians to the Epistle to the Hebrews, 148; manuscripts and editions of the letter, 151; exposition of his theology, 153; resemblance between Epistle of Clemens and that of Polycarp, 231.
Clementine Homilies, 117, 124, 148.
Clementine Recognitions, 118, 119, 124, 148.
Clericus, 108, 151, 382.
Codex Alexandrinus, 124, 158.

INDEX.

Codex Frederico-Augustanus, 385.
Codex Sinaiticus, 384.
Colomesius, 151.
Columna, Cardinal, 313.
Constantius, 152.
Constitutions, Apostolical, 124, 148, 151, 198, 275.
Contogones, Professor, 38.
Corinth, Church in, 65, 113, 125, 134, 136, 143.
Corinthians, First Epistle to, 134, 136.
Cornwallis, Miss, 94.
Cossartius, 151.
Cotelerius, 108, 151, 247, 251, 314, 335, 377, 380, 382, 391.
Cox, Rev. Robert, 41.
Cressollius, 313.
Criticism, principles of, 12; want of critical faculty in the ancients, Pagan or Christian, 15.
Cunningham, Dr., 79.
Cyprian. 28, 29, 377.

D.

Dachery, 313.
Daillé, 19, 20, 21, 30, 71, 84, 227.
Damascus, John of, 25.
Danz, 34.
Danaids, 121.
Davidson, Dr., 95, 398.
Deacons appointed by Apostles, 171; their function in Clemens Romanus, 177; mentioned in the Epistle of Polycarp, 241; in Hermas, 377.
De Quincey, 24, 138.
Deutinger, 38.
Devil, in Clemens Romanus, 165; in Polycarp, 238; in Barnabas, 293; in Hermas, 363.
Dindorf, Louis, 23.
Dindorf Wilhelm, 23, 383.
Dionysius the Areopagite, 18, 227, 229.
Dionysius of Corinth, 28, 115, 125.
Dirce, 121.
Doctrines, difficulties in the exposition of, 58.
Docetes, 104, 225, 271.
Dodwell, 21, 134.

Dogma, development of, 6, 70, 92.
δόγμα, 283.
Döllinger, 70.
Domitian, 271, 332.
Domitilla, Flavia, 133.
Dorner, 158, 159, 160, 240, 274, 276, 333, 337, 357.
Dressel, 110, 114, 246, 247, 312, 314, 315, 376, 383, 384, 391.
Du Pin, 36.

E.

Early Christian writings, their value, 4; their help in solving present difficulties, 7; their testimony to the New Testament, 8; their worth in the interpretation of the New Testament, 9; their value for the philosopher, 9; for the scholar, 10.
Ebion, 195.
Ebionites, 271, 273, 333.
Education of children, 162, 190.
Edwards, Edward, 402.
Ekker, 127, 158, 189.
ἐκσφενδονᾶν, 316.
Election, 168.
Elias, Revelation of, 183.
Engelhardt, 41.
English Church, 82.
Epagathus, Vetus, 208.
Epictetus, 395.
ἐπινομή, 172.
Epiphanius, 20, 119, 184, 195.
Erdmann, 10.
Esdras, Fourth Book of, 272.
Eucharist, 177.
εὐχαριστία, 194.
Eumathius, 316.
Eusebius, 9, 32, 113, 116, 120, 130, 148, 195, 198, 211, 213, 216, 223, 224, 249, 321, 393, 395; value of his history, the Chronicon, 16, 22, 23.
Eustathius, 316.
Evarestus, 199.
Evangelical School of Theology, 71.
Evans, Rev. R. W., 18, 41, 205.
Evidence, Internal, 26; fundamental principles, 30.

F.

Faber, Jacobus Stapulensis, 247, 391.
Fabricius, his collection of works on the Ecclesiastical writers, 19, 272, 391.
Faith, 166.
Fasts, 242, 380.
Fell, Bishop, 151, 314, 382, 391.
Fessler, 38.
Florinus, 191, 224.
Forbes, Professor, 81, 83.
Forged writings, 27.
Free-will, 364.
Freppel, Abbé, 103, 111.
Frey, 247.
Friedländer, 106.
Future state, opinions of Clemens Romanus, 178; Polycarp, 242; Barnabas, 298; Hermas, 380.

G.

Gaâb, 325.
Gaius, 215.
Gallandi, 43, 247, 267, 314, 391, 402.
Gasparin, Count de, 63, 335.
Genoude, 43.
Gerhard, 41.
Gerius, R., 40.
Germanicus a Martyr, 220.
Gfrörer, 104.
Giles, Dr., 44.
Gilly, Dr., 19.
Gilse, 112, 190, 326.
Glabrio, Ancilius, 133.
Gnosis, 129, 189, 273, 282.
Goarus, 23.
Gobarus, 395.
God in nature, 139; idea of Clemens Romanus in regard to God, 153; God propitiated, 155, 352; sufferings of God, 157; ideas of Polycarp, 234; of Barnabas, 288; of the Pastor of Hermas, 351.
Godwin, Professor, 60, 61.
Goldwitzer, 38.
Goode's Rule of Faith, 74.

Grabe, 149, 400, 402.
γραφεῖον, 184.
Grapte, 330.
Guillon, 43.
Gundert, 136.

H.

Hadrian, 272, 332.
Hailes, Lord, 89.
Halloix, 247, 312, 395, 402.
Heaven, 107.
Hebrews, Epistle to the, 134, 141, 148, 272, 323, 372.
Hefele, 109, 131, 216, 247, 248, 251, 268, 271, 272, 280, 282, 285, 291, 314, 320, 391.
Hegel, 8.
Hegesippus, 114.
Heinichen, 28.
Heldam, 381.
Helvidius, 19.
Henke, 249.
Heresy, historians of, 20, 21; attitude of the Apostolical Fathers to, 104.
Hermas, Pastor, its authorship, 318; external testimony, 318; internal evidence, 325; its date, 330; the place, 332; its theological character, 332; its object, 337; its value, 339; abstract, 340; doctrines, 351; manuscripts, 382; editions, 391.
Hermes, Professor, 68.
Herod, 206, 214, 217; the Irenarch, 221.
Herodotus, 123.
Heunisch, 41.
Heyns, 112, 190.
Hilarion, 19.
Hilgenfeld, 56, 57, 110, 111, 135, 142, 159, 165, 187, 189, 197, 218, 225, 226, 232, 252, 265, 268, 271, 272, 276. 280, 285, 298, 305, 315, 332, 333, 334, 340, 357, 391.
Hinds, Bishop, 112.
Hodius, 24.
Holstenius, Lucas, 314, 315.
Hoole, Charles H., M.A., 152, 392.

Horsley, Bishop, 89.
Huber, Dr., 10.
Hülsemannus, 41.
Hyginus, 324.

I.

Ignatius, 32, 102, 151, 224, 226, 232, 271.
Inspiration, 8; Clemens Romanus regarded by some as inspired, 130; theory of inspiration in Clemens Romanus, 181.
Irenæus, 115, 125, 191, 193, 215, 223, 224, 318, 393, 395, 401.
Ittigius, 109, 151, 247.

J.

Jachmann, 337, 357, 364, 374, 380.
Jacobson, Dr., 109, 152, 215, 246, 247.
James, St., 394, 400.
James, the Less, 400.
James, Rev. Thomas, 29.
Jamieson, Dr., 89.
Jerome, 29, 117, 130, 184, 224, 249, 272, 275, 322, 401; his book, De Illustribus Viris, 18; his critical powers, 19; his version of the Chronicon of Eusebius, 22.
Jerusalem, 267.
John, St., 133, 191, 193, 194, 393, 394, 400.
John Mark, 258.
John the Presbyter, 393.
John of Trittenheim, 38.
Jortin, 204, 219.
Jovinian, 19.
Judaism, 103, 129.
Judas, 397, 399.
Judith, Book of, 135.
Junius, F. J. J. A., 111, 190, 246.
Junius, Patricius (Patrick Young), 151, 158.
Justification by Faith, 96, 141, 142; justified or made righteous by faith in God, 166; in Hermas, 369.
Justin Martyr, 123, 165, 208, 272.
Justus, named Barsabas, 399.

K.

Kaufmann, 38.
Kayser, 141, 265, 272.
Kayser, Aug., 276.
Kestner, 138.
Killen's, Professor, Ancient Church, 79.
Knox, John, 76.
Köstlin, 142, 394.

L.

Labbé, 35, 151.
Lang, 38.
Lange, 111.
Lardner, Dr., 91, 114, 301.
Laurent, 152, 157.
Lechler, 111, 160.
Lewis, Sir G. Cornewall, 13.
Liberianus, Catalogus, 323.
Lightfoot, Professor, 135, 152, 157, 169, 184.
Linus, 115.
Lipsius, 114, 136, 141, 158, 160, 324, 335.
Locherer, 38.
Locke, 88.
Loescher, 41.
Logos, doctrine of the, 158.
Lord's Supper, see *Eucharist*.
Love in Christ saves, 168.
Lucius, 208.
Lücke, 184.
Luke, St., 149.
Lumper, 37.
Luther, 76.
Lycurgus, Alexander, 383.

M.

Macarius a S. Elia, 38.
Mader, 151, 314.
Magon, 38.
Mai, Cardinal, 22.
Maitland, 19.
Malalas, Joannes, 23, 24.
Man: original sin not mentioned in Clemens Romanus, 165; nor in

INDEX.

Polycarp, 238; nor in Barnabas, 294; nor in Hermas, 364; method of salvation in Clemens Romanus, 165; in Polycarp 239; in Barnabas, 295; in Hermas, 366.
Marcion, 105, 193, 226.
Marcionites, 225, 396.
Marcus, 199.
Margarinus de la Bigne. 43.
Mark, St., 398.
Marriage, 374.
μαρτυρέω, 188.
Mary: the four Scripture Maries, 400.
Matthew, St., 394, 398.
Maurice, 94, 205.
Maximus, 17, 229.
McCrie, 76.
Meelführer, 41.
Melancthon, 41.
Menard, 402.
Menardus, Hugo, 313.
Merivale, 15.
μετάνοια, 366.
Metrodorus of Lampsacus, 103.
Michael, 362.
Migne, J. P., 43, 391, 402.
Middleton, Bishop, 219.
Millennium, 106, 396.
Milman, Dean, 95.
Milton, 72, 88, 219.
Miracles, 399.
Miræus, 38.
Moehler, 37, 63, 114.
Modal, 381.
Morality of Clemens, 190; of Polycarp, 246; of Barnabas, 311.
Mosheim, 91, 128.
Moyne, Le, 247, 260, 314.
Müller, J. G., 272, 305, 315.
Muratori, 323.
Muralto, 314.

N.

Neander, 63, 68, 92, 129, 264, 309.
Nero, 332.
Nerva, 271.
Newman, Dr. Henry, 69, 85.
Newton, 88.

Nicephorus, 20, 382.
Nicetas, 206, 221.
Nourry, 36.

O.

Œcumenius, 399.
Oehler, 21, 272.
Old Testament saints baptised in the lower world, 379.
Olearius, 41.
Origen, 29, 63, 116, 117, 119, 148, 149, 261, 270, 275, 319, 321, 390.
Original sin, see *Man*.
Osburn W., 335.
Oudin, 35.

P.

Papias, 107; his life, 393; his writings, 395; theology, 401.
Passover, 193, 197.
Paschale, Chronicon, 23.
Patripassianism, 158.
Paul, St., 115, 132, 141, 149, 184, 188, 231, 232; his allegorical interpretations, 103; First Epistle to the Corinthians, 134.
Pearson, 18, 401.
Permaneder, 34, 395.
Perseverance of Saints, 296.
Pestalozzi, 41.
Petavius, 68, 86.
Peter, St., 115, 131, 148, 187, 394, 398.
Philastrius, 272.
Philip, St., 394, 399.
Philip the Trallian, 214, 222.
Philippi, Church in, 224, 230.
Philo, 103, 104, 165.
Philomelium, 211.
Phœnix, The, 123.
Photius, 24, 155.
Photographic Facsimile of Clemens, 152.
Pionios, 214, 215, 216, 229.
Pius, 325.
Plato on Allegory, 104.
Pliny the Elder, 123.
Polycarp, 246, 260, 270, 312, 315, 393; his life, 191; facts stated

INDEX. 409

by Irenæus, 193 ; his observance of the Passover, 196 ; the Martyrium discussed, 198 ; writings, 224 ; Letter to the Philippians, genuineness, 225 ; his other works, 229 ; the object of the letter, 229 ; date, 230 ; value, 231 ; theology, 231 ; abstract of letter, 232.
Possevinus, 35.
Prayer, 374.
Pressensé, 108.
Priestley, 89.
Propitiation, 369.
Protestant writers on early Christian Literature, 41, 42, 71.

Q.

Quadratus, Statius, 214, 224.

R.

Rahab, 189.
Redemption, see *Death of Christ;* redemption by suffering, 212.
Reithmayr, 37, 247, 314.
Repentance, 370.
Resurrection, 65, 137 ; the opinions of Clemens Romanus, 178.
Reuss, 108, 111, 141.
Revelation of Elias, 183.
Riches, the possession of by Christians, 373.
Riddle, 42.
Ritschl, Albrecht, 48, 55, 111, 161, 228, 332, 335.
Ritter, 10.
Rivetus, 372.
Rome, Church in, 113, 125, 143.
Rössler, 43, 246.
Rothe, 110, 172, 376.
Routh, 234, 247, 400, 402.
Rueff, 38.
Rufinus, 20, 29, 118, 119, 322.
Russel, 247, 314, 391.

S.

Sabbath, 286, 297.
Sadness, 375 ; a sin, 340.
Sacrifices, 129.
Saints, Clemens Romanus supposed by some to state that saints after death hear prayers, 179.
Salmasius, 313.
Salvation, see *Man*.
Sandius, 41, 86.
Sardagna, 38.
Saussay, 35.
Scaliger, 219 ; Thesaurus Temporum Eusebii, 23.
Schenkel, 136, 260, 264, 274.
Schleiermarcher, 92, 398.
Schliemann, 117.
Schleichert, 38.
Schmidt, 106.
Schopf, 41.
Schöne's Canon of Eusebius, 22.
Schottus, Andreas, 247, 313.
Schwegler, 15, 142, 225, 332 ; his Nachapostolisches Zeitalter, 49.
Scripture : the Old Testament inspired according to Clemens Romanus, 180 : misquotation of Scripture by Clemens Romanus, 181 ; Clemens Romanus quotes from the Septuagint, 182 ; statements not found in our Bible by Clemens Romanus, 182 ; passages quoted by him and not found in our Bible, 182 ; Scriptures in Polycarp, 242 ; Scriptures in Barnabas, 304 ; books mentioned in the Epistle of Barnabas, 300; differences from Septuagint, 300, 303 ; Old Testament inspired, 302 ; interpretation of Old Testament, 307 ; inspiration of the Pastor of Hermas, 318 ; no quotation from the Scriptures in Hermas, 381.

Genesis ii. 2, p. 286; 297; xv. 6, 285; xxv. 23, 284; xlviii. 11, 285.
Exodus xvii. 14, 304; xx. 8, 285.
Leviticus xvi. 27, 255 ; xxiii. 29, 255.
Numbers xi. 26, 27, 381 ; xviii. 27, 181 ; xix. 2, 282 ; xxi. 9, 303.
Deuteronomy v. 12, 285 ; xxxii. 8, 165.

2 Chronicles xxxi. 14, 181.
Job xix. 25, 26, 190.
Psalm i., 284; iii. 5, 190; iv. 5, 243; xxii. 17, 281; xxxiv. 11-18, 189; xli. 3, 281; ciii. 11, 182; cx. 1, 284; cxviii. 12, 22, 281; cxix. 120, 280.
Proverbs i. 17, 280.
Isaiah i. 18, 182; 11-14, 278; v. 5, 305; viii. 14, 280; 300; xiii. 22, 163; xvi. 1, 2, 283; xxvi. 20, 183; xxviii. 16, 300; xxxiii. 16, 283; xl. 12, 286; xlii. 6, 7, 285; xlv. 1, 284; 304; 2, 3, 283; xlix. 6, 285; 17, 286; l. 8, 9, 280; liii. 5, 7, 162; 280; lviii. 4, 5, 279; lxi. 1, 2, 285; lxiv. 4, 183; lxv. 2, 284; lxvi. i. 286.
Jeremiah ii. 12, 13, 283; iii. 4, 19, 182; iv. 4, 282; vii. 22, 23, 278; 26, 282; xxv. 36, 305.
Ezekiel xviii. 30, 182; xxxvii. 12, 184; xlvii. 12, 284.
Daniel, Book of, 271.
Daniel, vii. 7, 8, 24, 279.
Habakkuk ii. 3, 163.
Zephaniah iii. 19, 284.
Malachi iii. 1, 163.
Gospel of Matthew, 244, 306, 398.
Matthew vi. 14, 185; vii. 2, 12, 185; x. 33, 381; xi. 5, 187; xviii. 6, 186; xx. 16, 300; xxii. 14, 300; xxvi. 24, 186.
Gospel of Mark, 244, 398.
Mark ix. 42, 186; xiv. 21, 186.
Luke vi. 31, 37, 38, 185; vii. 22, 187; xvii. 2, 186.
Gospel of John, 218.
The Acts of the Apostles, 187, 244, 399.
Acts ii. 24, 244; xx. 35, 187.
Romans xvi. 14, 319.
First Epistle to the Corinthians mentioned by Clemens Romanus, 184.
1 Corinthians ii. 9, 183; vi. 2, 244; 9, 10, 244.
Galatians i. 1, 244; ii. 12, 334; 13, 252; iv. 26, 244; vi. 7, 244.

Ephesians ii. 8, 9, 244; iv. 26, 243; vi. 5, 241.
Epistle to the Philippians, 245.
Philippians ii. 6, 163.
2 Thessalonians iii. 15, 244.
1 Timothy ii. 2, 226; vi. 7, 244; 10, 244.
2 Timothy ii. 12, 244.
Titus iii. 10, 193.
Hebrews i. 3, 4, 5, 7, 13, 150; iii. 2, 150; iv. 14, 150; vi. 4-6, 372; xi. 37, 150; xiii. 17, 150.
James i. 8, 183.
First Epistle of Peter, 224, 399.
1 Peter i. 8, 244; 13, 244; 21, 244; ii. 11, 238, 244; ii. 12, 244; 22, 244; 24, 244; iii. 9, 244.
Second Epistle of Peter, 244.
2 Peter iii. 3, 4, 183.
First Epistle of John, 399.
1 John ii. 20, 243; iv. 3, 244.
Revelation of John, 401.
Revelation xxii. 12, 301.
Words of Christ quoted by Clemens Romanus, 185; in Polycarp, 245; in Barnabas, 301.

APOCRYPHAL.

Fourth Book of Ezra, 337.
4 Ezra ii. 16, 184; v. 5, 284; 305.
Sirach iv. 31, 305; 26, 306.
Book of Enoch, 304, 305.
Revelation of Elias, 183.
Tobit iv. 10, 243; xii. 9, 243.
Gospel according to the Hebrews, 399.
Gospel of the Nazarenes, 185.
Gospel of Peter, 186.
Eldad and Medad, 381.

Scultetus, 41, 81, 372.
Semler, Johann Salomo, 92, 219.
Severus, Sulpicius, 20, 269.
Sibyl, inspired, 123.
Simeon Metaphrastes, 25.
Simon de Voyon, 38.
Simonides, 315, 383.
Sinaitic Manuscript, 315, 384.

INDEX. 411

Sin, see *Man.*
Sirmond, Jacob, 247, 312.
Sixtus, Senensis, 38.
Smith, Thomas, 247.
Smyrna, Letter of the Church in, 191, 198.
Socrates of Corinth, 215.
Sophocles, 44.
Soter, 125.
Spirit, Holy, the opinions of Clemens Romanus, 164; Scriptures inspired by Holy Spirit, 181; not mentioned in Polycarp's Epistle, 238; the meaning of Holy Spirit in Hermas, 333; the relation of Christ to Holy Spirit, 353; the Holy Spirit in Hermas, 358.
Sprenger, 43.
Spurious works of the first three centuries, 26.
Steitz, 395.
Stephanus Lusignanus, 38.
Stöckl, 10.
Stoics, 9, 104.
Stolle, 41.
Strataias, 198.
Stoughton, Dr., 79, 103, 336.
Subintroductæ, 330.
Suffridis, Petri, 38.
Suicer, 44.
Suidas, 198, 229, 316.
Sunday, 125, 130, 286, 297.
Supererogation, Works of, 369.
Syncellus, Georgius, 23.

T.

Tacitus, 123.
Tatian, 10.
Taylor, Isaac, 19, 74.
Teachers in the Church, 377.
Tentzel, 41.
Tertullian, 10, 117, 196, 212, 272, 322, 323.
Testament, New, 8.
Theodoret, 21, 195.
Theophylact, 400.
Thiersch, 111, 326.
Thomas, St., 394.
Thönnissen, 127, 176.
Tillemont, 35, 118, 119, 121, 219.

Tischendorf, 152, 277, 315, 383.
Tobenz, 38.
Trajan, 271, 332.
Trinity, doctrine of the, 71, 78, 85, 87, 164.
Tübingen School, 45.
Tulloch, Principal, 76.
Turrianus, 312.

U.

Ueberweg, 10.
Unitarians, 88.
Uhlhorn, 136, 142.
Usher, Archbishop, 214, 224, 247, 313.
Urbicus, 208.

V.

Valens, 229.
Valentinus, 193,
Valesius, 209, 210, 393.
Varenius, 41.
Vaughan, Dr., 79.
Vespasian, 271.
Victor of Capua, 229.
Virginity, letter on, ascribed to Clemens, 148.
Volkmar, 135, 271, 272, 305, 315.
Vossius, 247.

W.

Wake, Archbishop, 152, 392.
Walch, 13, 219; his Bibliotheca, 34.
Waterland, 83, 86, 87.
Weizsäcker, 263, 266, 271, 272.
Westcott, Canon, 95, 333, 335, 393, 398, 401.
Wharton, 40.
Whiston, Professor, 90.
Wiest, 38.
Wilhelmus, 38.
Wilson, Rev. W., 42.
Winter, 38.
Wisdom, some think that Clemens Romanus identified Christ with the, 158.
Women to love all Christian men equally, 190, 246.

Wordsworth, 122.
Worlds beyond ocean, 140.
Wotton, Henry, 151, 183, 185.

Y.

Young, Patrick, 151, 158.

Z.

Zeller, 15.
Zöckler, 19.
Zohrab, 22.
Zahn, 324, 327, 357, 369, 398.